D1373612

# Living Psalms and Proverbs

## With The
## MAJOR PROPHETS

### Paraphrased
by Kenneth N. Taylor

Second Printing, July, 1967
*175,000 copies*

# CONTENTS

*From Wm. Tyndale's Prologue to the First Printed English New Testament:*

Exhortynge instantly and besechynge those that are better sene in the tongues than I, and that have higher gifts of grace to interpret the sense of Scripture, and meaning of the Spirit, than I, to consider and ponder my labor, and that with the spirit of meekness. And if they perceive in any places that I have not attained the very sense of the tongue, or meaning of the Scripture, or have not given the right English word, that they put to their hands to amend it, remembering that so is their duty to do. For we have not received the gifts of God for ourselves only, or for to hide them; but for to bestow them unto the honoring of God and Christ and edifying of the congregation, which is the body of Christ.

**LIVING PSALMS
AND PROVERBS
With The
Major Prophets
Paraphrased**

# PREFACE

**I** have never been much of a reader of the Psalms! Oh, occasionally I have read them when I was on a "through-the-Bible" reading spree. Or perhaps in family devotions, or when visiting the sick. But a regular reader I was not.

Neither did the Proverbs attract me, although I dipped into them occasionally because Billy Graham and several others, including my father-in-law, claimed that to read a chapter a day from the Proverbs along with five daily Psalms (so that both books are read completely once a month) is a spiritual tonic *par excellence*. But I never tried it myself . . .

Until . . . well, until I *had* to read these books *intently, repeatedly,* and *constantly* in order to paraphrase them for this "Living Series" of Bible portions.

Then something happened. For these marvelous portions of the Word of God have become my meat and drink! Now I ask sincerely how anyone can live without these precious messages of hope and trust. It's true that other parts of the Bible give the same assurance, warnings, and joy—but no others are quite like the Psalms; no others have such exciting, thoughtful wisdom as the Proverbs. No others contain the awesome pathos of the Prophets.

Having made this great discovery, naturally I long that others, too, who have not yet found this open secret, will begin to enjoy the tender grass of these green pastures of God's Word. I even hope that this new translation will help the entire English-speaking world to begin to look afresh at these living portions of the Word of God and be transformed by them.

## The Major Prophets

But what can I say to encourage you to read the "major prophets"—Isaiah, Jeremiah (with the Lamentations), and Ezekiel?*

They are long, but not windy! They are intense, but not difficult—at least, not in this paraphrase. Read them and feel God's horror of sin. See His dreadful anger in action. See His divine plan working inexorably for Israel and against the nations who are her enemies. See how eager God is to welcome back His people to Himself from their sinning and errors. See how He loves *you!* See how He longs for *your* love! Let love and awe for God grow strong in your life; let there be horror, anger, and love for God's ancient people; and simultaneously the realization that you yourself have erred as often, yes, sinned as grievously—yet God remains gracious and forgives freely when you return to Him, for you are protected from His judgment by His mercy found in Christ.

---

*The book of Daniel, usually included among the major prophets, has already been paraphrased in "Living Prophecies."

These are my dreams for all readers of this book: Read, enjoy, grow—in grace, in faith, in love.

And now a word to those many readers who have long preceded me in the discovery of the wonders of these Bible books and have been enjoying them perhaps for many years: I hope that this new rendering will prove helpful, rather than disturbing. The replowing of the fertile soil should increase the fruit, not lessen it; may this prove true as you read this volume.

Kenneth N. Taylor

Tyndale House
March, 1967

# The Psalms

## PSALM 1

O h, the joys of those who do not follow evil men's advice, who do not hang around with sinners, scoffing at the things of God:

2    But they delight in doing everything God wants them to, and day and night are always meditating on His laws and thinking about ways to follow Him more closely.

3    They are like trees along a river bank bearing luscious fruit each season without fail. Their leaves shall never wither, and all they do shall prosper.

4    But for sinners, what a different story! They blow away like chaff before the wind!

5    They are not safe on Judgment Day; they shall not stand among the godly.

6    For the Lord watches over all the plans and paths of godly men, but the paths of the godless lead to doom.

## PSALM 2

W hat fools[1] the nations are to rage against the Lord! How strange that men should try to out-wit God![2]

[1] Implied; literally, "Why do the heathen rage?"
[2] Literally, "meditate a vain thing."

2    For a summit conference of the nations has been called to plot against the Lord and His Messiah, Christ the King.[3]

3    "Come, let us break His chains," they say, "and free ourselves from all this slavery to God."

4    But God in heaven merely laughs! He is amused by all their puny plans.

5    And then in fierce fury He rebukes them and fills them with fear.

6    For the Lord declares,[4] "This is the King of My choice, and I have enthroned Him in Jerusalem, My holy city."[5]

7    His chosen One replies,[4] "I will reveal the everlasting purposes of God, for the Lord has said to Me, 'You are My Son. This is Your Coronation Day.[6] Today I am giving You Your glory.'"

8    "Only ask, and I will give You all the nations of the world.

9    Rule them with an iron rod; smash them like clay pots!"

10    O kings and rulers of the earth, listen while there is time.

11    Serve the Lord with reverent fear; rejoice with trembling.

12    Fall down before His Son and kiss His feet[4] before His anger is roused and you perish. I am warning you—His wrath will soon begin. But, oh, the joys of those who put their trust in Him!

---

[3]Literally, "His anointed."
[4]Implied.
[5]Literally, "Upon Zion, My holy mountain."
[6]Literally, "This day have I begotten You."

## PSALM 3

*A Psalm of David when he fled from his son Absalom*

O Lord, so many are against me. So many seek to harm me. I have so many enemies.

2 So many say that God will never help me.

3 But Lord, You are my shield, my glory, and my only hope. You alone can lift my head, now bowed in shame.[4]

4 I cried out to the Lord, and He heard me from His Temple in Jerusalem.[7]

5 Then I lay down and slept in peace and woke up safely, for the Lord was watching over me.

6 And now, although ten thousand enemies surround me on every side, I am not afraid!

7 I will cry to Him, "Arise, O Lord! Save me, O my God!" And He will slap them in the face, insulting[8] them and breaking off their teeth.

8 For salvation comes from God. What joys He gives to all His people.

## PSALM 4

O God, You have declared me perfect in Your eyes;[9] You have always cared for me in my dis-

---

[7]Literally, "from His holy mountain."
[8]Implied.
[9]Literally, "God of my righteousness."

tress; now hear me as I call again. Have mercy on me. Hear my prayer.

2 The Lord God asks, "Sons of men, will you forever turn My glory into shame by worshiping these silly idols, when every claim that's made for them is false?"

3 Mark this well: The Lord has set apart the redeemed for Himself. Therefore He will listen to me and answer when I call to Him.

4 Stand before the Lord in awe,[1] and do not sin against Him. Lie quietly upon your bed in silent meditation.

5 Put your trust in the Lord, and offer Him pleasing sacrifices.

6 Many say that God will never help us. Prove them wrong,* O Lord, by letting the light of Your face shine down upon us.

7 Yes, the gladness You have given me is far greater than their joys at harvest time as they gaze at their bountiful crops.

8 I will lie down in peace and sleep, for though I am alone, O Lord, You will keep me safely.


## PSALM 5

O Lord, hear me praying; listen to my plea, O God my King, for I will never pray to anyone but You.

3 Each morning I will look to You in heaven and lay my requests before You, praying earnestly.

---

[1]Or, "Be ye angry"
*Implied

4   I know You get no pleasure from wickedness and cannot tolerate the slightest sin.

5   Therefore proud sinners will not survive Your searching gaze; for how You hate their evil deeds.

6   You will destroy them for their lies; how You abhor all murder and deception.

7   But as for me, I will come into Your Temple protected by Your mercy and Your love; I will worship You with deepest awe.

8   Lord, lead me as You promised me You would; otherwise my enemies will conquer me. Tell me clearly what to do, which way to turn.

9   For they cannot speak one truthful word. Their hearts are filled to the brim with wickedness. Their suggestions are full of the stench of sin and death. Their tongues are filled with flatteries to gain their wicked ends.

10   O God, hold them responsible. Catch them in their own traps; let them fall beneath the weight of their own transgressions, for they rebel against You.

11   But make everyone rejoice who puts his trust in You. Keep them shouting for joy because You are defending them. Fill all who love You with Your happiness.

12   For You bless the godly man, O Lord; You protect him with Your shield of love.

## PSALM 6

No, Lord! Don't punish me in the heat of Your anger.

2   Pity me, O Lord, for I am weak. Heal me, for my body is sick,

3   And I am upset and disturbed. My mind is filled with apprehension and with gloom. Oh, restore me soon.

4   Come, O Lord, and make me well. In Your kindness save me.

5   For if I die I cannot give You glory by praising You before my friends.[2]

6   I am worn out with pain; every night my pillow is wet with tears.

7   My eyes are growing old and dim with grief because of all my enemies.

*     *     *     *     *

8   Go, leave me now, you men of evil deeds, for the Lord has heard my weeping

9   And my pleading. He will answer all my prayers.

10   All my enemies shall be suddenly dishonored, terror-stricken, and disgraced. God will turn them back in shame.

## PSALM 7

I am depending on You, O Lord my God, to save me from my persecutors.

2   Don't let them pounce upon me as a lion would and maul me and drag me away with no one to rescue me.

---

[2]Literally, "In the grave, who shall give You thanks?" Isaiah 57:1,2 may indicate that Old Testament saints believed in a conscious and pleasant hereafter for those who love God.

3   It would be different, Lord, if I were doing evil things—

4   If I were paying back evil for good or unjustly attacking those I dislike.

5   Then it would be right for You to let my enemies destroy me, crush me to the ground, and trample my life in the dust.

6   But Lord! Arise in anger against the anger of my enemies. Awake! Demand justice for me, Lord!

7, 8   Gather all peoples before You; sit high above them, judging their sins. But justify me publicly; establish my honor and truth before them all.

9   End all wickedness, O Lord, and bless all who truly worship God;[3] for You, the righteous God, look deep within the hearts of men and examine all their motives and their thoughts.

10   God is my shield; He will defend me. He saves those whose hearts and lives are true and right.[4]

11   God is a judge who is perfectly fair, and He is angry with the wicked every day.

12   Unless they repent, He will sharpen His sword and slay them. He has bent and strung His bow

13   And fitted it with deadly arrows made from shafts of fire.

14   The wicked man conceives an evil plot, labors with its dark details, and brings to birth his treachery and lies;

15   Let him fall into his own trap.

---

[3]Literally, "the just."
[4]Literally, "the upright in heart."

16 May the violence he plans for others boomerang upon himself; let him die.

17 Oh, how grateful and thankful I am to the Lord because He is so good. I will sing praise to the name of the Lord who is above all lords.

## PSALM 8

O Lord our God, the majesty and glory of Your name fills all the earth and overflows the heavens.

2 You have taught the little children to praise You perfectly. May their example shame and silence Your enemies!

3 When I look up into the night skies and see the work of Your fingers—the moon and the stars You have made—

4 I cannot understand how You can bother with mere puny man, to pay any attention to him!

5 And yet You have made him only a little lower than the angels,[5] and placed a crown of glory and honor upon his head.

6 You have put him in charge of everything You made; everything is put under his authority:

7 All sheep and oxen, and wild animals too,

8 The birds and fish, and all the life in the sea.

9 O Jehovah, our Lord, the majesty and glory of Your name fills the earth.

---

[5]Or, "only a little lower than God!"

# PSALM 9

O Lord, I will praise You with all my heart, and tell everyone about the marvelous things You do.

2   I will be glad, yes, filled with joy because of You. I will sing Your praises, O Lord God above all gods.[6]

3   My enemies will fall back and perish in Your presence;

4   You have vindicated me; You have endorsed my work, declaring from Your throne that it is good.[7]

5   You have rebuked the nations and destroyed the wicked, blotting out their names for ever and ever.

6   O enemies of mine, you are doomed forever. The Lord will destroy your cities; even the memory of them will disappear.

7, 8   But the Lord lives on forever; He sits upon His throne to judge justly the nations of the world.

9   All who are oppressed may come to Him. He is a refuge for them in their times of trouble.

10   All those who know Your mercy, Lord, will count on You for help. For You have never yet forsaken those who trust in You.

11   Oh, sing out your praises to the God who lives in Jerusalem.[8] Tell the world about His unforgettable deeds.

12   He who avenges murder has an open ear to

---

[6]Literally, "O Most High."
[7]Literally, "You sit on the throne judging righteously."
[8]Literally, "in Zion."

those who cry to Him for justice. He does not ignore the prayers of men in trouble when they call to Him for help.

13 And now, O Lord, have mercy on me; see how I suffer at the hands of those who hate me. Lord, snatch me back from the jaws of death.

14 Save me, so that I can praise You publicly before all the people at Jerusalem's[8] gates and rejoice that You have rescued me.

15 The nations fall into the pitfalls they have dug for others; the trap they set has snapped on them.

16 The Lord is famous for the way He punishes the wicked in their own snares![9]

17 The wicked shall be sent away to hell; this is the fate of all the nations forgetting the Lord.

18 For the needs of the needy shall not be ignored forever; the hopes of the poor shall not always be crushed.

19 O Lord, arise and judge and punish the nations; don't let them conquer You!

20 Make them tremble in fear; put the nations in their place until at last they know they are but puny men.

## PSALM 10

Lord, why are You standing aloof and far away? Why do you hide when I need You the most?

---

[8]Literally, "in the gates of the daughter of Zion."
[9]The Hebrew text adds here: "Higgaion. Selah." The meanings of these words are not known.

2    Come and deal with all these proud and wicked men who viciously persecute the poor. Pour upon these men the evil they planned for others!

3    For these men brag of all their evil lusts; they revile God and congratulate those the Lord abhors, whose only goal in life is money.

4    These wicked men, so proud and haughty, seem to think that God is dead.[1] They wouldn't think of looking for Him!

5    Yet there is success in everything they do, and their enemies fall before them. They do not see Your punishment awaiting them.

6    They boast that neither God nor man can ever keep them down—somehow they'll find a way!

7    Their mouths are full of profanity and lies and fraud. They are always boasting of their evil plans.

8    They lurk in dark alleys of the city and murder passersby.

9    Like lions they crouch silently, waiting to pounce upon the poor. Like hunters they catch their victims in their traps.

10    The unfortunate are overwhelmed by their superior strength and fall beneath their blows.

11    "God isn't watching," they say to themselves; "He'll never know!"

12    O Lord, arise! O God, crush them! Don't forget the poor or anyone else in need.

13    Why do You let the wicked get away with this

---

[1]Literally, "that there is no God."

contempt for God? For they think that God will never call them to account.

14 Lord, You see what they are doing. You have noted each evil act. You know what trouble and grief they have caused. Now punish them. O Lord, the poor man trusts himself to You; You are known as the helper of the helpless.

15 Break the arms of these wicked men. Go after them until the last of them is destroyed.

16 The Lord is King forever and forever. Those who follow other gods shall be swept from His land.

17 Lord, You know the hopes of humble people. Surely You will hear their cries and comfort their hearts by helping them.

18 You will be with the orphans and all who are oppressed, so that mere earthly man will terrify them no longer.

## PSALM 11

How dare you tell me, "Flee[2] to the mountains for safety," when I am trusting in the Lord?

2 For the wicked have strung their bows, drawn their arrows tight against the bowstrings, and aimed from ambush at the people of God.

3 "Law and order have collapsed,"[3] we are told. "What can the righteous do but flee?"

4 But the Lord is still in His holy temple; He still

[2]Literally, "Flee as a bird."
[3]Literally, "If the foundations have been torn down."

rules from heaven. He closely watches everything that happens here on earth.

5 He puts the righteous and the wicked to the test; He hates those loving violence.

6 He will rain down fire and brimstone on the wicked and scorch them with His burning wind.

7 For God is good, and He loves goodness; the godly shall see His face.⁴

## PSALM 12

Lord! Help! Godly men are fast disappearing. Where in all the world can dependable men be found?

2 Everyone deceives and flatters and lies. There is no sincerity left.

3, 4 But the Lord will not deal gently with people who act like that; He will destroy those proud liars who say, "We will lie to our hearts' content. Our lips are our own; who can stop us?"

5 The Lord replies, "I will arise and defend the oppressed, the poor, the needy. I will rescue them as they have longed for Me to do."

6 The Lord's promise is sure. He speaks no careless word; all He says is purest truth, like silver seven times refined.

7 O Lord, we know that You will forever preserve Your own from the reach of evil men,

---

⁴Or, "His face shines down in mercy and joy upon the good."

8 Although they prowl on every side and vileness is praised throughout the land.

## PSALM 13

How long will You forget me, Lord? Forever? How long will You look the other way when I am in need?

2 How long must I be hiding daily anguish in my heart? How long shall my enemy have the upper hand?

3 Answer me, O Lord my God; give me light in my darkness lest I die.

4 Don't let my enemies say, "We have conquered him!" Don't let them gloat that I am down.

5 But I will always trust in You and in Your mercy and shall rejoice in Your salvation.

6 I will sing to the Lord because He has blessed me so richly.

## PSALM 14

That man is a fool who says to himself, "There is no God!" Anyone who talks like that is warped and evil and cannot really be a good person at all.

2 The Lord looks down from heaven on all mankind to see if there are any who are wise, who want to please God.

3 But no, all have strayed away; all are rotten with sin. Not one is good, not one!

4   They eat my people like bread and wouldn't think of praying! Don't they really know any better?

5   Terror shall grip them, for God is with those who love Him.

6   He is the refuge of the poor and humble when evildoers are oppressing them.

7   Oh, that the time of their rescue were already here; that God would come from Zion now to save His people. What gladness when the Lord has rescued Israel!

## PSALM 15

Lord, who may go and find refuge and shelter in Your tabernacle up on Your holy hill?

2   Anyone who leads a blameless life and is truly sincere.

3   Anyone who refuses to slander others, does not listen to gossip, never harms his neighbor,

4   Speaks out against sin, criticizes those committing it, commends the faithful followers of the Lord, keeps a promise even if it ruins him,

5   Does not crush his debtors with high interest rates, and refuses to testify against the innocent despite the bribes offered him—such a man shall stand firm forever.

## PSALM 16

Save me, O God, because I have come to You for refuge.

2 I said to Him, "You are my Lord; I have no other help but Yours."

3 I want the company of the godly men and women in the land; they are the true nobility.

4 Those choosing other gods shall all be filled with sorrow; I will not offer the sacrifices they do or even speak the names of their gods.

5 The Lord Himself is my inheritance, my prize! He is my food and drink, my highest joy! He guards all that is mine.

6 He sees that I am given pleasant brooks and meadows as my share![5] What a wonderful inheritance!

7 I will bless the Lord who counsels me; He gives me wisdom in the night. He tells me what to do.

8 I am always thinking of the Lord; and because He is so near, I never need to stumble or to fall.

9 Heart, body, and soul are filled with joy.

10 For You will not leave me among the dead; You will not allow Your beloved one to rot in the grave.

11 You have let me experience the joys of life and the exquisite pleasures of Your own eternal presence.

## PSALM 17

I am pleading for Your help, O Lord; for I have been honest and have done what is right, and You must listen to my earnest cry!

---

[5]Literally, "The boundary lines are fallen unto me in pleasant places."

2   Publicly acquit me, Lord, for You are always fair.

3   You have tested me and seen that I am good. You have come even in the night and found nothing amiss and know that I have told the truth.

4   I have followed Your commands and have not gone along with cruel and evil men.

5   My feet have not slipped from Your paths.

6   Why am I praying like this? Because I know You will answer me, O God! Yes, listen as I pray.

7   Show me Your strong love in wonderful ways, O Savior of all those seeking Your help against their foes.

8   Protect me as You would the pupil of Your eye; hide me in the shadow of Your wings as You hover over me.

9   My enemies encircle me with murder in their eyes.

10   They are pitiless and arrogant. Listen to their boasting.

11   They close in upon me and are ready to throw me to the ground.

12   They are like lions eager to tear me apart, like young lions hiding and waiting their chance.

13, 14   Lord, arise and stand against them! Push them back! Come and save me from these men of the world whose only concern is earthly gain—these men whom You have filled with Your treasures so that their children and grandchildren are rich and prosperous.

15   But as for me, my contentment is not in wealth

but in seeing You and knowing all is well between us. And when I awake in heaven, I will be fully satisfied, for I will see You face to face.

## PSALM 18

*(This song of David was written at a time when the Lord had delivered him from his many enemies, including Saul.)*

Lord, how I love You! For You have done such tremendous things for me.

2 The Lord is my fort where I can enter and be safe; no one can follow me in and slay me. He is a rugged mountain where I hide; He is my Savior, a rock where none can reach me, and a tower of safety. He is my shield. He is like the strong horn of a mighty fighting bull.

3 All I need to do is cry to Him—oh, praise the Lord—and I am saved from all my enemies!

4 Death bound me with chains, and the floods of ungodliness mounted a massive attack against me.

5 Trapped and helpless, I struggled against the ropes that drew me on to death.

6 In my distress I screamed to the Lord for His help. And He heard me from heaven;[6] my cry reached His ears.

7 Then the earth rocked and reeled, and mountains shook and trembled. How they quaked! For He was angry.

---

[6]Literally, "out of His temple."

8　Fierce flames leaped from His mouth, setting fire to the earth;[7] smoke blew from His nostrils.

9　He bent the heavens down and came to my defense;[8] thick darkness was beneath His feet.

10　Mounted on the cherubim* He sped swiftly to my aid with wings of wind.

11　He enshrouded Himself with darkness, veiling His approach with dense clouds dark as murky waters.

12　Suddenly the brilliance of His presence broke through the clouds with lightning[9] and a mighty storm of hail.

13　The Lord thundered in the heavens; the God above all gods has spoken—oh, the hailstones; oh, the fire!

14　He flashed His fearful arrows of lightning and routed all my enemies. See how they run!

15　Then at Your command, O Lord, the sea receded from the shore. At the blast of Your breath the depths were laid bare.

16　He reached down from heaven and took me and drew me out of my great trials. He rescued me from deep waters.

17　He delivered me from my strong enemy, from those who hated me—I who was helpless in their hands.

18　On the day when I was weakest, they attacked. But the Lord held me steady.

---

[7]Literally, "coals were kindled by it."
[8]Implied.
*Literally, "a cherub."
[9]Literally, "coals of fire."

19 He led me to a place of safety, for He delights in me.

20 The Lord rewarded me for doing right and being pure.

21 For I have followed His commands and have not sinned by turning back from following Him.

22 I kept close watch on all His laws; I did not refuse a single one.

23 I did my best to keep them all, holding myself back from doing wrong.

24 And so the Lord has paid me with His blessings, for I have done what is right, and I am pure of heart. This He knows, for He watches my every step.

25 Lord, how merciful You are to those who are merciful. And You do not punish those who run from evil.[1]

26 You give blessings to the pure but pain to those who leave Your paths.

27 You deliver the humble but condemn the proud and haughty ones.

28 You have turned on my light! The Lord my God has made my darkness turn to light.

29 Now in Your strength I can scale any wall, attack any troop.

30 What a God He is! How perfect in every way! All His promises prove true. He is a shield for everyone who hides behind Him.

31 For who is God except our Lord? Who but He is as a rock?

---

[1]Literally, "with the upright You show Yourself upright."

32 He fills me with strength and protects me wherever I go.

33 He gives me the surefootedness of a mountain goat upon the crags. He leads me safely along the top of the cliffs.

34 He prepares me for battle and gives me strength to draw an iron[2] bow!

35 You have given me Your salvation as my shield. Your right hand, O Lord, supports me; Your gentleness has made me great.

36 You have made wide steps beneath my feet so that I need never slip.

37 I chased my enemies; I caught up with them and did not turn back until all were conquered.

38 I pinned them to the ground; all were helpless before me. I placed my feet upon their necks!

39 For You have armed me with strong armor for the battle. My enemies quail before me and fall defeated at my feet.

40 You made them turn and run; I destroyed all who hated me.

41 They shouted for help but no one dared to rescue them; they cried to the Lord, but He refused to answer them.

42 So I crushed them fine as dust and cast them to the wind. I threw them away like sweepings from the floor.

43, 44, 45 You gave me victory in every battle! The nations came and served me.

---

[2]Literally, "a bow of bronze."

Even those I didn't know before come now and bow before me. Foreigners who have never seen me submit instantly. They come trembling from their strongholds.

46 God is alive! Praise Him who is the great rock of protection.

47 He is the God who pays back those who harm me and subdues the nations before me.

48 He rescues me from my enemies; He holds me safely out of their reach and saves me from these powerful opponents.

49 For this, O Lord, I will praise You among the nations.

50 Many times You have miraculously rescued me, the king You appointed. You have been loving and kind to me and will be to my descendants.

## PSALM 19

The heavens are telling the glory of God; they are a marvelous display of His craftsmanship.

2 Day and night they keep on telling about God.

3, 4 Without a sound or word, silent in the skies, their message reaches out to all the world.

The sun lives in the heavens where God placed it

5 And moves out across the skies as radiant[3] as a bridegroom going to his wedding,[4] or as joyous as an athlete looking forward to a race!

---

[3]Implied. Literally, "is like a bridegroom."
[4]Implied. Literally, "going forth from his chamber."

6   It crosses the heavens from end to  end, and nothing can hide from its heat.

\*     \*     \*     \*     \*

7, 8   God's laws are perfect. They protect us, make us wise, and give us joy and light.

9   God's laws are just and perfect. Reverence for God keeps us pure and leads us on to heaven.[6]

10   His laws are more desirable than gold. They are sweeter than honey dripping from a honeycomb.

11   For they warn us away from harm and give success to those who obey them!

12   But how can I ever know what sins are lurking in my heart? Cleanse me from these hidden faults.

13   And keep me from deliberate wrongs; help me to stop doing them.  Only then can I be free of guilt and innocent of some great crime.

14   May my spoken words and unspoken thoughts be pleasing even to You, O Lord my Rock and my Redeemer.

## PSALM 20

In your day of trouble, may the Lord be with you! May the God of Jacob keep you from all harm.

2   May He send you aid from His sanctuary in Zion.

3   May He remember with pleasure the gifts you have given Him, your sacrifices and burnt offerings.

---

[6]Or, "The rules governing the worship of the Lord are pure and need never be changed."

4 May He grant you your heart's desire and fulfill all your plans.

5 May there be shouts of joy when we hear the news of your victory, flags flying with praise to God for all that He has done for you. May He answer all your prayers!

6 "God save the king"—I know He does! He hears me from highest heaven and sends great victories.

7 Some nations boast of armies and of weaponry, but our boast is in the Lord our God.

8 Those nations will collapse and perish; we will arise to stand firm and sure!

9 Give victory to our king, O Lord; oh, hear our prayer.

## PSALM 21

How the king rejoices in Your strength, O Lord! How he exults in Your salvation.

2 For You have given him his heart's desire, everything he asks You for!

3 You welcomed him to the throne with success and prosperity. You set a kingly crown of purest gold upon his head.

4 He asked for a long, good life, and You have granted his request; the days of his life stretch on and on forever!

5 You have given him fame and honor. You have clothed him with splendor and majesty.

6 You have endowed him with eternal happiness. You have given him the unquenchable joy of Your presence.

7 And because the king trusts in the Lord, he will never stumble, never fall; for he depends upon the steadfast love of the God who is above all gods.

8 Your hand, O Lord, will find Your enemies, all who hate You.

9, 10 When You appear, they will be destroyed in the fierce fire of Your presence. The Lord will destroy them and their children.

11 For these men plot against You, Lord, but they cannot possibly succeed.

12 They will turn and flee when they see Your arrows aimed straight at them.

13 Accept our praise, O Lord, for all Your glorious power! We will write songs to celebrate Your mighty acts!

## PSALM 22

My God, my God, why have You forsaken me? Why do You refuse to help me or even to listen to my groans?

2 Day and night I keep on weeping, crying for Your help, but there is no reply—

3, 4 For *You are holy.*

\* \* \* \* \*

The praises of our fathers surrounded Your throne; they trusted You and You delivered them.

5    You heard their cries for help and saved them; they were never disappointed when they sought Your aid.

6    But I am a worm, not a man, scorned and despised by my own people and by all mankind.

7    Everyone who sees me mocks and sneers and shrugs;

8    "Is this the one who rolled his burden on the Lord?" they laugh. "Is this the one who claims the Lord delights in him? We'll believe it when we see God rescue him!"

9, 10, 11    Lord, how You have helped me before![7] You took me safely from my mother's womb and brought me through the years of infancy. I have depended upon You since birth; You have always been my God. Don't leave me now, for trouble is near and no one else can possibly help.

12    I am surrounded by fearful enemies, strong as the giant bulls from Bashan.

13    They come at me with open jaws, like roaring lions attacking their prey.

14    My strength has drained away like water, and all my bones are out of joint. My heart melts like wax;

15    My strength has dried up like sun-baked clay; my tongue sticks to my mouth, for You have laid me in the dust of death.

16    The enemy, this gang of evil men, circles me like a pack of dogs; they have pierced my hands and feet.

---

[7] Implied.

17 I can count every bone in my body. See these men of evil gloat and stare;

18 They divide my clothes among themselves by a toss of the dice.

19 O Lord, don't stay away. O God my Strength, hurry to my aid.

20 Rescue me from death; spare my precious life from all these evil men.[8]

21 Save me from these lions' jaws and from the horns of these wild oxen; yes, God will answer me and rescue me.

22 I will praise You to all my brothers; I will stand up before the congregation and testify of the wonderful things You have done.

23 "Praise the Lord, each one of you who fears Him," I will say. "Each of you[9] must fear and reverence His name. Let all Israel sing His praises,

24 For He has not despised my cries of deep despair; He has not turned and walked away. When I cried to Him, He heard and came."

25 Yes, I will stand and praise You[1] before all the people. I will publicly fulfill my vows in the presence of all who reverence Your name.

26 The poor[2] shall eat and be satisfied; all who seek the Lord shall find Him and shall praise His name. Their hearts shall rejoice with everlasting joy.

---

[8] Literally, "Deliver my soul from the sword, my only one from the power of the dog!"
[9] Literally, "all you sons of Jacob."
[1] Literally, "praise from you."
[2] Literally, "the afflicted."

27 The whole earth shall see it and return to the Lord; the people of every nation shall worship Him.

28 For the Lord is King and rules the nations.

29 Both proud and humble together, all who are mortal—born to die—shall worship Him.

30 Our children too shall serve Him, for they shall hear from us about the wonders of the Lord;

31 Generations yet unborn shall hear of all the miracles He did for us.

## PSALM 23

B ecause the Lord is my shepherd, I have everything I need!

2, 3 He lets me rest in the meadow grass and leads me beside the quiet streams. He restores my failing health. He helps me do what honors Him the most.

\*     \*     \*     \*     \*

4 Even when walking through the Dark Valley of death I will not be afraid, for You are close beside me, guarding, guiding all the way.[3]

5 You provide delicious food for me in the presence of my enemies. You have welcomed me as Your guest;[5] blessings overflow!

6 Your goodness and unfailing kindness shall be with me all of my life, and afterwards I will live with You forever in Your home.

---

[3]Literally, "Your rod and Your staff comfort me."
[5]Literally, "You have anointed my head with oil, my cup runs over."

## PSALM 24

The earth belongs to God! Everything in all the world is His!

2 He is the One who pushed the oceans back to let dry land appear.[6]

3 Who may climb the mountain of the Lord and enter where He lives? Who may stand before the Lord?

4 Only those with pure hands and hearts, who do not practice dishonesty and lying.

5 They will receive God's own goodness[7] as their blessing from Him, planted in their lives by God Himself, their Savior.

6 These are the ones who are allowed to stand before the Lord and worship the God of Jacob.

7 Open up, O ancient gates, and let the King of Glory in.

8 Who is this King of Glory? The Lord, strong and mighty, invincible in battle.

9 Yes, open wide the gates and let the King of Glory in.

10 Who is this King of Glory? The Commander of all of heaven's armies!

## PSALM 25

To You, O Lord, I pray!

2 Don't fail me, Lord, for I am trusting You.

---

[6]Literally, "He has founded it upon the seas."
[7]Literally, "righteousness," right standing with God.

Don't let my enemies succeed. Don't give them victory over me.

3  None who have faith in God will ever be disgraced for trusting Him. But all who harm the innocent shall be defeated.

4  Show me the path where I should go, O Lord; point out the right road for me to walk.

5  Lead me; teach me; for You are the God who gives me salvation. I have no hope except in You.

6, 7  Overlook my youthful sins, O Lord! Look at me instead through eyes of mercy and forgiveness, through eyes of everlasting love and kindness.

8  The Lord is good and glad to teach the proper path to all who go astray;

9  He will teach the ways that are right and best to those who humbly turn to Him.

10  And when we obey Him, every path He guides us on is fragrant with His lovingkindness and His truth.

11  But Lord, my sins! How many they are. Oh, pardon them for the honor of Your name.

12  Where is the man who fears the Lord? God will teach him how to choose the best!

13  He shall live within God's circle of blessing, and his children shall inherit the earth!

14  Friendship with God is reserved for those who reverence Him. With them alone He shares the secrets of His promises.

15  My eyes are ever looking to the Lord for help, for He alone can rescue me.

16   Come, Lord, and show me Your mercy, for I am helpless, overwhelmed, in deep distress;

17   My problems go from bad to worse. Oh, save me from them all!

18   See my sorrows; feel my pain; forgive my sins.

19   See how many enemies I have and how viciously they hate me!

20   Save me from them! Deliver my life from their power! Oh, let it never be said that I trusted You in vain!

21   Assign me Godliness and Integrity as my bodyguards, for I expect You to protect me,

22   And to ransom Israel from all her troubles.


## PSALM 26

Dismiss all the charges against me, Lord, for I have tried to keep Your laws and have trusted You without wavering.

2   Cross-examine me, O Lord, and see that this is so; test my motives and affections too.

3   For I have taken Your lovingkindness and Your truth as my ideals.

4   I do not have fellowship with tricky, two-faced men; they are false and hypocritical.

5   I hate the sinners' hangouts and refuse to enter them.

6   I wash my hands to prove my innocence and come before Your altar

7  Singing a song of thanksgiving and telling about Your miracles.

8  Lord, I love Your home, this shrine where the brilliant, dazzling splendor of Your presence lives.

9, 10  Don't treat me as a common sinner or murderer who plots against the innocent and demands bribes.

11  No, I am not like that, O Lord; I try to walk a straight and narrow path of doing what is right; therefore in mercy save me.

12  I publicly praise the Lord for keeping me from slipping and falling.


## PSALM 27

The Lord is my light and my salvation; whom shall I fear?

2  When evil men come to destroy me, they will stumble and fall!

3  Yes, though a mighty army marches against me, my heart shall know no fear! I am confident that God will save me.

4  The one thing I want from God, the thing I seek most of all, is the privilege of meditating in His temple, living in His presence every day of my life, delighting in His incomparable perfections and glory.

5  There I'll be when troubles come! He will hide me. He will set me on a high rock

6 Out of reach of all my enemies. Then I will bring Him sacrifices and sing His praises with much joy.

7 Listen to my pleading, Lord! Be merciful and send the help I need.

8 My heart has heard You say, "Come and talk with Me, O My people." And my heart responds, "Lord, I am coming."

9 Oh, do not hide Yourself when I am trying to find You. Do not angrily reject Your servant! You have been my help in all my trials before; don't leave me now. Don't forsake me, O God of my salvation.

10 For if my father and mother should abandon me, You would welcome and comfort me.

11 Tell me what to do, O Lord, and make it plain because I am surrounded by waiting enemies.

12 Don't let them get me, Lord! Don't let me fall into their hands! For they accuse me of things I never did, and all the while are plotting cruelty.

13 I am expecting the Lord to rescue me again, so that once again I will see His goodness to me here in the land of the living!

\* \* \* \* \*

14 Don't be impatient! Wait for the Lord, and He will come and save you! Be brave, stout-hearted and courageous. Yes, wait and He will help you.

## PSALM 28

I plead with You to help me, Lord, for You are my Rock of safety. If you refuse to answer me, I might as well give up and die.

2   Lord, I lift my hands to heaven[8] and implore Your help. Oh, listen to my cry.

3   Don't punish me with all the wicked ones who speak so sweetly to their neighbors while planning to murder them.

4   Give them the punishment they so richly deserve! Measure it out to them in proportion to their wickedness; pay them back for all their evil deeds.

5   They care nothing for God or what He has done or what He has made; therefore God will dismantle them like old buildings, never to be rebuilt again.

*     *     *     *     *

6   Oh, praise the Lord, for He has listened to my pleadings!

7   He is my strength, my shield from every danger. I trusted in Him, and He helped me! Joy rises in my heart until I burst out in songs of praise to Him.

8   The Lord protects His people and gives victory to His anointed king.

9   Defend Your people, Lord; defend and bless Your chosen ones. Lead them like a shepherd and carry them forever in Your arms.

## PSALM 29

Praise the Lord, you angels of His; praise His glory and His strength.

---

[8]Literally, "Your innermost shrine," i.e., the Holy of Holies within the tabernacle.

2 Praise Him for His majestic glory, the glory of His name. Come before Him clothed in sacred garments.

3 The voice of the Lord echoes from the clouds. The God of Glory thunders through the skies.

4 So powerful is His voice; so full of majesty.

5, 6 It breaks down the cedars! It splits the giant trees of Lebanon. It shakes Mount Lebanon and Mount Sirion. They leap and skip before Him like young calves!

7 The voice of the Lord thunders through the lightning.

8 It resounds through the deserts and shakes the wilderness of Kadesh.

9 The voice of the Lord spins and topples the mighty oaks.[9] It strips the forests bare! They whirl and sway beneath the blast. But in His temple all are praising, "Glory, glory to the Lord."

10 At the Flood, the Lord showed His control of all creation. Now He continues to unveil His power.

11 He will give His people strength. He will bless them with peace.

## PSALM 30

I will praise You, Lord, for You have saved me from my enemies. You refuse to let them triumph over me.

2 O Lord my God, I pled with You, and You gave me my health again.

---

[9]Or, "makes the hinds to calve."

3 You brought me back from the brink of the grave, from death itself, and here I am alive!

4 Oh, sing to Him you saints of His; give thanks to His holy name.

5 His anger lasts a moment; His favor lasts for life! Weeping may go on all night, but in the morning there is joy.

6, 7 In my prosperity I said, "This is forever; nothing can stop me now! The Lord has shown me His favor. He has made me steady as a mountain."

Then, Lord, You turned Your face away from me and cut off Your river of blessings.[1] Suddenly my courage was gone; I was terrified and panic-stricken.

8 I cried to You, O Lord; oh, how I pled:

9 "What will You gain, O Lord, from killing me? How can I praise You then to all my friends?[1] How can my dust in the grave speak out and tell the world about Your faithfulness?

10 Hear me, Lord; oh, have pity and help me."

11 Then He turned my sorrow into joy! He took away my clothes of mourning and gave me gay and festive garments to rejoice in

12 So that I might sing glad praises to the Lord instead of lying in silence in the grave. O Lord my God, I will keep on thanking You forever!

## PSALM 31

Lord, I trust in You alone. Don't let my enemies defeat me. Rescue me because You are the God who always does what is right.

---

[1]Implied.

2  Answer quickly when I cry to You; bend low and hear my whispered[2] plea. Be for me a great Rock of safety from my foes.

3  Yes, You are my Rock and my fortress; honor Your name by leading me out of this peril.

4  Pull me from the trap my enemies have set for me. For You alone are strong enough.[3]

5, 6  Into Your hand I commit my spirit . . .

\*     \*     \*     \*     \*

You have rescued me, O God who keeps His promises! for I worship only You; and how You hate all those who worship idols, those imitation gods.

7  I am radiant with joy because of Your mercy, for You have listened to my troubles and have seen the crisis in my soul.

8  You have not handed me over to my enemy, but have given me open ground in which to maneuver.

\*     \*     \*     \*     \*

9, 10  O Lord, have mercy on me in my anguish. My eyes are red from weeping; my health is broken from sorrow. I am pining away with grief; my years are shortened, drained away because of sadness. My sins have sapped my strength; I stoop with sorrow and with shame.[4]

11  I am scorned by all my enemies and even more by my neighbors and friends. They dread meeting me and look the other way when I go by.

12  I am forgotten like a dead man, like a broken and discarded pot.

---

[2]Implied.
[3]Literally, "for You are my refuge."
[4]Literally, "Even my bones are rotting away."

13  I heard the lies about me, the slanders of my enemies. Everywhere I looked I was afraid, for they were plotting against my life.

14, 15  But I was trusting You, O Lord. I said, "You alone are my God; my times are in Your hands. Rescue me from those who hunt me down relentlessly.

16  Let Your favor shine again upon Your servant; save me just because You are so kind!

17  Don't disgrace me, Lord, by not replying when I call to You for aid. But let the wicked be shamed by what they trust in; let them lie silently in their graves,

18  Their lying lips quieted at last—the lips of these arrogant men who are accusing honest men of evil deeds."

19  Oh, how great is Your goodness to those who publicly declare that You will rescue them. For You have stored up great blessings for those who trust and reverence You.

20  Hide Your loved ones in the shelter of Your presence, safe beneath Your hand, safe from all conspiring men.

21  Blessed is the Lord, for He has shown me that His never-failing love protects me like the walls of a fort!

22  I spoke too hastily when I said, "The Lord has deserted me," for You listened to my plea and answered me.

23  Oh, love the Lord all of you who are His people; for the Lord protects those who are loyal to Him, but harshly punishes all who haughtily reject Him.

24 So cheer up! Take courage if you are depending on the Lord!

## PSALM 32

What happiness for those whose guilt has been forgiven! What joys when sins are covered over! What relief for those who have confessed their sins and God has cleared their record.

3 There was a time when I wouldn't admit what a sinner I was.[5] But my dishonesty made me miserable and filled my days with frustration.

4 All day and all night Your hand was heavy on me. My strength evaporated like water on a sunny day

5 Until I finally admitted all my sins to You and stopped trying to hide them. I said to myself, "I will confess them to the Lord." And You forgave me! All my guilt is gone!

6 After this experience, I say that every believer should confess his sins to God as soon as he becomes aware of them, while there is yet time to be forgiven. If he does this, judgment will not touch him.[6]

7 You are my hiding place from every storm of life; You even keep me from getting into trouble! You surround me with songs of victory.

8 I will instruct you (says the Lord) and guide you along the best pathway for your life; I will advise you and watch your progress.

---

[5]Literally. "When I kept silence."
[6]Literally, "When the great waters overflow they shall not reach him."

9   Don't be like a senseless horse or mule that has to have a bit in its mouth to keep it in line!

10   Many sorrows come to the wicked, but abiding love surrounds those who trust in the Lord.

11   So rejoice in Him, all those who are His,[7] and shout for joy, all those who try to obey Him.[8]

## PSALM 33

Let all the joys of the godly well up in praise to the Lord, for it is right to praise Him.

2   Play joyous melodies of praise upon the lyre and on the harp!

3   Compose new songs of praise to Him, accompanied skillfully on the harp; sing joyfully.

4   For all God's words are right, and everything He does is worthy of our trust.

5   He loves whatever is just and good; the earth is filled with His tender love.

6   He merely spoke, and the heavens were formed, and all the galaxies of stars.

7   He made the oceans, pouring them into His vast reservoirs.

8   Let everyone in all the world—men, women and children—fear the Lord and stand in awe of Him.

9   For when He but spoke, the world began! It appeared at His command!

[7]Literally, "You righteous."
[8]Literally, "All who are upright in heart."

10   And with a breath He can scatter the plans of all the nations who oppose Him,

11   But His own plan stands forever. His intentions are the same for every generation.

12   Blessed is the nation whose God is the Lord, whose people He has chosen as His own.

13, 14, 15   The Lord gazes down upon mankind from heaven where He lives. He has made their hearts and closely watches everything they do.

16, 17   The best-equipped army cannot save a king —for great strength is not enough to save anyone. A war horse is a poor risk for winning victories—it is strong but it cannot save.

18, 19   But the eyes of the Lord are watching over those who fear Him, who rely upon His steady love. He will keep them from death even in times of famine!

20   We depend upon the Lord alone to save us. Only He can help us, He protects us like a shield.

21   No wonder we are happy in the Lord! For we are trusting Him! We trust His holy name.

22   Yes, Lord, let Your constant love surround us, for our hopes are in You alone.


## PSALM 34

I will praise the Lord no matter what happens. I will constantly speak of His glories and grace.[9]

---
[9]Literally, "His praise shall continually be in my mouth."

2   I will boast of all His kindness to me. Let all who are discouraged take heart!

3   Let us praise the Lord together, and exalt His name.

4   For I cried to Him and He answered me! He freed me from all my fears.

5   Others too were radiant at what He did for them. Theirs was no downcast look of rejection!

6   This poor man cried to the Lord—and the Lord heard him and saved him out of his troubles.

7   For the Angel of the Lord guards and rescues all who reverence Him.

8   Oh, put God to the test and see how kind He is! See for yourself the way His mercies shower down on all who trust in Him!

9   If you belong to the Lord, reverence Him; for everyone who does this has everything he needs.

10   Even strong young lions sometimes go hungry, but those of us who reverence the Lord will never lack any good thing.

11   Sons and daughters, come and listen and let me teach you the importance of trusting and fearing the Lord.

12   Do you want a long, good life?

13   Then watch your tongue! Keep your lips from lying.

14   Turn from all known sin and spend your time in doing good. Try to live in peace with everyone; work hard at it.

15   For the eyes of the Lord are intently watching

all who live good lives, and He gives attention when they cry to Him.

16 But the Lord has made up His mind to wipe out even the memory of evil men from the earth.

17 Yes, the Lord hears the good man when he calls to Him for help, and saves him out of all his troubles.

18 The Lord is close to those whose hearts are breaking; He rescues those who are humbly sorry for their sins.

19 The good man does not escape all troubles—he has them too. But the Lord helps him in each and every one.

20 God even protects him from accidents.

21 Calamity will surely overtake the wicked; heavy penalties are meted out to those who hate the good.

22 But as for those who serve the Lord, He will redeem them; everyone who takes refuge in Him will be freely pardoned.

## PSALM 35

O Lord, fight those fighting me; declare war on them for their attacks on me.

2 Put on Your armor, take Your shield and protect me by standing in front.

3 Lift Your spear in my defense, for my pursuers are getting very close. Let me hear You say that You will save me from them!

4 Dishonor those who are trying to kill me! Turn them back and confuse them.

5 Blow them away like chaff in the wind—wind sent by the Angel of the Lord.

6 Make their path dark and slippery before them, with the Angel of the Lord pursuing them.

7 For though I did them no wrong, yet they laid a trap for me and dug a pitfall in my path.

8 Let them be overtaken by sudden ruin, caught in their own net, and destroyed.

9 But I will rejoice in the Lord. He shall rescue me!

10 From the bottom of my heart praise rises to Him. Where is His equal in all of heaven and earth? Who else protects the weak and helpless from the strong, and the poor and needy from those who would rob them?

11 These evil men swear to a lie. They accuse me of things I have never even heard about.

12 I do them good, but they return me harm. I am sinking down to death.

13 When they were ill, I mourned before the Lord in sackcloth, asking Him to make them well; I refused to eat; I prayed for them with utmost earnestness, but God did not listen.

14 I went about sadly as though it were my mother, friend or brother who was sick and nearing death.

15 But now that I am in trouble they are glad; they come together in meetings filled with slander against me—I didn't even know some of those who were there.

16 For they gather with the worthless fellows of the town and spend their time cursing me.

17 Lord, how long will You stand there, doing

nothing? Act now and rescue me, for I have but one life and these young lions are out to get it.

18   Save me, and I will thank You publicly before the entire congregation, before the largest crowd I can find.

19   Don't give victory to those who fight me without any reason! Don't let them rejoice[1] at my fall—let them die.

20   They don't talk of peace and doing good, but of plots against innocent men who are minding their own business.

21   They shout that they have seen *me* doing wrong! "Aha!" they say, "With our own eyes we saw him do it."

22   Lord, You know all about it. Don't stay silent! Don't desert me now!

23   Rise up, O Lord my God; vindicate me.

24   Declare me "not guilty," for You are just.[2] Don't let my enemies rejoice over me in my troubles.

25   Don't let them say, "Aha! Our dearest wish against him will soon be fulfilled!" and, "At last we have him!"

26   Shame them; let these who boast against me and who rejoice at my troubles be themselves overcome by misfortune that strips them bare of everything they own. Bare them to dishonor.

27   But give great joy to all who wish me well. Let them shout with delight, "Great is the Lord who enjoys helping His child!"[3]

---

[1]Literally, "Wink with the eye."
[2]Literally, "Judge me according to Your righteousness."
[3]Literally, "Servant."

28   And I will tell everyone how great and good You are; I will praise You all day long.

## PSALM 36

Sin lurks deep in the hearts of the wicked, forever urging them on to evil deeds. They have no fear of God to hold them back.

2   Instead, in their conceit, they think they can hide their evil deeds and not get caught.

3   Everything they say is crooked and deceitful; they are no longer wise and good.

4   They lie awake at night to hatch their evil plots, instead of planning how to keep away from wrong.

5   Your steadfast love, O Lord, is as great as all the heavens. Your faithfulness reaches beyond the clouds!

6   Your justice is as solid as God's mountains. Your decisions are as full of wisdom as the oceans are with water. You are concerned[4] for men and animals alike!

7   How precious is Your constant love, O God! All humanity takes refuge in the shadow of Your wings!

8   You feed them with blessings from Your own table and let them drink from Your rivers of delight.

9   For You are the Fountain of Life; our light is from Your Light.

10   Pour out Your unfailing love on those who know You! Never stop giving Your salvation[5] to those who long to do Your will.

---

[4]Literally, "You preserve."
[5]Literally, "Your righteousness."

11   Don't let these proud men trample me. Don't let their wicked hands push me around.

12   Look! They have fallen. They are thrown down and will not rise again.

## PSALM 37

Never envy the wicked!
2   Soon they fade away like grass and disappear.

3   Trust in the Lord instead. Be kind and good to others; then you will live safely here in the land and prosper, feeding in safety.

4   Be delighted with the Lord! Then He will give you all your heart's desires.

5   Commit everything you do to the Lord. Trust Him to help you do it and He will.

6   Your innocence will be clear to everyone. He will vindicate you with the blazing light of justice shining down as from the noonday sun.

7   Rest in the Lord; wait patiently for Him to act. Don't be envious of evil men who prosper.

8   Stop your anger! Turn off your wrath. Don't fret and worry—it only leads to harm.

9   For the wicked shall be destroyed, but those who trust the Lord shall be given every blessing.

10   Only a little while and the wicked shall disappear. You will look for them in vain.

11 But all who humble themselves before the Lord shall be given every blessing, and shall have wonderful peace.

12, 13 The Lord is laughing at those who plot against the godly, for He knows their judgment day is coming.

14 Evil men take aim to slay the poor; they are ready to butcher those who do right.

15 But their swords will be plunged into their own hearts and all their weapons will be broken.

16 It is better to have little and be godly than to own an evil man's wealth;

17 For the strength of evil men shall be broken, but the Lord takes care of those He has forgiven.[6]

18 Day by day the Lord observes the good deeds done by godly men,[7] and gives them eternal rewards.

19 He cares for them when times are hard; even in famine, they will have enough.

20 But evil men shall perish. These enemies of God will wither like grass, and disappear like smoke.

21 Evil men borrow and "cannot pay it back"! But the good man returns what he owes with some extra besides.

22 Those blessed by the Lord shall inherit the earth; but those cursed by Him shall die.

23 The steps of good men are directed by the Lord. He delights in each step they take.

24 If they fall it isn't fatal, for the Lord holds them with His hand.

---

[6]Literally, "the righteous."
[7]Literally, "knows the days of the upright."

25   I have been young and now I am old. And in all my years I have never seen the Lord forsake a man who loves Him; nor have I seen the children of the godly go hungry.

26   Instead, the godly are able to be generous with their gifts and loans to others, and their children are a blessing.

27   So if you want an eternal home, leave your evil, low-down ways and live good lives.

28   For the Lord loves justice and fairness; He will never abandon His people. They will be kept safe forever; but all who love wickedness shall perish.

29   The godly shall be firmly planted in the land, and live there forever.

30, 31   The godly man is a good counselor because he is just and fair and knows right from wrong.

32   Evil men spy on the godly, waiting for an excuse to accuse them and then demanding their death!

33   But the Lord will not let these evil men succeed, or let the godly be condemned when they are brought before the judge.

34   Don't be impatient for the Lord to act! Keep steadily along His pathway and in due season He will honor you with every blessing,[8] and you will see the wicked destroyed.

35, 36   I myself have seen it happen: a proud and evil man, towering like a cedar of Lebanon, but when I looked again, he was gone! I searched but could not find him!

_____
[8]Literally, "to possess the land."

37  But the good man—what a different story! For the good man—the blameless, the upright, the man of peace—he has a wonderful future ahead of him. For him there is a happy ending.

38  But evil men shall be destroyed, and their posterity shall be cut off.

39  The Lord saves the godly! He is their salvation and their refuge when trouble comes.

40  Because they trust in Him, He helps them and delivers them from the plots of evil men.


## PSALM 38

O Lord, don't punish me while You are angry!
2  Your arrows have struck deep; Your blows are crushing me.

3, 4  Because of Your anger my body is sick, my health is broken beneath my sins. They are like a flood, higher than my head; they are a burden too heavy to bear.

5, 6  My wounds are festering and full of pus. Because of my sins I am bent and racked with pain. My days are filled with anguish.

7  My loins burn with inflammation[9] and my whole body is diseased.

8  I am exhausted and crushed; I groan in despair.[1]

9  Lord, You know how I long for my health once more. You hear my every sigh.

---

[9]Implied.
[1]Or, "Because of the pains in my heart."

10 My heart beats wildly, my strength fails, and I am going blind.

11 My loved ones and friends stay away, fearing my disease. Even my own family stands at a distance.

12 Meanwhile my enemies are trying to kill me. They plot my ruin and spend all their waking hours planning treachery.

13, 14 But I am deaf to all their threats; I am silent before them as a man who cannot speak. I have nothing to say.

15 For I am waiting for You, O Lord my God. Come and protect me.

16 Put an end to their arrogance, these who gloat when I am cast down!

17 How constantly I find myself upon the verge of sin;[2] this source of sorrow always stares me in the face.

18 I confess my sins; I am sorry for what I have done.

19 But my enemies persecute with vigor, and continue to hate me—though I have done nothing against them to deserve it.

20 They repay me evil for good and hate me for standing for the right.

21 Don't leave me, Lord! Don't go away!

22 Come quickly! Help me, O my Savior.


## PSALM 39

I said to myself, I'm going to quit complaining! I'll keep quiet, especially when the ungodly are around me.

---

[2]Literally, "I am ready to fall."

2, 3   But as I stood there silently, the turmoil within me grew to the bursting point. The more I mused, the hotter the fires inside. Then at last I spoke, and pled with God:

4   Lord, help me to realize how brief my time on earth will be! Help me to know that I am here for but a moment more.

5, 6   My life is no longer than my hand! My whole lifetime is but a moment to You. Proud man! Frail as breath! A shadow! And all his busy rushing ends in nothing. He heaps up riches for someone else to spend.

7   And so, Lord, my only hope is in You.

8   Save me from being overpowered by my sins, for even fools will mock me then.

9   Lord, I am speechless before You. I will not open my mouth to speak one word of complaint, for my punishment is from You.[3]

10   Lord, don't hit me anymore—I am exhausted beneath Your hand.

11   When You punish a man for his sins, he is destroyed; for he is as fragile as a moth-infested cloth; yes, man is frail as breath.

12   Hear my prayer, O Lord; listen to my cry! Don't sit back, unmindful of my tears! For I am Your guest! I am a traveler passing through the earth, as all my fathers were!

13   Spare me, Lord! Let me recover and be filled with happiness again before my death.

---

[3]Literally, "for You have done it."

## PSALM 40

I waited patiently for God to help me; then He listened and heard my cry.

2 He lifted me out of the pit of despair, out from the bog and the mire, and set my feet on a hard, firm path and steadied me as I walked along.

3 He has given me a new song to sing, of praises to our God. Now many will hear of the glorious things He did for me, and stand in awe before the Lord, and put their trust in Him.

4 Many blessings are given to those who trust the Lord, and have no confidence in those who are proud, or who trust in idols.

5 O Lord my God, many and many a time You have done great miracles for us, and we are ever in Your thoughts. Who else can do such glorious things? No one else can be compared with You. There isn't time to tell of all Your wonderful deeds.

6 It isn't sacrifices and offerings which You really want from Your people. Burnt animals bring no special joy to Your heart. But You have accepted the offer of my lifelong service.[4]

7 Then I[5] said, "See, I have come, just as all the prophets foretold.

8 And I delight to do Your will, my God; for Your law is written upon My heart!"

[4]Literally, "My ears You have dug."
[5]This verse was quoted by Christ as applying to Himself. See John 4:34.

9  I have told everyone the Good News that You forgive men's sins.[6] I have not been timid about it, as You well know, O Lord.

10  I have not kept this Good News[6] hidden in my heart, but have proclaimed Your lovingkindness and truth to all the congregation.

11  O Lord, don't hold back Your tender mercies from me! My only hope is in Your love and faithfulness!

12  Otherwise I perish, for problems far too big for me to solve are piled higher than my head. Meanwhile my sins, too many to count, have all caught up with me and I am ashamed to look up. My heart quails within me.

13  Please, Lord, rescue me! Quick! Come and help me!

14, 15  Confuse them! Turn them around and send them sprawling—all these who are trying to destroy me. Disgrace these scoffers with their utter failure!

16  But may the joy of the Lord be given to everyone who loves Him and His salvation. May they constantly exclaim, "How great God is!"

17  I am poor and needy, yet the Lord is thinking about me right now! O my God, You are my helper; You are my Savior; come quickly, and save me. Please don't delay!

## PSALM 41

God blesses those who are kind to the poor. He helps them out of their troubles!

---

[6]Literally, "Your righteousness."

2 He protects them and keeps them alive; He publicly honors them and destroys the power of their enemies.

3 He nurses them when they are sick, and soothes their pains and worries.[7]

4 "O Lord," I prayed, "be kind and heal me, for I have confessed my sins."

5 But my enemies say, "May he soon die and be forgotten!"

6 They act so friendly when they come to visit me while I am sick; but all the time they hate me and are glad that I am lying there upon my bed of pain. And when they leave, they laugh and mock.

7 They whisper together about what they will do when I am dead.

8 "It's fatal, whatever it is," they say. "He'll never get out of that bed!"

9 Even my best friend has turned against me— a man I completely trusted; how often we ate together.

10 Lord, don't You desert me! Be gracious, Lord, and make me well again so I can pay them back!

11 I know You are pleased with me because You haven't let my enemies triumph over me.

12 You have preserved me because I was honest; You have admitted me forever to Your presence.

13 Bless the Lord, the God of Israel, who exists from everlasting ages past—and on into everlasting eternity ahead. Amen and Amen!

---

[7]Literally, "You make all his bed in his sickness."

## PSALM 42

As the deer pants for water, so I long for You, O God.

2 I thirst for God, the living God. Where can I find Him to come and stand before Him?

3 Day and night I weep for His help, and all the while my enemies taunt me. "Where is this God of yours?" they scoff.

4, 5 Take courage, my soul! Do you remember those times (but how could you ever forget them!) when you led a great procession to the Temple on festival days, singing with joy, praising the Lord? Why then be downcast? Why be discouraged and sad? Hope in God! I shall yet praise Him again! Yes, I shall again praise Him for His help.[8]

6 Yet I am standing here depressed and gloomy; but I will meditate upon Your kindness to this lovely land where the Jordan River flows and where Mount Hermon and Mount Mizar stand.

7 All your waves and billows have gone over me, and floods of sorrow pour upon me like a thundering cataract.[9]

8 Yet day by day the Lord also pours out His steadfast love upon me, and through the night I sing His songs and pray to God who gives me life.

9 "O God my Rock," I cry, "why have You for-

[8]Literally, "for the help of His countenance."
[9]Literally, "deep calls to deep at the noise of Your waterfalls."

saken me? Why must I suffer these attacks from my
enemies?"

10 Their taunts pierce me like a fatal wound; again
and again they scoff, "Where is that God of yours?"

11 But O my soul, don't be discouraged! Don't be
upset! Expect God to act! For I know that I shall again
have plenty of reason to praise Him for all that He will
do! He is my help! He is my God!

## PSALM 43

O God, defend me from the charges of these merciless, deceitful men.

2 For You are God, my only place of refuge. Why
have You tossed me aside? Why must I mourn at the
oppression of my enemies?

3 Oh, send out Your light and Your truth—let
them lead me. Let them lead me to Your Temple on
Your holy mountain, Zion.

4 There I will go to the altar of God my exceeding
joy, and praise Him with my harp. O God—my God!

5 O my soul, why be so gloomy and discouraged?
Trust in God! I shall again praise Him for His won-
drous help; He will make me smile again,[1] *for He is my
God!*

## PSALM 44

O God, we have heard of the glorious miracles You
did in the days of long ago. Our forefathers have

[1]Literally, "He is the help of my countenance."

told us how You drove the heathen nations from this land and gave it all to us, spreading Israel from one end of the country to the other.

3   They did not conquer by their own strength and skill; but by Your mighty power and because You smiled upon them and favored them.

4   You are my King and my God. Decree victories for Your people!

5   For it is only by Your power and through Your name that we tread down our enemies;

6   I do not trust my weapons! They could never save me.

7   Only You can give us the victory over those who hate us.

8   My constant boast is God. I can never thank You enough!

9   And yet for a time, O Lord, You have tossed us aside in dishonor, and have not helped us in our battles.

10   You have actually fought against us and defeated us before our foes. Our enemies have invaded our land and pillaged the countryside.

11   You have treated us like sheep in a slaughter pen, and scattered us among the nations.

12   You sold us for a pittance. You valued us at nothing at all.

13   The neighboring nations laugh and mock at us because of all the evil You have sent.

14   You have made the word "Jew" a byword of contempt and shame among the nations, disliked by all.

15, 16 I am constantly despised, mocked, taunted and cursed by my vengeful enemies.

17 And all this has happened, Lord, despite our loyalty to You. We have not violated Your covenant.

18 Our hearts have not deserted You! We have not left Your path by a single step.

19 If we had, we could understand Your punishing us in the barren wilderness and sending us into darkness and death.

20 If we had turned away from worshiping our God, and were worshiping idols,

21 Would God not know it? Yes, He knows the secrets of every heart.

22 But that is not our case! For we are facing death threats constantly because of serving You! We are like sheep awaiting slaughter.

23 Waken! Rouse Yourself! Don't sleep, O Lord! Are we cast off forever?

24 Why do You look the other way? Why do You ignore our sorrows and oppression?

25 We lie face downward in the dust.

26 Rise up, O Lord, and come and help us. Save us by Your constant love.

## PSALM 45

My heart is overflowing with a beautiful thought! I will write a lovely poem to the King, for I am as full of words as the speediest writer pouring out his story.

2    You are the fairest of all;
     Your words are filled with grace;
     God Himself is blessing You forever!

3    Arm Yourself, O Mighty One,
     So glorious, so majestic!

4    And in Your majesty
     Go on to victory,
     Defending truth, humility, and justice.
     Go forth to awe-inspiring deeds!

5    Your arrows are sharp
     In Your enemies' hearts;
     They fall before You.

6    Your throne, O God, endures forever.
     Justice is Your royal scepter.

7    You love what is good
     And hate what is wrong.
     Therefore God, Your God,
     Has given You more gladness
     Than anyone else.

        \*    \*    \*    \*    \*

8   Your robes are perfumed with myrrh, aloes and cassia. In your inlaid palaces of ivory, lovely music is being played for your enjoyment.

9   Kings' daughters are among your concubines.[2] Standing beside you is the queen, wearing jewelry of finest gold from Ophir.

10, 11   "I advise you, O daughter, not to fret about

[2] Literally, "honorable women."

your parents in your homeland far away. Your royal husband delights in your beauty. Reverence him, for he is your lord.

12 The people of Tyre, the richest people of our day, will shower you with gifts and entreat your favors."

13 The bride,[3] a princess, waits within her chamber, robed in beautiful clothing woven with gold.

14 Lovely[4] she is, led beside her maids of honor to the king!

15 What a joyful, glad procession as they enter in the palace gates!

16 "Your sons will some day be kings like their father. They shall sit on thrones around the world!

17 I will cause your name to be honored in all generations; the nations of the earth will praise you forever."

## PSALM 46

God is our refuge and strength, a tested help in times of trouble.

2 And so we need not fear even if the world blows up, and the mountains crumble into the sea.

3 Let the oceans roar and foam; let the mountains tremble!

4 There is a river of joy flowing through the City of our God—the sacred home of the God above all gods.

---

[3]Literally, "The king's daughter."
[4]Literally, "embroidered work."

5 God Himself is living in that City; therefore it stands unmoved despite the turmoil everywhere. He will not delay His help.

6 The nations rant and rave in anger—but when God speaks, the earth melts in submission and kingdoms totter into ruin.

7 The Commander of the armies of heaven is here among us. He, the God of Jacob, has come to rescue us.

8 Come, see the glorious things that our God does, how He brings ruin upon the world,

9 And causes wars to end throughout the earth, breaking and burning every weapon.

10 "Stand silent! Know that I am God! I shall be honored by every nation in the world!"

11 The Commander of the heavenly armies is here among *us!* He, the God of Jacob, has come to rescue *us!*

## PSALM 47

C ome everyone, and clap for joy! Shout triumphant praises to the Lord!

2 For the Lord, the God above all gods, is awesome beyond words; He is the great King of all the earth.

3 He subdues the nations before us,

4 And will personally select His choicest blessings

for His Jewish people[5]—the very best for those He loves.

5 God has ascended (into heaven)[6] with a mighty shout, with trumpets blaring.

6, 7 Sing out your praises to our God, our King. Yes, sing your highest praises to our King, the King of all the earth. Sing thoughtful praises!

8 He reigns above the nations, sitting on His holy throne.

9 The Gentile rulers of the world have joined with us in praising[7] Him—praising[7] the God of Abraham—for the battle shields of all the armies of the world are His trophies. He is highly honored everywhere.

## PSALM 48

How great is the Lord! How much we should praise Him. He lives upon Mount Zion in Jerusalem.

2 What a glorious sight! See Mount Zion rising north of the city[8] high above the plains for all to see—Mount Zion, joy of all the earth, the residence of the great King.

3 God Himself is the defender of Jerusalem.[9]

4 The kings of the earth have arrived together to inspect the city.

---

[5]Literally, "the pride of Jacob."
[6]Implied
[7]Implied.
[8]Literally, "on the sides of the north."
[9]Literally, "God has made Himself known in her palaces for a high tower."

5   They marvel at the sight and hurry home again,

6   Afraid of what they have seen; they are filled with panic like a woman in travail!

7   For God destroys the mightiest warships with a breath of wind!

8   We have heard of the city's glory—the city of our God, the Commander of the armies of heaven. And now we see it for ourselves! God has established Jerusalem forever.

9   Lord, here in Your Temple we meditate upon Your kindness and Your love.

10   Your name is known throughout the earth, O God. You are praised everywhere for the salvation[1] You have scattered throughout the world.

11   O Jerusalem,[2] rejoice! O people of Judah, rejoice! For God will see to it that you are finally treated fairly.

12   Go, inspect the city! Walk around and count her many towers!

13   Note her walls and tour her palaces, so that you can tell your children!

14   For this great God is our God forever and ever. He will be our guide until we die.


## PSALM 49

Listen, everyone! High and low, rich and poor, all around the world—listen to my words,

---

[1]Literally, "Your right hand is filled with righteousness."
[2]Literally, "Mount Zion."

3  For they are wise and filled with insight.

4  I will tell in song accompanied by harps the answer to one of life's most perplexing problems:

5  *There is no need to fear when times of trouble come,* even though surrounded by enemies!

6  For they trust in their wealth and boast about how rich they are!

7  Yet not one of them, though rich as kings, can ransom his own brother from the penalty of sin! For God's forgiveness does not come that way![3]

8, 9  For a soul is far too precious to be ransomed by mere earthly wealth. There is not enough of it in all the earth to buy eternal life for just one soul, to keep it out of hell.[4]

10  Rich man! Proud man! Wise man! You must die like all the rest! You have no greater lease on life than foolish, stupid men. You must leave your wealth to others!

11  You name your estates after yourselves as though your lands could be forever yours, and you could live on them eternally!

12  But man with all his pomp must die like any animal!

13  Such is the folly of these men, though after they die they will be quoted as having great wisdom!

14  Death is the shepherd of all mankind. And "in the morning" those who are evil will be the slaves of those who are good. For the power of their wealth[5] is gone when they die; they cannot take it with them.

---

[3]Implied from text.
[4]Literally, "so that he should not see the Pit."
[5]Literally, "their beauty shall be for Sheol to consume."

15 But as for me, God will redeem my soul from the power of death, for He will receive me.

16 So do not be dismayed when evil men grow rich and build their lovely homes.

17 For when they die they carry nothing with them! Their honors will not follow them.

18 Though a man calls himself happy all through his life—and the world loudly applauds success—

19 Yet in the end he dies like everyone else, and enters eternal darkness.

20 For man with all his pomp[6] must die like any animal!

## PSALM 50

The mighty God, the Lord, has summoned all mankind from east to west!

2 God's glory-light shines from the beautiful Temple[7] on Mount Zion.

3 He comes with the noise of thunder,[8] surrounded by devastating fire; a great storm rages round about Him.

4 He has come to judge His people. To heaven and earth He shouts,

5 "Gather together My own people who by their sacrifice upon My altar have promised to obey[9] Me."

---

[6]Literally, "but without insight." It is uncertain whether this phrase was part of the original text.
[7]Literally, "Out of Zion, the perfection of beauty."
[8]Literally, "comes, and does not keep silence."
[9]Literally, "who made a covenant with me by sacrifice."

6   God will judge them with complete fairness, for all heaven declares that He is just.

7   O My people, listen! For I am your God. Listen! Here are My charges against you:

8   I have no complaint about the sacrifices you bring to My altar, for you bring them regularly.

9   But it isn't sacrificial bullocks and goats that I really want from you!

10, 11   For all the animals of field and forest are Mine! The cattle on a thousand hills! And all the birds upon the mountains!

12   If I were hungry, I would not mention it to you—for all the world is Mine, and everything in it.

13   No, I don't need your sacrifices of flesh and blood!

14, 15   What I want from you is your true thanks; I want your promises fulfilled. *I want you to trust Me in your times of trouble, so I can rescue you, and you can give Me glory!*

16   But God says to evil men: Recite My laws no longer, and stop claiming My promises,

17   For you have refused My discipline, disregarding My laws.

18   You see a thief and help him, and spend your time with evil and immoral men.

19   You curse and lie, and vile language streams from your mouths.

20   You slander your own brother.

21   I remained silent—you thought I didn't care—

but now your time of punishment has come, and I list all the above charges against you.

22　This is the last chance, for all of you who have forgotten God before I tear you apart—and no one can help you then.

23　But true praise is a worthy sacrifice; this really honors Me. Those who walk My paths will receive salvation from the Lord.

## PSALM 51

*(Written after Nathan the prophet had come to inform David of God's judgment against him because of his adultery with Bathsheba, and his murder of Uriah, her husband.)*

O loving and kind God, have mercy. Have pity upon me and take away the awful stain of my transgressions.

2　Oh, wash me, cleanse me from this guilt. Let me be pure again.

3　For I admit my shameful deed—it haunts me day and night.

4　It is against You and You alone I sinned, and did this terrible thing. You saw it all, and Your sentence against me is just.

5　But I was born a sinner, yes, from the moment my mother conceived me.

6　You deserve honesty from the heart; yes, utter sincerity and truthfulness. Oh, give me this wisdom.

7   Sprinkle me with the cleansing blood[2] and I shall be clean again. Wash me and I shall be whiter than snow.

8   And after You have punished me, give me back my joy again.

9   Don't keep looking at my sins—erase them from Your sight.

10   Create in me a new, clean heart, O God, filled with clean thoughts and right desires.

11   Don't toss me aside, banished forever from Your presence. Don't take Your Holy Spirit from me.

12   Restore to me again the joy of Your salvation, and make me willing to obey You.

13   Then I will teach Your ways to other sinners, and they—guilty like me—will repent and return to You.

14, 15   Don't sentence me to death. O my God, You alone can rescue me. Then I will sing of Your forgiveness,[3] for my lips will be unsealed—oh, how I will praise You.

16   You don't want penance;[4] if You did, how gladly I would do it! You aren't interested in offerings burned before You on the altar.

17   It is a broken spirit You want—remorse and penitence. A broken and a contrite heart, O God, You will not ignore.

18   And Lord, don't punish Israel for my sins—help Your people and protect Jerusalem.[5]

---

[2]Literally, "purge me with hyssop." See Exodus 12:22, Hebrews 9:18-22.
[3]Literally, "righteousness."
[4]Literally, "a sacrifice."
[5]Literally, "Do good in Your good pleasure unto Zion; build the walls of Jerusalem."

19    And when my heart is right,[6] then You will rejoice in the good that I do[7] and in the bullocks I bring to sacrifice upon Your altar.


## PSALM 52


*Written by David to protest against his enemy Doeg (I Samuel 22), who later slaughtered 85 priests and their families.*

Y ou call yourself a *hero,* do you? You *boast* about this evil deed of yours against God's people.[8]

2    You are sharp as a tack in plotting your evil tricks.

3    How you love wickedness—far more than good! And lying more than truth!

4    You love to slander—you love to say anything that will do harm, O man with the lying tongue!

5    But God will strike you down and pull you from your home, and drag you away from the land of the living.

6    The followers of God will see it happen. They will watch in awe. Then they will laugh and say,

7    "See what happens to those who despise God and trust in their wealth, and become ever more bold in their wickedness."[9]

8    But I am like a sheltered olive tree protected

---

[6]Implied.
[7]Literally, "then you will delight in the sacrifice of righteousness."
[8]Literally, "the lovingkindness of God continually."
[9]Literally, "strengthened himself in his wickedness."

by the Lord Himself. I trust in the mercy of God forever and ever.

9 O Lord, I will praise You forever and ever for Your punishment.[1] And I will wait for Your mercies—for everyone knows what a merciful God You are.

## PSALM 53

Only a fool would say to himself, "There is no God." And why does he say it?[2] Because of his wicked heart, his dark and evil deeds. His life is corroded with sin.

2 God looks down from heaven, searching among all mankind to see if there is a single one who does right and really seeks for God.

3 But all have turned their backs on Him; they are filthy with sin—corrupt and rotten through and through. Not one is good, not one!

4 How can this be? Can't they understand anything? For they devour My people like bread and refuse to come to God.

5 But soon unheard-of terror will fall on them. God will scatter the bones of these, your enemies! They are doomed, for God has rejected them.

6 Oh, that God would come from Zion now and save Israel! Only when the Lord Himself restores them can they ever be really happy again.

---

[1]Literally, "because You have done it."
[2]Implied.

## PSALM 54

*Written by David at the time the men of Ziph tried to betray him to Saul.*

Come with great power,[3] O God, and save me! Defend me with Your might!

2 Oh, listen to my prayer.

3 For violent men have risen against me—ruthless men who care nothing for God are seeking my life.

4 But God is my helper! He is a friend of mine![4]

5 He will cause the evil deeds of my enemies to boomerang upon them. Do as You promised and put an end to these wicked men, O God.

6 Gladly I bring my sacrifices to You; I will praise Your name, O Lord, for it is good.

7 God has rescued me from all my trouble, and triumphed over my enemies.

## PSALM 55

Listen to my prayer, O God; don't hide Yourself when I cry to You!

2 Hear me, Lord! Listen to me! For I groan and weep beneath my woe.

3 My enemies shout against me and threaten me

---

[3]Literally, "Your name."
[4]Literally, "The Lord is of them that uphold my soul."

with death. They surround me with terror and plot to kill me. Their fury and hatred rise to engulf me.

4 My heart is in anguish within me. Stark fear overpowers me.

5 Trembling and horror overwhelm me.

6 Oh, for wings like a dove, to fly away and rest!

7 I would fly to the far off deserts and stay there.

8 I would flee to some refuge from all this storm.

9 O Lord, make these enemies begin to quarrel among themselves—destroy them with their own violence and strife.[5]

10 Though they patrol their walls night and day against invaders, their real problem is internal—wickedness and dishonesty are entrenched in the heart of the city.

11 There is murder and robbery there, and cheating in the markets and everywhere one looks.

\*    \*    \*    \*    \*

12 It was not an enemy who taunted me—then I could have borne it; I could have hidden and escaped.

13 But it was you, a man like myself, my companion and my friend.

14 What fellowship we had, what wonderful discussions as we walked together to the Temple of the Lord on holy days.

\*    \*    \*    \*    \*

15 Let death seize them and cut them down in their prime, for there is sin in their homes, and they are polluted to the depths of their souls.

---

[5]Literally, "for I have seen violence and strife in the city."

16   But I will call upon the Lord to save me—and He will.

17   I will pray morning, noon and night pleading aloud with God; and He will hear and answer.

18   Though the tide of battle runs strongly against me, for so many are fighting me, yet He will rescue me.

19   God Himself—God from everlasting ages past —will answer them! For they refuse to fear Him or even honor His commands.

\*       \*       \*       \*       \*

20   This friend of mine betrayed me—I who was at peace with him. He broke his promises.

21   His words were oily smooth, but in his heart was war. His words were sweet, but underneath were daggers.

\*       \*       \*       \*       \*

22   Give your burdens to the Lord. He will carry them. He will not permit the godly to slip or fall.

23   He will send my enemies to the pit of destruction. Murderers and liars will not live out half their days. But I am trusting You to save me.


## PSALM 56

Lord, have mercy on me; all day long the enemy troops press in. So many are proud to fight against me; how they long to conquer me.

3, 4   But when I am afraid, I will put my confidence in You. Yes, I will trust the promises of God.

And since I am trusting Him, what can mere man do to me?

5   They are always twisting what I say. All their thoughts are how to harm me.

6   They meet together to perfect their plans; they hide beside the trail, listening for my steps, waiting to kill me.

7   They expect to get away with it. Don't let them, Lord. In anger cast them to the ground.

8   You have seen me tossing and turning through the night. You have collected all my tears and preserved them in Your bottle! You have recorded every one in Your book.

\*      \*      \*      \*      \*

9   The very day I call for help, the tide of battle turns! My enemies flee! This one thing I *know: God is for me!*

10, 11   I am trusting God—oh, praise His promises! I am not afraid of anything mere man can do to me! Yes, praise His promises.

12   I will surely do what I have promised, Lord, and thank You for Your help.

13   For You have saved me from death and my feet from slipping, so that I can walk before the Lord in the land of the living.


## PSALM 57

O God, have pity, for I am trusting You! I will hide beneath the shadow of Your wings until this storm is past.

2 I will cry to the God of heaven who does such wonders for me.

3 He will send down help from heaven to save me, because of His love and His faithfulness. He will rescue me from these liars who are so intent upon destroying me.

4 I am surrounded by fierce lions—hotheads whose teeth are sharp as spears and arrows. Their tongues are like swords.

5 Lord, be exalted above the highest heavens! Show Your glory high above the earth.

6 My enemies have set a trap for me. Frantic fear grips me. They have dug a pitfall in my path. But look! They themselves have fallen into it!

7 O God, my heart is quiet and confident. No wonder I can sing Your praises!

8 Rouse yourself, my soul! Arise, O harp and lyre! Let us greet the dawn with song!

9 I will thank You publicly throughout the land. I will sing Your praises among the nations.

10 Your kindness and love are as vast as the heavens. Your faithfulness is higher than the skies.

\* \* \* \* \*

11 Yes, be exalted, O God, above the heavens. May Your glory shine throughout the earth.

## PSALM 58

Justice? You high and mighty politicians don't even know the meaning of the word! Fairness? Which

of you has any left? Not one! All your dealings are
crooked: you give "justice" in exchange for bribes.[6]

3   These men are born sinners, lying from their
earliest words!

4, 5   They are poisonous as deadly snakes, cobras
that close their ears to the most expert of charmers.

6   O God, break off their fangs. Tear out the teeth
of these young lions, Lord.

7   Let them disappear like water into thirsty
ground. Make their weapons useless in their hands.[7]

8   Let them be as snails that dissolve into slime;
and as those who die at birth, who never see the sun.

9   God will sweep away both old and young. He
will destroy them more quickly than a cooking pot can
feel the blazing fire of thorns beneath it.

10   The godly shall rejoice in the triumph of right;[8]
they shall walk the blood-stained fields of slaughtered,
wicked men.

11   Then at last everyone will know that good is
rewarded, and that there is a God who judges justly
here on earth.

## PSALM 59

*(Written by David at the time King Saul set guards at his
home to capture and kill him. I Samuel 19:11)*

O my God, save me from my enemies. Protect me
from these who have come to destroy me.

---

[6]Literally, "you deal out the violence of your hands in the land."
[7]Or, "Let them be trodden down and wither like grass."
[8]Literally, "when he sees the vengeance."

2 Preserve me from these criminals, these murderers.

3 They lurk in ambush for my life. Strong men are out there waiting. And not, O Lord, because I've done them wrong.

4 Yet they prepare to kill me. Lord, waken! See what is happening! Help me!

5 (And O Jehovah, God of heaven's armies, God of Israel, arise and punish the heathen nations surrounding us.) Do not spare these evil, treacherous men.

6 At evening they come to spy, slinking around like dogs that prowl the city.

7 I hear them shouting insults and cursing God, for "No one will hear us," they think.

8 Lord, laugh at them! (And scoff at these surrounding nations too.)

9 O God my Strength! I will sing Your praises, for You are my place of safety.

10. My God is changeless in His love for me and He will come and help me. He will let me see my wish come true upon my enemies.

11 Don't kill them—for my people soon forget such lessons—but stagger them with your power and bring them to their knees. Bring them to the dust, O Lord our shield.

12, 13 They are proud, cursing liars. Angrily destroy them. Wipe them out. (And let the nations find out too that God rules in Israel and will reign throughout the world.)

14, 15 Let these evil men slink back at evening,

and prowl the city all night before they are satisfied, howling like dogs and searching for food.

16    But as for me, I will sing each morning about Your power and mercy. For You have been my high tower of refuge, a place of safety in the day of my distress.

17    O my Strength, to You I sing my praises; for You are my high tower of safety, my God of mercy.


## PSALM 60

*(Written by David at the time he was at war with Syria, with the outcome still uncertain; this was when Joab, captain of his forces, slaughtered 12,000 men of Edom in the Valley of Salt.)*

O God, You have rejected us and broken our defenses; You have become angry and deserted us. Lord, restore us again to Your favor.

2    You have caused this nation to tremble in fear; You have torn it apart. Lord, heal it now, for it is shaken to its depths.

3    You have been very hard on us and made us reel beneath Your blows.

4, 5    But You have given us a banner to rally to; all who love truth[9] will rally to it; then You can deliver Your beloved people. Use Your strong right arm to rescue us!

6, 7    God has promised to help us! He has vowed it

---

[9]Literally, "that it may be displayed because of the truth."

by His holiness! No wonder I exult! "Shechem, Succoth, Gilead, Manasseh—still are Mine!" He says. "Judah shall continue to produce kings, and Ephraim great warriors.

8 Moab shall become My lowly servant, and Edom My slave. And I will shout in triumph over the Philistines."

9, 10 Who will bring me in triumph into Edom's strong cities? God will! He who cast us off! He who abandoned us to our foes!

11 Yes, Lord, help us against our enemies, for man's help is useless.

12 With God's help we shall do mighty things, for He will trample down our foes.

## PSALM 61

O God, listen to me! Hear my prayer!
2 For wherever I am, though faraway at the ends of the earth, I will cry to You for help. When my heart is faint and overwhelmed, lead me to the mighty, towering Rock of safety.

3 For You are my refuge, a high tower where my enemies can never reach me.

4 I shall live forever in Your tabernacle; oh, to be safe beneath the shelter of Your wings.

5 For You have heard my vows, O God, to praise[1] You every day, and You have given me the blessings You reserve for those who reverence Your name.

[1] Implied from verse 8.

6   You will give me[2] added years of life, as rich
and full as those of many generations, all packed into
one!

7   And I shall live before the Lord forever. Oh,
send Your lovingkindness and truth to guard and
watch over me,

8   And I will praise Your name continually, fulfilling my vow of praising You each day.

## PSALM 62

I stand silently before the Lord, waiting for Him to
rescue me. For salvation comes from Him alone.

2   Yes, He alone is my Rock, my rescuer, defense
and fortress. Why then should I be tense with fear when
troubles come?

\*      \*      \*      \*      \*

3, 4   But what is this? They pick on me at a time
when my throne[3] is tottering; they plot my death and
use lies and deceit to try to force me from the throne.[3]
They are so friendly to my face while cursing in their
hearts!

5   But I stand silently before the Lord, waiting for
Him to rescue me. For salvation comes from Him
alone.

6   Yes, He alone is my Rock, my rescuer, defense
and fortress—why then should I be tense with fear
when troubles come?

---

[2]Literally, "to the days of the king."
[3]Implied.

7 My protection and success[4] come from God alone. He is my refuge, a Rock where no enemy can reach me.

8 O my people, trust Him all the time. Pour out your longings before Him, for He can help!

9 The greatest of men, or the lowest—both alike are nothing in His sight. They weigh less than air on scales!

10, 11 Don't become rich by extortion and robbery. And don't let the rich men be proud.

12 He is loving and kind and rewards each one of us according to the work we do for Him.


## PSALM 63


*(A Psalm of David when he was hiding in the wilderness of Judea.)*

O God, *my* God! How I search for You! How I thirst for You in this parched and weary land where there is no water! How I long to find You!

2 How I wish I could go into Your sanctuary to see Your strength and glory!

3 For Your love and kindness are better to me than life itself. How I praise You!

4 I will bless You as long as I live, lifting up my hands to You in prayer.

5 At last I shall be fully satisfied; I will praise You with great joy!

---

[4]Literally, "glory."

6 I lie awake at night thinking of You—

7 Of how much You have helped me—and how I rejoice through the night beneath the protecting shadow of Your wings.

8 I follow close behind You, protected by Your strong right arm.

9 But those plotting to destroy me shall go down to the depths of hell.

10 They are doomed to die by the sword, to become the food of jackals.

11 But I[5] will rejoice in God! All who trust in Him exult, while liars shall be silenced.

## PSALM 64

Lord, listen to my complaint: Oh, preserve my life from the conspiracy of these wicked men, these gangs of criminals.

3 They cut me down with sharpened tongues; they aim their bitter words like arrows straight at my heart.

4 They shoot from ambush at the innocent. Suddenly the deed is done, yet they are not afraid.

5 They encourage each other to do evil. They meet in secret to set their traps. "He will never notice them here," they say.

6 They keep a sharp lookout for opportunities of crime. They spend long hours with all their endless evil thoughts and plans.[6]

---

[5]Literally, "the king."
[6]Literally, "And the inward thought and the heart of everyone is deep."

7   But God Himself will shoot them down. Suddenly His arrow will pierce them.

8   They will stagger backward, destroyed by those they spoke against. All who see it happening will scoff at them.

9   Then everyone shall stand in awe and confess the greatness of the miracles of God; at last they will realize what amazing things He does!

10   And the godly shall rejoice in the Lord, and trust and praise Him.

## PSALM 65

O God in Zion, we wait before You in silent praise, and thus fulfill our vow. And because You answer prayer, all mankind will come to You with their requests.

3   Though sins fill our hearts, You forgive them all.

4   How greatly to be envied are those You have chosen to come and live with You within the holy tabernacle courts! What joys await us among all the good things there.

5   With dread deeds and awesome power You will defend us from our enemies,[7] O God who saves us. You are the only hope of all mankind throughout the world and far away upon the sea.

\*     \*     \*     \*     \*

---

[7] Literally, "will answer us in righteousness."

6   He formed the mountains by His mighty strength.

7   He quiets the raging oceans and all the world's clamor.

8   In the farthest corners of the earth the glorious acts of God shall startle everyone. The dawn and sunset shout for joy!

9   He waters the earth to make it fertile. The rivers of God will not run dry! He prepares the earth for His people and sends them rich harvests of grain.

10   He waters the furrows with abundant rain. Showers soften the earth, melting the clods and causing seeds to sprout across the land.

11, 12   Then He crowns it all with green, lush pastures in the wilderness; hillsides blossom with joy.

13   The pastures are filled with flocks of sheep, and the valleys are carpeted with grain. All the world shouts with joy, and sings.

## PSALM 66

Sing to the Lord, all the earth!
    2   Sing of His glorious name! Tell the world how wonderful He is.

3   How awe-inspiring are Your deeds, O God! How great Your power! No wonder Your enemies surrender!

4   All the earth shall worship You and sing of Your glories.

5   Come, see the glorious things God has done. What marvelous miracles happen to His people!

6   He made a dry road through the sea for them. They went across on foot. What excitement and joy there was that day!

7   Because of His great power He rules forever. He watches every movement of the nations. O rebel lands, He will deflate your pride.

8   Let everyone bless God and sing His praises,

9   For He holds our lives in His hands! And He holds our feet to the path!

10   You have purified us with fire,[8] O Lord, like silver in a crucible.

11   You captured us in Your net and laid great burdens on our backs.

12   You sent troops to ride across our broken bodies.[9] We went through fire and flood. But in the end, You brought us into wealth and great abundance.

13   Now I have come to Your Temple with burnt-offerings to pay my vows.

14   For when I was in trouble I promised You many offerings.

15   That is why I am bringing You these fat he-goats, rams and calves. The smoke of their sacrifice shall rise before You.

16   Come and hear, all of you who reverence the Lord, and I will tell you what He did for me:

17   For I cried to Him for help, with praises ready on my tongue.

---

[8]Implied.
[9]Literally, "You caused men to ride over our heads."

18 He would not have listened if I had not confessed my sins.

19 But He listened! He heard my prayer! He paid attention to it!

20 Blessed be God who didn't turn away when I was praying, and didn't refuse me His kindness and love.

## PSALM 67

O God, in mercy bless us; let Your face beam with joy as You look down at us.

2 Send us around the world with the news of Your saving power and Your eternal plan for all mankind.

3 How everyone throughout the earth will praise the Lord!

4 How glad the nations will be, singing for joy because You are their King[1] and will give true justice to their people!

5 Praise God, O world! May all the peoples of the earth give thanks to You.

6, 7 For the earth has yielded abundant harvests. God, even our own God, will bless us. And peoples from remotest lands will worship Him.

## PSALM 68

Arise, O God, and scatter all Your enemies! Chase them away!

---

[1]Literally, "govern the nations."

2    Drive them off like smoke before the wind; melt them like wax in fire! So let the wicked perish at the presence of God.

3    But may the godly man exult! May he rejoice and be merry!

4    Sing praises to the Lord! Raise your voice in song to Him who rides upon the clouds![2] Jehovah is His name—Oh, rejoice in His presence.

5    He is a father to the fatherless; He gives justice to the widows; for He is holy.[3]

6    He gives families to the lonely, and releases prisoners from jail, singing with joy! But for rebels there is famine and distress.

7    O God, when You led Your people through the wilderness,

8    The earth trembled and the heavens shook. Mount Sinai quailed before You—the God of Israel.

9, 10    You sent abundant rain upon Your land, O God, to refresh it in its weariness! There Your people lived, for You gave them this home when they were destitute.

11, 12, 13    The Lord speaks. The enemy flees. The women at home[5] cry out the happy news: "The armies that came to destroy us have fled!" Now all the women of Israel are dividing the booty. See them sparkle with jewels of silver and gold, covered all over as wings cover doves!

[2]Or, "deserts."
[3]Literally, "in His holy habitation."
[5]Literally, "among the sheepfolds."

14  God scattered their enemies like snowflakes melting in the forests of Zalmon.

15, 16  O mighty mountains in Bashan! O splendid many-peaked ranges! Well may you look with envy at Mount Zion, the mount where God has chosen to live forever.

17  Surrounded by unnumbered chariots, the Lord moves on from Mount Sinai and comes to His holy temple high upon Mount Zion.

18  He ascends the heights, leading many captives in His train. He receives gifts for[6] men, even those who once were rebels. God will live among us here.

19  What a glorious Lord! He who daily bears our burdens also gives us our salvation!

20  He frees us! He rescues us from death.

21  But He will crush His enemies, for they refuse to leave their guilty, stubborn ways.

22  The Lord says, "Come," to all His people's enemies;[7] they are hiding on Mount Hermon's highest slopes and deep within the sea!

23  His people must destroy them. Cover your feet with their blood; dogs will eat them.

24  The procession of God my King moves onward to the sanctuary—

25  Singers in front, musicians behind, girls playing the timbrels in between.

26  Let all the people of Israel praise the Lord, who is Israel's fountain.

27  The little tribe of Benjamin leads the way. The

---

[6] Implied from Ephesians 4:8.
[7] Literally, "I will bring back from Bashan."

princes and elders of Judah, and the princes of Zebulon and Naphtali are right behind.[8]

28 Summon Your might; display Your strength, O God, for You have done such mighty things for us.

29 The kings of the earth are bringing their gifts to Your temple in Jerusalem.

30 Rebuke our enemies, O Lord. Bring them— submissive, tax in hand.[9] Scatter all who delight in war.

31 Egypt will send gifts of precious metals. Ethiopia will stretch out her hands to God in adoration.

32 Sing to the Lord, O kingdoms of the earth— sing praises to the Lord,

33 To Him who rides upon the ancient heavens, whose mighty voice thunders from the sky.

34 Power belongs to God! His majesty shines down on Israel; His strength is mighty in the heavens.

35 What awe we feel, kneeling here before Him in the sanctuary. The God of Israel gives strength and mighty power to His people. Blessed be God!


## PSALM 69

Save me, O my God. The floods have risen. Deeper and deeper I sink in the mire; the waters rise around me.

---

[8]Implied.
[9]Literally, "Everyone submitting himself with pieces of silver." An alternate rendering of verse 30 could be, "Trample upon those who lust after the tribute of smaller nations, and who delight in aggressive wars."

3   I have wept until I am exhausted; my throat is dry and hoarse; my eyes are swollen with weeping, waiting for my God to act.

4   I cannot even count all those who hate me without cause. They are influential men, these who plot to kill me though I am innocent. They demand that I be punished for what I didn't do.

5   O God, You know so well how stupid I am, and You know all my sins.

6   O Lord God of the armies of heaven, don't let me be a stumbling block to those who trust in You. O God of Israel, don't let me cause them to be confused,

7   Though I am mocked and cursed and shamed for Your sake.

8   Even my own brothers pretend they don't know me!

9   My zeal for God and His work[2] burns hot within me. And because I advocate Your cause, Your enemies insult me even as they insult You.

10   How they scoff and mock me when I mourn and fast before the Lord!

11   How they talk about me when I wear sackcloth to show my humiliation and sorrow for my sins!

12   I am the talk of the town and the song of the drunkards.

13   But I keep right on praying to you, Lord. For now is the time—You are bending down to hear! You are ready with a plentiful supply of love and kindness!

---

[2]Literally, "for Your house."

Now answer my prayer and rescue me as You promised.[3]

14  Pull me out of this mire. Don't let me sink in. Rescue me from those who hate me, and from these deep waters I am in.

15  Don't let the floods overwhelm me, or the ocean swallow me; save me from the pit that threatens me.

16  O Jehovah, answer my prayers, for Your loving kindness is wonderful; Your mercy is so plentiful, so tender and so kind.

17  Don't hide from me;[4] for I am in deep trouble. Quick! Come and save me.

18  Come, Lord, and rescue me. Ransom me from all my enemies.

19  You know how they talk about me, and how they so shamefully dishonor me. You see them all and know what each has said.

20  Their contempt has broken my heart; my spirit is heavy within me. If even one would show some pity, if even one would comfort me!

21  For food they gave me poison; for my awful thirst they offered me vinegar.

22  Let their joys[5] turn to ashes and their peace disappear;

23  Let darkness, blindness and great feebleness be theirs.

---

[3]Literally, "in the truth of Your salvation."
[4]Literally, "Your servant."
[5]Literally, "their table."

24    Pour out Your fury upon them; consume them with the fierceness of Your anger.

25    Let their homes be desolate and abandoned.

26    For they persecute the one You have smitten; and scoff at the pain of the one You have pierced.

27    Pile their sins high and do not overlook them.

28    Let these men be blotted from the list[6] of the living; do not give them the joys of life with the righteous.

29    But rescue me, O God, from my poverty and pain.

30    Then I will praise God with my singing! My thanks will be His praise—

31    That will please Him more than sacrificing a bullock or an ox.

32    The humble shall see their God at work for them. No wonder they will be so glad! All who seek for God shall live in joy.

33    For Jehovah hears the cries of His needy ones, and does not look the other way.

34    Praise Him, all heaven and earth! Praise Him, all the seas and everything in them!

35    For God will save Jerusalem;[7] He rebuilds the cities of Judah. His people shall live in them and not be dispossessed.

36    Their children shall inherit the land; all who love His name shall live there safely.

---

[6]Or, "Let them be blotted out of the book of life."
[7]Literally, "Zion."

## PSALM 70

**R**escue me, O God! Lord, hurry to my aid!

2, 3 They are after my life, and delight in hurting me. Confuse them! Shame them! Stop them! Don't let them keep on mocking me!

4 But fill the followers of God with joy! Let those who love Your salvation exclaim, "What a wonderful God He is!"

5 But I am in deep trouble. Rush to my aid, for only You can help and save me. O Lord, don't delay.

## PSALM 71

**L**ord, You are my refuge! Don't let me down!

2 Save me from my enemies, for You are just! Rescue me! Bend down Your ear and listen to my plea and save me.

3 Be to me a great protecting rock, where I am always welcome, safe from all attacks. For You have issued the order to save me.

4 Rescue me, O God, from these unjust and cruel men.

5 O Lord, You alone are my hope; I've trusted You from childhood.

6 Yes, You have been with me from birth and have helped me constantly—no wonder I am always praising You!

7   My success—at which so many stand amazed—
is because You are my mighty protector.

8   All day long I'll praise and honor You, O God,
for all that You have done for me.

9   And now, in my old age, don't set me aside!
Don't forsake me now when my strength is failing!

10   My enemies are whispering,

11   "God has forsaken him! Now we can get him.
There is no one to help him now!"

12   O God, don't stay away! Come quickly! Help!

13   Destroy them! Cover them with failure and disgrace—these enemies of mine.

14   I will keep on expecting You to help me. I
praise You more and more.

15   I cannot count the times when You have faithfully rescued me from danger. I will tell everyone how
good You are, and of Your constant, daily care.

16   I walk in the strength of the Lord God. I tell
everyone that You alone are just and good.

17   O God, You have helped me from my earliest
childhood—and I have constantly testified to others of
the wonderful things You do.

18   And now that I am old and gray, don't forsake
me. Give me time to tell this new generation (and their
children too) about all Your mighty miracles.

19   Your power and goodness, Lord, reach to the
highest heavens. You have done such wonderful things.
Where is there another God like You?

20   You have let me sink down deep in desperate

problems. But You will bring me back to life again, up from the depths of the earth.

21 You will give me greater honor than before, and turn again and comfort me.

22 I will praise You with music, telling of Your faithfulness to all Your promises, O Holy One of Israel.

23 I will shout and sing Your praises for redeeming me.

24 I will talk to others all day long about Your justice and Your goodness. For all who tried to hurt me have been disgraced and dishonored.

## PSALM 72

O God, help the king to judge as You would, and help his son to walk in godliness.

2 Help him to give justice to Your people, even to the poor!

3 May the mountains and hills flourish in prosperity because of his good reign.

4 Help him to defend the poor and needy and to crush their oppressors.

5 May the poor and needy revere You constantly, as long as sun and moon continue in the skies! Yes, forever!

6 May the reign of this Son[8] of mine be as gentle and fruitful as the springtime rains upon the grass— like showers that water the earth!

---

[8]The reference seems to look beyond Solomon's son to Jesus the Messiah.

7   May all good men flourish in His reign, with abundance of peace to the end of time.

8   Let Him reign from sea to sea, and from the Euphrates River to the ends of the earth.

9   The desert nomads shall bow before Him; His enemies shall fall face downward in the dust.

10   Kings along the Mediterranean coast—the kings of Tarshish and the islands—and those from Sheba and from Seba—all will bring their gifts.

11   Yes, kings from everywhere! All will bow before Him! All will serve Him!

12   He will take care of the helpless and poor when they cry to Him; for they have no one else to defend them.

13   He feels pity for the weak and needy, and will rescue them.

14   He will save them from oppression and from violence, for their lives are precious to Him.

15   And He shall live; and to Him will be given the gold of Sheba, and there will be constant praise[9] for Him. His people[1] will bless Him all day long.

16   Bless us with abundant crops throughout the land, even on the highland plains; may there be fruit like that of Lebanon; may the cities be as full of people as the fields are of grass.

17   His name will be honored forever; it will continue as the sun; and all will be blessed in Him; all nations will praise Him.

---

[9]Literally, "men shall pray for him continually."
[1]Implied. Literally, "they" or "he."

18 Blessed be Jehovah God, the God of Israel, who only does wonderful things!

19 Blessed be His glorious name forever! Let the whole earth be filled with His glory. Amen, and amen!

20 (This ends the psalms of David, son of Jesse.)

\*     \*     \*     \*     \*

## PSALM 73

How good God is to Israel—to those whose hearts are pure.

2 But as for me, I came *so* close to the edge of the cliff! My feet were slipping and I was almost gone.

3 For I was envious of the prosperity of the proud and wicked.

4 Yes, all through life their road is smooth![2] They grow sleek and fat.

5 They aren't always in trouble and plagued with problems like everyone else,

6 So their pride sparkles like a jeweled necklace, and their clothing is woven of cruelty!

7 These fat cats have everything their hearts could ever wish for!

8 They scoff at God and threaten His people. How proudly they speak!

9 They boast against the very heavens, and their words strut through the earth.

---

[2]Or, "they never have any pains."

10   And so God's people are dismayed and confused, and drink it all in.

11   "Does God realize what is going on?" they ask.

12   "Look at these men of arrogance; they never have to lift a finger—theirs is a life of ease; and all the time their riches multiply."

13   Have I been wasting my time? Why take the trouble to be pure?

14   All I get out of it is trouble and woe—every day and all day long!

15   If I had really said that, I would have been a traitor to Your people.

16   Yet it is so hard to explain it—this prosperity of those who hate the Lord.

17   Then one day I went into God's sanctuary to meditate, and thought about the future of these evil men.

18   What a slippery path they are on—suddenly God will send them sliding over the edge of the cliff and down to their destruction:

19   An instant end to all their happiness, an eternity of terror.

20   Their present life is only a dream! They will awaken to the truth as one awakens from a dream of things that never really were!

21   When I saw this, what turmoil filled my heart!

22   I saw myself so stupid and so ignorant; I must seem like an animal to You, O God.

23    But even so, You love me! You are holding my right hand!

24    You will keep on guiding me all my life with Your wisdom and counsel; and afterwards receive me into the glories of heaven![3]

25    Whom have I in heaven but You? And I desire no one on earth as much as You!

26    My health fails; my spirits droop, yet God remains! He is the strength of my heart; He is mine forever!

27    But those refusing to worship God will perish, for He destroys those serving other gods.

28    But as for me, I get as close to Him as I can! I have chosen Him and I will tell everyone about the wonderful ways He rescues me.

## PSALM 74

O God, why have You cast us away forever? Why is Your anger hot against us—the sheep of Your own pasture?

2    Remember that we are Your people—the ones You chose in ancient times from slavery and made the choicest of Your possessions. You chose Jerusalem[4] as Your home on earth!

3    Walk through the awful ruins of the city, and see what the enemy has done to Your sanctuary.

---

[3]Or, "You will bring me unto honor."
[4]Literally, "Mount Zion."

4 There they shouted their battle cry and erected their idols to flaunt their victory.

5, 6 Everything lies in shambles like a forest chopped to the ground. They came with their axes and sledgehammers and smashed and chopped the carved paneling,

7 And set the sanctuary on fire, and razed it to the ground—Your sanctuary, Lord.

8 "Let's wipe out every trace of God," they said, and went through the entire country burning down the assembly places where we worshiped You.

9, 10 There is nothing left to show that we are Your people. The prophets are gone, and who can say when it all will end? How long, O God, will You allow our enemies to dishonor Your name? Will You let them get away with this forever?

11 Why do You delay? Why hold back Your power? Unleash Your fist and give them a final blow.

12 God is my King from ages past; You have been actively helping me everywhere throughout the land.

13, 14 You divided the Red Sea with Your strength; You crushed the sea-god's heads! You gave him to the desert tribes to eat!

15 At Your command the springs burst forth to give Your people water; and then You dried a path for them across the everflowing Jordan.

16 Day and night alike belong to You; You made the starlight and the sun.

17 All nature is within Your hands; You make the summer and the winter too.

18 Lord, see how these enemies scoff at You. O Jehovah, an arrogant nation has blasphemed Your name.

19 O Lord, save me! Protect Your turtle-dove from the hawks.[5] Save Your beloved people from these beasts.

20 Remember Your promise! For the land is full of darkness and cruel men.

21 O Lord, don't let Your downtrodden people be constantly insulted. Give cause for these poor and needy ones to praise Your name!

22 Arise, O God, and state Your case against our enemies. Remember the insults these rebels have hurled against You all day long.

23 Don't overlook the cursing of these enemies of Yours; it grows louder and louder.


## PSALM 75

How we thank You, Lord! Your mighty miracles give proof that You care.

2 "Yes," the Lord replies, "And when I am ready, I will punish the wicked!

3 Though the earth shakes and all its people live in turmoil, yet its pillars are firm, for I have set them in place!"

4 I warned the proud to cease their arrogance! I told the wicked to lower their insolent gaze,[6]

---

[5]Literally, "the wild beasts."
[6]Literally, "lift not up the horn."

5   And to stop being stubborn and proud.

6, 7   For promotion and power come from no-where on earth, but only from God. He promotes one and deposes another.

8   In Jehovah's hand there is a cup of pale and sparkling wine. It is His judgment, poured out upon the wicked of the earth. They must drain that cup to the dregs.

9   But as for me, I shall forever declare the praises of the God of Jacob.

10   "I will cut off the strength of evil men," says the Lord,[7] "and increase the power of good men in their place."

## PSALM 76

God's reputation is very great in Judah and in Israel!

2   His home is in Jerusalem! He lives upon Mount Zion.

3   There He breaks the weapons of our enemies.

4   The everlasting mountains cannot compare with You in glory!

5   The mightiest of our enemies are conquered; they lie before us in the sleep of death; not one can lift a hand against us.

6   When You rebuked them, God of Jacob, steeds and riders fell.

---

[7]Implied.

7   No wonder You are greatly feared! Who can stand before an angry God?

8   You pronounce sentence on them from heaven; the earth trembles and stands silently before You;

9   You stand up to punish the evil-doers and to defend the meek of the earth.

10   Man's futile wrath will bring You glory! You will use it as an ornament!

\*      \*      \*      \*

11   Fulfill all your vows that you have made to Jehovah your God. Let everyone bring Him presents. He should be reverenced and feared,

12   For He cuts down princes and does awesome things to the kings of the earth.

## PSALM 77

I cry to the Lord; I call and call to Him. Oh, that He would listen.

2   I am in deep trouble and I need His help so badly. All night long I pray, lifting my hands to heaven, pleading. There can be no joy for me until He acts.

3   I think of God and moan, overwhelmed with longing for His help.

4   I cannot sleep until You act. I am too distressed even to pray!

5   I keep thinking of the good old days of the past, long since ended.

6   Then my nights were filled with joyous songs. I search my soul and meditate upon the difference now.

7   Has the Lord rejected me forever? Will He never again be favorable?

8   Is His lovingkindness gone forever? Has His promise failed?

9   Has He forgotten to be kind to one so undeserving? Has He slammed the door in anger on His love?

10   And I said: This is my fate, that the blessings of God have changed to hate.[8]

11   I recall the many miracles He did for me so long ago.

12   Those wonderful deeds are constantly in my thoughts. I cannot stop thinking about them.

\*      \*      \*      \*      \*

13   O God, Your ways are holy. Where is there any other as mighty as You?

14   You are the God of miracles and wonders! You still demonstrate Your awesome power.

\*      \*      \*      \*      \*

15   You have redeemed us who are the sons of Jacob and of Joseph by Your might.

16   When the Red Sea saw You, how it feared! It trembled to its depths!

17   The clouds poured down their rain, the thunder rolled and crackled in the sky. Your lightning flashed.

18   There was thunder in the whirlwind; the lightning lighted up the world! The earth trembled and shook.

---

[8]Literally, "that the right hand of the Most High has changed."

19   Your road led by a pathway through the sea—a pathway no one knew was there!

20   You led Your people along that road like a flock of sheep, with Moses and Aaron as their shepherds.

## PSALM 78

O my people, listen to my teaching. Open your ears to what I am saying.

2, 3   For I will show you lessons from our history, stories handed down to us from former generations.

4   I will reveal these truths to you so that you can describe these glorious deeds of Jehovah to your children, and tell them about the mighty miracles He did.

5   For He gave His laws to Israel, and commanded our fathers to teach them to their children,

6   So that they in turn could teach their children too. Thus His laws pass down from generation to generation.

7   In this way each generation has been able to obey His laws and to set its hope anew on God and not forget His glorious miracles.

8   Thus they did not need to be as their fathers were—stubborn, rebellious, unfaithful, refusing to give their hearts to God.

9   The people of Ephraim, though fully armed, were defeated in battle

10   Because they didn't obey His laws. They refused to follow His ways.

11, 12 And they forgot about the wonderful miracles God had done for them, and for their fathers back in Egypt.

13 For He divided the sea before them and led them through! The water stood banked up along both sides of them!

14 In the daytime He led them by a cloud, and at night by a pillar of fire.

15 He split open the rocks in the wilderness to give them plenty of water, as though gushing from a spring.

16 Streams poured from the rock, flowing like a river!

17 Yet they kept on with their rebellion, sinning against the God who is above all gods.

18 They murmured and complained, demanding other food than God was giving them.

19, 20 They even spoke against God Himself. "Why can't He give us decent food as well as water?" they grumbled.

21 Jehovah heard them and was angry; the fire of His wrath burned against Israel,

22 Because they didn't believe in God or trust in Him to care for them,

23 Even though He commanded the skies to open —He opened the windows of heaven—

24 And rained down manna for their food. He gave them bread from heaven!

25 They ate angel's food! He gave them all that they could hold.

26 And He led forth the east wind and guided the south wind by His mighty power.

27 He rained down birds as thick as dust, clouds of them like sands along the shore!

28 He caused the birds to fall to the ground among the tents!

29 The people ate their fill. He gave them what they asked for.

30 But they had hardly finished eating, and the meat was yet in their mouths,

31 When the anger of the Lord rose against them and killed the finest of Israel's young men.

32 Yet even so the people kept on sinning and refused to believe in miracles.

33 So He cut their lives short and gave them years of terror and disaster.

34 Then at last, when He had ruined them, they walked awhile behind Him; how earnestly they turned around and followed Him!

35 Then they remembered that God was their Rock—that their Savior was the God above all gods.

36 But it was only with their words they followed Him, not with their hearts;

37 Their hearts were far away. They did not keep their promises.

38 Yet He was merciful and forgave their sins and didn't destroy them all. Many and many a time He held back His anger.

39 For He remembered that they were merely mortal men, gone in a moment like a breath of wind.

40 Oh, how often they rebelled against Him in those desert years and grieved His heart.

41 Again and again they turned away and tempted God to kill them, and limited the Holy One of Israel from giving them His blessings.

42 They forgot His power and love, and how He had rescued them from their enemies;

43 They forgot the plagues He sent upon the Egyptians in Tanis[9]—

44 How He turned their rivers into blood, so that no one could drink;

45 And how He sent vast swarms of flies to fill the land, and how the frogs had covered all of Egypt!

46 He gave their crops to caterpillars. Their harvest was consumed by locusts.

47 He destroyed their grapevines and their sycamores with hail.

48 Their cattle died in the fields, mortally wounded by iceballs from heaven. Their sheep were killed by lightning.

49 He loosed on them the fierceness of His anger, sending sorrow and trouble. He dispatched against them a band of destroying angels.

50 He gave free course to His anger and did not spare the Egyptians' lives, but handed them over to plagues and sickness.

51 Then He killed the eldest son[2] in each Egyptian family—he who was the beginning of its strength and joy.

[9]Literally, "the plains of Zoan."
[2]Literally, "all the first-born."

52   But He led forth His own people like a flock, guiding them safely through the wilderness.

53   He kept them safe, so they were not afraid. But the Sea closed in upon their enemies and overwhelmed them.

54   He brought them to the border of His land of blessing, to this land of hills He made for them.

55   He drove out the nations occupying the land, and gave each tribe of Israel its apportioned place as its home.

56   Yet though He did all this for them, they still rebelled against the God above all gods, and refused to follow His commands.

57   They turned back from entering the Promised Land and disobeyed as their fathers had. Like a crooked arrow, they missed the target of God's will.

58   They made Him angry by erecting idols and altars to other gods.

59   When God saw their deeds, His wrath was strong and He despised His people.

60   Then He abandoned His tabernacle at Shiloh, where He had lived among mankind,

61   And allowed His ark to be captured; He surrendered His glory into enemy hands.

62   He caused His people to be butchered because His anger was intense.

63   Their young men were killed by fire and their girls died before they were old enough to sing their wedding songs.

64   The priests were slaughtered and their widows died before they could even begin their lament.

65   Then the Lord rose up as though awakening from sleep, and like a mighty man aroused by wine

66   He routed His enemies and drove them back and sent them to eternal shame.

67   But He rejected Joseph's family, the tribe of Ephraim,

68   And chose the tribe of Judah—and Mount Zion which He loved.

69   There He built His towering temple, solid and enduring as the heavens and the earth.

70   He chose His servant David, taking him from feeding sheep,

71, 72   And from following the ewes with lambs; God presented David to His people as their shepherd and he cared for them with a true heart and skillful hands.

## PSALM 79

O God, Your land has been conquered by the heathen nations. Your Temple is defiled and Jerusalem is a heap of ruins.

2   The bodies of Your people lie exposed—food for birds and animals.

3   The enemy has butchered the entire population of Jerusalem; blood has flowed like water; no one is left even to bury them.

4    The nations all around us scoff. They heap contempt on us.

5    O Jehovah, how long will You be angry with us? Forever? Will Your jealousy burn till every hope is gone?

6    Pour out Your wrath upon the godless nations, not on us! And on kingdoms that refuse to pray, that will not call upon Your name!

7    For they have destroyed Your people Israel, invading every home.

8    Oh, do not hold us guilty for our former sins! Let Your tenderhearted mercies meet our needs, for we are brought low to the dust.

9    Help us, God of our salvation! Help us for the honor of Your name! Oh, save us and forgive our sins.

10    Why should the heathen nations be allowed to scoff, "Where is their God?" Publicly avenge this slaughter of Your people!

11    Listen to the sighing of the prisoners and those condemned to die. Demonstrate the greatness of Your power by saving them.

12    O Lord, take sevenfold vengeance on these nations scorning You.

13    Then we Your people, the sheep of Your pasture, will thank You forever and forever, praising Your greatness from generation to generation.


## PSALM 80

O Shepherd of Israel who leads Israel like a flock; O God enthroned above the cherubim, bend down

Your ear and listen as I plead. Display Your power and radiant glory.

2  Let Ephraim, Benjamin and Manasseh see You rouse Yourself and use Your mighty power to rescue us.

3  Turn us again to Yourself, O God. Look down on us in joy and love;[3] only then shall we be saved.

4  O Jehovah, God of heaven's armies, how long will You be angry and reject our prayers?

5  You have fed us with sorrow and tears,

6  And have made us the scorn of the neighboring nations. They laugh among themselves.

7  Turn us again to Yourself, O God of Hosts. Look down on us in joy and love;[3] only then shall we be saved.

8  You brought us from Egypt as though we were a tender vine and drove away the heathen from Your land and planted us.

9  You cleared the ground and tilled the soil and we took root and filled the land.

10  The mountains were covered with our shadow; we were like the mighty cedar trees,[4]

11  Covering the entire land from the Mediterranean Sea to the Euphrates River.

12  But now You have broken down our walls leaving us without protection.

13  The boar from the forest roots around us, and the wild animals feed on us.

---
[3]Literally, "cause Your face to shine upon us."
[4]Literally, "the cedars of God."

14 Come back, we beg of You, O God of the armies of heaven, and bless us. Look down from heaven and see our plight and care for this Your vine!

15 Protect what You Yourself have planted, this son You have raised for Yourself.

16 For we are chopped and burned by our enemies. May they perish at Your frown.

17 Strengthen the man You love,[5] the son of Your choice,[6]

18 And we will never forsake You again. Revive us to trust in You.

19 Turn us again to Yourself, O God of the armies of heaven. Look down on us, Your face aglow with joy and love—only then shall we be saved.

## PSALM 81

The Lord makes us strong! Sing praises! Sing to Israel's God!

2 Sing, accompanied by drums; pluck the sweet lyre and harp.

3 Sound the trumpet! Come to the joyous celebrations at full moon, new moon and all the other holidays!

4 For God has given us these times of joy; they are scheduled in the laws of Israel.

5 He gave them as reminders of His war against

---

[5]Literally, "the man of Your right hand."
[6]Literally, "the son of man You made strong for Yourself."

Egypt where we were slaves on foreign soil. I heard an unknown voice that said,

6    "Now I will relieve your shoulder of its burden; I will free your hands from their heavy tasks."

7    He said, "You cried to Me in trouble and I saved you; I answered from Mount Horeb[8] where the thunder hides. I tested your faith at Meribah, when you complained there was no water.

8    Listen to Me, O My people, while I give you stern warnings. O Israel, if you will only listen!

9    *You must never worship any other god,* nor ever have an idol in your home.[7]

10   For it was I, Jehovah your God, who brought you out of the land of Egypt. Only test Me![8] Open your mouth wide and see if I won't fill it! You will receive every blessing you can use!

11   But no, My people won't listen. Israel doesn't want Me around.

12   So I am letting them go their blind and stubborn way, living according to their own desires.

13   But oh, that My people would listen to Me! Oh, that Israel would follow Me, walking in My paths!

14   How quickly then I would subdue her enemies! How soon My hands would be upon her foes!

15   Those who hate the Lord would cringe before Him; their desolation would last forever.

16   But He would feed you with the choicest foods. He would satisfy you with honey for the taking.[9]

---

[7]Literally, "There shall no foreign god be in you."
[8]Implied.
[9]Literally, "honey out of the rock."

# PSALM 82

**G**od stands up to open heaven's court. He pronounces judgment on the judges.[1]

2 How long will you judges refuse to listen to the evidence? How long will you shower special favors on the wicked?

3 Give fair judgment to the poor man, the afflicted, the fatherless, the destitute.

4 Rescue the poor and needy from the grasp of evil men.

5 But you are so foolish and so ignorant! Because you are in darkness, all the foundations of society[2] are shaken to the core.

6 I have called you all "gods" and "sons of the Most High."

7 But in death you are mere men. You will fall as any prince—for all must die.

8 Stand up, O God, and judge the earth. For all of it belongs to You. All nations are in Your hands.

# PSALM 83

**O** God, don't sit idly by, silent and inactive when we pray. Answer us! Deliver us!

---

[1]Implied from verses 2-4 and 6. Literally, "He judges among the gods."
[2]Literally, "of the earth."

2   Don't You hear the tumult and commotion of
Your enemies? Don't You see what they are doing,
these proud men who hate the Lord?

3   They are full of craftiness and plot against Your
people, laying plans to slay Your precious ones.

4   Come, they say, and let us wipe out Israel as a
nation—we will destroy the very memory of her exist-
ence.

5   This was their unanimous decision at their summit conference—they signed a treaty to ally themselves
against Almighty God—

6   These Ishmaelites and Edomites and Moabites
and Hagrites;

7   People from the lands of Gebal, Ammon,
Amalek, Philistia and Tyre;

8   Assyria has joined them too, and is allied with
the descendants of Lot.[3]

9   Do to them as once You did to Midian, or as
You did to Sisera and Jabin at the river Kishon,

10  And as You did to Your enemies at Endor,
whose decaying corpses fertilized the soil.

11  Make their mighty nobles die as Oreb did,[4] and
Zeeb;[4] let all their princes die like Zebah[5] and Zal-
munna,[5]

12  Who said, "Let us seize for our own use these
pasturelands of God!"

13  O my God, blow them away like dust; like chaff
before the wind—

---

[3]The Moabites and Ammonites were among Lot's descendants.
[4]Judges 7:25.
[5]Judges 8:21.

14   As a forest fire that roars across a mountain.

15   Chase them with Your fiery storms, tempests and tornados.

16   Utterly disgrace them until they recognize Your power and name, O Lord.

17   Make them failures in everything they do; let them be ashamed and terrified

18   Until they learn that You alone, Jehovah, are the God above all gods in supreme charge of all the earth.

## PSALM 84

How lovely is Your Temple, O Lord of the armies of heaven.

2   I long, yes, faint with longing to be able to enter Your courtyard and come near to the Living God.

3   Even the sparrows and swallows are welcome to come and nest among Your altars and there have their young, O Lord of heaven's armies, my King and my God!

4   How happy are Your priests who can always be in Your Temple, singing Your praises.

5   Happy are those who are strong in the Lord, who want above all else to follow Your steps.

6   When they walk through the Valley of Weeping it will become a place of springs where pools of blessing and refreshment collect after rains!

7   They will grow constantly in strength and each of them is invited to meet with the Lord in Zion!

8   O Jehovah, God of the heavenly armies, hear my prayer! Listen, God of Israel.

9   O God, our Defender and our Shield, have mercy on the one You have anointed as Your king.[6]

10   A single day spent in Your Temple is better than a thousand anywhere else! I would rather be a doorman of the Temple of my God than live in palaces[7] of wickedness.

11   For Jehovah God is our Light and our Protector. He gives us grace and glory. No good thing will He withhold from those who walk along His paths.[8]

12   O Lord of the armies of heaven, blessed are those who trust in You.

## PSALM 85

Lord, You have poured out amazing blessings on this land! You have restored the fortunes[9] of Israel,

2   And forgiven the sins of Your people—yes, covered over each one,

3   So that all Your wrath, Your blazing anger, is now ended.

4   Now bring us back to loving You[1], O Lord, so that Your anger will never need rise against us again.

[6]Literally, "Your anointed."
[7]Literally, "tents."
[8]Literally, "walk uprightly."
[9]Literally, "brought back the captivity."
[1]Or, "Turn to us."

5  (Or will You be always angry—on and on to distant generations?)

6  Oh, revive us! Then Your people can rejoice in You again.

7  Pour out Your love and kindness on us, Lord, and grant us Your salvation.

8  I am listening carefully to all the Lord is saying—for He speaks peace to His people, His saints, if they will only stop their sinning.

9  Surely His salvation is near to those who reverence Him; our land will be filled with His glory!

10  Mercy and truth have met together. Grim justice[2] and peace have kissed!

11  Truth rises from the earth and righteousness smiles down from heaven.

12  Yes, the Lord pours down His blessings on the land and it yields its bountiful crops.

13  Justice goes before Him to make a pathway for His steps.[3]

## PSALM 86

Bend down and hear my prayer, O Lord, and answer me, for I am deep in trouble.

2  Protect me from death, for I try to follow all Your laws. Save me, for I am serving You and trusting You.

[2]Literally, "righteousness."
[3]Or, "set us in the way of His steps."

3   Be merciful, O Lord, for I am looking up to You in constant hope.

4   Give me happiness, O Lord, for I worship only You.

5   O Lord, You are so good and kind, so ready to forgive; so full of mercy for all who ask Your aid.

6   Listen closely to my prayer, O God. Hear my urgent cry.

7   I will call to You whenever trouble strikes, and You will help me.

8   Where among the heathen gods is there a God like You? Where are their miracles?

9   All the nations—and You made each one—will come and bow before You, Lord, and praise Your great and holy name.

10   For You are great, and do great miracles. You alone are God.

11   Tell me where You want me to go and I will go there. May every fiber of my being unite in reverence to Your name.

12   With all my heart I will praise You. I will give glory to Your name forever,

13   For You love me so much! And You are constantly so kind! And You have rescued me from deepest hell.

14   O God, proud and insolent men defy me; violent, godless men are trying to kill me.

15   But You are merciful and gentle, Lord, slow in

getting angry, full of constant lovingkindness and of truth;

16 So look down in pity and grant strength to Your servant and save me.

17 Send me a sign of Your favor. When those who hate me see it they will lose face because You help and comfort me.

## PSALM 87

**H**igh on His holy mountain stands Jerusalem,[4] the city of God, the city He loves more than any other!

3 O City of God, what wondrous tales are told of you!

4 Nowadays when I mention among my friends the names of Egypt and Babylonia, Philistia and Tyre, or even distant Ethiopia, someone boasts that he was born in one or another of those countries.

5 But someday the highest honor will be to be a native of Jerusalem! For the God above all gods will personally bless this city.

6 When He registers her citizens He will place a checkmark beside the names of those who were born here!

7 And in the festivals they'll sing, "All my heart is in Jerusalem."

---

[4] Literally, "Zion."

## PSALM 88

O Jehovah, God of my salvation, I have wept before You day and night.

2   Now hear my prayers; oh, listen to my cry,

3   For my life is full of troubles, and death draws near.

4   They say my life is ebbing out—a hopeless case.

5   They have left me here to die, like those slain on battlefields, from whom Your mercies are removed.

6   You have thrust me down to the darkest depths.

7   Your wrath lies heavy on me; wave after wave engulfs me.

8   You have made my friends to loathe me, and they have gone away. I am in a trap with no way out.

9   My eyes grow dim with weeping. Each day I beg Your help; O Lord, I reach my pleading hands to You for mercy.

10   Soon it will be too late! Of what use are Your miracles when I am in the grave? How can I praise You then?

11   Can those in the grave declare Your lovingkindness? Can they proclaim Your faithfulness?

12   Can the darkness speak of Your miracles? Can anyone in the Land of Forgetfulness talk about Your help?

13   O Lord, I plead for my life and shall keep on pleading day by day.

14  O Jehovah, why have You thrown my life away? Why are You turning Your face from me, and looking the other way?

15  From my youth I have been sickly and ready to die. I stand helpless before Your terrors.

16  Your fierce wrath has overwhelmed me. Your terrors have cut me off.

17  They flow around me all day long.

18  Lover, friend, acquaintance—all are gone. There is only darkness everywhere.

## PSALM 89

Forever and ever I will sing about the tender kindness of the Lord! Young and old shall hear about Your blessings.

2  Your love and kindness are forever; Your truth is as enduring as the heavens.

3, 4  The Lord God says,[5] "I have made a solemn agreement with My chosen servant David. I have taken an oath to establish his descendants as kings forever on his throne, from now until eternity!"

5  All heaven shall praise Your miracles, O Lord; myriads of angels[6] will praise You for Your faithfulness.

6  For who in all of heaven can be compared with God? What mightiest angel[7] is anything like Him?

---

[5]Implied.
[6]Literally, "the assembly of the holy ones."
[7]Literally, "the sons of the mighty."

7  The highest of angelic powers[6] stand in dread and awe of Him. Who is as revered as He by those surrounding Him?

8  O Jehovah, commander of the heavenly armies, where is there any other Mighty One like You? Faithfulness is Your very character.

9  You rule the oceans when their waves arise in fearful storms; You speak, and they lie still.

10  You have cut haughty Egypt[8] to pieces. Your enemies are scattered by Your awesome power.

11  The heavens are Yours, the world, everything—for You created them all.

12  You created north and south! Mount Tabor and Mount Hermon rejoice to be signed by Your name as their maker!

13  Strong is Your arm! Strong is Your hand! Your right hand is lifted high in glorious strength.

14, 15  Your throne is founded on two strong pillars—the one is Justice and the other Righteousness. Mercy and Truth walk before You as Your attendants. Blessed are those who hear the joyful blast of the trumpet, for they shall walk in the light of Your presence.

16  They rejoice all day long in Your wonderful reputation and in Your perfect righteousness.

17  You are their strength! What glory! Our power is based on Your favor!

18  Yes, our protection is from the Lord Himself and He, the Holy One of Israel has given us our king.

[8]Literally, "Rahab."

19 In a vision You spoke to Your prophet[9] and said, "I have chosen a splendid young man from the common people to be the king—

20 He is My servant David! I have anointed him with My holy oil.

21 I will steady him and make him strong.

22 His enemies shall not outwit him, nor shall the wicked overpower him.

23 I will beat down his adversaries before him, and destroy those who hate him.

24 I will protect and bless him constantly and surround him with my love; he will be great because of Me.

25 He will hold sway from the Euphrates River to the Mediterranean Sea.

26 And he will cry to Me, 'You are my Father, my God, and my Rock of Salvation.'

27 I will treat him as My firstborn son, and make him the mightiest king in all the earth.

28 I will love him forever, and be kind to him always; My covenant with him will never end.

29 He will always have an heir; his throne will be as endless as the days of heaven.

30, 31, 32 If his children forsake My laws and don't obey them, then I will punish them,

33 But I will never completely take away My lovingkindness from them, nor let My promise fail.

---

[9]Literally, "Your saint;" apparently a reference to Samuel, who was sent to anoint David as king.

34  No, I will not break My covenant; I will not take back one word of what I said.

35, 36  For I have sworn to David, (and a holy God can never lie), that his dynasty will go on forever, and his throne will continue to the end of time.[1]

37  It shall be eternal as the moon, My faithful witness in the sky!"

\*     \*     \*     \*     \*

38  Then why cast me off, rejected? Why be so angry with the one You chose as king?

39  Have You renounced Your covenant with him? For You have thrown his crown in the dust.

40  You have broken down the walls protecting him and laid in ruins every fort defending him.

41  Everyone who comes along has robbed him while his neighbors mock.

42  You have strengthened his enemies against him and made them rejoice.

43  You have struck down his sword and refused to help him in battle.

44  You have ended his splendor and overturned his throne.

45  You have made him old before his time and publicly disgraced him.

\*     \*     \*     \*     \*

46  O Jehovah, how long will this go on? Will You hide Yourself from me forever? How long will Your wrath burn like fire?

47  Oh, remember how short You have made man's

---

[1]Literally, "his throne as the sun before me."

lifespan. Is it an empty, futile life You give the sons of men?

48 No man can live forever. All will die. Who can rescue his life from the power of the grave?

49 Lord, where is the love You used to have for me? Where is Your kindness that You promised to David with a faithful pledge?

50 Lord, see how all the people are despising me.

51 Your enemies joke about me, the one You anointed as their king.

52 And yet—blessed be the Lord forever! Amen and Amen!

## PSALM 90

*A Prayer of Moses, the Man of God*

Lord, through all the generations You have been our home!

2 Before the mountains were created, before the earth was formed, You are God without beginning or end.

3 You speak, and man turns back to dust.

4 A thousand years are but as yesterday to You! They are like a single hour![2]

5, 6 We glide along the tides of time as swiftly as a racing river, and vanish as quickly as a dream. We are like grass that is green in the morning but mowed down and withered before the evening shadows fall.

---

[2]Literally, "as a watch in the night."

7 We die beneath Your anger; we are overwhelmed by Your wrath.

8 You spread out our sins before You—our secret sins—and see them all.

9 No wonder the years are long and heavy here beneath Your wrath. All our days are filled with sighing.

10 Seventy years are given us! And some may even live to 80. But even the best of these years are often emptiness and pain; soon they disappear, and we are gone.

11 Who can realize the terrors of Your anger? Which of us can fear You as he should?

12 Teach us to number our days and recognize how few they are; help us to spend them as we should.

13 O Jehovah, come and bless us! How long will You delay? Turn away Your anger from us.

14 Satisfy us in our earliest youth* with Your lovingkindness, giving us constant joy to the end of our lives.

15 Give us gladness in proportion to our former misery! Replace the evil years with good.

16 Let us see Your miracles again; let our children see glorious things, the kind You used to do,

17 And let the Lord our God favor us and give us success.

## PSALM 91

We live within the shadow of the Almighty, sheltered by the God who is above all gods.

---
*Literally, "early."

2 This I declare, that He alone is my refuge, my place of safety; He is my God, and I am trusting Him.

3 For He rescues you from every trap, and protects you from the fatal plague.

4 He will shield you with His wings! They will shelter you. His faithful promises are your armor.

5 Now you don't need to be afraid of the dark any more, nor fear the dangers of the day;

6 Nor dread the plagues of darkness, nor disasters in the morning.[3]

\* \* \* \* \*

7 Though a thousand fall at my side, though ten thousand are dying around me, the evil will not touch me.

8 I will see how the wicked are punished but I will not share it.

9 For Jehovah is my refuge! I choose the God above all gods to shelter me.

10 How then can evil overtake me or any plague come near?

\* \* \* \* \*

11 For He orders His angels to protect you wherever you go.

12 They will steady you with their hands to keep you from stumbling against the rocks on the trail.

13 You can safely meet a lion or step on poisonous snakes; yes, even trample them beneath your feet!

14 For the Lord says, "Because he loves Me, I will

---

[3]Literally, "at noonday."

rescue him; I will make him great because he trusts in My name."

15   When he calls on Me I will answer; I will be with him in trouble, and rescue him and honor him.

16   I will satisfy him with a full life[4] and give him My salvation."

## PSALM 92

### *A Song To Sing On The Lord's Day*[5]

It is good to say, "Thank You" to the Lord, to sing praises to the God who is above all gods.

2   Every morning tell Him, "Thank You for Your kindness," and every evening rejoice in all His faithfulness.

3   Sing His praises, accompanied by music from the harp and lute and lyre.

4   You have done so much for me, O Lord. No wonder I am glad! I sing for joy.

5   O Lord, what miracles you do! And how deep are Your thoughts!

6   Unthinking people do not understand them! No fool can comprehend this:

7   That although the wicked flourish like weeds, there is only eternal destruction ahead of them.

8   But the Lord continues forever, exalted in the heavens,

---

[4]Literally, "with long life."
[5]Literally, "for the Sabbath day."

9  While His enemies—all evil-doers—shall be scattered.

10  But You have made me as strong as a wild bull. How refreshed I am by your blessings![6]

11  I have heard the doom of my enemies announced and seen them destroyed.

12  But the godly shall flourish like palm trees, and grow tall as the cedars of Lebanon.

13  For they are transplanted into the Lord's own garden, and are under His personal care.

14  Even in old age they will still produce fruit and be vital and green.

15  This honors the Lord, and exhibits His faithful care. He is my shelter. There is nothing but goodness in Him!


## PSALM 93

Jehovah is King! He is robed in majesty and strength. The world is His throne.[7] O Lord, you have reigned from prehistoric times, from the everlasting past.

3  The mighty oceans thunder Your praise.

4  You are mightier than all the breakers pounding on the seashores of the world!

5  Your royal decrees cannot be changed. Holiness is forever the keynote of Your reign.

---

[6]Literally, "anointed with fresh oil."
[7]Literally, "The world is established . . . Your throne is established."

## PSALM 94

Lord God, to whom vengeance belongs, let Your glory shine out. Arise and judge the earth; sentence the proud to the penalties they deserve.

3 Lord, how long shall the wicked be allowed to triumph and exult?

4 Hear their insolence! See their arrogance! How these men of evil boast!

5 See them oppressing Your people, O Lord, afflicting those You love.

6, 7 They murder widows, immigrants, and orphans, for "The Lord isn't looking," they say, "and besides, He[8] doesn't care."

8 Fools!

9 Is God deaf and blind—He who makes ears and eyes?

10 He punishes the nations—won't He also punish you? He knows everything—doesn't He also know what you are doing?

11 The Lord is fully aware of how limited and futile the thoughts of mankind are,

12, 13 So He helps us by punishing us. This makes us follow His paths, and gives us respite from our enemies while God traps them and destroys them.

14 The Lord will not forsake His people, for they are His prize.

---

[8]Literally, "the God of Jacob."

15 Judgment will again be just and all the upright will rejoice.

16 Who will protect me from the wicked? Who will be my shield?

17 I would have died unless the Lord had helped me.

18 I screamed, "I'm slipping, Lord!" and He was kind and saved me.

19 Lord, when doubts fill my mind, when my heart is in turmoil, quiet me and give me renewed hope and cheer.

20 Will You permit a corrupt government to rule under Your protection—a government permitting wrong to defeat right?

21, 22 Do You approve of those who condemn the innocent to death? No! The Lord my God is my fortress—the mighty Rock where I can hide.

23 God has made the sins of evil men to boomerang upon them! He will destroy them by their own plans! Jehovah our God will cut them off.

## PSALM 95

Oh, come, let us sing to the Lord! Give a joyous shout in honor of the Rock of our salvation!

2 Come before Him with thankful hearts. Let us sing Him psalms of praise.

3 For the Lord is a great God, the great King of[9] all gods.

4 He controls the formation of the depths of the earth and the mightiest mountains; all are His.

5 He made the sea and formed the land; they too are His.

6 Come, kneel before the Lord our Maker,

7 For He is our God. We are His sheep and He is our shepherd! Oh, that you would hear Him calling you today and come to Him!

8 Don't harden your hearts as Israel did in the wilderness[1] at Meribah and Massah.

9 For there your fathers doubted Me, though they had seen so many of My miracles before. My patience was severely tried by their complaints.

10 "For forty years I watched them in disgust," the Lord God says. "They were a nation whose thoughts and heart were far away from Me. They refused to accept My laws.

11 Therefore in mighty wrath I swore that they would never enter the Promised Land, the place of rest I planned for them."

## PSALM 96

Sing a new song to the Lord! Sing it everywhere around the world!

---

[9]Literally, "above."
[1]Exodus 17:7.

2 Sing out His praises! Bless His name. Each day tell someone that He saves.

3 Publish His glorious acts throughout the earth. Tell everyone about the amazing things He does.

4 For the Lord is great beyond description, and greatly to be praised. Worship only Him among the gods!

5 For the gods of other nations are merely idols, but our God made the heavens!

6 Honor and majesty surround Him; strength and beauty are in His Temple.

7 O nations of the world, confess that God alone is glorious and strong.

8 Give Him the glory He deserves! Bring your offering and come to worship Him.[2]

9 Worship the Lord with the beauty of holy lives.[3] Let the earth tremble before Him.

10 Tell the nations that Jehovah reigns! He rules the world. His power can never be overthrown. He will judge all nations fairly.

11 Let the heavens be glad, the earth rejoice; let the vastness of the roaring seas demonstrate His glory.

12 Praise Him for the growing fields, for they display His greatness. Let the trees of the forest rustle with praise.

13 For the Lord is coming to judge the earth; He will judge the nations fairly and with truth!

[2]Literally, "enter His courts."
[3]Or, "in the priestly robes."

## PSALM 97

Jehovah is King! Let all the earth rejoice! Tell the farthest islands to be glad.

2   Clouds and darkness surround Him! Righteousness and justice are the foundation of His throne.

3   Fire goes forth before Him and burns up all His foes.

4   His lightning flashes out across the world. The earth sees and trembles.

5   The mountains melt like wax before the Lord of all the earth.

6   The heavens declare His perfect righteousness; every nation sees His glory.

7   Let those who worship idols be disgraced—all who brag about their worthless gods—for every god must bow to Him!

8, 9   Jerusalem and all the cities of Judah have heard of Your justice, Lord, and are glad that You reign in majesty over the entire earth and are far greater than these other gods.

10   The Lord loves those who hate evil; He protects the lives of His people, and rescues them from the wicked.

11   Light is sown for the godly and joy for the good.

12   May all who are godly be happy in the Lord and crown[4] Him, our holy God.

---

[4]Literally, "give glory to His holy name."

## PSALM 98

Sing a new song to the Lord telling about His mighty deeds! For He has won a mighty victory by His power and holiness.

2, 3   He has announced this victory and revealed it to every nation by fulfilling His promise to be kind to Israel. The whole earth has seen God's salvation of His people.

4   That is why the earth breaks out in praise to God, and sings for utter joy!

5   Sing your praise accompanied by music from the harp.

6   Let the cornets and trumpets shout! Make a joyful symphony before the Lord, the King!

7   Let the sea in all its vastness roar with praise! Let the earth and all those living on it shout, "Glory to the Lord."

8, 9   Let the waves clap their hands in glee, and the hills sing out their songs of joy before the Lord, for He is coming to judge the world with perfect justice.

## PSALM 99

Jehovah is King! Let the nations tremble! He is enthroned upon the cherubim. Let the whole earth shake.

2   Jehovah sits in majesty in Zion, supreme above all rulers of the earth.

3   Let them reverence Your great and holy name.

4   This mighty King is determined to give justice. Fairness is the touchstone of everything He does. He gives justice throughout Israel.

5   Exalt the Lord our holy God! Bow low before His feet.

6   When Moses and Aaron and Samuel, His prophet, cried to Him for help, He answered them.

7   He spoke to them from the pillar of cloud and they followed his instructions.

8   O Jehovah our God! You answered them and forgave their sins, yet punished them when they went wrong.

9   Exalt the Lord our God, and worship at His holy mountain in Jerusalem for He is holy.


## PSALM 100

Shout with joy before the Lord, O earth!
2   Obey Him gladly; come before Him singing with joy.

3   Try to realize what this means—the Lord is God! He made us—we are His people, the sheep of His pasture.

4   Go through His open gates with great thanksgiving; enter His courts with praise. Give thanks to Him and bless His name.

5  For the Lord is always good. He is always loving and kind, and His faithfulness goes on and on to each succeeding generation.

## PSALM 101

I will sing about Your lovingkindness and Your justice, Lord. I will sing Your praises!

2  I will try to walk a blameless path, but how I need Your help; especially in my own home, where I long to act as I should.

3  Help me to refuse the low and vulgar things; help me to abhor all crooked deals of every kind, to have no part in them.

4  I will reject all selfishness and stay away from every evil.

5  I will not tolerate any slander of my neighbors; I will not permit conceit and pride.

6  I will make the godly of the land my heroes, and invite them to my home. Those who are truly good shall be my examples.

7  But I will not allow those who deceive and lie to stay in my house.

8  My daily task will be to ferret out criminals and free the city of God from their grip.

## PSALM 102

*A prayer when overwhelmed with trouble.*

Lord, hear my prayer! Listen to my plea!

2  Don't turn away from me in this time of my distress. Bend down Your ear and give me speedy answers,

3, 4   For my days disappear like smoke. My health
is broken and my heart is sick; it is trampled like grass
and is withered. My food is tasteless, and I have lost
my appetite.

5   I am reduced to skin and bones because of all my
groaning and despair.

6   I am like a vulture in a far-off wilderness, or
like an owl alone in the desert.

7   I lie awake, lonely as a solitary sparrow on the
roof.

8   My enemies taunt me day after day and curse at
me.

9, 10   I eat ashes instead of bread. My tears run
down into my drink because of Your anger against me,
because of Your wrath. For You have rejected me and
thrown me out.

11   My life is passing swiftly as the evening
shadows. I am withering like grass,

12   While you, Lord, are a famous King forever.
Your fame will endure to every generation.

13   I know that You will come and have mercy on
Jerusalem—and now is the time to pity her—the time
You promised help.

14   For Your people love every stone in her walls
and feel sympathy for every grain of dust in her streets.

15   Now let the nations and their rulers tremble
before the Lord, before His glory.

16   For Jehovah will rebuild Jerusalem! He will
appear in His glory!

17  He will listen to the prayers of the destitute, for He is never too busy to heed their requests.

18  I am recording this so that future generations will also praise the Lord for all that He has done. And a people that shall be created shall praise the Lord.

19  Tell them that God looked down from His Temple in heaven,

20  And heard the groans of His people in slavery —they were children of death—and released them,

21, 22  So that multitudes would stream to the Temple to praise Him, and His praises were sung throughout the city of Jerusalem; and many rulers throughout the earth came to worship Him.

\*     \*     \*     \*     \*

23  He has cut me down in middle life, shortening my days.

24  But I cried to Him, "O God, You live forever and forever! Don't let me die half through my years!

25  In ages past You laid the foundations of the earth, and made the heavens with Your hands!

26  They shall perish, but You go on forever. They will grow old, like worn-out clothing, and You will change them as a man putting on a new shirt and throwing away the old one!

27  But You Yourself never grow old. You are forever, and Your years never end.

\*     \*     \*     \*     \*

28  But our families will continue; generation after generation will be preserved by Your protection.

## PSALM 103

I bless the holy name of God with all my heart.

2   Yes, I will bless the Lord and not forget the glorious things He does for me.

3   He forgives all my sins! He heals me!

4   He ransoms me from hell! He surrounds me with lovingkindness and tender mercies!

5   He fills my life with good things! My youth is renewed like the eagle's!

6   He gives justice to all who are treated unfairly.

7   He revealed His will and nature to Moses and the people of Israel.

8   He is merciful and tender toward those who don't deserve it; He is slow to get angry and full of kindness and love!

9   He never bears a grudge, nor remains angry forever.

10   He has not punished us as we deserve for all our sins,

11   For His mercy towards those who fear and honor Him is as great as the height of the heavens above the earth.

12   He has removed our sins as far away from us as the east is from the west.

13   He is like a father to us, tender and sympathetic to those who reverence Him.

14   For He knows we are but dust,

15    And that our days are few and brief, like grass, like flowers,

16    Blown by the wind and gone forever.

17, 18    But the lovingkindness of the Lord is from everlasting to everlasting, to those who reverence Him; His salvation is to children's children of those who are faithful to His covenant and remember to obey Him!

19    The Lord has made the heavens His throne; from there He rules over everything there is.

20    Bless the Lord, you mighty angels of His who carry out His orders, listening for each of His commands.

21    Yes, bless the Lord, you armies of His angels who serve Him constantly.

22    Let everything everywhere bless the Lord. And how I bless Him too!

## PSALM 104

I bless the Lord: O Lord my God, how great You are! You are robed with honor and with majesty and light! You stretched out the starry curtain of the heavens,

3    And hollowed out the surface of the earth to form the seas. The clouds are His chariots! He rides upon the wings of the wind!

4    The angels[6] are His messengers—His servants of fire!

\*    \*    \*    \*    \*

---

[6] Literally, "spirits."

5 You bound the world together so that it would never fall apart.

6 You clothed the earth with floods of waters covering up the mountains.

7, 8 You spoke, and at the sound of Your shout the water collected into its vast ocean beds, and mountains rose and valleys sank to the levels You decreed.

9 And then You set a boundary for the seas, so that they would never again cover the earth.

*    *    *    *    *

10 He placed springs in the valleys, and streams that gush from the mountains.

11 They gave water for all the animals to drink. There the wild donkeys quench their thirst,

12 And the birds nest beside the streams and sing among the branches of the trees.

13 He sends rain upon the mountains and fills the earth with fruit.

14 The tender grass grows up at His command to feed the cattle, and there are fruit trees, vegetables and grain for man to cultivate,

15 And wine to make him glad, and olive oil as lotion for his skin, and bread to give him strength.

16 The Lord planted the cedars of Lebanon. They are tall and flourishing.

17 There the birds make their nests, the storks in the firs.

18 High in the mountains are pastures for the wild goats; and rock-badgers burrow in among the rocks and find protection there.

19 He assigned the moon to mark the months, and the sun to mark the days.

20 He sends the night and darkness, when all the forest folk come out.

21 Then the young lions roar for their food; but they are dependent on the Lord.

22 At dawn they slink back into their dens to rest,

23 And men go off to work until the evening shadows fall again.

24 O Lord, what a variety You have made! And in wisdom You have made them all! The earth is full of Your riches.

25 There before me lies the mighty ocean, teeming with life of every kind, both great and small.

26 And look! See the ships! And over there, the whale You made to play in the sea!

27 Every one of these depends on You to give them daily food.

28 You supply it, and they gather it! You open wide Your hand to feed them and they are satisfied with all Your bountiful provision.

29 But if You turn away from them, then all is lost. And when You gather up their breath, they die and turn again to dust.

30 Then You send Your Spirit, and new life is born[7] to replenish all the living of the earth.

31 Praise God forever! How He must rejoice in all His work!

---

[7]Literally, "created."

32 The earth trembles at His glance; the mountains burst into flame at His touch.

33 I will sing to the Lord as long as I live! I will praise God to my last breath!

34 May He be pleased by all these thoughts about Him, for He is the source of all my joy.

35 Let all sinners perish—all who refuse to praise Him. But I will praise Him. Hallelujah!

## PSALM 105

Thank the Lord for all the glorious things He does; proclaim them to the nations.

2 Sing His praises and tell everyone about His miracles.

3 Glory in the Lord; O worshipers of God, rejoice.

4 Search for Him and for His strength, and keep on searching!

5, 6 Think of the mighty deeds He did for us, His chosen ones—descendants of God's servant Abraham, and of Jacob. Remember how He destroyed our enemies.

7 He is the Lord our God. His goodness[8] is seen everywhere throughout the land.

8 Though a thousand generations pass He never forgets His promise, His covenant with Abraham and Isaac,

---

[8]Literally, "His judgments."

10, 11   And confirmed with Jacob. This is His never-ending treaty with the people of Israel:
*"I will give you the land of Canaan as your inheritance."*

12   He said this when they were but few in number, very few, and were only visitors in Canaan.

13   Later they were dispersed among the nations, and were driven from one kingdom to another;

14   But through it all He would not let one thing be done to them apart from His decision.[9] He destroyed many a king who tried!

15   "Touch not these chosen ones of Mine," He warned, "and do not hurt My prophets."

16   He called for a famine on the land of Canaan, cutting off its food supply.

17   Then He sent Joseph as a slave to Egypt to save His people from starvation.

18   There in prison they hurt his feet with fetters, and placed his neck in an iron collar,

19   Until God's time finally came—how God tested his patience!

20   Then the king sent for him and set him free.

21   He was put in charge of all the king's possessions.

22   At his pleasure he could imprison the king's aides and teach the king's advisors.

23   Then Jacob (Israel) arrived in Egypt and lived there with his sons.

24   In the years that followed, the people of Israel

---

[9] Literally, "He suffered no man to do them wrong."

multiplied explosively, until they were a greater nation than their rulers.

25   At that point God turned the Egyptians against the Israeli; they hated and enslaved them.

26   But God sent Moses as His representative, and Aaron with him,

27   To call down miracles of terror upon the land of Egypt.

28   They[1] followed His instructions and He sent thick darkness through the land,

29   And turned the nation's water into blood, poisoning the fish.

30   Then frogs invaded in enormous numbers; they were found even in the king's private rooms.

31   When Moses spoke, the flies and other insects swarmed in vast clouds from one end of Egypt to the other.

32   Instead of rain He sent down murderous hail, and lightning flashes overwhelmed the nation.

33   Their grape vines and fig trees were ruined; all the trees lay broken on the ground.

34   He spoke, and hordes of locusts came,

35   And ate up everything green, destroying all the crops.

36   Then He killed the oldest child in each Egyptian home, their pride and joy—

37   And brought His people safely out from Egypt, loaded with silver and gold; there were no sick and feeble folk among them then.

---

[1] Implied.

38    Egypt was glad when they were gone, for the dread of them was great.

39    He spread out a cloud above them to shield them from the burning sun, and gave them a pillar of flame at night to give them light.

40    They asked for meat and He sent them quail, and gave them manna—bread from heaven.

41    He opened up a rock, and water gushed out to form a river through the dry and barren land;

42    For He remembered His sacred promises to Abraham His servant.

43    So He brought His chosen ones singing into the Promised Land.[2]

44    He gave them the lands of the Gentiles, complete with their growing crops; they ate what others planted.

45    This was done to make them faithful and obedient to His laws. Hallelujah!


## PSALM 106


Hallelujah! Thank You, Lord! How good You are! Your love for us keeps growing.

2    Who can ever list the glorious miracles of God? Who can ever praise Him half enough?

3    Happiness comes to those who are fair to others and are always just and good.

---

[2]Implied.

4 Remember me too, O Lord, while You are blessing and saving Your people.

5 Let me share in Your chosen ones' prosperity and rejoice in all their joys, and receive the glory You give to them.

6 Both we and our fathers have sinned so much.

7 They weren't impressed by the wonder of Your miracles in Egypt, and soon forgot Your many acts of kindness to them. Instead they rebelled against You at the Red Sea.

8 Even so You saved them—to defend the honor of Your name and demonstrate Your power to all the world.

9 You commanded the Red Sea to divide, forming a dry road across its bottom. Yes, as dry as any desert!

10 Thus You rescued them from their enemies.

11 Then the water returned and covered the road and drowned their foes; not one survived.

12 Then at last His people believed Him. Then they finally sang His praise.

13 Yet how quickly they forgot again! They wouldn't wait for Him to act,

14 But demanded better food,[3] testing God's patience to the breaking point.

15 So He gave them their demands, but sent them leanness in their souls.[4]

16 They were envious of Moses; yes, and Aaron, too, the man anointed[5] by God as His priest.

---

[3]Literally, "lusted exceedingly."
[4]Or, "but sent a plague to punish them."
[5]Literally, "the holy one of Jehovah."

17   Because of this the earth opened and swallowed Dathan, Abiram and his friends;

18   And fire fell from heaven to consume these wicked men.

19, 20   For they preferred a statue of an ox that eats grass, to the glorious presence of God Himself.

21, 22   Thus they despised their Savior who had done such mighty miracles in Egypt and at the Sea.

23   So the Lord declared He would destroy them. But Moses, His chosen one, stepped into the breach between the people and their God and begged Him to turn from His wrath, and not destroy them.

24   They refused to enter the Promised Land, for they wouldn't believe His solemn oath to care for them.

25   Instead, they pouted in their tents and mourned and despised His command.

26   Therefore He swore that He would kill them in the wilderness

27   And send their children away to distant lands as exiles.

28   Then our fathers joined the worshipers of Baal at Peor and even offered sacrifices to the dead![6]

29   With all these things they angered Him—and so a plague broke out upon them

30   And continued until Phineas executed those whose sins had caused the plague to start.

31   (For this good deed Phineas will be remembered forever.)

---

[6]Or, "to lifeless idols."

32   At Meribah, too, Israel angered God, causing Moses serious trouble,

33   For he became angry and spoke foolishly.

34   Nor did Israel destroy the nations in the land as God had told them to,

35   But mingled in among the heathen and learned their evil ways,

36   Sacrificing to their idols, and were led away from God.

37, 38   They even sacrificed their little children to the demons—the idols of Canaan—shedding innocent blood and polluting the land with murder.

39   Their evil deeds defiled them, for their love of idols was adultery in the sight of God.

40   That is why Jehovah's anger burned against His people, and He abhorred them.

41, 42   That is why He let the heathen nations crush them. They were ruled by those who hated them and oppressed by their enemies.

43   Again and again He delivered them from their slavery, but they continued to rebel against Him, and were finally destroyed by their sin.

44   Yet, even so, He listened to their cries and heeded their distress;

45   He remembered His promises to them and relented because of His great love,

46   And caused even their enemies who captured them to pity them.

47   O Lord God, save us! Regather us from the

nations so we can thank Your holy name and rejoice and praise You.

\* \* \* \* \*

48 Blessed be the Lord, the God of Israel, from everlasting to everlasting. Let all the people say, "Amen!" Hallelujah!

## PSALM 107

Say "Thank You" to the Lord for being so good, for always being so loving and kind.

2 Has the Lord redeemed you? Then speak out! Tell others He has saved you from your enemies.

3 He brought the exiles back from the farthest corners of the earth.

4 They were wandering homeless in the desert,

5 Hungry and thirsty and faint.

6 "Lord, help!" they cried, and He did!

7 He led them straight to safety and a place to live.

8 Oh, that these men would praise the Lord for His lovingkindness, and for all of His wonderful deeds!

9 For He satisfies the thirsty soul and fills the hungry soul with good.

10 Who are these who sit in darkness, in the shadow of death, crushed by misery and slavery?

11 They rebelled against the Lord, scorning Him who is the God above all gods.

12 That is why He broke them with hard labor; they fell and none could help them rise again.

13   Then they cried to the Lord in their troubles, and He rescued them!

14   He led them from the darkness and shadow of death and snapped their chains!

15   Oh, that these men would praise the Lord for His lovingkindness and for all of His wonderful deeds!

16   For He broke down their prison gates of brass and cut apart their iron bars.

\*        \*        \*        \*        \*

17   Others, the fools, were ill because of their sinful ways.

18   Their appetites were gone and death was near.

19   Then they cried to the Lord in their troubles, and He helped them and delivered them.

20   He spoke, and they were healed—snatched from the door of death.

21   Oh, that these men would praise the Lord for His lovingkindness and for all of His wonderful deeds!

22   Let them tell Him "Thank You" as their sacrifice, and sing about His glorious deeds.

\*        \*        \*        \*        \*

23   And then there are the sailors sailing the seven seas, plying the trade routes of the world.

24   They, too, observe the power of God in action.

25   He calls to the storm winds; the waves rise high.

26   Their ships are tossed to the heavens and sink again to the depths; the sailors cringe in terror.

27   They reel and stagger like drunkards and are at their wit's end.

28  Then they cry to the Lord in their trouble, and He saves them!

29  He calms the storm and stills the waves.

30  What a blessing is that stillness, as He brings them safely into harbor!

31  Oh, that these men would praise the Lord for His lovingkindness for all of His wonderful deeds!

32  Let them praise Him publicly before the congregation, and before the leaders of the nation.

\* \* \* \* \*

33  He dries up rivers,

34  And turns the good land of the wicked into deserts of salt.

35  Again, He turns deserts into fertile, watered valleys!

36  He brings the hungry to settle there and build their cities,

37  To sow their fields and plant their vineyards, and reap their bumper crops!

38  How He blesses them! They raise big families there, and many cattle!

39  But others become poor through oppression, trouble and sorrow.

40  For God pours contempt upon the haughty and causes princes to wander among ruins;

41  But He rescues the poor who are godly and gives them many children and much prosperity.

42  Good men everywhere will see it and be glad, while evil men are stricken silent.

43  Listen, if you are wise, to what I am saying. Think about the lovingkindness of the Lord!

## PSALM 108

O God, my heart is ready to praise You! I will sing and rejoice before You.

2   Wake up, O harp and lyre! We will meet the dawn with song.

3   I will praise You everywhere around the world, in every nation.

4   For Your lovingkindness is great beyond measure, high as the heavens! Your faithfulness reaches the skies!

5   His glory is far more vast than the heavens! It towers above the earth.

6   Hear the cry of Your beloved child—come with mighty power and rescue me.

7   God has given sacred promises; no wonder I exult! He has promised to give us all the land of Shechem, and also Succoth Valley!

8   "Gilead is Mine to give to you," He says, "and Manasseh as well; the land of Ephraim is the helmet on My head. Judah is My scepter.

9   But Moab and Edom are despised;[7] and I will shout in triumph over the Philistines."

10   Who but God can give me strength to conquer these fortified cities? Who else can lead me into Edom?

11   Lord, have You thrown us away? Have You deserted our army?

12   Oh, help us fight against our enemies, for men are useless allies.

---

[7]Literally, "Moab is my washbasin; upon Edom I cast My shoe."

13   But with the help of God we shall do mighty acts of valor! For He treads down our foes.


## PSALM 109

O God of my praise, don't stand silent and aloof
      2   While the wicked slander me and tell their lies.
3   They have no reason to hate and fight me, yet they do!
4   I love them, but even while I am praying for them, they are trying to destroy me.
5   They return evil for good, and hatred for love!

     *     *     *     *     *

6   Show him how it feels![8] Let lies be told about him, and bring him to court before an unfair judge.
7   When his case is called for judgment, let him be pronounced guilty! Count his prayers as sins!
8   Let his years be few and brief; let others step forward to replace him.
9, 10   May his children become fatherless and his wife a widow, and be evicted from the ruins of their home.
11   May creditors seize his entire estate and strangers take all he has earned.
12, 13   Let no one be kind to him; let no one pity his fatherless children. May they die. May his family name be blotted out in a single generation.
14   Punish the sins of his father and mother. Don't overlook them.

---

[8]Implied.

15 Think constantly about the evil things he has done, and cut off his name from the memory of man.

16 For he refused all kindness to others, and persecuted those in need, and hounded brokenhearted ones to death.

17 He loved to curse others; now You curse him. He never blessed others; now don't You bless him.

18 Cursing is as much a part of him as his clothing, or as the water he drinks, or the rich food he eats!

19 Now may those curses return and cling to him like his clothing or his belt.

20 This is the Lord's punishment upon my enemies who tell lies about me and threaten me with death.

\* \* \* \* \*

21 But as for me, O Lord, deal with me as Your child, as one who bears Your name! Because You are so kind, O Lord, deliver me.

22, 23 I am slipping down the hill to death; I am shaken off from life as easily as a man brushes a grasshopper from his arm.

24 My knees are weak from fasting and I am skin and bones.

25 I am a symbol of failure to all mankind; when they see me they shake their heads.

26 Help me, O Lord my God! Save me because You are loving and kind.

27 Do it publicly, so all will see that You Yourself have done it.

28 Then let them curse me if they like—I won't mind that if You are blessing me! For then all their

efforts to destroy me will fail, and I shall go right on rejoicing!

29    Make them fail in everything they do. Clothe them with disgrace.

30    But I will give repeated thanks to the Lord, praising Him to everyone.

31    For He stands beside the poor and hungry to save them from their enemies.

## PSALM 110

Jehovah said to my Lord the Messiah,[9] "Rule as My regent—I will subdue Your enemies and make them bow low before You."

2    Jehovah has established Your throne[1] in Jerusalem[2] to rule over Your enemies.

3    In that day of Your power Your people shall come to You willingly, dressed in holy altar robes.[3] And Your strength shall be renewed day by day like morning dew.

4    Jehovah has taken oath, and will not rescind His vow, that You are a priest forever like[4] Melchizedek.

5    God stands beside You to protect You. He will strike down many kings in the day of His anger.

---

[9]Implied. In Matthew 22:41-45, Jesus applies these words to Himself.
[1]Literally, "The Lord will send forth the rod of your strength out of Zion."
[2]Literally, "from Zion."
[3]Literally, "in holy array."
[4]Literally, "after the manner of."

6 He will punish the nations, and fill them with their dead. He will crush many heads.

7 But He Himself shall be refreshed from springs along the way.

## PSALM 111

**H**allelujah! I want to express publicly before His people my heartfelt thanks to God for His mighty miracles! All who are thankful should ponder them with me.

3 For His miracles demonstrate His honor, majesty, and eternal goodness.

4 Who can forget the wonders He performs— deeds of mercy and of grace?

5 He gives food to those who trust Him; He never forgets His promises!

6 He has shown His great power to His people by giving them the land of Israel, though it was the home of many nations living there.

7 All He does is just and good, and all His laws are right,

8 For they are formed from truth and goodness, and stand firm forever.

9 He has paid a full ransom for His people; now they are always free to come to God (what a holy, awe-inspiring name that is).

10 How can men be wise? The only way to begin is by reverence for God. For growth in wisdom comes from obeying His laws. Praise His name forever.

# PSALM 112

Praise the Lord! For all who fear God and trust in Him are blessed beyond expression. Yes, happy is the man who delights in doing His commands.

2 His children shall be honored everywhere, for good men's sons have a special heritage.

3 He himself shall be wealthy, and his good deeds will never be forgotten.[5]

4 When darkness overtakes him, light will come bursting in. He is kind and merciful—

5 And all goes well for the generous man who conducts his business fairly.

6 Such a man will not be overthrown by evil circumstances. God's constant care of him will make a deep impression on all who see it.

7 He does not fear bad news, nor live in dread of what may happen. For he is settled in his mind that Jehovah will take care of him.

8 That is why he is not afraid, but can calmly face his foes.

9 He gives generously to those in need. His deeds will never be forgotten.[5] He shall have influence and honor.

10 Evil-minded men will be infuriated when they see all this; they will gnash their teeth in anger and slink away, their hopes thwarted.

---

[5]Literally, "his righteousness endures forever."

## PSALM 113

Hallelujah!  O servants of Jehovah, praise His name.
    2    Blessed is His name forever and forever.

3    Praise Him from sunrise to sunset!

4    For He is high above the nations; His glory is far greater than the heavens.

5    Who can be compared with God enthroned on high?

6    Far below Him are the heavens and the earth; He stoops to look,

7    And lifts the poor from the dirt, and the hungry from the garbage dump,

8    And sets them among princes!

9    He gives children to the childless wife, so that she becomes a happy mother. Hallelujah! Praise the Lord.

## PSALM 114

Long ago when the Israeli escaped from Egypt, from that land of foreign tongue,

2    Then the lands of Judah and of Israel became God's new home and kingdom.

3    The Red Sea saw them coming and quickly broke apart before them! The Jordan River opened up a path for them to cross!

4    The mountains skipped like rams, the little hills like lambs!

5    What's wrong, Red Sea, that made you cut yourself in two? What happened, Jordan River, to your waters? Why were they held back?

6    Why, mountains, did you skip like rams? Why, little hills, like lambs?

7    Tremble, O earth, at the presence of the Lord, the God of Jacob.

8    For He caused gushing streams to burst from flinty rock.

## PSALM 115

Glorify Your name, not ours O Lord! Cause everyone to praise Your lovingkindness and Your truth.

2    Why let the nations say, "Their God is dead!"[6]

3    For He is in the heavens, and does as He wishes.

4    Their gods are merely man-made things of silver and of gold.

5    They can't talk or see, despite their eyes and mouths!

6    Nor can they hear, nor smell,

7    Nor use their hands or feet! Nor speak!

8    And those who make and worship them are just as foolish as their idols are.

9    O Israel, trust the Lord! He is your helper. He is your shield.

---

[6]Literally, "Where is their God?"

10    O priests of Aaron, trust the Lord! He is your helper; He is your shield.

11    All of you His people, trust in Him. He is your helper; He is your shield.

12    Jehovah is constantly thinking about us and He will surely bless us! He will bless the people of Israel and the priests of Aaron,

13    And all, both great and small, who reverence Him.

14    May the Lord bless you richly both you and your children.

15    Yes, Jehovah who made heaven and earth will personally bless you!

16    The heavens belong to the Lord, but He has given the earth to all mankind.

17    The dead cannot sing praises to Jehovah here on earth,[7]

18    But we can! We praise Him forever! Hallelujah! Praise the Lord!

## PSALM 116

I love the Lord because He hears my prayers and answers them.

2    Because He bends down and listens, I will pray as long as I breathe!

3    Death stared me in the face—I was frightened and sad.

4    Then I cried, "Lord, save me!"

[7]Implied.

5 How kind He is! How good He is! So merciful, this God of ours!

6 The Lord protects the simple and the childlike: I was facing death and then He saved me.

7 Now I can relax. For the Lord has done this wonderful miracle for me.

8 He has saved me from death, my eyes from tears, my feet from stumbling.

9 I shall live! Yes, in His presence—here on earth!

10, 11 In my discouragement I thought, "They are lying when they say I will recover."[9]

12 But now what can I offer Jehovah for all He has done for me?

13 I will bring Him an offering of wine[1] and praise His name.

14 I will publicly bring Him the sacrifice I vowed I would.

15 His loved ones are very precious to Him and He does not lightly let them die.[2]

16 O Lord, You have freed me from my bonds and I will serve you forever.

17 I will worship You and offer You a sacrifice of thanksgiving.

18, 19 Here in the courts of the Temple in Jerusalem, before all the people, I will pay everything I vowed to the Lord. Praise the Lord.

[1]Literally, "the cup of salvation" i.e., the thank-offering of wine for saving me.
[9]Literally, "I said in my alarm, all men are liars."
[2]Literally, "Precious in the sight of the Lord is the death of His saints." See context for validity of the paraphrase.

## PSALM 117

Praise the Lord, all nations everywhere. Laud Him, all the peoples of the earth.

2   For He loves us very dearly, and His truth endures. Praise the Lord.

## PSALM 118

Oh, thank the Lord, for He's so good! His lovingkindness is forever.

2   Let the congregation of Israel praise Him with these same words: "His lovingkindness is forever."

3   And let the priests of Aaron chant, "His lovingkindness is forever."

4   Let the Gentile converts chant, "His lovingkindness is forever."

\*     \*     \*     \*     \*

5   In my distress I prayed to the Lord and He answered me and rescued me.

6   He is for me! How can I be afraid? What can mere man do to me?

7   The Lord is on my side, He will help me. Let those who hate me beware.

8   It is better to trust the Lord than to put confidence in men.

9   It is better to take refuge in Him than in the mightiest king!

10    Though all the nations of the world attack me, I will march out behind His banner and destroy them.

11    Yes, they surround and attack me; but with His flag flying above me I will cut them off.

12    They swarm around me like bees; they blaze against me like a roaring flame. Yet beneath His flag I shall destroy them.

13    You did your best to kill me, O my enemy, but the Lord helped me.

14    He is my strength and song in the heat of battle, and now He has given me the victory.

15, 16    Songs of joy at the news of our rescue are sung in the homes of the godly. The strong arm of the Lord has done glorious things!

17    I shall not die, but live to tell of all His deeds.

18    The Lord has punished me, but not handed me over to Death.

19    Open the gates of the Temple[1]—I will go in and give Him my thanks.

20    Those gates are the way into the presence of the Lord, and the godly enter there.

21    O Lord, thank you so much for answering my prayer and saving me.

22    The stone rejected by the builders has now become the capstone of the arch![2]

23    This is the Lord's doing, and it is marvelous to see!

---

[1]Literally, "the gates of righteousness."
[2]Literally, "the head of the corner."

24 This is the day the Lord has made. We will rejoice and be glad in it.

25 O Lord, please help us. Save us. Give us success.

26 Blessed is the One who is coming, the One sent[3] by the Lord. We bless You from the Temple.

27, 28 Jehovah God is our light. I present to Him my sacrifice upon the altar, for You are my God, and I shall give You this thanks and this praise.

29 Oh, give thanks to the Lord, for He is so good! For His lovingkindness is forever.

## PSALM 119

Happy are all who perfectly follow the laws of God. 2 Happy are all who search for God, and always do His will,

3 Rejecting compromise with evil, and walking only in His paths.

4 You have given us Your laws to obey—

5 Oh, how I want to follow them consistently.

6 Then I will not be disgraced, for I will have a clean record.

7 After You have corrected[4] me I will thank You by living as I should!

8 I *will* obey! Oh, don't forsake me and let me slip back into sin again.[5]

---

[3]Literally, "in the name of the Lord."
[4]Literally, "when I learn (have experienced) Your righteous judgments."
[5]Literally, "Oh forsake me not utterly."

9 How can a young man stay pure? By reading Your word and following its rules.

10 I have tried my best to find You—don't let me wander off from Your instructions.

11 I have thought much about Your words, and stored them in my heart so that they would hold me back from sin.

12 Blessed Lord, teach me Your rules.

13 I have recited Your laws,

14 And rejoiced in them more than in riches.

15 I will meditate upon them and give them my full respect.

16 I will delight in them and not forget them.

17 Bless me with life⁶ so that I can continue to obey You.

18 Open my eyes to see wonderful things in Your word.

19 I am but a pilgrim here on earth: how I need a map—and Your commands are my chart and guide.

20 I long for Your instructions more than I can tell.

21 You rebuke those cursed proud ones who refuse Your commands—

22 Don't let them scorn me for obeying You.

23 For even princes sit and talk against me, but I will continue in Your plans.

24 Your laws are both my light and my counselors.

---

⁶Literally, "deal bountifully that I may live."

25 I am completely discouraged—I lie in the dust. Revive me by Your Word.

26 I told You my plans and You replied. Now give me Your instructions.

27 Make me understand what You want; for then I shall see Your miracles.

28 I weep with grief; my heart is heavy with sorrow; encourage and cheer me with Your words.

29, 30 Keep me far from every wrong; help me, undeserving as I am, to obey Your laws, for I have chosen to do right.

31 I cling to Your commands and follow them as closely as I can. Lord, don't let me make a mess of things.

32 If You will only help me to want Your will, then I will follow Your laws even more closely.

33, 34 Just tell me what to do and I will do it, Lord. As long as I live I'll wholeheartedly obey.

35 Make me walk along the right paths for I know how delightful they really are.

36 Help me to prefer obedience to making money!

37 Turn me away from wanting any other[7] plan than Yours. Revive my heart toward You.

38 Reassure me that Your promises are for me; for I trust and revere You.

39 How I dread being mocked for obeying; for Your laws are right and good.

40, 41, 42 I long to obey them! Therefore in

---

[7]Literally, "from beholding vanity."

fairness renew my life, for this was Your promise—yes,
Lord, to save me! Now spare me this kindness and love.
Then I will have an answer for those who taunt me, for
I trust Your promises.

43    May I never forget Your words; for they are my
only hope.

44, 45, 46    Therefore I will keep on obeying You
forever and forever, free within the limits of Your laws.
I will speak to kings about their value, and they will
listen with interest and respect.

47    How I love Your laws! How I enjoy Your commands!

48    "Come, come to me," I call to them, for I love
them and will let them fill my life.

49, 50    Never forget Your promises to me Your
servant; for they are my only hope. They give me
strength in all my troubles; how they refresh and revive
me!

51    Proud men hold me in contempt for obedience
to God, but I stand unmoved.

52    From my earliest youth I have tried to obey
You; Your Word has been my comfort.

53    I am very angry with those who spurn Your
commands.

54    For these laws of Yours have been my source of
joy and singing through all these years of my earthly
pilgrimage.

55    I obey them even at night and keep my
thoughts, O Lord, on You.

56   What a blessing this has been to me—to constantly obey.

57   Jehovah is mine! And I promise to obey!

58   With all my heart I want Your blessings. Be merciful just as You promised.

59, 60   I thought about the wrong direction in which I was headed, and turned around and came running back to You.

61   Evil men have tried to drag me into sin, but I am firmly anchored to Your laws.

62   At midnight I will rise to give my thanks to You for Your good laws.

63   Anyone is my brother who fears and trusts the Lord and obeys Him.

64   O Lord, the earth is full of Your lovingkindness! Teach me Your good paths.

65   Lord, I am overflowing with Your blessings, just as You promised!

66   Now teach me good judgment as well as knowledge! For Your laws are my guide.

67   I used to wander off until You punished me; now I closely follow all You say.

68   You are good and do only good; make me follow Your lead!

69   Proud men have made up lies about me, but the truth is that I obey Your laws with all my heart.

70   Their minds are dull and stupid, but I have sense enough to follow You.

71, 72   The punishment You gave me was the best

thing that could have happened to me, for it taught me to pay attention to Your laws. They are more valuable to me than millions in silver and gold!

73  You made my body, Lord; now give me sense to heed Your laws.

74  All those who fear and trust in You will welcome me because I too am trusting in Your Word.

75, 76, 77  I know, O Lord, that Your decisions are right and that Your punishment was right and did me good. Now let Your lovingkindness comfort me, just as You promised. Surround me with Your tender mercies, that I may live. For Your law is my delight.

78  Let the proud be disgraced, for they have cut me down with all their lies. But I will concentrate my thoughts upon Your laws.

79  Let all others join me, who trust and fear You, and we will discuss Your laws.

80  Help me to love Your every wish; then I will never have to be ashamed of myself!

81  I faint for Your salvation; but I expect Your help, for You have promised it.

82  My eyes are straining to see Your promises come true. When will You comfort me with Your help?

83  I am shriveled like a wineskin in the smoke, exhausted with waiting. But still I cling to Your laws and obey them.

84  How long must I wait before You punish those who persecute me?

85, 86  These proud men who hate Your truth and laws have dug deep pits for me to fall in. Their lies have brought me into deep trouble. Help me, for You love only truth.

87   They had almost finished me off, yet I refused to yield and disobey Your laws.

88   In Your kindness, spare my life; then I can continue to obey You.

89   Forever, O Lord, Your Word stands firm in heaven.

90, 91   Your faithfulness extends to every generation, like the earth You created; it endures by Your decree, for everything serves Your plans.

92   I would have despaired and perished unless Your laws had been my deepest delight.

93   I will never lay aside Your laws, for You have used them to restore my joy and health.

94   I am Yours! Save me! For I have tried to live according to Your desires.

95   Though the wicked hide along the way to kill me, I will quietly keep my mind upon Your promises.

96   Nothing is perfect except Your words.

97   Oh, how I love them. I think about them all day long.

98   They make me wiser than my enemies, because they are my constant guide.

99   Yes, wiser than my teachers; for I am ever thinking of Your rules.

100   They make me even wiser than the aged.

101   I have refused to walk the paths of evil for I will remain obedient to Your Word.

102, 103 No, I haven't turned away from what You taught me: Your words are sweeter than honey.

104 And since only Your rules can give me wisdom and understanding, no wonder I hate every false teaching.

105 Your words are a flashlight to light the path ahead of me, and keep me from stumbling.

106 I've said it once and I'll say it again and again: I will obey these wonderful laws of Yours.

107 I am close to death at the hands of my enemies; oh, give me back my life again, just as You promised me.

108 Accept my grateful thanks and teach me Your desires.

109 My life hangs in the balance, but I will not give up obedience to Your laws.

110 The wicked have set their traps for me along Your path, but I will not turn aside.

111 Your laws are my joyous treasure forever.

112 I am determined to obey You until I die.

113 I hate those who are undecided whether or not to obey You; but my choice is clear—I love Your law.

114 You are my refuge and my shield, and Your promises are my only source of hope.

115 Begone, you evil-minded men. Don't try to stop me from obeying God's commands.

116 Lord, You promised to let me live! Never let it be said that God failed me.

117 Hold me safe above the heads of all my enemies; then I can continue to obey Your laws.

118  But You have rejected all who reject Your laws. They are only fooling themselves.

119  The wicked are the scum You skim off and throw away; no wonder I love to obey Your laws!

120  I tremble in fear of You; I fear Your punishments.

121  Don't leave me to the mercy of my enemies, for I have done what is right; I've been perfectly fair.

122  Commit Yourself to bless me! Don't let the proud oppress me!

123  My eyes grow dim with longing for You to fulfill Your wonderful promise to rescue me.

124  Lord, deal with me in lovingkindness, and teach me, Your servant, to obey;

125  For I am Your servant; therefore give me common sense to apply Your rules to everything I do.

126  Lord, it is time for You to act. For these evil men have violated Your laws,

127  While I love Your commandments more than the finest gold.

128  Every law of God is right, whatever it concerns. I hate every other way.

129  Your laws are wonderful; no wonder I obey them.

130  As Your plan unfolds, even the simple can understand it.

131  No wonder I wait expectantly for each of Your commands.

132  Come and have mercy on me as is Your way with those who love You.

133 Guide me with Your laws so that I will not be overcome by evil.

134 Rescue me from the oppression of evil men; then I can obey You.

135 Look down in love upon me and teach me all Your laws.

136 I weep because Your laws are disobeyed.

137 O Lord, You are just and Your punishments are fair.

138 Your demands are just and right.

139 I am indignant and angry because of the way my enemies have disregarded Your laws.

140 I have thoroughly tested Your promises and that is why I love them so much.

141 I am worthless and despised, but I don't despise Your laws.

142 Your justice is eternal for Your laws are perfectly fair.

143 In my distress and anguish, Your commandments comfort me.

144 Your laws are always fair; help me to understand them and I shall live.

145 I am praying with great earnestness; answer me, O Lord, and I will obey Your laws.

146 "Save me," I cry, "for I am obeying."

147 Early in the morning, before the sun is up, I was praying and pointing out how much I trust in You.

148 I stay awake through the night to think about Your promises.

149 Because You are so loving and kind, listen to me and make me well again.

150 Here come these lawless men to attack me;

151 But You are near, O Lord; all Your commandments are based on truth.

152 I have known from earliest days that Your will never changes.

153 Look down upon my sorrows and rescue me, for I am obeying Your commands.

154 Yes, rescue me and give me back my life again just as You have promised.

155 The wicked are far from salvation for they do not care for Your laws.

156 Lord, how great is Your mercy: oh, give me back my life again.

157 My enemies are so many. They try to make me disobey; but I have not swerved from Your will.

158 I loathed these traitors because they care nothing for Your laws.

159 Lord, see how much I really love Your demands. Now give me back my life and health because You are so kind.

160 There is utter truth in all Your laws; Your decrees are eternal.

161 Great men have persecuted me, though they have no reason to, but I stand in awe of only Your words.

162 I rejoice in Your laws like one who finds a great treasure.

163 How I hate all falsehood but how I love Your laws.

164 I will praise You seven times a day because of Your wonderful laws.

165 Those who love Your laws have great peace of heart and mind and do not stumble.

166 I long for Your salvation, Lord, and so I have obeyed Your laws.

167 I have looked for Your commandments and I love them very much;

168 Yes, I have searched for them. You know this because everything I do is known to You.

169 O Lord, listen to my prayers; give me the common sense You promised.

170 Hear my prayers; rescue me as You said You would.

171 I praise You for letting me learn Your laws.

172 I will sing about their wonder, for each of them is just.

173 Stand ready to help me because I have chosen to follow Your will.

174 O Lord, I have longed for Your salvation and Your law is my delight.

175 If You will let me live, I will praise You; let Your laws assist me.

176 I have wandered away like a lost sheep; come and find me for I have not turned away from Your commandments.

## PSALM 120

In my troubles I pled with God to help me and He did!

2 Deliver me, O Lord, from liars.

3 O lying tongue, what shall be your fate?

4 You shall be pierced with sharp arrows and burned with glowing coals.[9]

5, 6 My troubles pile high among these haters of the Lord, these men of Meshech and Kedar. I am tired of being here among these men who hate peace.

7 I am for peace, but they are for war, and my voice goes unheeded in their councils.

## PSALM 121

Shall I look to the mountain gods for help?

2 No! My help is from Jehovah who made the mountains! And the heavens too!

3, 4 He will never let me stumble, slip or fall. For He is always watching, never sleeping.

5 Jehovah Himself is caring for you! He is your defender.[1]

6 He protects you day and night.

7 He keeps you from all evil, and preserves your life.

8 He keeps His eye upon you as you come and go, and always guards you.

---

[9]Literally, "with coals of the broom tree."
[1]Literally, "your shade at your right hand."

## PSALM 122

I was glad for the suggestion of going to Jerusalem, to the Temple of the Lord.

2, 3 Now we are standing here inside the crowded city.

4 All Israel—Jehovah's people—have come to worship as the law requires, to thank and praise the Lord.

5 Look! There are the judges holding court beside the city gates, deciding all the people's arguments.

6 Pray for the peace of Jerusalem. May all who love this city prosper.

7 O Jerusalem, may there be peace within your walls and prosperity in your palaces.

8 This I ask for the sake of all my brothers and my friends who live here;

9 And may there be peace as a protection to the Temple of the Lord.

## PSALM 123

O God enthroned in heaven, I lift my eyes to You. 2 We look to Jehovah our God for His mercy and kindness just as a servant keeps his eyes upon his master or a slave girl watches her mistress for the slightest signal.

3, 4 Have mercy on us, Lord, have mercy. For we have had our fill of contempt and of the scoffing of the rich and proud.

## PSALM 124

If the Lord had not been on our side (let all Israel admit it), if the Lord had not been on our side,

2, 3   We would have been swallowed alive by our enemies, destroyed by their anger.

4, 5   We would have drowned beneath the flood of these men's fury and pride.

6   Blessed be Jehovah who has not let them devour us.

7   We have escaped with our lives as a bird from a hunter's snare. The snare is broken and we are free!

8   Our help is from the Lord who made heaven and earth!

## PSALM 125

Those who trust in the Lord are steady as Mount Zion, unmoved by any circumstance.

2   Just as the mountains surround and protect Jerusalem, so the Lord surrounds and protects His people.

3   For the wicked shall not rule the godly, lest the godly be forced to do wrong.

4   O Lord, do good to those who are good, whose hearts are right with the Lord;

5   But lead evil men to execution. And let Israel have quietness and peace.

## PSALM 126

When Jehovah brought back His exiles to Jerusalem, it was like a dream!

2 How we laughed and sang for joy. And the other nations said, "What amazing things the Lord has done for them."

3 Yes, glorious things! What wonder! What joy!

4 May we be refreshed[2] as by streams in the desert.

5 Those who sow tears shall reap joy.

6 Yes, they go out weeping, carrying seed for sowing and return singing, carrying their sheaves.

## PSALM 127

Unless the Lord builds a house, the builders' work is useless. Unless the Lord protects a city, sentries do no good.

2 It is senseless for you to work so hard from early morning until late at night, fearing you will starve to death; for God wants His loved ones to get their proper rest.

3 Children are a gift from God; they are His reward.

---

[2]Literally, "Restore our fortunes, Lord."

4   Children born to a young man are like sharp arrows to defend him.

5   Happy is the man who has his quiver full of them. That man shall have the help he needs when arguing with his enemies.[3]

## PSALM 128

Blessings on all who reverence and trust the Lord—on all who obey Him!

2   Their reward shall be prosperity and happiness.

3   Your wife shall be contented in your home. And look at all those children! There they sit around the dinner table as vigorous and healthy as young olive trees.

4   That is God's reward to those who reverence and trust Him.

5   May the Lord continually bless you with heaven's blessings[4] as well as with human joys.[5]

6   May you live to enjoy your grandchildren! And may God bless Israel!

## PSALM 129

Persecuted from my earliest youth (Israel is speaking),

---

[3]Literally, "When they speak with their enemies in the gate."
[4]Literally, "from Zion."
[5]Literally, "of Jerusalem."

2   And faced with never-ending discrimination—but not destroyed! My enemies have never been able to finish me off!

3, 4   Though my back is cut to ribbons with their whips, the Lord is good. For He has snapped the chains that evil men had bound me with.

5   May all who hate the Jews be brought to ignominious defeat.

6, 7   May they be as grass in shallow soil, turning sear and yellow when half grown, ignored by the reaper, despised by the binder.

8   And may those passing by refuse to bless them by saying, "Jehovah's blessings be upon you; we bless you in Jehovah's name."


## PSALM 130

O Lord, from the depths of despair I cry for Your help:

2   "Hear me! Answer! Help me!"

3, 4   Lord, if You keep in mind our sins then who can ever get an answer to his prayers? But You forgive! What an awesome thing this is!

5   That is why I wait expectantly, trusting God to help, for He has promised.

6   I long for Him more than sentinels long for the dawn.

7   O Israel, hope in the Lord; for He is loving and kind, and comes to us with armloads of salvation.

8   He Himself shall ransom Israel from her slavery to sin.

## PSALM 131

Lord, I am not proud and haughty. I don't think myself better than others. I don't pretend to "know it all."

2   I am quiet now before the Lord, just as a child who is weaned from the breast. Yes, my begging has been stilled.

3   O Israel, you too should quietly trust in the Lord—now, and always.

## PSALM 132

Lord, do You remember that time when my[6] heart was so filled with turmoil?

2, 3, 4, 5   I couldn't rest, I couldn't sleep, thinking how I ought to build a permanent home for the Ark[7] of the Lord, a Temple for the mighty One of Israel. Then I vowed that I would do it; I made a solemn promise to the Lord.

6   First the Ark was in[8] Ephrathah, then in the distant countryside of Jaar.

7   But now it will be settled in the Temple, in God's

---

[6]Literally, "David's soul."
[7]Implied.
[8]Literally, "Lo, we heard of it in Ehprathah."

permanent home here on earth. That is where we will go to worship Him.[9]

8 Arise, O Lord, and enter Your Temple with the Ark, the symbol of Your power.

9 We will clothe the priests in white, the symbol of all purity. May our nation shout for joy.

\* \* \* \* \*

10 Do not reject Your servant David—the king You chose for Your people.

11 For You promised me that my son would sit on my throne and succeed me. And surely You will never go back on a promise!

12 You also promised that if my descendants will obey the terms of Your contract with me, then the dynasty of David shall never end.

13 O Lord, You have chosen Jerusalem[1] as Your home:

14 "This is My permanent home where I shall live," You said, "for I have always wanted it this way.

15 I will make this city prosperous and satisfy her poor with food.

16 I will clothe her priests with salvation; her saints shall shout for joy.

17 David's power shall grow, for I have decreed for him a mighty Son.[2]

18 I'll clothe His enemies with shame, but He shall be a glorious King."

---

[9]Literally, "We will go into His tabernacles; we will worship at His footstool."
[1]Literally, "Zion."
[2]Literally, "a progeny."

## PSALM 133

How wonderful it is, how pleasant, when brothers live in harmony!

2 For harmony is as precious as the fragrant anointing oil that was poured over Aaron's head, and ran down onto his beard, and onto the border of his robe.

3 Harmony is as refreshing as the dew on Mount Hermon, on the mountains of Israel. And God has pronounced this eternal blessing on Jerusalem,[3] even life forevermore.

## PSALM 134

Oh, bless the Lord, you who serve Him as watchmen in the Temple every night.

2 Lift your hands in holiness and bless the Lord.

3 The Lord bless you from Zion—the Lord who made heaven and earth.

## PSALM 135

Hallelujah! Yes, let His people praise Him, as they stand in His Temple courts.

3 Praise the Lord because He is so good; sing to His wonderful name.

---

[3]Literally, "Zion."

4   For the Lord has chosen Israel as His personal possession.

5   I know the greatness of the Lord—that He is greater far than any other god.

6   He does whatever pleases Him throughout all of heaven and earth, and in the deepest seas.

7   He makes mists rise throughout the earth and sends the lightning to bring down the rain; and sends the winds from His treasuries.

8   He destroyed the eldest child in each Egyptian home, along with the firstborn of the flocks.

9   He did great miracles in Egypt before Pharaoh and all his people.

10   He smote great nations, slaying mighty kings—

11   Sihon, king of Amorites; and Og, the king of Bashan; and the kings of Canaan—

12   And gave their land as an eternal gift to His people Israel.

13   O Jehovah, Your name endures forever; Your fame is known to every generation.

14   For Jehovah will vindicate His people, and have compassion on His servants.

15   The heathen worship idols of gold and silver, made by men—

16   Idols with speechless mouths and sightless eyes

17   And ears that cannot hear; they cannot even breathe.

18   Those who make them become like them! And so do all who trust in them!

19   O Israel, bless Jehovah! High priests of Aaron, bless His name.

20   O Levite priests, bless the Lord Jehovah! Oh, bless His name, all of you who trust and reverence Him.

21   All people of Jerusalem,[4] praise the Lord, for He lives here in Jerusalem. Hallelujah!

## PSALM 136

Oh, give thanks to the Lord, for He is good; His lovingkindness continues forever.

2   Give thanks to the God of gods, for His lovingkindness continues forever.

3   Give thanks to the Lord of lords, for His lovingkindness continues forever.

4   Praise Him who alone does mighty miracles, for His lovingkindness continues forever.

5   Praise Him who made the heavens, for His lovingkindness continues forever.

6   Praise Him who planted the water within the earth,[5] for His lovingkindness continues forever.

7   Praise Him who made the heavenly lights, for His lovingkindness continues forever:

8   The sun to rule the day, for His lovingkindness continues forever;

---

4 Literally, "the Lord be blessed from Zion."
5 Or, "who separated the earth from the oceans."

9   And the moon and stars at night, for His loving-kindness continues forever.

10   Praise the God who smote the firstborn of Egypt, for His lovingkindness to Israel[6] continues forever.

11, 12   He brought them out with mighty power and upraised fist to strike their enemies, for His loving-kindness to Israel[6] continues forever.

13   Praise the Lord who opened the Red Sea to make a path before them, for His lovingkindness continues forever,

14   And led them safely through, for His loving-kindness continues forever—

15   But drowned Pharaoh's army in the sea, for His lovingkindness to Israel[6] continues forever.

16   Praise Him who led His people through the wilderness for His lovingkindness continues forever.

17   Praise Him who saved His people from the power of mighty kings, for His lovingkindness continues forever,

18   And killed famous kings who were their enemies, for His lovingkindness to Israel[6] continues forever:

19   Sihon, king of Amorites—for God's loving-kindness to Israel[6] continues forever—

20   And Og, king of Bashan—for His lovingkind-ness to Israel[6] continues forever.

21   God gave the land of these kings to Israel as a

[6]Implied.

gift forever, for His lovingkindness to Israel[7] continues forever;

22　Yes, a permanent gift to His servant Israel, for His lovingkindness continues forever.

23　He remembered our utter weakness, for His lovingkindness continues forever.

24　And saved us from our foes, for His loving-kindness continues forever.

25　He gives food to every living thing, for His lov-ingkindness continues forever.

26　Oh, give thanks to the God of heaven, for His lovingkindness continues forever.

## PSALM 137

Weeping, we sat beside the rivers of Babylon think-ing of Jerusalem.

2　We have put away our lyres, hanging them upon the branches of the willow trees,

3, 4　For how can we sing? Yet our captors, our tormentors, demand that we sing for them the happy songs of Zion!

5, 6　If I forget you, O Jerusalem, let my right hand forget her skill upon the harp. If I fail to love her more than my highest joy, let me never sing again.

7　O Jehovah, do not forget what these Edomites did on that day when the armies of Babylon captured Jerusalem. "Raze her to the ground!" they yelled.

---
[7]Implied.

8  O Babylon, evil beast, you shall be destroyed. Blessed is the man who destroys you as you have destroyed us.

9  Blessed is the man who takes your babies and smashes them against the rocks![8]

## PSALM 138

Lord, with all my heart I thank You.  I will sing Your praises before the armies of angels[9] in heaven.

2  I face Your Temple as I worship, giving thanks to You for all Your lovingkindness and Your faithfulness, for Your promises are backed by all the honor of Your name.[1]

3  When I pray, You answer me, and encourage me by giving me the strength I need.

4  Every king in all the earth shall give You thanks, O Lord, for all of them shall hear Your voice.

5  Yes, they shall sing about Jehovah's glorious ways, for His glory is very great.

6  Yet though He is so great, He respects the humble; but proud men must keep their distance.

7  Though I am surrounded by troubles, You will bring me safely through them. You will clench Your fist against my angry enemies! Your power will save me.

8  The Lord will work out His plans for my life— for Your lovingkindness, Lord, continues forever. Don't abandon me—for You made me.

---

[8]Perhaps this could be paraphrased, "Blessed is he who invades and sacks your city."
[9]Literally, "before the gods," or "before the idols."
[1]Literally, "You have exalted Your word above all Your name."

## PSALM 139

O Lord, You have examined my heart and know everything about me.

2　You know when I sit or stand. When far away You know my every thought.

3　You chart the path ahead of me, and tell me where to stop and rest! Every moment, You know where I am!

4　You know what I am going to say before I even say it.

5　You both precede and follow me, and place Your hand of blessing on my head.

6　This is too glorious, too wonderful to believe!

7　I can *never* be lost to Your Spirit! I can *never* get away from God!

8　If I go up to heaven You are there; if I go down to the place of the dead, You are there.

9　If I ride the morning winds to the farthest oceans,

10　Even there Your hand will guide me, Your strength will support me.

11　If I try to hide in the darkness, the night becomes light around me!

12　For even darkness cannot hide from God; to You the night shines as bright as day. Darkness and light are both alike to You.

13　You made all the delicate, inner parts of my body, and knit them together in my mother's womb.

14 Thank You for making me so wonderfully complex! It is amazing to think about. Your workmanship is marvelous—and how well I know it.

15 You were there while I was being formed in utter seclusion!

16 You saw me before I was born and scheduled each day of my life before I began to breathe. Every day was recorded in Your Book!

17, 18 How precious it is, Lord, to realize that You are thinking about me constantly! I can't even count how many times a day Your thoughts turn towards me!² And when I waken in the morning, You are still thinking of me!

\* \* \* \* \*

19 Surely You will slay the wicked, Lord! Away, bloodthirsty men! Begone!

20 They blaspheme Your name and stand in arrogance against You—how silly can they be?

21 O Lord, shouldn't I hate those who hate You? Shouldn't I be grieved with them?

22 Yes, I hate them, for Your enemies are my enemies too.

23 Search me, O God, and know my heart, test my thoughts.

24 Point out anything You find in me that makes You sad, and lead me along the path of everlasting life.

## PSALM 140

O Lord, deliver me from evil men. Preserve me from the violent,

---

²Literally, "how precious are Your thoughts to me."

2    Who plot and stir up trouble all day long.

3    Their words sting like poisonous snakes.

4    Keep me out of their power. Preserve me from their violence, for they are plotting against me.

5    These proud men have set a trap to catch me, a noose to yank me up and leave me dangling in the air; they wait in ambush with a net to throw over and hold me helpless in its meshes.

6, 7, 8    O Jehovah, my Lord and Savior, my God and my shield—hear me as I pray! Don't let these wicked men succeed; don't let them prosper and be proud.

9    Let their plots boomerang! Let them be destroyed by the very evil they have planned for me.

10    Let burning coals fall down upon their heads, or throw them into the fire, or into deep pits from which they can't escape.

11    Don't let liars prosper here in our land; quickly punish them.

12    But the Lord will surely help those they persecute; He will maintain the rights of the poor.

13    Surely the godly are thanking You, for they shall live in Your presence.

## PSALM 141

Quick, Lord, answer me—for I have prayed. Listen when I cry to You for help!

2    Regard my prayer as my evening sacrifice and as incense wafting up to You.

3    Help me, Lord, to keep my mouth shut and my lips sealed.

4    Take away my lust for evil things; don't let me want to be with sinners, doing what they do, sharing their dainties.

5    Let the godly smite me! It will be a kindness! If they reprove me, it is medicine! Don't let me refuse it. But I am in constant prayer against the wicked and their deeds.

6, 7    When their leaders are condemned, and their bones are strewn across the ground,[3] then these men will finally listen to me and know that I am trying to help them.

8    I look to You for help, O Lord God. You are my refuge. Don't let them slay me.

9    Keep me out of their traps.

10    Let them fall into their own snares, while I escape.


## PSALM 142

How I plead with God, how I implore His mercy, pouring out my troubles before Him.

3    For I am overwhelmed and desperate, and You alone know which way I ought to turn to miss the traps my enemies have set for me.

---

[3]Literally, "As when one plows and cleaves the earth, our bones are scattered at the mouth of Sheol."

4    (There's one—just over there to the right!) No one gives me a passing thought. No one will help me; no one cares one whit what happens to me.

5    Then I prayed to Jehovah. "Lord," I pled, "You are my only place of refuge. Only You can keep me safe.

6    Hear my cry, for I am very low. Rescue me from my persecutors, for they are too strong for me.

7    Bring me out of prison, so that I can thank You. The godly will rejoice with me for all Your help."

## PSALM 143

Hear my prayer, O Lord; answer my plea, because You are faithful to Your promises.[4]

2    Don't bring me to trial! For as compared with You, no one is perfect.

3    My enemies chased and caught me. They have knocked me to the ground. They force me to live in the darkness like those in the grave.

4    I am losing all hope; I am paralyzed with fear.

5    I remember the glorious miracles You did in days of long ago.

6    I reach out for You. I thirst for You as parched land thirsts for rain.

7    Come quickly, Lord, and answer me, for my depression deepens; don't turn away from me or I shall die.

---

[4]Literally, "answer me in faithfulness and righteousness."

8    Let me see Your kindness to me in the morning, for I am trusting You. Show me where to walk, for my prayer is sincere.

9    Save me from my enemies, O Lord, I run to You to hide me.

10    Help me to do Your will, for You are my God. Lead me in good paths, for Your Spirit is good.

11    Lord, saving me will bring glory to Your name. Bring me out of all this trouble because You are true to Your promises.

12    And because You are loving and kind to me, cut off all my enemies and destroy those who are trying to harm me; for I am Your servant.

## PSALM 144

Bless the Lord who is my immovable Rock. He gives me strength and skill in battle.

2    He is always kind and loving to me; He is my fortress, my tower of strength and safety, my deliverer. He stands before me as a shield. He subdues my people under me.

3    O Lord, what is man that You even notice him? Why bother at all with the human race?[5]

4    For man is but a breath; his days are like a passing shadow.

5    Bend down the heavens, Lord, and come. The mountains smoke beneath Your touch.

[5]Literally, "or the son of man that You take account of him?"

6   Let loose Your lightning bolts, Your arrows,
Lord, upon Your enemies, and scatter them.

7   Reach down from heaven and rescue me; deliver
me from deep waters, from the power of my enemies.

8   Their mouths are filled with lies; they swear to
the truth of what is false.

9   I will sing You a new song, O God, with a ten-
stringed harp.

10   For You grant victory to kings! You are the one
who will rescue Your servant David from the fatal
sword.

11   Save me! Deliver me from these enemies, these
liars, these treacherous men.

\*     \*     \*     \*

12, 13, 14, 15   Here is my description of[6] a truly
happy land where Jehovah is God:

Sons vigorous and tall as growing plants.
Daughters of graceful beauty like the pil-
    lars of a palace wall.
Barns full to the brim with crops of every
    kind.
Sheep by the thousands out in our fields.
Oxen loaded down with produce.
No enemy attacking the walls, but peace
    everywhere.
No crime in our streets.
Yes, happy are those whose God is Jeho-
    vah.

[6]Implied.

## PSALM 145

I will praise You, my God and King, and bless Your name each day and forever.

3 Great is Jehovah! Greatly praise Him! His greatness is beyond discovery!

4 Let each generation tell its children what glorious things He does.

5 I will meditate about Your glory, splendor, majesty and miracles.

6 Your awe-inspiring deeds shall be on every tongue; I will proclaim Your greatness.

7 Everyone will tell about how good You are, and sing about Your righteousness.

8 Jehovah is kind and merciful, slow to get angry, full of love.

9 He is good to everyone, and His compassion is intertwined with everything He does.

10 All living things shall thank You, Lord, and Your people will bless You.

11 They will talk together about the glory of Your kingdom and mention examples of Your power.

12 They will tell about Your miracles and about the majesty and glory of Your reign.

13 For Your kingdom never ends. You rule generation after generation.

14 The Lord lifts the fallen and those bent beneath their loads.

15 The eyes of all mankind look up to You for help; You give them their food as they need it.

16 You constantly satisfy the hunger and thirst of every living thing.

17 The Lord is fair in everything He does, and full of kindness.

18 He is close to all who call on Him sincerely.

19 He fulfills the desires of those who reverence and trust Him; He hears their cries for help and rescues them.

20 He protects all those who love Him, but destroys the wicked.

21 I shall praise the Lord and call on all men everywhere to bless His holy name forever and forever.


## PSALM 146


Praise the Lord! Yes, really praise Him!
2 I will praise Him as long as I live, yes, even with my dying breath.

3 Don't look to men for help; their greatest leaders fail;

4 For every man must die. His breathing stops, life ends, and in a moment all he planned for himself is ended.

5 But happy is the man who has the God of Jacob as his helper, whose hope is in the Lord his God—

6 The God who made both earth and heaven, the

seas and everything in them. He is the God who keeps every promise,

7  And gives justice to the poor and oppressed, and food to the hungry. He frees the prisoners,

8  And opens the eyes of the blind; He lifts the burdens from those bent down beneath their loads. For the Lord loves good men.

9  He protects the immigrants, and cares for the orphans and widows. But He turns topsy-turvy the plans of the wicked.

10  The Lord will reign forever. O Jerusalem,[7] your God is King in every generation! Hallelujah! Praise the Lord!

## PSALM 147

Hallelujah! Yes, praise the Lord! How good it is to sing His praises! How delightful, and how right!

2  He is rebuilding Jerusalem and bringing back the exiles.

3  He heals the broken-hearted, binding up their wounds.

4  He counts the stars and calls them all by name.

5  How great He is! His power is absolute! His understanding is unlimited.

6  The Lord supports the humble, but brings the wicked into the dust.

7  Sing out your thanks to Him; sing praises to our God, accompanied by harps.

[7]Literally, "Zion."

8   He covers the heavens with clouds, sends down the showers and makes the green grass grow in mountain pastures.

9   He feeds the wild animals and the young ravens cry to Him for food.

10   The speed of a horse is nothing to Him. How puny in His sight is the strength of a man.

11   But His joy is in those who reverence Him; those who expect Him to be loving and kind.

12   Praise Him, O Jerusalem! Praise Your God, O Zion!

13   For He has fortified your gates against all enemies, and blessed your children.

14   He sends peace across your nation, and fills your barns with plenty of the finest wheat.

15   He sends His orders to the world. How swiftly His word flies.

16   He sends the snow in all its lovely whiteness, and scatters the frost upon the ground,

17   And hurls the hail upon the earth. Who can stand before His freezing cold?

18   But then He calls for warmer weather, and the spring winds blow and all the river ice is broken.

19   He has made known His laws and ceremonies of worship to Israel—

20   Something He has not done with any other nation; they have not known His commands.

\*        \*        \*        \*        \*

Hallelujah! Yes, praise the Lord!

## PSALM 148

Praise the Lord, O heavens! Praise Him from the skies!

2 Praise Him, all His angels, all the armies of heaven.

3 Praise Him sun and moon, and all you twinkling stars.

4 Praise Him, skies above. Praise Him, vapors high above the clouds.

5 Let everything He has made give praise to Him! For He issued His command, and they came into being;

6 He established them forever and forever. His orders will never be revoked.

7 And praise Him down here on earth, you creatures of the ocean depths.

8 Let fire and hail, snow, rain, wind and weather, all obey.

9 Let the mountains and hills, the fruit trees and cedars,

10 The wild animals and cattle, the snakes and birds,

11 The kings and all the people, with their rulers and their judges,

12 Young men and maidens, old men and children—

13 All praise the Lord together. For He alone is

worthy. His glory is far greater than all of earth and heaven.

14   He has made His people strong, honoring His godly ones—the people of Israel, the people closest to Him.

\*          \*          \*          \*          \*

Hallelujah! Yes, praise the Lord!

## PSALM 149

Hallelujah! Yes, praise the Lord! Sing Him a new song. Sing His praises, all His people.

2   O Israel, rejoice in your Maker. O people of Jerusalem, exult in Your King.

3   Praise His name by marching together to the Temple,[8] accompanied by drums and lyre.

4, 5   For Jehovah enjoys His people; He will save the humble. Let His people rejoice in this honor. Let them sing for joy as they lie upon their beds.

6, 7   Adore Him, O His people! And take a double-edged sword to execute His punishment upon the nations.

8   Bind their kings and leaders with iron chains,

9   And execute their sentences.

\*          \*          \*          \*          \*

He is the glory of His people. Hallelujah! Praise Him!

---

[8]Literally, "Let them praise His name in the dance."

# PSALM 150

**H**allelujah! Yes, praise the Lord! Praise Him in His Temple, and in the heavens He made with mighty power.[9]

2    Praise Him for His mighty works. Praise His unequalled greatness.

3    Praise Him with the trumpet and with lute and harp.

4    Praise Him with the timbrels and processional. Praise Him with stringed instruments and horns.

5    Praise Him with the cymbals, yes, loud clanging cymbals.

6    Let everything alive give praises to the Lord! *You* praise Him!

\*     \*     \*     \*

Hallelujah!

---

[9] Literally, "in the firmament of His power."

# Proverbs

## CHAPTER 1

These are the proverbs of King Solomon of Israel, David's son:

2  He wrote them to teach his people how to live— how to act in every circumstance,

3  For he wanted them to be understanding, just and fair in everything they did.

4  "I want to make the simple-minded wise!" he said. "I want to warn young men about some problems they will face.

5, 6  I want those already wise to become the wiser and become leaders by exploring the depths of meaning in these nuggets of truth."

\*    \*    \*    \*    \*

7, 8, 9  How does a man become wise? The first step is to trust and reverence the Lord!

Only fools refuse to be taught. Listen to your father and mother. What you learn from them will stand you in good stead; it will gain you many honors.\*

10  If young toughs tell you, "Come and join us"— turn your back on them!

---

\*Literally, "a fair garland and adornment."

11 "We'll hide and rob and kill," they say;

12 "Good or bad, we'll treat them all alike!

13 And the loot we'll get! All kinds of stuff!

14 Come on, throw in your lot with us; we'll split with you in equal shares."

15 Don't do it, son! Stay far from men like that,

16 For crime is their way of life, and murder is their specialty.

17 When a bird sees a trap being set, it stays away,

18 But not these men; they trap themselves! They lay a booby trap for their own lives.

19 Such is the fate of all who live by violence and murder.[1] They will die a violent death.

\* \* \* \* \*

20 Wisdom shouts in the streets for a hearing.

21 She calls out to the crowds along Main Street, and to the judges in their courts, and to everyone in all the land:

22 "You simpletons!" she cries, "how long will you go on being fools? How long will you scoff at wisdom and fight the facts?

23 Come here and listen to me! I'll pour out the spirit of Wisdom upon you, and make you wise.

24 I have called you so often but still you won't come. I have pleaded, but all in vain.

25 For you have spurned my counsel and reproof.

26 Some day you'll be in trouble, and I'll laugh! Mock me, will you?—I'll mock you!

---

[1]Literally, "all who are greedy of gain."

27   When a storm of terror surrounds you, and when you are engulfed by anguish and distress,

28   Then I will not answer your cry for help. It will be too late though you search for me ever so anxiously.

29   For you closed your eyes to the facts and did not choose to reverence and trust the Lord,

30   And you turned your back on me, spurning my advice.

31   That is why you must eat the bitter fruit of having your own way, and experience the full terrors of the pathway you have chosen.

32   For you turned away from me—to death; your own complacency will kill you. Fools!

33   But all who listen to me shall live in peace and safety, unafraid."

## CHAPTER 2

E very young man who listens to me and obeys my instructions will be given wisdom and good sense.

3, 4, 5   Yes, if you want better insight and discernment, and are searching for them as you would for lost money or hidden treasure, then wisdom will be given you and knowledge of God Himself; you will soon learn the importance of reverence for the Lord and of trusting Him.

6   For the Lord grants wisdom! His every word is a treasure of knowledge and understanding.

7, 8   He grants good sense to the godly—His

saints. He is their shield, protecting them and guarding their pathway.

9 He shows how to distinguish right from wrong, how to find the right decision every time.

10 For wisdom and truth will enter the very center of your being, filling your life with joy.

11, 12, 13 You will be given the sense to stay away from evil men who want you to be their partners in crime—men who turn from God's ways to walk down dark and evil paths,

14 And exult in doing wrong, for they thoroughly enjoy their sins.

15 Everything they do is crooked and wrong.

\* \* \* \* \*

16, 17 Only wisdom from the Lord can save a man from the flattery of prostitutes; these girls have abandoned their husbands and flouted the laws of God.

18 Their houses lie along the road to death and hell.

19 The men who enter them are doomed. None of these men will ever be the same again.*

20 Follow the steps of the godly instead, and stay on the right path,

21 For only good men enjoy life to the full;²

22 Evil men lose the good things they might have had;³ and they themselves shall be destroyed.

---

*Literally, "never return to the ways of life."
²Literally, "shall dwell in the land."
³Literally, "shall be cut off from the land."

# CHAPTER 3

**M**y son, never forget the things I've taught you. If you want a long and satisfying life, closely follow my instructions.

3   Never forget to be truthful and kind. Hold these virtues tightly. Write them deep within your heart.

4, 5   If you want favor with both God and man, and a reputation for good judgment and common sense, then trust the Lord completely; don't ever trust yourself.

6   In everything you do, put God first, and He will direct you and crown your efforts with success.

7, 8   Don't be conceited, sure of your own wisdom. Instead, trust and reverence the Lord, and turn your back on evil; when you do that, then you will be given renewed health and vitality.

9, 10   Honor the Lord by giving Him the first part of all your income, and He will fill your barns with wheat and barley and overflow your wine vats with the finest wines.

11, 12   Young man, do not resent it when God chastens and corrects you, for His punishment is proof of His love. Just as a father punishes a son he delights in to make him better, so the Lord corrects you.

13, 14, 15   The man who knows right from wrong[4] and has good judgment and common sense is

---

[4]Literally, "the man that finds wisdom."

happier than the man who is immensely rich! For such wisdom is far more valuable than precious jewels. Nothing else compares with it.

16, 17 Wisdom gives:

A long, good life
Riches
Honor
Pleasure
Peace

18 Wisdom is a tree of life to those who eat her fruit; happy is the man who keeps on eating it.

19 The Lord's wisdom founded the earth; **His** understanding established all the universe and space.

20 The deep fountains of the earth were broken open by His knowledge, and the skies poured down rain.

21 Have two goals: wisdom—that is, knowing and doing right—and common sense. Don't let them slip away,

22 For they fill you with living energy, and are a feather in your cap.[5]

23 They keep you safe from defeat and disaster and from stumbling off the trail.

24, 25, 26 With them on guard you can sleep without fear; and you need not be afraid of disaster or the plots of wicked men; for the Lord is with you; He protects you.

27, 28 Don't withhold repayment of your debts. Don't say "some other time," if you can pay now.

29 Don't plot against your neighbor; he is trusting you.

---

[5]Literally, "be an ornament to your neck."

30    Don't get into needless fights.

31    Don't envy violent men. Don't copy their ways.

32    For such men are an abomination to the Lord, but He gives His friendship to the godly.

33    The curse of God is on the wicked, but His blessing is on the upright.

34    The Lord mocks at mockers, but helps the humble.

35    The wise are promoted to honor, but fools are promoted to shame!


## CHAPTER 4


Young men, listen to me as you would to your father. Listen, and grow wise, for I speak the truth—don't turn away.

3    For I, too, was once a son, tenderly loved by my mother as an only child, and the companion of my father.

4    He told me never to forget his words. "If you follow them," he said, "you will have a long and happy life."

5    *"Learn to be wise,"* he said, *"and develop good judgment and common sense! I cannot overemphasize this point.*[6]*"*

6    Cling to wisdom—she will protect you. Love her—she will guard you.

7    Determination to be wise is the first step toward

---
[6]Literally, "Forget not nor turn from the words of my mouth."

becoming wise! And with your wisdom, develop common sense and good judgment.

8, 9   If you exalt wisdom, she will exalt you. Hold her fast and she will lead you to great honor; she will place a beautiful crown upon your head.

10   My son, listen to me and do as I say, and you will have a long, good life.

11   I would have you learn this great fact: that a life of doing right is the wisest life there is.

12   If you live that kind of life, you'll not limp or stumble as you run.

13   Carry out my instructions; don't forget them, for they will lead you to real living.

14   Don't do as the wicked do.

15   Avoid their haunts—turn away, go somewhere else,

16   For evil men don't sleep until they've done their evil deed for the day. They can't rest unless they cause someone to stumble and fall.

17   They eat and drink wickedness and violence!

18   But the good man walks along in the ever brightening light of God's favor; the dawn gives way to morning splendor,

19   While the evil man gropes and stumbles in the dark.

20   Listen, son of mine, to what I say. Listen carefully.

21   Keep these thoughts ever in mind; let them penetrate deep within your heart:

22 For they will mean real life for you, and radiant health.

23 *Above all else, guard your affections*. For they influence everything else in your life.

24 Spurn the careless kiss of a prostitute.[7] Stay far from her.

25 Look straight ahead; don't even turn your head to look.

26 Watch your step. Stick to the path and be safe.

27 Don't side-track; pull back your foot from danger.

## CHAPTER 5

Listen to me, my son! I know what I am saying; listen!

2 Watch yourself, lest you be indiscreet and betray some vital information.

3 For the lips of a prostitute are as sweet as honey, and smooth flattery is her stock in trade.

4 But afterwards only a bitter conscience[8] is left to you, sharp as a double-edged sword.

5 She leads you down to death and hell.

6 For she does not know the path to life. She staggers down a crooked trail, and doesn't even realize where it leads.

7 Young men, listen to me, and never forget what I'm about to say:

8 *Run from her! Don't go near her house,*

9 Lest you fall to her temptation and lose your

---

[7]Implied; literally, "Put away from you a wayward mouth."
[8]Literally, "But in the end she is bitter as wormwood."

honor, and give the remainder of your life to the cruel and merciless;[1]

10 Lest strangers obtain your wealth, and you become a slave of foreigners.

11 Lest afterwards you groan in anguish and in shame, when syphilis[2] consumes your body,

12 And you say, "Oh, if only I had listened! If only I had not demanded my own way!

13 Oh, why wouldn't I take advice? Why was I so stupid?

14 For now I must face public disgrace."

15 Drink from your own well, my son—be faithful and true to your wife.

16 Why should you beget children with women of the street?

17 Why share your children with those outside your home?

18 Let your manhood be a blessing; rejoice in the wife of your youth.

19 Let her charms[3] and tender embrace[4] satisfy you. Let her love alone fill you with delight.

20 Why delight yourself with prostitutes, embracing what isn't yours?

21 *For God is closely watching you,* and He weighs carefully everything you do.

22 The wicked man is doomed by his own sins; they are ropes that catch and hold him.

---

[1]Perhaps the reference is to blackmail, or to fear of vengeance from the wronged husband.
[2]Literally, "disease."
[3]Literally, "as a loving hind and a pleasant doe."
[4]Literally, "breasts."

23 He shall die because he will not listen to the truth; he has let himself be led away into incredible folly.

## CHAPTER 6

Son, if you endorse a note for someone you hardly know, guaranteeing his debt, you are in serious trouble.

2 You may have trapped yourself by your agreement.

3 Quick! Get out of it if you possibly can! Swallow your pride; don't let embarrassment stand in the way. Go and beg to have your name erased.

4 Don't put it off. Do it now. Don't rest until you do.

5 If you can get out of this trap you have saved yourself like a deer that escapes from a hunter, or a bird from the net.

\* \* \* \* \*

6 Take a lesson from the ants, you lazy fellow. Learn from their ways and be wise!

7 For though they have no king to make them work,

8 Yet they labor hard all summer, gathering food for the winter.

9 But you—all you do is sleep. When will you wake up?

10 "Let me sleep a little longer!" Sure, just a little more!

11  And as you sleep, poverty creeps upon you like a robber and destroys you; want attacks you in full armor.

*   *   *   *   *

12, 13  Let me describe for you a worthless and a wicked man; first, he is a constant liar; he signals his true intentions to his friends with eyes and feet and fingers.

14  Next, his heart is full of rebellion. And he spends his time thinking of all the evil he can do, and stirring up discontent.

15  But he will be destroyed suddenly, broken beyond hope of healing.

16-19  For there are six things the Lord hates—no, seven:

> Haughtiness
> Lying
> Murdering
> Plotting evil
> Eagerness to do wrong
> A false witness
> Sowing discord among brothers

20  Young man, obey your father and your mother.

21  Tie their instructions around your finger so you won't forget. Take to heart all of their advice.

22  Every day and all night long their counsel will lead you and save you from harm; when you wake up in the morning, let their instructions guide you into the new day.

23  For their advice is a beam of light directed into

the dark corners of your mind to warn you of danger and to give you a good life.

24   Their counsel will keep you far away from prostitutes with all their flatteries.

25   Don't lust for their beauty. Don't let their coyness seduce you.

26   For a prostitute will bring a man to poverty, and an adulteress may cost him his very life.

27   Can a man hold fire against his chest and not be burned?

28   Can he walk on hot coals and not blister his feet?

29   So it is with the man who commits adultery with another's wife. He shall not go unpunished for this sin.

30   Excuses might even be found for a thief, if he steals when he is starving!

31   But even so, he is fined seven times as much as he stole, though it may mean selling everything in his house to pay it back.

32   But the man who commits adultery is an utter fool, for he destroys his own soul.

33   Wounds and constant disgrace are his lot,

34   For the woman's husband will be furious in his jealousy, and he will have no mercy on you in his day of vengeance.

35   You won't be able to buy him off no matter what you offer.

# CHAPTER 7

Follow my advice, my son; always keep it in mind and stick to it.

2　Obey me and live! Guard my words as your most precious possession.

3　Write them down,[5] and also keep them deep within your heart.

4　Love wisdom like a sweetheart; make her a beloved member of your family;

5　Let her hold you back from visiting a prostitute, from listening to her flattery.

6　I was looking out the window of my house one day,

7　And saw a simple-minded lad, a young man lacking common sense,

8, 9　Walking at twilight down the street to the house of this wayward girl, a prostitute.

10　She approached him, saucy and pert, and dressed seductively.

11, 12　She was the brash, coarse type, seen often in the streets and markets, soliciting at every corner for men to be her lovers.

13　She put her arms around him and kissed him, and with a saucy look she said,

14　"I've decided to forget our quarrel![6]

---

[5]Literally, "Bind them upon your fingers."
[6]Literally, "Sacrifices of peace offerings were due from me; this day have I paid my vows." If she meant this literally, she was telling him that she had plenty of food on hand, left from her sacrifice at the Temple.

15　I was just coming to look for you and here you are!

16, 17　My bed is spread with lovely, colored sheets of finest linen imported from Egypt, perfumed with myrrh, aloes and cinnamon.

18　Come on, let's take our fill of love until morning,

19　For my husband is away on a long trip.

20　He has taken a wallet full of money with him, and won't return for several days."

21　So she seduced him with her pretty speech, her coaxing and her wheedling, until he yielded to her. He couldn't resist her flattery.

22　He followed her as an ox going to the butcher, or as a stag that is trapped,

23　Waiting to be killed with an arrow through its heart. He was as a bird flying into a snare, not knowing the fate awaiting it there.

24　Listen to me, young men, and not only listen but obey;

25　Don't let your desires get out of hand; don't let yourself think about her; don't go near her; stay away from where she walks, lest she tempt you and seduce you.

26　For she has been the ruin of multitudes—a vast host of men have been her victims.

27　If you want to find the road to hell, look for her house.

## CHAPTER 8

Can't you hear the voice of wisdom? She is standing at the city gates and at every fork in the road, and at the door of every house. Listen to what she says:

4, 5 "Listen, men!" she calls. "How foolish and naive you are! Let me give you understanding. O foolish ones, let me show you common sense!

6, 7 Listen to me! For I have important information for you. Everything I say is right and true, for I hate lies and every kind of deception.

8 My advice is wholesome and good. There is nothing of evil in it.

9 My words are plain and clear to anyone with half a mind—if it is only open!

10 My instruction is far more valuable than silver or gold."

11 For the value of wisdom is far above rubies; nothing can be compared with it.

12 Wisdom and good judgment live together, for wisdom knows where to discover knowledge and understanding.

13 If anyone respects and fears God, he will hate evil. For wisdom hates pride, arrogance, corruption and deceit of every kind.

14, 15 "I, Wisdom, give good advice and common sense. Because of my strength, kings reign in power. I show the judges who is right and who is wrong.

16 Rulers rule well with my help.

17 I love all who love me. Those who search for me shall surely find me.

18 Unending riches, honor, justice and righteousness are mine to distribute.

19 My gifts are better than the purest gold or sterling silver!

20 My paths are those of justice and right.

21 Those who love and follow me are indeed wealthy. I fill their treasuries.

22 The Lord formed me in the beginning, before He created anything else.

23 From ages past, I am. I existed before the earth began.

24 I lived before the oceans were created, before the springs bubbled forth their waters onto the earth;

25 Before the mountains and the hills were made.

26 Yes, I was born before God made the earth and fields, and high plateaus.

27, 28, 29 I was there when He established the heavens and formed the great springs in the depths of the oceans. I was there when He set the limits of the seas and gave them His instructions not to spread beyond their boundaries. I was there when He made the blueprint for the earth and oceans.

30 I was always at His side like a little child.[7] I was His constant delight, laughing and playing in His presence.

---

[7]Or, "like a master workman."

31 And how happy I was with what He created—His wide world and all His family of mankind!

32 And so, young men, listen to me, for how happy are all who follow my instructions.

33 Listen to my counsel—oh, don't refuse it—and be wise.

34. Happy is the man who is so anxious to be with me that he watches for me daily at my gates, or waits for me outside my home!

35 For whoever finds me finds Life and wins approval from the Lord.

36 But the one who misses me has injured himself irreparably. Those who refuse me show that they love death."

## CHAPTER 9

Wisdom has built a palace supported on seven pillars,

2 And has prepared a great banquet, and mixed the wines,

3 And sent out her maidens inviting all to come. She calls from the busiest intersections in the city,

4 "Come, you simple ones without good judgment;

5 Come to wisdom's banquet and drink the wines that I have mixed.

6 Leave behind your foolishness and begin to live; learn how to be wise."

\* \* \* \* \*

7, 8 If you rebuke a mocker, you will only get a

smart retort; yes, he will snarl at you. So don't bother
with him; he will only hate you for trying to help him.
But a wise man, when rebuked, will love you all the
more.

9     Teach a wise man, and he will be the wiser; teach
a good man, and he will learn more;

10     *For the reverence and fear of God are basic to
all wisdom. Knowing God results in every other kind of
understanding.*

11     I, Wisdom, will make the hours of your day
more profitable and the years of your life more fruitful.

12     Wisdom is its own reward, and if you scorn her,
you hurt only yourself.

\*          \*          \*          \*          \*

13     A prostitute is loud and brash, and never has
enough of lust and shame.

14     She sits at the door of her house or stands at the
street corners of the city,

15     Whispering to men going by, and to those minding their own business.

16     "Come home with me," she urges simpletons;

17     "Stolen melons[8] are the sweetest; stolen apples[9]
taste the best!"

18     But they don't realize that her former guests are
now citizens of hell.

## CHAPTER 10

*These are the proverbs of Solomon:*

Happy is the man with a level-headed son; sad the
mother of a rebel.

---

[8] Literally, "water."
[9] Literally, "food."

2 Ill-gotten gain brings no lasting happiness; right living does.

3 The Lord will not let a good man starve to death, nor will He let the wicked man's riches continue forever.

4 Lazy men are soon poor; hard workers get rich.

5 A wise youth makes hay while the sun shines, but what a shame to see a lad who sleeps away his hour of opportunity.

6 The good man is covered with blessings from head to foot, but an evil man inwardly curses his luck.[1]

7 We all have happy memories of good men gone to their reward, but the names of wicked men stink after them.

8 The wise man is glad to be instructed, but a self-sufficient fool falls flat on his face.

9 A good man has firm footing, but a crook will slip and fall.

10 Winking at sin leads to sorrow; bold reproof leads to peace.

11 There is living truth in what a good man says, but the mouth of the evil man is filled with curses.

12 Hatred stirs old quarrels, but love overlooks insults.

13 Men with common sense are admired[2] as counselors; those without it are beaten as servants.

14 A wise man holds his tongue. Only a fool blurts out everything he knows; that only leads to sorrow and trouble.

---

[1] Literally, "but the mouth of the wicked conceals violence."

15  The rich man's wealth is his only[2] strength. The poor man's poverty is his only[2] curse.

16  The good man's earnings advance the cause of righteousness. The evil man squanders his on sin.

17  Anyone willing to be corrected is on the pathway to life. Anyone refusing has lost his chance.

18  To hate is to be a liar; to slander is to be a fool.

19  Don't talk so much. You keep putting your foot in your mouth. Be sensible and turn off the flow!

20  When a good man speaks, he is worth listening to, but the words of fools are a dime a dozen.

21  A godly man gives good advice, but a rebel is destroyed by lack of common sense.

22  The Lord's blessing is our greatest wealth. All our work adds nothing to it![3]

23  A fool's fun is being bad; a wise man's fun is being wise!

24  The wicked man's fears will all come true, and so will the good man's hopes.

25  Disaster strikes like a cyclone and the wicked are whirled away. But the good man has a strong anchor.

26  A lazy fellow is a pain to his employers—like smoke in their eyes or vinegar that sets the teeth on edge.

27  Reverence for God adds hours to each day;[4] so how can the wicked expect a long, good life?

---

[2]Implied.
[3]Or, "and he adds no sorrow therewith."
[4]Literally, "prolongs days."

28 The hope of good men is eternal happiness; the hopes of evil men are all in vain.

29 God protects the upright but destroys the wicked.

30 The good shall never lose God's blessings, but the wicked shall lose everything.

31 The good man gives wise advice, but the liar's counsel is shunned.

32 The upright speak what is helpful; the wicked speak rebellion.

## CHAPTER 11

The Lord hates cheating and delights in honesty.

2 Proud men end in shame, but the meek become wise.

3 A good man is guided by his honesty; the evil man is destroyed by his dishonesty.

4 Your riches won't help you on Judgment Day; only righteousness counts then.

5 The upright are directed by their honesty; the wicked shall fall beneath their load of sins.

6 The good man's goodness delivers him; the evil man's treachery is his undoing.

7 When an evil man dies, his hopes all perish, for they are based upon this earthly life.

8 God rescues good men from danger while letting the wicked fall into it.

9 Evil words destroy. Godly skill rebuilds.[5]

---

[5]Or, "When a godless man slanders his neighbor, the charges won't stick because everyone knows his reputation."

10    The whole city celebrates a good man's success
—and also the godless man's death.

11    The good influence of godly citizens causes a
city to prosper, but the moral decay of the wicked
drives it downhill.

12    To quarrel with a neighbor is foolish; a man
with good sense holds his tongue.

13    A gossip goes around spreading rumors, while a
trustworthy man tries to quiet them.

14    Without wise leadership, a nation is in trouble;
but with good counselors there is safety.

15    Be sure you know a person well before you
vouch for his credit! Better refuse than suffer later.

16    Honor goes to kind and gracious women, mere[6]
money to cruel men.

17    Your own soul is nourished when you are kind;
it is destroyed when you are cruel.

18    The evil man gets rich for the moment, but
the good man's reward lasts forever.

19    The good man finds Life; the evil man, Death.

20    The Lord hates the stubborn but delights in
those who are good.

21    You can be very sure that the evil man will not
go unpunished forever. And you can also be very sure
that God will rescue the children of the godly.

22    A beautiful woman lacking discretion and
modesty is like a fine gold ring in a pig's snout.

23    The good man can look forward to happiness,
while the wicked can expect only wrath.

---

[6]Implied.

24, 25  It is possible to give away and become richer! It is also possible to hold on too tightly and lose everything. Yes, the liberal man shall be rich! By watering others, he waters himself.

26  People curse the man who holds his grain for higher prices, but they bless the man who sells it to them in their time of need.

27  If you search for good you will find God's favor; if you search for evil you will find His curse.

28  Trust in your money and down you go! Trust in God and flourish as a tree!

29  The fool who provokes his family to anger and resentment will finally have nothing worthwhile left. He shall be the servant of a wiser man.

30  Godly men are growing a tree that bears life-giving fruit, and all who win souls are wise.[7]

31  Even the godly shall be rewarded here on earth; how much more the wicked!

## CHAPTER 12

To learn, you must want to be taught. To refuse reproof is stupid.

2  The Lord blesses good men and condemns the wicked.

3  Wickedness never brings real success; only the godly have that.

4  A worthy wife is her husband's joy and crown;

[7]Or, "He that is wise wins souls."

the other kind corrodes his strength and tears down everything he does.

5    A good man's mind is filled with honest thoughts; an evil man's mind is crammed with lies.

6    The wicked accuse; the godly defend.

7    The wicked shall perish; the godly shall stand.

8    Everyone admires a man with good sense, but a man with a warped mind is despised.

9    It is better to get your hands dirty—and eat,[8] than to be too proud to work—and starve.

10    A good man is concerned for the welfare of his animals, but even the kindness of godless men is cruel.

11    Hard work means prosperity;[9] only a fool idles away his time.

12    Crooks are jealous of each other's loot, while good men long to help each other.

13    Lies will get any man into trouble, but honesty is its own defense.

14    Telling the truth gives a man great satisfaction, and hard work returns many blessings to him.

15    A fool thinks he needs no advice, but a wise man listens to others.

16    A fool is quick-tempered; a wise man stays cool when insulted.

17    A good man is known by his truthfulness; a false man by deceit and lies.

18    Some people like to make cutting remarks, but the words of the wise soothe and heal.

---

[8]Implied.
[9]Literally, "he who tills his ground shall have his fill of bread."

19 Truth stands the test of time; lies are soon exposed.

20 Deceit fills hearts that are plotting for evil; joy fills hearts that are planning for good!

21 No real[1] harm befalls the good, but there is constant trouble for the wicked.

22 God loves those who keep their promises, and hates those who don't.

23 A wise man doesn't display his knowledge, but a fool displays his foolishness.

24 Work hard and become a leader; be lazy and never succeed.

25 Anxious hearts are very heavy but a word of encouragement does wonders!

26 The good man asks advice from friends; the wicked plunge ahead—and fall.

27 A lazy man won't even dress the game he gets while hunting, but the diligent man makes good use of everything he finds.

28 The path of the godly leads to Life. So why fear Death?

## CHAPTER 13

A wise youth accepts his father's rebuke; a young mocker doesn't.

2 The good man wins his case by careful argument; the evil-minded only wants to fight.

---

[1]Implied.

3  Self-control means controlling the tongue! A quick retort can ruin everything.

4  Lazy people want much but get little, while the diligent are prospering.

5  A good man hates lies; wicked men lie[2] constantly and come to shame.

6  A man's goodness helps him all through life, while evil men are being destroyed by their wickedness.

7  Some rich people are poor, and some poor people have great wealth!

8  Being kidnapped and held for ransom never worries the poor man!

9  The good man's life is full of light. The sinner's road is dark and gloomy.

10  Pride leads to arguments; be humble, take advice and become wise.

11  Wealth from gambling quickly disappears; wealth from hard work grows.

12  Hope deferred makes the heart sick; but when dreams come true at last, there is life and joy.[3]

13  Despise God's word and find yourself in trouble. Obey it and succeed.

14  The advice of a wise man refreshes like water from a mountain spring. Those accepting it become aware of the pitfalls on ahead.

15  A man with good sense is appreciated. A treacherous man must walk a rocky road.

16  A wise man thinks ahead; a fool doesn't, and even brags about it!

---

[2]Implied.
[3]Literally, "it is a tree of life."

17   An unreliable messenger can cause a lot of trouble. Reliable communication permits progress.

18   If you refuse criticism you will end in poverty and disgrace; if you accept criticism you are on the road to fame.

19   It is pleasant to see plans develop. That is why fools refuse to give them up even when they are wrong.

20   Be with wise men and become wise. Be with evil men and become evil.

21   Curses chase sinners, while blessings chase the righteous!

22   When a good man dies, he leaves an inheritance to his grandchildren; but when a sinner dies, his wealth is stored up for the godly.

23   A poor man's farm may have good soil, but injustice robs him of its riches.

24   If you refuse to discipline your son, it proves you don't love him; for if you love him you will be prompt to punish him.

25   The good man eats to live, while the evil man lives to eat.[4]

## CHAPTER 14

A wise woman builds her house, while a foolish woman tears hers down by her own efforts.

2   To do right honors God; to sin is to despise Him.

3   A rebel's foolish talk should prick his own pride! But the wise man's speech is respected.

---

[4]Literally, "but the wicked never get enough."

4  An empty stable stays clean—but there is no income from an empty stable.

5  A truthful witness never lies; a false witness always lies.

6  A mocker never finds the wisdom he claims he is looking for, yet it comes easily to the man with common sense.

7  If you are looking for advice, stay away from fools.

8  The wise man looks ahead. The fool attempts to fool himself and won't face facts.

9  The common bond of rebels is their guilt.* The common bond of godly people is good will.

10  Only the person involved can know his own bitterness or joy—no one else can really share it.

11  The work of the wicked will perish; the work of the godly will flourish.

12  Before every man there lies a wide and pleasant road that seems right but ends in death.

13  Laughter cannot mask a heavy heart. When the laughter ends, the grief remains.

14  The backslider gets bored with himself; the godly man's life is exciting.

15  Only a simpleton believes what he is told! A prudent man checks to see where he is going.

16  A wise man is cautious and avoids danger; a fool plunges ahead with great confidence.

17  A short-tempered man is a fool. He hates the man who is patient.

---

*Or, "Fools make a mock at sin." The Hebrew is obscure.

18   The simpleton is crowned with folly; the wise man is crowned with knowledge.

19   Evil men shall bow before the godly.

20   Even his own neighbors despise the poor man, while the rich have many "friends."

21   To despise the poor is to sin. Blessed are those who pity them.

22   Those who plot evil shall wander away and be lost, but those who plan good shall be granted mercy and quietness.

23   Work brings profit; talk brings poverty!

24   Wise men are praised for their wisdom; fools are despised for their folly.

25   A witness who tells the truth saves good men from being sentenced to death, but a false witness is a traitor.

26   Reverence for God gives a man deep strength; his children have a place of refuge and security.

27   Reverence for the Lord is a fountain of life; its waters keep a man from death.

28   A growing population is a king's glory; a dwindling nation is his doom.

29   A wise man controls his temper. He knows that anger causes mistakes.

30   A relaxed attitude lengthens a man's life; jealousy rots it away.

31   Anyone who oppresses the poor is insulting God who made them. To help the poor is to honor God.

32   The godly have a refuge when they die, but the wicked are crushed by their sins.

33   Wisdom is enshrined in the hearts of men of common sense, but it must shout loudly before fools will hear it.

34   Godliness exalts a nation, but sin is a reproach to any people.

35   A king rejoices in servants who know what they are doing; he is angry with those who cause trouble.


## CHAPTER 15

A soft answer turns away wrath, but harsh words cause quarrels.

2   A wise teacher makes learning a joy; a rebellious teacher spouts foolishness.

3   The Lord is watching everywhere and keeps His eye on both the evil and the good.

4   Gentle words cause life and health; griping brings discouragement.

5   Only a fool despises his father's advice; a wise son considers each suggestion.

6   There is treasure in being good, but trouble dogs the wicked.

7   Only the good can give good advice. Rebels can't.

8   The Lord hates the gifts of the wicked, but delights in the prayers of His people.

9, 10   The Lord despises the deeds of the wicked, but loves those who try to be good. If they stop trying, the Lord will punish them; if they rebel against that punishment, they will die.

11   The depths of hell are open to God's knowledge. How much more the hearts of all mankind!

12   A mocker stays away from wise men because he hates to be scolded.

13   A happy face means a glad heart; a sad face means a breaking heart.

14   A wise man is hungry for truth, while the mocker feeds on trash.

15   When a man is gloomy, everything seems to go wrong; when he is cheerful, everything seems right!

16   Better a little with reverence for God, than great treasure and trouble with it.

17   It is better to eat soup with someone you love than steak with someone you hate.

18   A quick-tempered man starts fights; a cool-tempered man tries to stop them.

19   A lazy fellow has trouble all through life; the good man's path is easy!

20   A sensible son gladdens his father. A rebellious son saddens his mother.[5]

21   If a man enjoys folly, something is wrong! The sensible stay on the pathways of right.

22   Plans go wrong with too few counselors; many counselors bring success.

23   Everyone enjoys giving good advice, and how

---

[5]Literally, "despises his mother."

wonderful it is to be able to say the right thing at the right time!

24 The road of the godly leads upward, leaving hell behind.

25 The Lord destroys the possessions of the proud but cares for widows.

26 The Lord hates the thoughts of the wicked but delights[6] in kind words.

27 Dishonest money brings grief to all the family, but hating bribes brings happiness.[7]

28 A good man thinks before he speaks; the evil man pours out his evil words without a thought.

29 The Lord is far from the wicked, but He hears the prayers of the righteous.

30 Pleasant sights and good reports give happiness and health.

31, 32 If you profit from constructive criticism you will be elected to the wise men's hall of fame. But to reject criticism is to harm yourself and your own best interests.

33 Humility and reverence for the Lord will make you both wise and honored.

## CHAPTER 16

We can make our plans, but the final outcome is in God's hands.

---

[6]Literally, "but kind words are pure."
[7]Literally, "you will live."

2  We can always "prove" that we are right, but is the Lord convinced?

3  Commit your work to the Lord, then it will succeed.

4  The Lord has made everything for His own purposes—even the wicked, for punishment.

5  Pride disgusts the Lord. Take my word for it— *proud men shall be punished.*

6  Iniquity is atoned for by mercy and truth; being good comes from reverence for God.

7  When a man is trying to please God, He makes even his worst enemies to be at peace with him.

8  A little, gained honestly, is better than great wealth gotten by dishonest means.

9  We should make plans—counting on God to direct us.

10  God will help the king to judge the people fairly; there need be no mistakes.

11  The Lord demands fairness in every business deal.[8] He established this principle.

12  It is a horrible thing for a king to do evil. His right to rule depends upon his fairness.[9]

13  The king rejoices when his people are truthful and fair.

14  The anger of the king is a messenger of death and a wise man will appease it.

15  Many favors are showered on those who please the king.

---

[8]Literally, "a just balance and scales are the Lord's; all the weights in the bag are His work."
[9]Literally, "for the throne is established by righteousness."

16 How much better is wisdom than gold, and understanding than silver!

17 The path of the godly leads away from evil; he who follows that path is safe.

18 Pride goes before destruction and haughtiness before a fall.

19 Better poor and humble than proud and rich.

20 God blesses those who obey Him; happy the man who trusts in the Lord.

21 The wise man is known by his common sense, and a pleasant teacher is the best.

22 Wisdom is a fountain of life to those possessing it, but a fool's burden is his folly.

23 From a wise mind comes careful and persuasive speech.

24 Kind words are like honey—enjoyable and healthful.

25 Before every man there lies a wide and pleasant road he thinks is right, but it ends in death.

26 Hunger is good—if it makes you work to satisfy it!

27 Idle hands are the devil's workshop; idle lips are his mouthpiece.[1]

28 An evil man sows strife; gossip separates the best of friends.

29 Wickedness loves company—and leads others into sin.[2]

---

[1]Literally, "a worthless man devises mischief; and in his lips there is a scorching fire."

[2]Or, "an evil man deceives his neighbor and leads him into loss."

30 The wicked man stares into space with pursed lips, deep in thought, planning his evil deeds.

31 White hair is a crown of glory and is seen most among the godly.

32 It is better to be slow-tempered than famous; it is better to have self-control than to control an army.

33 We toss the coin,⁴ but it is the Lord who controls its decision.

## CHAPTER 17

A dry crust eaten in peace is better then steak every day along with argument and strife.

2 A wise slave will rule his master's wicked sons and share their estate.

3 Silver and gold are purified by fire, but God purifies hearts.

4 The wicked enjoy fellowship with others who are wicked; liars enjoy liars.

5 Mocking the poor is mocking the God who made them. He will punish those who rejoice at others' misfortunes.

6 An old man's grandchildren are his crowning glory. A child's glory is his father.

7 Truth from a rebel or lies from a king are both unexpected.

8 A bribe works like magic. Whoever uses it will prosper!*

⁴Literally, "cast dice into the lap."
*This is a fact, but not to be encouraged!

9   Love forgets mistakes; nagging about them parts the best of friends.

10   A rebuke to a man of common sense is more effective than a hundred lashes on the back of a rebel.

11   The wicked live for rebellion; they shall be severely punished.[5]

12   It is safer to meet a bear robbed of her cubs than a fool caught in his folly.

13   If you repay evil for good, a curse is upon your home.

14   It is hard to stop a quarrel once it starts,[6] so don't let it begin.

15   The Lord despises those who say that bad is good, and good is bad.

16   It is senseless to pay tuition to educate a rebel who has no heart for truth.[7]

17   A true friend is always loyal, and a brother is born to help in time of need.

18   It is poor judgment to countersign another's note, to become responsible for his debts.

19   Sinners love to fight; boasting is looking for trouble.

20   An evil man is suspicious of everyone* and tumbles into constant trouble.

21   It's no fun to be a rebel's father.

22   A cheerful heart does good like medicine, but a broken spirit makes one sick.

[5]Literally, "a stern (ruthless) messenger will be sent against him."
[6]Literally, "as when one lets out water."
[7]Literally, "no heart."
*Or, "does not prosper."

23 It is wrong to accept a bribe to twist justice.

24 Wisdom is the main pursuit of sensible men, but a fool's goals are at the ends of the earth!

25 A rebellious son is a grief to his father and a bitter blow to his mother.

26 How short-sighted to fine the godly for being good! And to punish nobles for being honest!

27, 28 The man of few words and settled mind is wise; therefore, even a fool is thought to be wise when he is silent. It pays him to keep his mouth shut.

## CHAPTER 18

The selfish man quarrels against every sound principle of conduct by demanding his own way.

2 A rebel doesn't care about the facts. All he wants to do is yell.*

3 Sin brings disgrace.

4 A wise man's words express deep streams of thought.

5 It is wrong for a judge to favor the wicked and condemn the innocent.

6, 7 A fool gets into constant fights. His mouth is his undoing! His words endanger him.

8 What dainty morsels rumors are. They are eaten with great relish!

9 A lazy man is brother to the saboteur.

*Literally, "express his opinion."

10   The Lord[8] is a strong fortress. The godly run to Him and are safe.

11   The rich man thinks of his wealth as an impregnable defense, a high wall of safety. What a dreamer!

12   Pride ends in destruction; humility ends in honor.

13   What a shame—yes, how stupid!—to decide before knowing the facts!

14   A man's courage[9] can sustain his broken body, but when courage dies, what hope is left?

15   The intelligent man is always open to new ideas. In fact, he looks for them.

16   A bribe does wonders: it will bring you before men of importance!

17   Any story sounds true until someone tells the other side and sets the record straight.

18   A coin toss[1] ends arguments and settles disputes between powerful opponents.

19   It is harder to win back the friendship of an offended brother than to capture a fortified city.[2] His anger shuts you out like iron bars.

20   Ability to give wise advice satisfies like a good meal!

21   Those who love to talk will suffer the consequences. Men have died for saying the wrong thing!

22   The man who finds a wife finds a good thing; she is a blessing to him from the Lord.

[8]Literally, "The name of the Lord."
[9]Literally, "spirit."
[1]Literally, "the lot."
[2]The Hebrew of this verse is not clear.

23 The poor man pleads and the rich man answers with insults.

24 Some people are friends in name only. Others are closer than brothers.

## CHAPTER 19

Better be poor and honest than rich[3] and dishonest. 2 It is dangerous and sinful to rush into the unknown.

3 A man may ruin his chances by his own foolishness and then blame it on the Lord!

4 A wealthy man has many "friends"; the poor man has none left.

5 Punish false witnesses. Track down liars.

6 Many beg favors from a man who is generous; everyone is his friend!

7 A poor man's own brothers turn away from him in embarrassment;[4] how much more his friends! He calls after them, but they are gone.

8 He who loves wisdom loves his own best interest and will be a success.

9 A false witness shall be punished and a liar shall be caught.

10 It doesn't seem right for a fool to succeed or for a slave to rule over princes!

11 A wise man restrains his anger and overlooks insults. This is to his credit.

[3]Literally, "a fool."
[4]Literally, "despise him."

12 The king's anger is as dangerous as a lion's. But his approval is as refreshing as the dew on grass.

13 A rebellious son is a calamity to his father, and a nagging wife annoys like constant dripping.

14 A father can give his sons homes and riches, but only the Lord can give them understanding wives.

15 A lazy man sleeps soundly—and goes hungry!

16 Keep the commandments and keep your life; despising them means death.

17 When you help the poor you are lending to the Lord—and He pays wonderful interest on your loan!

18 Discipline your son in his early years while there is hope. If you don't you will ruin his life.

19 A short-tempered man must bear his own penalty; you can't do much to help him. If you try once you must try a dozen times!

20 Get all the advice you can and be wise the rest of your life.

21 Man proposes, but God disposes.

22 Kindness makes a man attractive. And it is better to be poor than dishonest.

23 Reverence for God gives life, happiness, and protection from harm.

24 Some men are so lazy they won't even feed themselves!

25 Punish a mocker and others will learn from his example. Reprove a wise man and he will be the wiser.

26 A son who mistreats his father or mother is a public disgrace.

27 Stop listening to teaching that contradicts what you know is right.

28 A worthless witness cares nothing for truth—he enjoys his sinning too much.

29 Mockers and rebels shall be severely punished.

## CHAPTER 20

Wine gives false courage; hard liquor leads to brawls; what fools men are to let it master them, making them reel drunkenly down the street!

2 The king's fury is like that of a roaring lion; to rouse his anger is to risk your life.

3 It is an honor for a man to stay out of a fight. Only fools insist on quarreling.

4 If you won't plow in the cold you won't eat at the harvest.

5 Though good advice lies deep within a counselor's heart, the wise man will draw it out.

6 Most people will tell you what loyal friends they are, but are they telling the truth?

7 It is a wonderful heritage to have an honest father.

8 A king sitting as judge weighs all the evidence carefully, distinguishing the true from false.

9 Who can ever say, "I have cleansed my heart; I am sinless."

10 The Lord despises every kind of cheating.[5]

---

[5]Literally, "diverse weights and diverse measures."

11 The character of even a child can be known by the way he acts—whether what he does is pure and right.

12 If you have good eyesight and good hearing, thank[6] God who gave them to you.

13 If you love sleep, you will end in poverty. Stay awake, work hard, and there will be plenty to eat!

14 "Utterly worthless!" says the buyer as he haggles over the price. But afterwards he brags about his bargain!

15 Good sense is far more valuable than gold or precious jewels.

16 It is risky to make loans to strangers!

17 Some men enjoy cheating, but the cake they buy with such ill-gotten gain will turn to gravel in their mouths.

18 Don't go ahead with your plans without the advice of others; don't go to war until they agree.

19 Don't tell[7] your secrets to a gossip unless you want them broadcast to the world.

20 God puts out the light of the man who curses his father or mother.

21 A fortune can be made from cheating,[8] but there is a curse that goes with it.

22 Don't repay evil for evil. Wait for the Lord to handle the matter.

23 The Lord loathes all cheating and dishonesty.[9]

---

[6]Implied.
[7]Literally, "company not with him."
[8]Literally, "quickly gathered."
[9]Literally, "diverse weights . . . false scales."

24 Since the Lord is directing our steps, why try to understand everything that happens along the way?

25 It is foolish and rash to make a promise to the Lord before counting the cost.

26 A wise king stamps out crime by severe punishment.

27 A man's conscience[1] is the Lord's searchlight exposing his hidden motives.

28 If a king is kind, honest and fair, his kingdom stands secure.

29 The glory of young men is their strength; of old men, their experience.[2]

30 Punishment that hurts chases evil from the heart.

## CHAPTER 21

Just as water is turned into irrigation ditches, so the Lord directs the king's thoughts. He turns them wherever He wants to.

2 We can justify our every deed but God looks at our motives.

3 God is more pleased when we are just and fair than when we give Him gifts.

4 Pride, lust, and evil actions[3] are all sin.

5 Steady plodding brings prosperity; hasty speculation brings poverty.

---

[1]Literally, "spirit."
[2]Literally, "the hoary head."
[3]Literally, "the tillage of the wicked."

6   Dishonest gain will never last, so why take the risk?

7   Because the wicked are unfair, their violence boomerangs and destroys them.

8   A man is known by his actions;* an evil man lives an evil life; a good man lives a godly life.

9   It is better to live in the corner of an attic than with a crabby woman in a lovely home.

10   An evil man loves to harm others; being a good neighbor is out of his line.

11   The wise man learns by listening; the simpleton can learn only by seeing scorners punished.

12   The godly learn by watching ruin overtake the wicked.

13   He who shuts his ears to the cries of the poor will be ignored in his own time of need.

14   An angry man is silenced by giving him a gift!

15   A good man loves justice, but it is a calamity to evil-doers.

16   The man who strays away from common sense will end up dead!

17   A man who loves pleasure becomes poor; wine and luxury are not the way to riches!

18   The wicked will finally lose; the righteous will finally win.[4]

19   Better to live in the desert than with a quarrelsome, complaining woman.

*Implied.
[4]Literally, "the wicked is a ransom for the righteous."

20   The wise man saves for the future,[5] but the foolish man spends whatever he gets.

21   The man who tries to be good, loving and kind finds life, righteousness and honor.

22   The wise man conquers the strong man and levels his defenses.

23   Keep your mouth closed and you'll stay out of trouble.

24   Mockers are proud, haughty and arrogant.

25, 26   The lazy man longs for many things but his hands refuse to work. He is greedy to get, while the godly love to give!

27   God loathes the gifts of evil men, especially if they are trying to bribe Him!

28   A false witness must be punished; an honest witness is safe.

29   An evil man is stubborn, but a godly man will reconsider.[6]

30   No one, regardless of how shrewd or well-advised he is, can stand against the Lord.

31   Go ahead and prepare for the conflict,[7] but victory comes from God.


## CHAPTER 22


If you must choose, take a good name rather than great riches; for to be held in loving esteem is better than silver and gold.

---

[5] Literally, "there is precious treasure and oil in the dwelling of the wise."
[6] Or, "the wicked man is brazen; the godly man is thoughtful."
[7] Literally, "the horse is prepared against the day of battle."

2   The rich and the poor are alike before the Lord who made them all.

3   A prudent man foresees the difficulties ahead and prepares for them; the simpleton goes blindly on and suffers the consequences.

4   True humility and respect for the Lord lead a man to riches, honor and long life.

5   The rebel walks a thorny, treacherous road; the man who values his soul will stay away.

6   Teach a child to choose the right path, and when he is older he will remain upon it.

7   Just as the rich rule the poor, so the borrower is servant to the lender.

8   The unjust tyrant will reap disaster and his reign of terror shall end.

9   Happy is the generous man, the one who feeds the poor.

10   Throw out the mocker, and you will be rid of tension, fighting and quarrels.

11   He who values grace and truth is the king's friend.

12   The Lord preserves the upright but ruins the plans[6] of the wicked.

13   The lazy man is full of excuses. "I can't go to work!" he says. "If I go outside I might meet a lion in the street and be killed!"

14   A prostitute is a dangerous trap; those cursed of God are caught in it.

----

[6]Literally, "the words."

**15** A youngster's heart is filled with rebellion, but punishment will drive it out of him.

**16** He who gains by oppressing the poor or by bribing the rich shall end in poverty.

\* \* \* \* \*

**17, 18, 19** Listen to this wise advice; follow it closely, for it will do you good, and you can pass it on to others: *Trust in the Lord.*

**20, 21** In the past, haven't I been right? Then believe what I am telling you now, and share it with others.

\* \* \* \* \*

**22, 23** Don't rob the poor and sick! For the Lord is their defender. If you injure them He will punish you.

**24, 25** Keep away from angry, short-tempered men, lest you learn to be like them and endanger your soul.

**26, 27** Unless you have the extra cash on hand, don't countersign a note. Why risk everything you own? They'll even take your bed!

**28** Do not move the ancient boundary marks. That is stealing.[9]

**29** Do you know a hard working man? He shall be successful and stand before kings!

## CHAPTER 23

When dining with a rich man,[1] be on your guard and don't stuff yourself, though it all tastes so

---

[9]Implied.
[1]Literally, "a ruler."

good; for he is trying to bribe you, and no good is going to come of his invitation.

4, 5 Don't weary yourself trying to get rich. Why waste your time? For riches can disappear as though they had the wings of a bird!

6, 7, 8 Don't become obligated[2] to evil men; don't long for their favors and gifts. Their kindness is a trick; they want to use you as their pawn. The delicious food they serve will turn sour in your stomach and you will vomit it, and have to take back your words of appreciation for their "kindness."

9 Don't waste your breath on a rebel. He will despise the wisest advice.

10, 11 Don't steal the land of defenseless orphans by moving their ancient boundary marks, for their Redeemer is strong; He Himself will accuse you.

12 Don't refuse to accept criticism; get all the help[3] you can.

13, 14 Don't fail to correct your children; discipline won't hurt them! They won't die if you use a stick on them! Punishment will keep them out of hell.

15, 16 My son, how I will rejoice if you become a man of common sense. Yes, my heart will thrill to your thoughtful, wise words.

17, 18 Don't envy evil men but continue to reverence the Lord all the time, for surely you have a wonderful future ahead of you. There is hope for you yet!

19, 20, 21 O my son, be wise and stay in God's paths; don't carouse with drunkards and gluttons, for

---

[2]More literally, "don't eat his bread."
[3]Literally, "knowledge."

they are on their way to poverty. And remember that too much sleep clothes a man with rags.

22    Listen to your father's advice and don't despise an old mother's experience.

23    Get the facts at any price, and hold on tightly to all the good sense you can get.

24, 25    The father of a godly man has cause for joy—what pleasure a wise son is! So give your parents joy!

26, 27, 28    O my son, trust my advice—stay away from prostitutes. For a prostitute is a deep and narrow grave. Like a robber, she waits for her victims as one after another become unfaithful to their wives.

29, 30    Whose heart is filled with anguish and sorrow? Who is always fighting and quarreling? Who is the man with bloodshot eyes and many wounds? It is the one who spends long hours in the taverns, trying out new mixtures.

31    Don't let the sparkle and the smooth taste of strong wine deceive you.

32    For in the end it bites like a poisonous serpent; it stings like an adder.

33    You will see hallucinations and have delirium tremens, and you will say foolish, silly things that would embarrass you no end when sober.

34    You will stagger like a sailor tossed at sea, clinging to a swaying mast.

35    And afterwards you will say, "I didn't even know it when they beat me up . . . Let's go and have another drink!"

# CHAPTER 24

Don't envy godless men; don't even enjoy their company.

2   For they spend their days plotting violence and cheating.

3, 4   Any enterprise is built by wise planning, becomes strong through common sense, and profits wonderfully by keeping abreast of the facts.

5   A wise man is mightier than a strong man. Wisdom is mightier than strength.

6   Don't go to war without wise guidance; there is safety in many counselors.

7   Wisdom is too much for a rebel. He'll not be chosen as a counselor!

8   To plan evil is as wrong as doing it.

9   The rebel's schemes are sinful, and the mocker is the scourge of all mankind.

10   You are a poor specimen if you can't stand the pressure of adversity.

11, 12   Rescue those who are unjustly sentenced to death; don't stand back and let them die. Don't try to disclaim responsibility by saying you didn't know about it. For God, who knows all hearts, knows yours, and He knows you knew! And He will reward everyone according to his deeds.

13, 14   My son, honey whets the appetite, and so

does wisdom! When you enjoy becoming wise, there is hope for you! A bright future lies ahead!

15, 16   O evil man, leave the upright man alone, and quit trying to cheat him out of his rights. Don't you know that this good man, though you trip him up seven times, will each time rise again? But one calamity is enough to lay you low.

17   Do not rejoice when your enemy meets trouble. Let there be no gladness when he falls—

18   For the Lord may be displeased with you and stop punishing him!

19, 20   Don't envy the wicked. Don't covet his riches. For the evil man has no future; his light will be snuffed out.

21, 22   My son, watch your step before the Lord and the king, and don't associate with radicals. For you will go down with them to sudden disaster, and who knows where it all will end?

\* \* \* \* \*

*Here are some additional proverbs:*

23   It is wrong to sentence the poor, and let the rich go free.

24   He who says to the wicked, "You are innocent," shall be cursed by many people of many nations;

25   But blessings shall be showered on those who rebuke sin fearlessly.

26   It is an honor to receive a frank reply.

27   Develop your business first before building your house.

28, 29   Don't testify spitefully against an innocent

neighbor. Why lie about him? Don't say, "Now I can pay him back for all his meanness to me!"

30, 31  I walked by the field of a certain lazy fellow and saw that it was overgrown with thorns, and covered with weeds; and its walls were broken down.

32   Then, as I looked, I learned this lesson:

33   "A little extra sleep,
       A little more slumber,
       A little folding of the hands to rest"

34   Means that poverty will break in upon you suddenly like a robber, and violently like a bandit.

## CHAPTER 25

These proverbs of Solomon[4] were discovered and copied by the aides of King Hezekiah[5] of Judah:

2, 3   It is God's privilege to conceal things, and the king's privilege to discover and invent. You cannot understand the height of heaven, the size of the earth, or all that goes on in the king's mind!

4, 5   When you remove dross from silver, you have sterling ready for the silversmith. When you remove corrupt men from the king's court, his reign will be just and fair.

6, 7   Don't demand an audience with the king as though you were some powerful prince. It is better to wait for an invitation rather than to be sent back to the end of the line, publicly disgraced!

[4] I Kings 4:32.
[5] Hezekiah lived 200 years after Solomon.

8, 9, 10   Don't be hot-headed and rush to court! You may start something you can't finish and go down before your neighbor in shameful defeat. So discuss the matter with him privately. Don't tell anyone else, lest he accuse you of slander and you can't withdraw what you said.

11   Timely advice is as lovely as golden apples in a silver basket.

12   It is a badge of honor to accept valid criticism.

13   A faithful employee is as refreshing as a cool day[6] in the hot summertime.

14   One who doesn't give the gift he promised is like a cloud blowing over a desert without dropping any rain.

15   Be patient and you will finally win, for a soft tongue can break hard bones.

16   Do you like honey? Don't eat too much of it, or it will make you sick!

17   Don't visit your neighbor too often, or you will outwear your welcome!

18   Telling lies about someone is as harmful as hitting him with an axe, or wounding him with a sword, or shooting him with a sharp arrow.

19   Putting confidence in an unreliable man is like chewing with a sore tooth, or trying to run on a broken foot.

20   Being happy-go-lucky around a person whose heart is heavy is as bad as stealing his jacket in cold weather, or rubbing salt in his wounds.[7]

---

[6]Literally, "snow."
[7]Literally, "like vinegar upon soda."

21, 22   If your enemy is hungry, give him food! If he is thirsty, give him something to drink! This will make him feel ashamed of himself, and God will reward you.

23   As surely as a wind from the north brings cold,[1] just as surely a retort causes anger!

24   It is better to live in a corner of an attic than in a beautiful home with a cranky, quarrelsome woman.

25   Good news from far away is like cold water to the thirsty.

26   If a godly man compromises with the wicked, it is like polluting a fountain or muddying a spring.

27   Just as it is harmful to eat too much honey, so also it is bad for men to think about all the honors they deserve!

28   A man without self-control is as defenseless as a city with broken-down walls.


## CHAPTER 26

Honor doesn't go with fools any more than snow with summertime or rain with harvest time!

2   An undeserved curse has no effect. Its intended victim will be no more harmed by it than by a sparrow or swallow flitting through the sky.

3   Guide a horse with a whip, a donkey with a bridle, and a rebel with a rod to his back!

4, 5   When arguing with a rebel, don't use foolish

---

[1]Literally, "rain."

arguments as he does, or you will become as foolish as he is! Prick[2] his conceit with silly replies!

6 To trust a rebel to convey a message is as foolish as cutting off your feet and drinking poison!

7 In the mouth of a fool a proverb becomes as useless as a paralyzed leg.

8 Honoring a rebel will backfire like a stone tied to a slingshot!

9 A rebel will misapply an illustration so that its point will no more be felt than a thorn in the hand of a drunkard.

10 The master may get better work from an untrained apprentice than from a skilled rebel!

11 As a dog returns to his vomit, so a fool repeats his folly.

12 There is one thing worse than a fool, and that is a man who is conceited.

13 The lazy man won't go out and work. "There might be a lion outside!" he says.

14 He sticks to his bed like a door to its hinges!

15 He is too tired even to lift his food from his dish to his mouth!

16 Yet in his own opinion he is smarter than seven wise men.

17 Yanking a dog's ears is no more foolish than interfering in an argument that isn't any of your business.

18, 19 A man who is caught lying to his neighbor

_____
[2]Implied. Literally, "Reply to a fool as his folly requires."

and says, "I was just fooling," is like a madman throwing around firebrands, arrows and death!

20 Fire goes out for lack of fuel, and tensions disappear when gossip stops.

21 A quarrelsome man starts fights as easily as a match³ sets fire to paper.

22 Gossip is a dainty morsel eaten with great relish.

23 Pretty words may hide a wicked heart, just as a pretty glaze covers a common clay pot.

24, 25, 26 A man with hate in his heart may sound pleasant enough, but don't believe him; for he is cursing you in his heart. Though he pretends to be so kind, his hatred will finally come to light for all to see.

27 The man who sets a trap for others will get caught in it himself. Roll a boulder down on someone, and it will roll back and crush you.

28 Flattery is a form of hatred and wounds cruelly.

## CHAPTER 27

Don't brag about your plans for tomorrow—wait and see what happens.

2 Don't praise yourself; let others do it!

3 A rebel's frustrations are heavier than sand and rocks.

4 Jealousy is more dangerous and cruel than anger.

5 Open rebuke is better than hidden love!

³Literally, "like hot embers to coals and wood to fire."

6 Wounds from a friend are better than kisses from an enemy!

7 Even honey seems tasteless to a man who is full; but if he is hungry, he'll eat anything!

8 A man who strays from home is like a bird that wanders from its nest.

9 Friendly suggestions are as pleasant as perfume.

10 Never abandon a friend—either yours or your father's. Then you won't need to go to a distant relative for help in your time of need.

11 My son, how happy I will be if you turn out to be sensible! It will be a public honor to me.

12 A sensible man watches for problems ahead and prepares to meet them. The simpleton never looks, and suffers the consequences.

13 The world's poorest credit risk is the man who agrees to pay a stranger's debts.

14 If you shout a pleasant greeting to a friend too early in the morning, he will count it as a curse!

15 A constant dripping on a rainy day and a cranky woman are much alike!

16 You can no more stop her complaints than you can stop the wind or hold onto anything with oil-slick hands.

17 A friendly discussion is as stimulating as the sparks that fly when iron strikes iron.

18 A workman may eat from the orchard he tends; anyone should be rewarded who protects another's interests.

19    A mirror reflects a man's face, but what he is really like is shown by the kind of friends he chooses.

20    Ambition[4] and death are alike in this: neither is ever satisfied.

21    The purity of silver and gold can be tested in a crucible, but a man is tested by his reaction to men's praise.

22    You can't separate a rebel from his foolishness though you crush him to powder.

23, 24    Riches can disappear fast. And the king's crown doesn't stay in his family forever—so watch your business[5] interests closely. Know the state of your flocks and your herds;

25, 26, 27    Then there will be lamb's wool enough for clothing, and goat's milk enough for food for all your household after the hay is harvested, and the new crop appears, and the mountain grasses are gathered in.


CHAPTER 28


The wicked flee when no one is chasing them! But the godly are bold as lions!

2    When there is moral rot within a nation, its government topples easily; but with honest, sensible leaders there is stability.

3    When a poor man oppresses those even poorer, he is like an unexpected flood sweeping away their last hope.

---

[4]Literally, "a man's eyes." Possibly the reference is to lust.
[5]Implied.

4 To complain about the law is to praise wickedness. To obey the law is to fight evil.

5 Evil men don't understand the importance of justice, but those who follow the Lord are much concerned about it.

6 Better to be poor and honest than rich and a cheater.

7 Young men who are wise obey the law; a son who is a member of a lawless gang is a shame to his father.

8 Income from exploiting the poor will end up in the hands of someone who pities them.

9 God doesn't listen to the prayers of men who flout the law.

10 A curse on those who lead astray the godly. But men who encourage the upright to do good shall be given a worthwhile reward.

11 Rich men are conceited, but their real poverty is evident to the poor.

12 When the godly are successful, everyone is glad. When the wicked succeed, everyone is sad.

13 A man who refuses to admit his mistakes can never be successful. But if he confesses and forsakes them, he gets another chance.

14 Blessed is the man who reveres God, but the man who doesn't care is headed for serious trouble.

15 A wicked ruler is as dangerous to the poor as a lion or bear attacking them.

16 Only a stupid prince will oppress his people, but

a king will have a long reign if he hates dishonesty and bribes.

17 A murderer's conscience will drive him into hell. Don't stop him!

18 Good men will be rescued from harm, but cheaters will be destroyed.

19 Hard work brings prosperity; playing around brings poverty.

20 The man who wants to do right will get a rich reward. But the man who wants to get rich quick will quickly fail.

21 Giving preferred treatment to rich people is a clear case of selling one's soul for a piece of bread.

22 Trying to get rich quick is evil and leads to poverty.

23 In the end, people appreciate frankness more than flattery.

24 A man who robs his parents and says, "What's wrong with that?" is no better than a murderer.

25 Greed causes fighting; trusting God leads to prosperity.

26 A man is a fool to trust himself! But those who use God's wisdom are safe.

27 If you give to the poor, your needs will be supplied! But a curse upon those who close their eyes to poverty.

28 When the wicked prosper, good men go away; when the wicked meet disaster, good men return.

# CHAPTER 29

The man who is often reproved but refuses to accept criticism will suddenly be broken and never have another chance.

2   With good men in authority, the people rejoice; but with the wicked in power, they groan.

3   A wise son makes his father happy, but a lad who hangs around with prostitutes disgraces him.

4   A just king gives stability to his nation, but one who demands bribes destroys it.

5, 6   Flattery is a trap; evil men are caught in it, but good men stay away and sing for joy.

7   The good man knows the poor man's rights; the godless don't care.

8   Fools start fights everywhere while wise men try to keep peace.

9   There's no use arguing with a fool. He only rages and scoffs, and tempers flare.

10   The godly pray for those who long to kill them.

11   A rebel shouts in anger; a wise man holds his temper in and cools it.

12   A wicked ruler will have wicked aides on his staff.

13   Rich and poor are alike in this: each depends on God for light.

14   A king who is fair to the poor shall have a long reign.

15 Scolding and spanking a child helps him to learn. Left to himself, he brings shame to his mother.

16 When rulers are wicked, their people are too; but good men will live to see the tyrant's downfall.

17 Discipline your son and he will give you happiness and peace of mind.

18 Where there is ignorance of God, the people run wild; but what a wonderful thing it is for a nation to know and keep His laws!

19 Sometimes[7] mere words are not enough—discipline is needed. For the words may not be heeded.

20 There is more hope for a fool than for a man of quick temper.

21 Pamper a servant from childhood, and he will expect you to treat him as a son!

22 A hot-tempered man starts fights and gets into all kinds of trouble.

23 Pride ends in a fall, while humility brings honor.

24 A man who assists a thief must really hate himself! For he knows the consequence but does it anyway.

25 Fear of man is a dangerous trap, but to trust in God means safety.

26 Do you want justice? Don't fawn on the judge, but ask the Lord for it!

27 The good hate the badness of the wicked. The wicked hate the goodness of the good.

## CHAPTER 30

These are the messages of Agur, son of Jakeh, from Massa, addressed to Ithiel and Ucal:

---
[7]Literally, "for a servant."

2 I am tired out, O God, and ready to die. I am too stupid even to call myself a human being!

3 I cannot understand man,[8] let alone God.

4 Who else but God goes back and forth to heaven? Who else holds the wind in His fists, and wraps up the oceans in his cloak? Who but God has created the world? If there is any other, what is his name—and his son's name—if you know it?

\* \* \* \* \*

5 Every word of God proves true. He defends all who come to Him for protection.

6 Do not add to his words, lest he rebuke you, and you be found a liar.

\* \* \* \* \*

7 O God, I beg two favors from you before I die:

8 First, help me never to tell a lie. Second, give me neither poverty nor riches! Give me just enough to satisfy my needs!

9 For if I grow rich, I may become content without God. And if I am too poor, I may steal, and thus insult God's holy name.

10 Never falsely accuse a man to his employer, lest he curse you for your sin.

\* \* \* \*

11, 12 There are those who curse their father and mother, and feel themselves faultless despite their many sins.

13, 14 They are proud beyond description, arro-

---

[8]Literally, "I have not learned wisdom."

gant, disdainful. They devour the poor with teeth as sharp as knives!

* * * * *

15 There are two things never satisfied, like a leech forever craving more: no, three things! no, four!

16   Hell
    The barren womb
    A barren desert
    Fire

* * * * *

17 A man who mocks his father and despises his mother shall have his eye plucked out by ravens and eaten by vultures.

* * * * *

18 There are three things too wonderful for me to understand—no, four!

19   How an eagle glides through the sky.
    How a serpent crawls upon a rock.
    How a ship finds its way across the heaving ocean.
    The growth of love between a man and a girl.[9]

20 There is another thing too: how a prostitute can sin and then say, "What's wrong with that?"

* * * * *

21 There are three things that make the earth tremble—no, four it cannot stand:

22, 23   A slave who becomes a king.
    A rebel who prospers.
    A bitter woman when she finally marries.

[9]Literally, "the way of a man with a maid." Some linguists believe the meaning is, "Why a girl will let herself be seduced."

A servant girl who marries her mistress' husband.[1]

\* \* \* \* \*

24, 25, 26, 27, 28 There are four things that are small but unusually wise:

Ants: they aren't strong, but store up food for the winter.

Cliff badgers: delicate little animals who protect themselves by living among the rocks.

The locusts: though they have no leader, they stay together in swarms.

The spiders: they are easy to catch and kill, yet are found even in king's palaces!

\* \* \* \* \*

29 There are three stately monarchs in the earth— no, four:

30, 31 The lion, king of the animals. He won't turn aside for anyone.

The peacock.

The he-goat.

A king as he leads his army.

32 If you have been a fool by being proud or plotting evil, don't brag about it—cover your mouth with your hand in shame.

33 As the churning of cream yields butter, and a blow to the nose causes bleeding, so anger causes quarrels.

---

[1]Literally, "who succeeds her mistress."

## CHAPTER 31

These are the wise sayings of King Lemuel of Massa,[2] taught to him at his mother's knee:

2    O my son, whom I have dedicated to the Lord,

3    Do not spend your time with women—the royal pathway to destruction.

4    And it is not for kings, O Lemuel, to drink wine and whiskey.

5    For if they drink they may forget their duties and be unable to give justice to those who are oppressed.

6, 7    Hard liquor is for sick men at the brink of death, and wine for those in deep depression. Let them drink to forget their poverty and misery.

8    You should defend those who cannot help themselves.

9    Yes, speak up for the poor and needy and see that they get justice.

*        *        *        *        *

10    If you can find a truly good wife, she is worth more than precious gems!

11    Her husband can trust her, and she will richly satisfy his needs.

12    She will not hinder him, but help him all her life.

13    She finds wool and flax and busily spins it.

---
[2]Or, "of King Lemuel the oracle."

14 She buys imported foods, brought by ship from distant ports.

15 She gets up before dawn to prepare breakfast for her household, and plans the day's work for her servant girls.

16 She goes out to inspect a field, and buys it; with her own hands she plants a vineyard.

17 She is energetic, a hard worker,

18 And watches for bargains. She works far into the night!

19, 20 She sews for the poor, and generously gives to the needy.

21 She has no fear of winter for her household, for she has made warm clothes for all of them.

22 She also upholsters with finest tapestry; her own clothing is beautifully made—a purple gown of pure linen.

23 Her husband is well known, for he sits in the council chamber with the other civic leaders.

24 She makes belted linen garments to sell to the merchants.

25 She is a woman of strength and dignity, and has no fear of old age.

26 When she speaks, her words are wise, and kindness is the rule for everything she says.

27 She watches carefully all that goes on throughout her household, and is never lazy.

28 Her children stand and bless her; so does her husband. He praises her with these words:

29   "There are many fine women in the world, but you are the best of them all!"

30   Charm can be deceptive and beauty doesn't last, but a woman who fears and reverences God shall be greatly praised.

31   Praise her for the many fine things she does. These good deeds of hers shall bring her honor and recognition from even the leaders of the nation.[3]

---

[3]Literally, "Give her of the fruit of her hands; and let her works praise her in the gates."

# Isaiah

## CHAPTER 1

These are the messages that came to Isaiah, son of Amoz, in the visions he saw during the reigns of King Uzziah, King Jotham, King Ahaz and King Hezekiah—all kings of Judah. In these messages God showed him what was going to happen to Judah and Jerusalem in the days ahead.

\* \* \* \*

2  Listen, O heaven and earth, to what the Lord is saying: The children I raised and cared for so long and tenderly have turned against Me.

3  Even the animals—the donkey and the ox—know their owner and appreciate his care for them, but not My people Israel. No matter what I do for them, they still don't care.

4  Oh, what a sinful nation they are! They walk bent-backed beneath their load of guilt. Their fathers before them were evil too. Born to be bad, they have turned their backs upon the Lord, and have despised the Holy One of Israel. They have cut themselves off from My help.

5, 6  Oh, my people, haven't you had enough of punishment? Why will you force Me to whip you again

and again? Must you forever rebel? From head to foot
you are sick and weak and faint, covered with bruises
and welts and infected wounds, unanointed and un-
bound.

7   Your country lies in ruins; your cities are burned;
while you watch, foreigners are destroying and plundering everything they see.

8   You stand there helpless and abandoned like a
watchman's shanty in the field when the harvest time is
over—or when the crop is stripped and robbed.

9   *If the Lord of Hosts had not stepped in to save a
few of us, we would have been wiped out as Sodom and
Gommorah were.*

10   An apt comparison![1] Listen, you leaders of
Israel, you men of Sodom and Gommorah, as I call you
now. Listen to the Lord. Hear what He is telling you!

11   I am sick of your sacrifices. Don't bring Me
any more of them. I don't want your fat rams; I don't
want to see the blood from your offerings.

12, 13   Who wants your sacrifices when you have
no sorrow for your sins? The incense you bring Me is a
stench in my nostrils. Your holy celebrations of the
new moon and the sabbath, and your special days for
fasting—even your most pious meetings—all are
frauds! I want nothing more to do with them.

14   I hate them all; I can't stand the sight of them.

15   From now on, when you pray with your hands
stretched out to heaven, I won't look or listen. Even
though you make many prayers, I will not hear, for

[1]Implied.

your hands are those of murderers; they are covered with the blood of your innocent victims.

16 O, wash yourselves! Be clean! Let Me no longer see you doing all these wicked things; quit your evil ways.

17 Learn to do good, to be fair and to help the poor, the fatherless, and widows.

18 Come, let's talk this over! says the Lord; no matter how deep the stain of your sins, I can take it out and make you as clean as freshly fallen snow. Even if you are stained as red as crimson, I can make you white as wool!

19 If you will only let Me help you, if you will only obey, then I will make you rich!

20 But if you keep on turning your backs and refusing to listen to Me, you will be killed by your enemies; I, the Lord, have spoken.

21 Jerusalem, once My faithful wife! And now a prostitute! Running after other gods! Once The City of Fair Play, but now a gang of murderers.

22 Once like sterling silver; now mixed with worthless alloy! Once so pure, but now diluted like watered-down wine!

23 Your leaders are rebels, companions of thieves; all of them take bribes and won't defend the widows and orphans.

24 Therefore the Lord of Hosts, the Mighty One of Israel, says: I will pour out My anger on you, My enemies!

25 I Myself will melt you in a smelting pot, and skim off your slag.

26 And afterwards I will give you good judges and wise counselors like those you used to have. Then your city shall again be called "The City of Justice," and "The Faithful Town."

27 Those who return to the Lord, who are just and good, shall be redeemed.

28 (But all sinners shall utterly perish, for they refuse to come to Me.)

29 Shame will cover you, and you will blush to think of all those times you sacrificed to idols in your groves of "sacred" oaks.

30 You will perish like a withered tree or a garden without water.

31 The strongest among you will disappear like burning straw; your evil deeds are the spark that sets the straw on fire, and no one will be able to put it out.

## CHAPTER 2

This is another message to Isaiah from the Lord concerning Judah and Jerusalem:

2 In the last days Jerusalem and the Temple of the Lord will become the world's greatest attraction,[2] and people from many lands will flow there to worship the Lord.

3 "Come," everyone will say, "let us go up the

---

[2]Literally, "shall be established as the highest of the mountains."

mountain of the Lord, to the Temple of the God of Israel; there He will teach us His laws, and we will obey them." For in those days the world will be ruled from Jerusalem.

4  The Lord will settle international disputes; all the nations will convert their weapons of war into implements of peace[3]. Then at the last all wars will stop and all military training will end.

5  O Israel, come, let us walk in the light of the Lord, and be obedient to His laws![4]

\*      \*      \*      \*      \*

6  The Lord has rejected you because you welcome foreigners from the East who practice magic and communicate with evil spirits, as the Philistines do.

7  Israel has vast treasures of silver and gold, and great numbers of horses and chariots

8  And idols—the land is full of them! They are man-made, and yet you *worship* them!

9  Small and great, all bow before them; God will not forgive you for this sin.

10  Crawl into the caves in the rocks and hide in terror from His glorious majesty,

11  For the day is coming when your proud looks will be brought low; the Lord alone will be exalted.

12  On that day the Lord of Hosts will move against the proud and haughty and bring them to the dust.

13  All the tall cedars of Lebanon and all the mighty oaks of Bashan shall bend low,

[3]Literally, "beat their swords into plowshares and their spears into pruning hooks."
[4]Implied.

14  And all the high mountains and hills,

15  And every high tower and wall,

16  And all the proud ocean ships and trim harbor craft—*all* shall be crushed before the Lord that day.

17  All the glory of mankind will bow low; the pride of men will lie in the dust, and the Lord alone shall be exalted.

18  And all idols shall be utterly abolished and destroyed.

19  When the Lord stands up from His throne to shake up the earth, His enemies will crawl with fear into the holes in the rocks and into the caves because of the glory of His majesty.

20  Then at last they will abandon their gold and silver idols to the moles and bats,

21  And crawl into the caverns to hide among the jagged rocks at the tops of the cliffs to try to get away from the terror of the Lord and the glory of His majesty when He rises to terrify the earth.

22  Puny man! Frail as his breath! Don't ever put your trust in him!

## CHAPTER 3

The Lord of Hosts will cut off Jerusalem's and Judah's food and water supplies

2  And kill her leaders; He will destroy her armies, judges, prophets, elders,

3  Army officers, businessmen, lawyers, magicians and politicians.

4   Israel's kings will be like babies, ruling child-ishly.

5   And the worst sort of anarchy will prevail—everyone stepping on someone else, neighbors fighting neighbors, youths revolting against authority, criminals sneering at honorable men.

6   In those days a man will say to his brother, "You have some extra clothing, so you be our king and take care of this mess."

7   "No!" he will reply, "I cannot be of any help! I have no extra food or clothes. Don't get me involved!"

8   Israel's civil government will be in utter ruin because the Jews have spoken out against their Lord and will not worship Him; they offend His glory.

9   The very look on their faces gives them away and shows their guilt. And they boast that their sin is equal to the sin of Sodom; they are not even ashamed. What a catastrophe! They have doomed themselves.

10   But all is well for the godly man. Tell him, "You lucky fellow!* What a reward you're going to get!"

11   But say to the wicked, "Your doom is sure. You too shall get your just deserts. Your well earned punishment is on the way."

12   O My people! Can't you see what fools your rulers are? Weak as women! Foolish as little children playing king. True leaders? No, misleaders! Leading you down the garden path to destruction.

13   The Lord stands up! He is the great Prosecuting Attorney presenting His case against His people!

14   First to feel His wrath will be the elders and the

---

*Literally, "that it shall be well with them."

princes, for they have defrauded the poor. They have filled their barns with grain extorted from the helpless peasants.

15   "How dare you grind My people in the dust like that?" the Lord of Hosts will demand of them.

16   Next, He will judge the haughty Jewish women, who mince along, noses in the air, tinkling bracelets on their ankles, with wanton eyes that rove among the crowds to catch the glances of the men.

17   The Lord will send a plague of scabs to ornament their heads! He will expose their nakedness for all to see.

18   No longer shall they tinkle with self assurance as they walk. For the Lord will strip away their artful beauty and their ornaments,

19   Their necklaces and bracelets and veils of shimmering gauze.

20   Gone shall be their scarves and ankle chains, headbands, earrings, and perfumes;

21   Their rings and jewels,

22   And party clothes and negligees and capes and ornate combs and purses;

23   Their mirrors, lovely lingerie, beautiful dresses and veils.

24   Instead of smelling of sweet perfume, they'll stink; for sashes they'll use ropes; their well-set hair shall all fall out; they'll wear sacks instead of robes. All their beauty shall be gone; all that will be left to them is shame and disgrace.

25, 26   Their husbands shall die in battle; the women, ravaged, shall sit crying on the ground.

## CHAPTER 4

At that time so few men will be left alive that seven women will fight over each of them and say, "Let us all marry you! We will furnish our own food and clothing; only let us be called by your name so that we won't be mocked as old maids."

\*          \*          \*          \*

2, 3, 4 Those whose names are written down to escape the destruction of Jerusalem will be washed and rinsed of all their moral filth by the horrors and the fire. They will be God's holy people. And the land will produce for them its lushest bounty and its richest fruit.[5]

5 Then the Lord will provide shade on all Jerusalem—over every home and all its public grounds—a canopy of smoke and cloud throughout the day, and clouds of fire at night, covering the Glorious Land,

6 Protecting it from daytime heat and from rains and storms.

## CHAPTER 5

Now I will sing a song about His vineyard to the One I love. *My Beloved has a vineyard on a very fertile hill.*

---

[5]The term used here, "branch of the Lord," sometimes refers to the coming Messiah (Jer. 23:5, Zech. 3:8). Here it is used differently to describe God's people, as explained by the parallel phrase, "fruit of the land." However, some may prefer to see here a reference to the presence of the Messiah in Jerusalem at that time.

2 *He plowed it and took out all the rocks and planted His vineyard with the choicest vines. He built a watchtower and cut a winepress in the rocks. Then He waited for the harvest, but the grapes that grew were wild and sour and not at all the sweet ones He expected.*

3 Now, men of Jerusalem and Judah, you have heard the case! You be the judges!

4 What more could I have done? Why did My vineyard give Me wild grapes instead of sweet?

5 I will tear down the fences and let My vineyard go to pasture to be trampled by cattle and sheep.

6 I won't prune it or hoe it, but let it be overgrown with briars and thorns. I will command the clouds not to rain on it any more.

7 I have given you the story of God's people. They are the vineyard that I spoke about. Israel and Judah are His pleasant acreage! He expected them to yield a crop of justice, but found bloodshed instead. He expected righteousness, but the cries of deep oppression met His ears.[6]

8 You buy up property so others have no place to live. Your homes are built on great estates so you can be alone in the midst of the earth!

9 But the Lord of Hosts has sworn your awful fate—with my own ears I heard Him say, "Many a beautiful home will lie deserted, their owners killed or gone."

---

[6]Here is an example of serious punning often used by the prophets: the Hebrew word for "judgment" and "bloodshed" sound very much alike, as do those in "righteousness" and "cry."

10    An acre of vineyard will not produce a gallon of juice! Ten bushels of seed will yield but a one-bushel crop!

11    Woe to you who get up early in the morning to go on long drinking bouts that last till late at night—woe to you drunken bums.

12    You furnish lovely music at your grand parties; the orchestras are superb! But for the Lord you have no thought or care.

13    Therefore I will send you into exile far away because you neither know nor care that I have done so much for you. Your great and honored men will starve, and the common people will die of thirst.

14    Hell is licking its chops in anticipation of this delicious morsel, Jerusalem. Her great and small shall be swallowed up, and all her drunken throngs.

15    In that day the haughty shall be brought down to the dust; the proud shall be humbled;

16    But the Lord of Hosts is exalted above all, for He alone is holy, just and good.

17    In those days flocks will feed among the ruins. Lambs and calves and kids will pasture there!

18    Woe to those who drag their sins behind them like a bullock[7] on a rope.

19    They even mock the Holy One of Israel and dare the Lord to punish them.[8] "Hurry up and punish us, O Lord," they say, "We want to see what You can do!"

20    They say that what is right is wrong, and what

---

[7]Or, "with cords of falsehood."
[8]Implied.

is wrong is right; that black is white and white is black; bitter is sweet and sweet is bitter.

21   Woe to those who are wise and shrewd in their own eyes!

22   Woe to those who are "heroes" when it comes to drinking, and boast about the liquor they can hold.

23   They take bribes to pervert justice, letting the wicked go free and putting innocent men in jail.

24   Therefore God will deal with them and burn them. They will disappear like straw on fire. Their roots will rot and their flowers wither, for they have thrown away the laws of God and despised the Word of the Holy One of Israel.

25   That is why the anger of the Lord is hot against His people; that is why He has reached out His hand to smash them. The hills will tremble, and the rotting bodies of His people will be thrown as refuse in the streets. But even so, His anger is not ended; His hand is heavy on them still.

26   He will send a signal to the nations far away, whistling to those at the ends of the earth, and they will come racing toward Jerusalem.

27   They never weary, never stumble, never stop; their belts are tight, their bootstraps strong; they run without stopping for rest or for sleep.

28   Their arrows are sharp; their bows are bent; sparks fly from their horses' hoofs, and the wheels of their chariots spin like the wind.

29   They roar like lions and pounce upon the prey.

They seize My people and carry them off into captivity with none to rescue them.

30   They growl over their victims like the roaring of the sea. Over all Israel lies a pall of darkness and sorrow and the heavens are black.

## CHAPTER 6

The year King Uzziah died I saw the Lord! He was sitting on a lofty throne, and the Temple was filled with His glory.

2   Hovering about Him were mighty, six-winged seraphs. With two of their wings they covered their faces; with two others they covered their feet, and with two they flew.

3   In a great antiphonal chorus they sang, "Holy, holy, holy is the Lord of Hosts; the whole earth is filled with His glory."

4   Such singing it was! It shook the Temple to its foundations, and suddenly the entire sanctuary was filled with smoke.

5   Then I said, "My doom is sealed, for I am a foul-mouthed sinner, a member of a sinful, foul-mouthed race; and I have looked upon the King, the Lord of heaven's armies."

6   Then one of the seraphs flew over to the altar and with a pair of tongs picked out a burning coal.

7   He touched my lips with it and said, "Now you

are pronounced 'Not guilty' because this coal has touched your lips. Your sins are all forgiven."

8  Then I heard the Lord asking, "Whom shall I send as a messenger to My people? Who will go?" And I said, "Lord, I'll go! Send *me*."

9  And He said, "Yes, go. But tell My people this: 'Though you hear My words repeatedly, you won't understand them. Though you watch and watch as I perform My miracles, still you won't know what they mean.'

10  Dull their understanding, close their ears and shut their eyes. I don't want them to see or to hear or to understand, or to turn to Me to heal them."[9]

11  Then I said, "Lord, how long will it be before they are ready to listen?" And He replied, "Not until their cities are destroyed—without a person left—and the whole country is an utter wasteland,

12  And they are all taken away as slaves to other countries far away, and all the land of Israel lies deserted!

13  Yet a tenth—a remnant—will survive; and though Israel is invaded again and again and destroyed, yet Israel will be like a tree cut down, whose stump still lives to grow again."

## CHAPTER 7

During the reign of Ahaz (the son of Jotham and grandson of Uzziah), Jerusalem was attacked by

---

[9]Apparently God's patience with their chronic rebellion was finally exhausted.

King Rezin of Syria and King Pekah of Israel (the son of Romaliah).[1] But it was not taken; the city stood.

2   However, when the news came to the royal court, "Syria is allied with Israel against us!" the hearts of the king and his people trembled with fear as the trees of a forest shake in a storm.

3   Then the Lord said to Isaiah, "Go out to meet King Ahaz, you and Shear-jashub, your son. You will find him at the end of the aqueduct which leads from Gihon Spring to the upper reservoir, near the road that leads down to the bleaching field.

4   Tell him to quit worrying," the Lord said. "Tell him he needn't be frightened by the fierce anger of those two has-beens, Rezin and Pekah.

5   Yes, the kings of Syria and Israel are coming against you. They say,

6   'We will invade Judah and throw her people into panic. Then we'll fight our way into Jerusalem and install the son of Tabeel as their king.'

7   But the Lord God says, This plan will not succeed,

8   For Damascus will remain the capital of Syria alone, and King Rezin's kingdom will not increase its boundaries. And within 65 years Ephraim, too, will be crushed and broken.[2]

9   Samaria is the capital of Ephraim alone and King Pekah's power will not increase. You don't believe Me? If you want Me to protect you, you must learn to believe what I say."

---

[1] "The usurper, the son of Pemaliah" is implied.
[2] Samaria, the capital of "Ephraim," fell to the Assyrian armies in 722 B.C., 13 years after this oracle—ending the Northern kingdom.

10 Not long after this, the Lord sent this further message to King Ahaz:

11 "Ask Me for a sign, Ahaz, to prove that I will indeed crush your enemies as I have said. Ask anything you like, in heaven or on earth."[3]

12 But the king refused. "No," he said, "I'll not bother the Lord with anything like that."

13 Then Isaiah said, O House of David, you aren't satisfied to exhaust *my* patience; you exhaust the Lord's as well!

14 All right then, the Lord Himself will choose the sign—a child shall be born to a virgin![4] And she shall call Him Immanuel (meaning, "God is with us").

15, 16 By the time this child is weaned[5] and knows right from wrong, the two kings you fear so much—the kings of Israel and Samaria—will both be dead.[6]

17 But later on,[7] the Lord will bring a terrible curse on you and on your nation and your family. There will be terror, such as has not been known since the division of Solomon's empire into Israel and Judah

[3]Literally, "let it be deep as Sheol or high as Heaven."
[4]The controversial Hebrew word used here sometimes means "virgin" and sometimes "young woman." Its immediate use here refers to Isaiah's young wife and her new-born son (Isaiah 8:1-4). This, of course, was not a virgin birth. God's sign was that before this child was old enough to talk (verse 4) the two invading kings would be destroyed. However, the Gospel of Matthew (1:23) tells us that there was a further fulfillment of this prophecy, in that a virgin (Mary) conceived and bore a son, Immanuel, the Christ. We have therefore properly used this higher meaning, "virgin," in verse 14, as otherwise the Matthew account loses its significance.
[5]Literally, "For before this child shall know (is old enough) to refuse the evil and to choose the good . . . and (is old enough) to eat curds and honey."
[6]Or, "the lands will be deserted (of their kings)."
[7]Implied.

—the mighty king of Assyria will come with his great army!

18    At that time the Lord will whistle for the army of Upper Egypt,[8] and of Assyria too, to swarm down upon you like flies and destroy you, like bees to sting and to kill.

19    They will come in vast hordes, spreading across the whole land, even into the desolate valleys and caves and thorny parts, as well as to all your fertile acres.

20    In that day the Lord will take this "razor"— these Assyrians you have hired to save you[9]—and use it on you to shave off everything you have: your land, your crops, your people.[1]

21, 22    When they finally stop plundering, the whole nation will be a pastureland; whole flocks and herds will be destroyed, and a farmer will be fortunate to have a cow and two sheep left. But the abundant pastureland will yield plenty of milk, and everyone left will live on curds and wild honey.

23    At that time the lush vineyards will become patches of briars.

24    All the land will be one vast thornfield, a hunting ground overrun by wildlife.

25    No one will go to the fertile hillsides where once the gardens grew, for thorns will cover them; cattle, sheep and goats will graze there.

---

[8]Literally, "sources of the streams of Egypt" refers to Upper Egypt where the powerful 25th Ethiopian Dynasty would soon arise.
[9]2 Kings 16:7-8.
[1]Implied. Literally, "head-hair, beard, body hair."

## CHAPTER 8

Again the Lord sent me a message: "Make a large signboard and write on it the birth announcement of the son I am going to give you. Use capital letters! His name will be Maher-shalal-hash-baz, which means 'Your enemies will soon be destroyed.' "[2]

2 I asked Uriah the priest and Zechariah the son of Jeberechiah, both known as honest men, to watch me as I wrote so they could testify that I had written it (before the child was even on the way).[3]

3 Then I had sexual intercourse with my wife and she conceived, and bore me a son, and the Lord said, "Call him Maher-shalal-hash-baz.

4 This name prophesies that within a couple of years, before this child is even old enough to say 'Daddy' or 'Mommy,' the king of Assyria will invade both Damascus and Samaria and carry away their riches."

5 Then the Lord spoke to me again and said:

6 "Since the people of Jerusalem are planning to refuse My gentle care[4] and are enthusiastic about asking King Rezin and King Pekah to come and aid them,

7, 8 Therefore I will overwhelm My people with Euphrates' mighty flood; the king of Assyria and all his mighty armies will rage against them. This flood

---

[2]Literally, "Blundering and despoiling (will) come quickly."
[3]Implied.
[4]Literally, "have refused the waters of Shiloah that go softly."

will overflow all its channels and sweep into your land of Judah, O Immanuel, submerging it from end to end."

9, 10  Do your worst, O Syria and Israel,[5] our enemies,[6] but you will not succeed—you will be shattered. Listen to me, all you enemies of ours: Prepare for war against us—and perish! Yes! Perish! Call your councils of war, develop your strategies, prepare your plans of attacking us, and perish! For God is with us.[7]

11  The Lord has said in strongest terms: Do not under any circumstances, go along with the plans of Judah to surrender to Syria and Israel.

12  Don't let people call you a traitor for staying true to God. Don't you panic as so many of your neighbors are doing when they think of Syria and Israel attacking you.

13  Don't fear anything except the Lord of the armies of heaven! If you fear Him, you need fear nothing else.

14, 15  He will be your safety; but Israel and Judah have refused His care and thereby stumbled against the Rock of their salvation and lie fallen and crushed beneath it: God's presence among them has endangered them!

16  Write down all these things I am going to do, says the Lord, and seal it up for the future. Entrust it to some godly man to pass on down to godly men of future generations."

[5]Literally, "O peoples."
[6]Implied.
[7]Or, "Immanuel."

17  I will wait for the Lord to help us, though He is hiding now. My only hope is in Him.

18  I and the children God has given me have symbolic names that reveal the plans of the Lord of heaven's armies for His people: "Isaiah" means "Jehovah will save (His people)," Shear-jashub means "A remnant shall return," and Maher-shalal-hash-baz means "Your enemies will soon be destroyed."

19  So why are you trying to find out the future by consulting witches and mediums? Don't listen to their whisperings and mutterings. Can the living find out the future from the dead? Why not ask your God?

20  "Check these witches' words against the Word of God!" He says. "If their messages are different than Mine, it is because I have not sent them; for they have no light or truth in them.

21  My people will be led away captive, stumbling, weary and hungry. And because they are hungry they will rave and shake their fists at heaven and curse their King and their God.

22  Wherever they look there will be trouble and anguish and dark despair. And they will be thrust out into the darkness."

## CHAPTER 9

Nevertheless, that time of darkness and despair shall not go on forever. Though soon the land of Zebulon and Naphtali will be under God's contempt and judgment, yet in the future these very lands—Galilee and Northern Transjordan, where lies the road to the Sea, will be filled with glory.

2   The people who walk in darkness shall see a great Light—a Light that will shine on all those who live in the land of the shadow of death.

3   For Israel will again be great, filled with joy like that of reapers when the harvest time has come, and like that of men dividing up the plunder they have won.

4   For God will break the chains that bind His people and the whip that scourges them, just as He did when He destroyed the vast host of the Midianites by Gideon's little band.

5   In that glorious day of peace there will no longer be the issuing of battle gear; no more the blood-stained uniforms of war; all such will be burned.

6   For unto us a Child is born; unto us a Son is given; and the government shall be upon His shoulder. These will be His royal titles: "Wonderful," "Counsellor," "The Mighty God," "The Everlasting Father," "The Prince of Peace."

7   His ever-expanding, peaceful government will never end. He will rule with perfect fairness and justice from the throne of His father David. He will bring true justice and peace to all the nations of the world. This is going to happen because the Lord of heaven's armies has dedicated Himself to do it!

\*     \*     \*     \*     \*

8, 9, 10   The Lord has spoken out against that braggart Israel who says that though our land lies in ruins now, we will rebuild it better than before. The sycamore trees are cut down, but we will replace them with cedars!

11, 12   The Lord's reply to your bragging is to

bring your[8] enemies against you—the Syrians on the east and the Philistines on the west. With bared fangs they will devour Israel. And even then the Lord's anger against you will not be satisfied—His fist will still be poised to smash you.

13 For after all this punishment you will not repent and turn to Him, the Lord of heaven's armies.

14, 15 Therefore the Lord, in one day, will destroy the leaders of Israel and the lying prophets.

16 For the leaders of His people have led them down the paths of ruin.

17 That is why the Lord has no joy in their young men, and no mercy upon even the widows and orphans; for they are all filthy-mouthed, wicked liars. That is why His anger is not yet satisfied, but His fist is still poised to smash them all.

18 He will burn up all this wickedness, these thorns and briers; and the flames will consume the forests, too, and send a vast cloud of smoke billowing up from their burning.

19, 20 The land is blackened by that fire, by the wrath of the Lord of heaven's armies. The people are fuel for the fire. Each fights against his brother to steal his food, but will never have enough. Finally they will even eat their own children!

21 Manassah against Ephraim and Ephraim against Manassah—and both against Judah. Yet even after all of this, God's anger is not yet satisfied. His hand is still heavy upon them, to crush them.

---

[8]Or, "Rezin's enemies," in some ancient versions.

## CHAPTER 10

Woe to unjust judges and to those who issue unfair laws, says the Lord,

2 So that there is no justice for the poor, the widows and orphans. Yes, it is true that they even rob the widows and fatherless children.

3 Oh, what will you do when I visit you in that day when I send desolation upon you from a distant land? To whom will you turn then for your help? Where will your treasures be safe?

4 I will not help you; you will stumble along as prisoners or lie among the slain. And even then My anger will not be satisfied, but My fist will still be poised to strike you.

5, 6 Assyria is the whip of My anger; his military strength is my weapon upon this godless nation, doomed and damned; he will enslave them and plunder them and trample them like dirt beneath his feet.

7 But the King of Assyria will not know that it is I who sent him. He will merely think he is attacking My people as part of his plan to conquer the world.

8 He will declare that every one of his princes will soon be a king, ruling a conquered land.

9 "We will destroy Calno just as we did Carchemish," he will say, "and Hamath will go down before us as Arpad did; and we will destroy Israel just as we did Damascus.

10 Yes, we have finished off many a kingdom

whose idols were far greater than those in Jerusalem and Samaria,

11   So when we have defeated Samaria and her idols we will destroy Jerusalem with hers."

12   After the Lord has used the King of Assyria to accomplish His purpose, then He will turn upon the Assyrians and punish them too—for they are proud and haughty men.

13   They boast, "We in our own power and wisdom have won these wars. We are great and wise. By our own strength we broke down the walls and destroyed the people and carried off their treasures.

14   In our greatness we have robbed their nests of riches and gathered up kingdoms as a farmer gathers eggs; and no one can move a finger or open his mouth to peep against us!"

15   But the Lord says, "Shall the axe boast greater power than the man who uses it? Is the saw greater than the man who saws? Can a rod strike unless a hand is moving it? Can a cane walk by itself?"

16   Because of all your evil boasting, O King of Assyria, the Lord of Hosts will send a plague among your proud troops, and strike them down.

17   God, the Light and Holy One of Israel, will be the fire and flame that will destroy them. In a single night He will burn those thorns and briers, the Assyrians who destroyed the land of Israel.[9]

18   Assyria's vast army is like a glorious forest, yet it will be destroyed. The Lord will destroy them, soul and body, as when a sick man wastes away.

[9]See 2 Kings 19:35 and Isaiah 37:36.

19    Only a few from all that mighty army will be left; so few a child could count them!

20    Then at last, those left in Israel and in Judah will trust the Lord, the Holy One of Israel, instead of fearing the Assyrians.

21    A remnant of them will return to the mighty God.

22    But though Israel be now as many as the sands along the shore, yet only a few of them will be left to return at that time; God has rightly decided to destroy His people:

23    Yes, it has already been decided by the Lord God of Hosts to consume them.

24    Therefore the Lord God of Hosts says, "O My people in Jerusalem, don't be afraid of the Assyrians when they oppress you just as the Egyptians did long ago.

25    It will not last very long; in a little while My anger against you will end, and then it will rise against them to destroy them."

26    The Lord of Hosts will send His angel to slay them in a mighty slaughter like the time when Gideon triumphed over Midian at the rock of Oreb or the time God drowned the Egyptian armies in the sea.

27    On that day God will end the bondage of His people. He will break the slave-yoke off their necks, and destroy it as decreed.[1]

28, 29    Look, the mighty armies of Assyria are coming! Now they are at Aiath, now at Migron; they

---

[1]Literally, "because of ointment." Some see here a reference to Messiah, the Anointed One.

are storing some of their equipment at Michmash and crossing over the pass; they are staying overnight at Geba; fear strikes the city of Ramah; all the people of Gibeah—the city of Saul—are running for their lives.

30 Well may you scream in terror, O people of Gallim. Shout out a warning to Laish, for the mighty army comes. O poor Anathoth, what a fate is yours!

31 There go the people of Madmenah, all fleeing, and the citizens of Gebim are preparing to run.

32 But the enemy stops at Nob for the remainder of that day. He shakes his fist at Jerusalem on Mount Zion.

33 Then, look, look! The Lord, the Lord of the armies of heaven, is chopping down the mighty tree! He is destroying all of that vast army, great and small alike, both officers and men.

34 He, the Mighty One, will cut down the enemy as a woodsman's axe cuts down the forest trees in Lebanon.

## CHAPTER 11

The royal line of David[2] will be cut off, chopped down like a tree; but from the stump will grow a Shoot[3]—yes, a new Branch[3] from the old root.

2 And the Spirit of the Lord shall rest upon Him, the Spirit of wisdom, understanding, counsel and might; the Spirit of knowledge and of the fear of the Lord.

---

[2]Literally, "Jesse."
[3]Christ, the Messiah.

3   His delight will be obedience to the Lord. He will not judge by appearance, false evidence, or hearsay,

4   But will defend the poor and the exploited. He will rule against the wicked who oppress them.

5   For He will be clothed with fairness and with truth.

6   In that day the wolf and the lamb will lie down together, and the leopard and goats will be at peace. Calves and fat cattle will be safe among lions, and a little child shall lead them all.

7   The cows will graze among bears; cubs and calves will lie down together, and lions will eat grass like the cows.

8   Babies will crawl safely among poisonous snakes, and a little child who puts his hand in a nest of deadly adders will pull it out unharmed.

9   Nothing will hurt or destroy in all My holy mountain; for as the waters fill the sea, so shall the earth be full of the knowledge of the Lord.

10   In that day He who created the royal dynasty of David[4] will be a banner of salvation to all the world. The nations will rally to Him, for the land where He lives will be a glorious place.

11   At that time the Lord will bring back a remnant of His people for the second time, returning them to the land of Israel from Assyria, Upper and Lower Egypt, Ethiopia, Elam, Babylonia, Hamath and all the distant coastal lands.

12   He will raise a flag among the nations for them

---

[4]Literally, "the Root of Jesse." Possibly the meaning is, "the Heir of David's royal line."

to rally to; He will gather the scattered Israelites from the ends of the earth.

13   Then, at last, the jealousy between Israel and Judah will end; they will not fight each other any more.

14   Together they will fly against the nations possessing their land on the east and on the west, uniting forces to destroy them; and they will occupy the nations of Edom and Moab and Ammon.

15   The Lord will dry a path through the Red Sea,[5] and wave His hand over the Euphrates,[6] sending a mighty wind to divide it into seven streams that can easily be crossed.

16   He will make a highway from Assyria for the remnant there, just as He did for all of Israel long ago when they returned from Egypt.

## CHAPTER 12

On that day you will say, "Praise the Lord! He was angry with me, but now He comforts me!

2   See, God has come to save me! I will trust and not be afraid, for the Lord is my strength and song; He is my salvation!

3   Oh, the joy of drinking deeply from the Fountain of Salvation!"

4   In that wonderful day you will say, "Thank the

[5]Literally, "the Sea of Egypt."
[6]Literally, "the River."

Lord! Praise His name! Tell the world about His wondrous love![7] How mighty He is!"

5 Sing to the Lord, for He has done wonderful things! Make known His praise around the world!

6 Let all the people of Jerusalem shout His praise with joy! For great and mighty is the Holy One of Israel, who lives among you!

## CHAPTER 13

This is the vision God showed Isaiah (son of Amoz) concerning Babylon's doom.

2 See the flags waving as their enemy attacks. Shout to them, O Israel, and wave them on as they march against Babylon to destroy the palaces of the rich and mighty.

3 I, the Lord, have set apart these armies for this task; I have called those rejoicing in their strength to do this work, to satisfy my anger.

4 Hear the tumult on the mountains! Listen as the armies march! It is the tumult and the shout of many nations: the Lord of Hosts has brought them here,

5 From countries far away. They are His weapons against you, O Babylon. They carry His anger with them and will destroy your whole land.

6 Scream in terror, for the Lord's time has come, the time for the Almighty to crush you.

---

[7]Literally, "Proclaim His doings among the nations."

7   Your arms lie paralyzed with fear; the strongest hearts melt,

8   And are afraid. Fear grips you with terrible pangs, like those of a woman in labor. You look at one another, helpless, as the flames of the burning city reflect upon your pallid faces.

9   For see, the day of the Lord is coming, the terrible day of His wrath and fierce anger. The land shall be destroyed, and all the sinners with it.

10   The heavens will be black above them. No light will shine from stars or sun or moon.

11   And I will punish the world for its evil, the wicked for their sin; I will crush the arrogance of the proud man and the haughtiness of the rich.

12   Few will live when I have finished up my work. Men will be as scarce as gold—of greater value than the gold of Ophir.

13   For I will shake the heavens in my wrath and fierce anger, and the earth will move from its place in the skies.

14   The armies of Babylon will run until exhausted, fleeing back to their own land like deer chased by dogs, wandering like sheep deserted by their shepherd.

15   Those who don't run will be butchered.

16   Their little children will be dashed to death against the pavement right before their eyes; their homes will be sacked, and their wives raped by the attacking hordes.

17   For I will stir up the Medes against Babylon, and no amount of silver or gold will buy them off.

18   The attacking armies will have no mercy on the young people of Babylon or the babies or the children.

19   And so Babylon, the most glorious of kingdoms, the flower of Chaldean culture, will be as utterly destroyed as Sodom and Gomorrah were when God sent fire from heaven;

20   Babylon will never rise again. Generation after generation will come and go, but the land will never again be lived in.[8] The nomads will not even camp there. The shepherds won't let their sheep stay overnight.

21   The wild animals of the desert will make it their home. The houses will be haunted by howling creatures. Ostriches will live there, and the demons will come there to dance.

22   Hyenas and jackals will den within the palaces. Babylon's days are numbered; her time of doom will soon be here.

## CHAPTER 14

But the Lord will have mercy on the Israeli; they are still His Special Ones. He will bring them back to settle once again in the land of Israel. And many nationalities will come and join them there and be their loyal allies.

2   The nations of the world will help them to return, and those coming to live in their land will serve them. Those enslaving Israel will be enslaved—Israel shall rule her enemies!

---

[8]Babylon, in Iraq, still lies in utter ruin today.

3 In that wonderful day when the Lord gives His people rest from sorrow and fear, from slavery and chains,

4 You will jeer at the king of Babylon and say, "You bully, you! At last you have what was coming to you!

5 For the Lord has crushed your wicked power, and broken your evil rule."

6 You persecuted My people with unceasing blows of rage and held the nations in your angry grip. You were unrestrained in tyranny.

7 But at last the whole earth is at rest and is quiet! All the world begins to sing!

8 Even the trees of the woods—the fir trees and cedars of Lebanon—sing out this joyous song: "Your power is broken; no one will bother us now; at last we have peace."

9 The denizens of hell crowd to meet you as you enter their domain. World leaders and earth's mightiest kings, long dead, are there to see you.

10 With one voice they all cry out, "Now you are as weak as we are!"

11 Your might and power are gone; they are buried with you; all the pleasant music in your palace has ceased; now maggots are your sheet, worms your blanket!

12 How you are fallen from heaven, O Lucifer, son of the morning! How you are cut down to the ground— mighty though you were against the nations of the world.

13 For you said to yourself, "I will ascend to heaven and rule the angels[9]. I will take the highest throne. I will preside on the Mount of Assembly far away in the north[1].

14 I will climb to the highest heavens and be like the Most High."

15 But instead you will be brought down to the pit of hell, down to its lowest depths.

16 Everyone there will stare at you and ask, "Can this be the one who shook the earth and the kingdoms of the world?

17 Can this be the one who destroyed the world and made it into a shambles and demolished its greatest cities and had no mercy on his prisoners?"

18 The kings of the nations lie in stately glory in their graves,

19 But your body is thrown out like a broken branch; it lies in an open grave, covered with the dead bodies of those slain in battle; it lies as a carcass in the road, trampled and mangled by horses' hoofs.

20 No monument will be given you, for you have destroyed your nation and slain your people. Your son will not succeed you as the king.

21 Slay the children of this sinner. Do not let them rise and conquer the land nor rebuild the cities of the world.

22 I, Myself, have risen against him, says the Lord of heaven's armies, and will cut off his children and his children's children from ever sitting on his throne.

---

[9]Literally, "the stars of God."
[1]Literally, "I will sit upon the mount of the congregation in the sides of the north" (Psalm 48:2); or, "on the slopes of Mt. Saphon."

23  I will make Babylon into a desolate land of porcupines, full of swamps and marshes. I will sweep the land with the broom of destruction, says the Lord of the armies of heaven.

24  He has taken an oath to do it! For this is His purpose and plan.

25  I have decided to break the Assyrian army when they are in Israel and to crush them on My mountains; My people shall no longer be their slaves.

26  This is My plan for the whole earth—I will do it by My mighty power that reaches everywhere around the world.

27  The Lord, the God of battle, has spoken—who can change His plans? When His hand moves, who can stop Him?

\*  \*  \*  \*  \*

28  This is the message that came to me the year King Ahaz died:

29  Don't rejoice, Philistines, that the king who smote you is dead.[2] That rod is broken, yes; but his son will be a greater scourge to you than his father ever was! From the snake will be born an adder, a fiery serpent to destroy you!

30  I will shepherd the poor of My people; they shall graze in My pasture! The needy shall lie down in peace. But as for you—I will wipe you out with famine and the sword.

31  Weep, Philistine cities—you are doomed. All

_____

[2]Shalmaneser V of Assyria.

your nation is doomed. For a perfectly trained army[s] is coming down from the north against you.

32   What then shall we tell the reporters? Tell them that the Lord has founded Jerusalem and is determined that the poor of His people will find a refuge within her walls.

## CHAPTER 15

Here is God's message to Moab: In one night your cities of Ar and Kir will be destroyed.

2   Your people in Dibon go mourning to their temples to weep for the fate of Nebo and Medeba; they shave their heads in sorrow and cut off their beards.

3   They wear sackcloth through the streets, and from every home comes the sound of weeping.

4   The cries from the cities of Heshbon and Elealeh are heard far away, even in Jahaz. The bravest warriors of Moab cry in utter terror.

5   My heart weeps for Moab! His people flee to Zoar and Eglath. Weeping, they climb the upward road to Luhith, and their crying will be heard all along the road to Horonaim.

6   Even Nimrim River is desolate! The grassy banks are dried up and the tender plants are gone.

7   The desperate refugees take only the possessions they can carry, and flee across the Brook of Willows.

8   The whole land of Moab is a land of weeping, from one end to the other.

---

[s]Sargon of Assyria.

9　The stream near Dibon will run red with blood, but I am not through with Dibon yet! Lions will hunt down the survivors, both those who escape and those who remain.

## CHAPTER 16

Moab's refugees at Sela send lambs as a token of alliance with the king of Judah.

2　The women of Moab are left at the fords of the Arnon River like homeless birds.

3　(The ambassadors, who accompany the gift to Jerusalem[4]) plead for advice and help. "Give us sanctuary. Protect us. Do not turn us over to our foes.

4, 5　Let our outcasts stay among you; hide them from our enemies! God will reward you for your kindness to us. If you let Moab's fugitives settle among you, then, when the terror is past, God will establish David's throne forever, and on that throne He will place a just and righteous King."

6　Is this proud Moab, concerning which we heard so much? His arrogance and insolence are all gone now!

7　Therefore all Moab weeps. Yes, Moab, you will mourn for stricken Kir-haraseth,

8　And for the abandoned farms of Heshbon and the vineyards at Sibmah. The enemy war-lords have cut down the best of the grape vines; their armies spread

---

[4]Implied.

out as far as Jazer in the deserts, and even down to the sea.

9 So I wail and lament for Jazer and the vineyards of Sibmah. My tears shall flow for Heshbon and Elealeh, for destruction has come upon their summer fruits and harvests.

10 Gone now is the gladness, gone the joy of harvest. The happy singing in the vineyards will be heard no more; the treading out of the grapes in the wine presses has ceased forever. I have ended all their harvest joys.

11 I will weep, weep, weep, for Moab; and my sorrow for Kir-haresh will be very great.

12 The people of Moab will pray in anguish to their idols at the tops of the hills, but it will do no good; they will cry to their gods in their idol temples, but none will come to save them.

13, 14 All this concerning Moab has been said before; but now the Lord says that within three years, without fail, the glory of Moab shall be ended, and few of all its people will be left alive.

## CHAPTER 17

This is God's message to Damascus, capital of Syria: Look, Damascus is gone! It is no longer a city—it has became a heap of ruins!

2 The cities of Aroer are deserted. Sheep pasture there, lying quiet and unafraid, with no one to chase them away.

3 The strength of Israel and the power of Damascus will end, and the remnant of Syria shall be destroyed. For as Israel's glory departed, so theirs, too, will disappear, declares the Lord of Hosts.

4 Yes, the glory of Israel will be very dim when poverty stalks the land.

5 Israel will be as abandoned as the harvested grain fields in the Valley of Rephaim.

6 Oh, a very few of her people will be left, just as a few stray olives are left on the trees when the harvest is ended, two or three in the highest branches, four or five out on the tips of the limbs. That is how it will be in Damascus and Israel—stripped bare of people except for a few of the poor who remain.

7 Then at last they will think of God their Creator and have respect for the Holy One of Israel.

8 They will no longer ask their idols for help in that day, neither will they worship what their hands have made! They will no longer have respect for the images of Ashteroth and the sun-idols.

9 Their largest cities will be as deserted as the distant wooded hills and mountain tops and become like the abandoned cities of the Amorites deserted when the Israelites approached (so long ago[5]).

10 Why? Because you have turned from the God who can save you—the Rock who can hide you; therefore, even though you plant a wonderful, rare crop of greatest value,

11 And though it grows so well that it will blossom

---

[5]Implied.

on the very morning that you plant it, yet you will never harvest it—your only harvest will be a pile of grief and incurable pain.

12 Look, see the armies thundering toward God's land.

13 But though they roar like breakers rolling upon a beach, God will silence them. They will flee, scattered like chaff by the wind, like whirling dust before a storm.

14 In the evening Israel waits in terror, but by dawn her enemies are dead. This is the just reward of those who plunder and destroy the people of God.

## CHAPTER 18

Ah, land beyond the upper reaches of the Nile,[6] where winged sailboats glide along the river!

2 Land that sends ambassadors in fast boats down the Nile! Let swift messengers return to you, O strong and supple nation feared far and wide, a conquering, destroying nation whose land the upper Nile[7] divides. And this is the message sent to you:

3 When I raise my battle flag upon the mountain, let all the world take notice! When I blow the trumpet, listen!

4 For the Lord has told me this: let your mighty army now advance against the land of Israel.[8] God will

---

[6]Literally, "land beyond the rivers of Ethiopia." Ethiopia was the seat of the powerful 25th Egyptian Dynasty (730-660 B.C.).
[7]Literally, "whose land the rivers divide."
[8]Implied.

watch quietly from His Temple in Jerusalem—serene as on a pleasant summer day or a lovely autumn morning during harvest time.

5 But before you have begun the attack, and while your plans are ripening like grapes, He will cut you off as though with pruning shears. He will snip the spreading tendrils.

6 Your mighty army will be left dead on the field for the mountain birds and wild animals to eat; the vultures will tear bodies all summer, and the wild animals will gnaw bones all winter.

7 But the time will come when that strong and mighty nation, a terror to all both far and near, that conquering, destroying nation whose land the rivers divide, will bring gifts to the Lord of Hosts in Jerusalem, where He has placed His name.

## CHAPTER 19

This is God's message concerning Egypt: Look, the Lord is coming against Egypt, riding on a swift cloud; the idols of Egypt tremble; the hearts of the Egyptians melt with fear.

2 I will set them to fighting against each other—brother against brother, neighbor against neighbor, city against city, province against province.

3 Her wise counselors are all at their wits' ends to know what to do; they plead with their idols for wisdom, and call upon mediums, wizards and witches to show them what to do.

4     I will hand over Egypt to a hard, cruel master, to a vicious king, says the Lord of Hosts.

5     And the waters of the Nile will fail to rise and flood the fields; the ditches will be parched and dry,

6     Their channels fouled with rotting reeds.

7     All green things along the river bank will wither and blow away. All crops will perish; everything will die.

8     The fishermen will weep for lack of work; those who fish with hooks and those who use the nets will all be unemployed.

9     The weavers will have no flax or cotton, for the crops will fail.

10     Great men and small—all will be crushed and broken.

11     What fools the counselors of Zoan are! Their best counsel to the King of Egypt is utterly stupid and wrong. Will they still boast of their wisdom? Will they dare tell Pharoah about the long line of wise men they have come from?

12     What has happened to your "wise counselors," O Pharoah? Where has their wisdom gone? If they are wise, let them tell you what the Lord is going to do to Egypt.

13     The "wise men" from Zoan are also fools, and those from Memphis are utterly deluded. They are the best you can find, but they have ruined Egypt with their foolish counsel.

14     The Lord has sent a spirit of foolishness on them, so that all their suggestions are wrong; they make Egypt stagger like a sick drunkard.

15 Egypt cannot be saved by anything or any-body—no one can show her the way.

16 In that day the Egyptians will be as weak as women, cowering in fear beneath the upraised fist of God.

17 Just to speak the name of Israel will strike deep terror in their hearts, for the Lord of Hosts has laid His plans against them.

18 At that time five of the cities of Egypt will follow the Lord of Hosts and will begin to speak the Hebrew language.⁹ One of these will be Heliopolis, "The City of the Sun."

19 And there will be an altar to the Lord in the heart of Egypt in those days, and a monument to the Lord at its border.

20 This will be for a sign of loyalty to the Lord of Hosts; then when they cry to the Lord for help against those who oppress them, He will send them a Saviour —and He shall deliver them.

21 In that day the Lord will make Himself known to the Egyptians. Yes, they will know the Lord and give their sacrifices and offerings to Him; they will make promises to God and keep them.

22 The Lord will smite Egypt and then restore her! For the Egyptians will turn to the Lord and He will listen to their plea and heal them.

23 In that day Egypt and Iraq¹ will be connected by a highway, and the Egyptians and the Iraqi will

⁹Literally, "the language of Canaan."
¹Literally, "Assyria."

move freely back and forth between their lands, and they shall worship the same God.

24 And Israel will be their ally; the three will be together, and Israel will be a blessing to them.

25 For the Lord will bless Egypt and Iraq because of their friendship[2] with Israel. He will say, "Blessed be Egypt, My people; Blessed be Iraq, the land I have made; Blessed be Israel, My inheritance!"

## CHAPTER 20

In the year when Sargon, king of Assyria, sent the commander-in-chief of his army against the Philistine city of Ashdod and captured it,

2 The Lord told Isaiah, the son of Amoz, to take off his clothing, including his shoes, and to walk around naked and barefoot. And Isaiah did as he was told.

3 Then the Lord said, My servant Isaiah, who has been walking naked and barefoot for the last three years, is a symbol of the terrible troubles I will bring upon Egypt and Ethiopia.

4 For the king of Assyria will take away the Egyptians and Ethiopians as prisoners, making them walk naked and barefoot, both young and old, their buttocks uncovered, to the shame of Egypt.

5, 6 Then how dismayed the Philistines[3] will be, who counted on "Ethiopia's power" and their "glorious ally," Egypt! And they will say, "If this can happen to Egypt, what chance have we?"

[2]Implied.
[3]Literally, "inhabitants of the coastland."

# CHAPTER 21

This is God's message concerning Babylon: [4] Disaster is roaring down upon you from the terrible desert, like a whirlwind sweeping from the Negeb.

2   I see an awesome vision: oh, the horror of it all! God is telling me what He is going to do. I see you plundered and destroyed. Elamites and Medes will take part in the siege. Babylon will fall, and the groaning of all the nations she enslaved will end.

3   My stomach constricts and burns with pain; sharp pangs of horror are upon me, like the pangs of a woman giving birth to a child. I faint when I hear what God is planning; I am terrified, blinded with dismay.

4   My mind reels; my heart races; I am gripped by awful fear. All rest at night—so pleasant once—is gone; I lie awake, trembling.

5   Look! They are preparing a great banquet! They load the tables with food; they pull up their chairs[5] to eat . . . . .

Quick, quick, grab your shields and prepare for battle! You are being attacked![6]

6, 7   Meanwhile (in my vision)[7] the Lord had told me, "Put a watchman on the city wall to shout out

---

[4]Implied from verse 9.
[5]Literally, "spread out the rugs."
[6]More details of the feast are seen in Daniel, chapter 5, as this prophecy was fulfilled when Cyrus captured the city.
[7]Implied.

what he sees. When he sees riders in pairs on donkeys and camels,[8] tell him, 'This is it!' "

8, 9   So I put the watchman on the wall, and at last he shouted, "Sir, day after day and night after night I have been here at my post. Now at last—look! Here come riders in pairs!" Then I heard a Voice shout out, "Babylon is fallen, is fallen; and all the idols of Babylon lie broken on the ground."

10   O my people, threshed and winnowed, I have told you all that the Lord of Hosts, the God of Israel has said.

\*          \*          \*          \*          \*

11   This is God's message to Edom![9] Someone from among you keeps calling, calling to me: "Watchman, what of the night? Watchman, what of the night? How much time is left?"

12   The watchman replies, "Your judgment day is dawning now. Turn again to God, so that I can give you better news. Seek for Him, then come and ask again!"

\*          \*          \*          \*          \*

13   This is God's message concerning Arabia: O caravans from Dedam, you will hide in the deserts of Arabia.

14   O people of Tema, bring food and water to these weary fugitives!

15   They have fled from drawn swords and sharp arrows and the terrors of war!

---

[8]Literally, "when he sees a troop, horsemen in pairs, riders on asses, riders on camels." Possibly the meaning is that the asses and camels were paired for the attack. The city fell to the Medes and Persians, perhaps represented by these paired riders.
[9]Literally, "Dumah."

16   "But a long year from now,"[1] says the Lord, "the great power of their enemy,[2] the mighty tribe of Kedar, will end.

17   Only a few of its stalwart archers will survive." The Lord, the God of Israel, has spoken.

## CHAPTER 22

This is God's message concerning Jerusalem![3] What is happening? Where is everyone going? Why are they running to the rooftops? What are they looking at?

2   The whole city is in terrible uproar. What's the trouble in this busy, happy city?[4] Bodies! Lying everywhere, slain by plague[4] and not by sword.

3   All your leaders flee; they surrender without resistance. The people slip away but they are captured, too.

4   Let me alone to weep. Don't try to comfort me—let me cry for my people as I watch them being destroyed.

5   Oh, what a day of crushing trouble! What a day of confusion and terror from the Lord God of heaven's armies! The walls of Jerusalem are breached and the cry of death echoes from the mountainsides.

6, 7   Elamites are the archers; Syrians drive the

---

[1]The Dead Sea manuscript reads, "within *three* years, according to the year of a hireling," like 16:14.
[2]Implied.
[3]Literally, "The Valley of Vision."
[4]Implied.

chariots; the men of Kir hold up the shields. They fill your choicest valleys and crowd against your gates.

8  God has removed His protecting care. You run to the armory for your weapons!

9, 10, 11  You inspect the walls of Jerusalem to see what needs repair! You check over the houses and tear some down for stone for fixing walls. Between the city walls, you build a reservoir for water from the lower pool! But all your feverish plans will not avail, for you never ask for help from God, who lets this come upon you. He is the One who planned it long ago.

12  The Lord God of Hosts called you to repent, to weep and mourn and shave your heads in sorrow for your sins, and to wear clothes made of sackcloth to show your remorse.

13  But instead, you sing and dance and play, and feast and drink. "Let us eat, drink, and be merry," you say: "What's the difference, for tomorrow we die."

14  The Lord of Hosts has revealed to me that this sin will never be forgiven you until the day you die.

15, 16  Furthermore, the same Lord God of the armies of heaven has told me this: Go and say to Shebna, the palace administrator: "And who do you think you are, building this beautiful sepulchre in the rock for yourself?

17  For the Lord who allowed you to be clothed so gorgeously will hurl you away, sending you into captivity, O strong man!

18  He will wad you up in His hands like a ball and toss you away into a distant, barren land; there you will die, O glorious one—you who disgrace your nation!

19   Yes, I will drive you out of office," says the Lord, "and pull you down from your high position.

20   And then I will call My servant Eliakim, the son of Hilkiah, to replace you.

21   He shall have your uniform and title and authority, and he will be a father to the people of Jerusalem and all Judah.

22   I will give him responsibility over all My people; whatever he says will be done; none will be able to stop him.

23, 24   I will make of him a strong and steady peg to support My people; they will load him with responsibility, and he will be an honor to his family name."

25   But the Lord will pull out that other peg that seems to be so firmly fastened to the wall! It will come out and fall to the ground, and everything it supports will fall with it, for the Lord has spoken.

## CHAPTER 23

This is God's message to Tyre: Weep, O ships of Tyre, returning home from distant lands![5] Weep for your harbor, for it is gone! The rumors that you heard in Cyprus are all true!

2, 3   Deathly silence is everywhere! Stillness reigns where once your hustling port was full of ships from Sidon, bringing merchandise from far across the ocean, from Egypt and along the Nile. You were the merchandise mart of the world.

---

[5]Tyre was originally a colony of the mother-city, Sidon.

4   Be ashamed, O Sidon,⁵ stronghold of the sea! For you are childless now!

5   When Egypt hears the news, there will be great sorrow.

6   Flee to Tarshish, men of Tyre, weeping as you go.

7   This silent ruin is all that's left of your once joyous land. What a history was yours! Think of all the colonists you sent to distant lands!

8   Who has brought this disaster on Tyre, empire builder and top trader of the world?

9   The Commander of the armies of heaven has done it to destroy your pride and show His contempt for all the greatness of mankind.

10   Sail on, O ships of Tarshish, for your harbor is gone!

11   The Lord holds out His hand over the seas; He shakes the kingdoms of the earth; He has spoken out against this great merchant city, to destroy its strength.

12   He says, "Never again, O dishonored virgin, daughter of Sidon, will you rejoice, will you be strong. Even if you flee to Cyprus, you will find no rest."

13   It will be the Babylonians, not the Assyrians, who consign Tyre to the wild beasts! They will lay siege to it, raze its palaces and make it a heap of ruins.

14   Wail, you ships that ply the oceans, for your home port is destroyed!

15, 16   For 70 years Tyre will be forgotten. Then, in the days of another king, the city will come back to life again; she will sing sweet songs as a harlot sings who, long absent from her lovers, walks the streets to look for them again and is remembered.

17 Yes, after 70 years, the Lord will revive Tyre, but she will be no different than she was before; she will return again to all her evil ways around the world.

18 Yet (the distant time will come when)[6] her businesses will give their profits to the Lord! They will not be hoarded but used for good food and fine clothes for the priests of the Lord!

## CHAPTER 24

Look! The Lord is overturning the land of Judah and making it a vast wasteland of destruction. See how He is emptying out all its people and scattering them over the face of the earth.

2 Priests and people, servants and masters, slave girls and mistresses, buyers and sellers, lenders and borrowers, bankers and debtors—none will be spared.

3 The land will be completely emptied and looted. The Lord has spoken.

4, 5 The land suffers for the sins of its people. The earth languishes, the crops wither, the skies refuse their rain. The land is defiled by crime; the people have twisted the laws of God and broken His everlasting commands.

6 Therefore the curse of God is upon them; they are left desolate, destroyed by the drought. Few will be left alive.

---

[6]Implied.

7   All the joys of life will go: the grape harvest will fail, the wine will be gone, the merrymakers will sigh and mourn.

8   The melodious chords of the harp and timbrel are heard no more; the happy days are ended.

9   No more are the joys of wine and song; strong drink turns bitter in the mouth.

10   The city lies in chaos; every home and shop is locked up tight to keep out looters.

11   Mobs form in the streets, crying for wine; joy has reached its lowest ebb; gladness has been banished from the land.

12   The city is left in ruins; its gates are battered down.

13   Throughout the land[7] the story is the same— only a remnant is left.

14   But all who are left will shout and sing for joy; those in the west will praise the majesty of God,

15, 16   And those in the east will respond with praise. Hear them singing to the Lord from the ends of the earth, singing glory to the Righteous One! But my heart is heavy with grief, for evil still prevails and treachery is everywhere.

17   Terror and the captivity of hell are still your lot, O men of the world.

18   When you flee in terror you will fall into a pit and if you escape from the pit you will step into a trap, for destruction falls from the heavens upon you; the world is shaken beneath you.

---

[7]Or possibly, "throughout the nations of the world."

19 The earth has broken down in utter collapse; everything is lost, abandoned and confused.

20 The world staggers like a drunkard; it shakes like a tent in a storm; it falls and will not rise again, for the sins of the earth are very great.

21 On that day the Lord will punish the fallen angels in the heavens, and the proud rulers of the nations on earth.

22 They will be rounded up like prisoners and imprisoned in a dungeon until they are tried and condemned.

23 Then the Lord of heaven's armies will mount His throne in Zion and rule gloriously in Jerusalem, in the sight of all the elders of His people. Such glory there will be that all the brightness of the sun and moon will seem to fade away.

## CHAPTER 25

O Lord, I will honor and praise Your Name, for You are my God; You do such wonderful things! You planned them long ago, and now You have accomplished them, just as You said!

2 You turn mighty cities into heaps of ruins. The strongest forts are turned to rubble. Beautiful palaces in distant lands disappear and never will be rebuilt.

3 Therefore strong nations will shake with fear before You; ruthless nations will obey and glorify Your name.

4   But to the poor, O Lord, You are a refuge from the storm, a shadow from the heat, a shelter from merciless men who are like a driving rain that melts down an earthen wall.

5   As a hot, dry land is cooled by clouds, You will cool the pride of ruthless nations.

6   Here on Mount Zion in Jerusalem, the Lord of Hosts will spread a wondrous feast for everyone around the world—a delicious feast of good food, with clear, well-aged wine and choice beef.

7   At that time He will remove the cloud of gloom, the pall of death that hangs over the earth;

8   He will swallow up death forever; the Lord God will wipe away all tears and take away forever all insults and mockery against His land and people. The Lord has spoken—He will surely do it!

9   In that day the people will proclaim, "This is our God, in whom we trust, for whom we waited. Now at last He is here." What a day of rejoicing!

10   For the Lord's good hand will rest upon Jerusalem, and Moab will be crushed as straw beneath His feet and left to rot.

11   God will push them down just as a swimmer pushes down the water with his hands. He will end their pride and all their evil works.

12   The high walls of Moab will be demolished and brought to dust.

## CHAPTER 26

Listen to them singing! In that day the whole land of Judah will sing this song:

"Our city is strong! We are surrounded by the walls of His salvation!"

2   Open the gates to everyone, for all may enter in who love the Lord.

3   He will keep in perfect peace all those who trust in Him, whose thoughts turn often to the Lord!

4   Trust in the Lord God always, for in the Lord Jehovah is your everlasting strength.

5   He humbles the proud and brings the haughty city to the dust; its walls come crashing down.

6   He presents it to the poor and needy for their use.

7   But for good men the path is not uphill and rough! God does not give them a rough and treacherous path, but smooths the road before them.

8   O Lord, we love to do Your will! Our hearts' desire is to glorify Your name.

9   All night long I search for You; earnestly I seek for God; for only when You come in judgment on the earth to punish it will people turn away from wickedness and do what is right.

10   Your kindness to the wicked doesn't make them good; they keep on doing wrong and take no notice of your majesty.

11   They do not listen when You threaten; they will not look to see Your upraised fist. Show them how much You love Your people. Perhaps then they will be ashamed! Yes, let them be burned up by the fire reserved for Your enemies.

12   Lord, grant us peace; for all we have and are has come from You.

13   O Lord our God, once we worshiped other gods; but now we worship You alone.

14   Those we served before are dead and gone; never again will they return. You came against them and destroyed them, and they are long forgotten.

15   O praise the Lord! He has made our nation very great. He has widened the boundaries of our land!

16   Lord, in their distress they sought for You. When Your punishment was on them, they poured forth a whispered prayer.

17   How we have missed Your presence, Lord! We suffered as a woman giving birth, who cries and writhes in pain.

18   We too have writhed in agony, but all to no avail. No deliverance has come from all our efforts.

19   Yet we have this assurance: Those who belong to God shall live again. Their bodies shall rise again! Those who dwell in the dust shall awake and sing for joy! For God's light of life will fall like dew upon them!

20   Go home, my people, and lock the doors! Hide for a little while until the Lord's wrath against your enemies has passed.

21   Look! The Lord is coming from the heavens to punish the people of the earth for their sins. The earth will no longer hide the murderers. The guilty will be found.

## CHAPTER 27

In that day the Lord will take His terrible, swift sword and punish leviathan, the swiftly moving serpent, the coiling, writhing serpent, the dragon of the sea.

2   In that day (of Israel's freedom[8]) let this anthem be their song:

3   Israel[8] is My vineyard; I, the Lord, will tend the fruitful vines; every day I'll water them, and day and night I'll watch to keep all enemies away.

4, 5   My anger against Israel[8] is gone. If I find thorns and briers bothering her, I will burn them up, unless these enemies of Mine surrender and beg for peace and My protection.

6   The time will come when Israel will take root and bud and blossom and fill the whole earth with her fruit!

7, 8   Has God punished Israel as much as He has punished her enemies? No, for He has devastated her enemies,[8] while he has punished Israel but a little, exiling her far from her own land as though blown away in a storm from the east.

9   And why did God do it? It was to purge away[9] her sins, to rid her of all her idol altars and her idols. They will never be worshiped again.

10   Her walled cities will be silent and empty, houses abandoned, streets grown up with grass, cows grazing through the city munching on twigs and branches.

11   My people are like the dead branches of a tree, broken off and used to burn beneath the pots. They are a foolish nation, a witless, stupid people, for they turn away from God. Therefore, He who made them will not have pity on them or show them His mercy.

---

[8]Implied.
[9]Literally, "atone for."

12  Yet the time will come when the Lord will gather them together one by one like handpicked grain, selecting them here and there from His great threshing floor that reaches all the way from the Euphrates River to the Egyptian boundary.

13  In that day the great trumpet will be blown, and many about to perish among their enemies, Assyria and Egypt, will be rescued and brought back to Jerusalem to worship the Lord in His holy mountain.


## CHAPTER 28

Woe to the city of Samaria, surrounded by her rich valley—Samaria, the pride and delight of the drunkards of Israel! Woe to her fading beauty, the crowning glory of a nation of men lying drunk in the streets!

2  For the Lord will send a mighty army (the Assyrians) against you; like a mighty hailstorm He will burst upon you and dash you to the ground.

3  The proud city of Samaria—yes, the joy and delight of the drunkards of Israel—will be hurled to the ground and trampled beneath the enemies' feet.

4  Once glorious, her fading beauty surrounded by a fertile valley will suddenly be gone, greedily snatched away as an early fig is hungrily snatched and gobbled up!

5  Then at last the Lord of Hosts himself will be their crowning glory, the diadem of beauty to His people who are left.

6 He will give a longing for justice to your judges and great courage to your soldiers who are battling to the last before your gates.

7 But Jerusalem is now led by drunks! Her priests and prophets reel and stagger, making stupid errors and mistakes.

8 Their tables are covered with vomit; filth is everywhere.

9 "Who does Isaiah think he is," the people say, "to speak to us like this! Are we little children, barely old enough to talk?

10 He tells us everything over and over again, a line at a time and in such simple words!"

11 But they won't listen; the only language they can understand is punishment! So God will punish them by sending against them foreigners who speak strange gibberish! Only then will they listen to Him!

12 They could have rest in their own land if they would obey Him, if they were kind and good. He told them that, but they wouldn't listen to Him.

13 So the Lord will spell it out for them again, repeating it over and over in simple words whenever He can; yet over this simple, straightforward message they will stumble and fall and be broken, trapped and captured.

14 Therefore hear the word of the Lord, you scoffing rulers in Jerusalem:

15 You have struck a bargain with Death, you say, and sold yourselves to the devil[1] in exchange for his

---
[1]Literally, "Sheol," "the underworld."

protection against the Assyrians. "They can never touch us," you say, "for we are under the care of one who will deceive and fool them."

16 But the Lord God says, See, I am placing a Foundation Stone in Zion—a firm, tested, precious Cornerstone that is safe to build on. He who believes need never run away again.

17 I will take the line and plummet of justice to check the foundation wall you built; it looks so fine, but it is so weak a storm of hail will knock it down! The enemy will come like a flood and sweep it away, and you will be drowned.

18 I will cancel your agreement of compromise with Death and the devil, so when the terrible enemy floods in, you will be trampled into the ground.

19 Again and again that flood will come and carry you off, until at last the unmixed horror of the truth of My warnings will finally dawn on you.

20 The bed you have made is far too short to lie on; the blankets are too narrow to cover you.

21 The Lord will come suddenly and in anger, as at Mount Perazim and Gibeon, to do a strange, unusual thing—to destroy His own people!

22 So scoff no more, lest your punishment be made even greater; for the Lord God of Hosts has plainly told me that He is determined to crush you.

23, 24 Listen to me, listen as I plead: Does a farmer always plow and never sow? Is he forever harrowing the soil and never planting it?

25 Does he not finally plant his many kinds of grain, each in its own section of his land?

26   He knows just what to do, for God has made him see and understand.

27   He doesn't thresh all grains the same. A sledge is never used on dill, but it is beaten with a stick. A threshing wheel is never rolled on cummin, but it is beaten softly with a flail.

28   Bread grain is easily crushed, so he doesn't keep on pounding it.

29   The Lord of Hosts is a wonderful teacher and gives the farmer wisdom.

## CHAPTER 29

Woe to Jerusalem,[2] the city of David. Year after year you make your many offerings,

2   But I will send heavy judgment upon you and there will be weeping and sorrow. For Jerusalem shall become as her name "Ariel" means—an altar covered with blood.

3   I will be your enemy. I will surround Jerusalem and lay siege against it, and build forts around it to destroy it.

4   Your voice will whisper like a ghost from the earth where you lie buried.

5   But suddenly your ruthless enemies will be driven away like chaff before the wind.

6   In an instant, I, the Lord of Hosts, will come upon them with thunder, earthquake, whirlwind and fire.

---

²Literally, "to Ariel."

7 And all the nations fighting Jerusalem will vanish like a dream!

8 As a hungry man dreams of eating, but is still hungry, and as a thirsty man dreams of drinking but is still faint from thirst when he wakes up, so your enemies will dream of victorious conquest, but all to no avail.

9 You are amazed, incredulous? You don't believe it? Then go ahead and be blind if you must! You are stupid—and not from drinking, either! Stagger, and not from wine!

10 For the Lord has poured out upon you a spirit of deep sleep. He has closed the eyes of your prophets and seers,

11 So all of these future events are a sealed book to them. When you give it to one who can read he says, "I can't, for it's sealed."

12 When you give it to another, he says, "Sorry, I can't read."

13 And so the Lord says, "Since these people say they are Mine but they do not obey Me, and since their worship amounts to mere words learned by rote,

14 Therefore I will take awesome vengeance on these hypocrites, and make their wisest counselors as fools."

15 Woe to those who try to hide their plans from God, who try to keep Him in the dark concerning what they do! "God can't see us," they say to themselves. "He doesn't know what is going on!"

16 How stupid can they be! Isn't He, the Potter, greater than you, the jars He makes? Will you say to

Him, "He didn't make us?" Does a machine call its inventor dumb?

17 Soon—and it will not be very long—the wilderness of Lebanon will be a fruitful field again, a lush and fertile forest.

18 In that day the deaf will hear the words of a book, and out of their gloom and darkness the blind will see My plans.

19 The meek will be filled with fresh joy from the Lord, and the poor shall exult in the Holy One of Israel.

20 Bullies will vanish and scoffers will cease, and all those plotting evil will be killed—

21 The violent man who fights at the drop of a hat, the man who waits in hiding to beat up the judge who sentenced him, and the men who use any excuse to be unfair.

22 That is why the Lord who redeemed Abraham says: My people will no longer pale with fear, or be ashamed.

23 For when they see the surging birth rate and the expanding economy,[3] then they will fear and rejoice in My name, and praise the Holy One of Israel, and stand in awe of Him.

24 Those in error will believe the truth, and complainers will be willing to be taught!

## CHAPTER 30

Woe to my rebellious children, says the Lord; you ask advice from everyone but Me, and decide to

---

[3]Literally, "when he sees his children, the work of My hands, in his midst."

do what I don't want you to do. You yoke yourselves with unbelievers, thus piling up your sins.

2 For without consulting Me you have gone down to Egypt to find aid and have put your trust in Pharoah for his protection.[4]

3 But in trusting Pharoah, you will be disappointed, humiliated and disgraced, for he can't deliver on his promises to save you.

4 For though his power extends to Zoan and Hanes,

5 Yet it will all turn out to your shame—he won't help one little bit!

6 See them moving slowly across the terrible desert to Egypt—donkeys and camels laden down with treasure to pay for Egypt's aid. On through the badlands they go, where lions and swift venomous snakes live— and Egypt will give you nothing in return!

7 For Egypt's promises are worthless! "The Reluctant Dragon,"[5] I call her!

8 Now go and write down this word of Mine concerning Egypt, so that it will stand until the end of time, forever and forever, as an indictment of Israel's unbelief.

9 For if you don't write it, they will claim I never warned them. "Oh, no," they'll say, "You never told us that!" For they are stubborn rebels.

10, 11 They tell My prophets, "Shut up—we don't want any more of your reports!" Or they say, "Don't tell us the truth; tell us nice things; tell us lies. Forget

---

[4]Hezakiah was seeking a defensive alliance with Ethiopia's Egyptian dynasty against Sennacherib of Assyria.
[5]Literally, "Rahab who sits still."

all this gloom; we've heard more than enough about your 'Holy One of Israel' and all He says."

12   This is the reply of the Holy One of Israel: Because you despise what I tell you and trust instead in frauds and lies and won't repent,

13   Therefore calamity will come upon you suddenly, as upon a bulging wall that bursts and falls; in one moment it comes crashing down.

14   God will smash you like a broken dish; He will not act sparingly. Not a piece will be left large enough to use for carrying coals from the hearth, or a little water from the well.

15   For the Lord God, the Holy One of Israel, says; Only in returning to Me and waiting for Me will you be saved; in quietness and confidence is your strength; but you'll have none of this.

16   "No," you say. "We will get our help from Egypt; they will give us swift horses for riding to battle." But the only swiftness you are going to see is the swiftness of your enemies chasing you!

17   One of them will chase a thousand of you! Five of them will scatter you until not two of you are left together. You will be like lonely trees in the distant mountain tops.

18   Yet the Lord still waits for you to come to Him, so He can show you His love; He will conquer you to bless you, just as He said. For the Lord is faithful to His promises. Blessed are all those who wait for Him to help them.

19   O my people in Jerusalem, you shall weep no

more; for He will surely be gracious to you at the sound of your cry. He will answer you.

20 Though He give you the bread of adversity and water of affliction, yet He will be with you to teach you—with your own eyes you will see your Teacher.

21 And if you leave God's paths and go astray, you will hear a Voice behind you say, "No, this is the way; walk here."

22 And you will destroy all your silver idols and golden images and cast them out like filthy things you hate to touch. "Ugh!" you'll say to them, "Be gone!"

23 Then God will bless you with rain at planting time and with wonderful harvests and with ample pastures for your cows.

24 The oxen and young donkeys that till the ground will eat clean straw, its chaff blown away by the wind.

25 In that day when God steps in to destroy your enemies, He will give you streams of water flowing down each mountain and every hill.

26 The moon will be as bright as the sun, and the sunlight brighter than seven days! So it will be when the Lord begins to heal His people and to cure the wounds He gave them.

27 See, the Lord comes from afar, aflame with wrath, surrounded by thick rising smoke. His lips are filled with fury; His words consume like fire.

28 His wrath pours out like floods upon them all, to sweep them all away. He will sift out the proud nations and bridle them and lead them off to their doom.

29  But the people of God will sing a song of solemn joy, like songs in the night when holy feasts are held; His people will have gladness of heart, as when a flutist leads a pilgrim band to Jerusalem to the Mountain of the Lord, the Rock of Israel.

30  And the Lord shall cause His majestic voice to be heard and shall crush down His mighty arm upon His enemies with angry indignation and with devouring flames and tornados and terrible storms and huge hailstones.

31  The voice of the Lord shall punish the Assyrians, who had been His rod of punishment.

32  And when the Lord smites them, His people will rejoice with music and song.

33  The funeral pyre has long been ready, prepared for Moloch, the Assyrian god; it is piled high with wood. The breath of the Lord, like fire from a volcano, will set it all on fire.


## CHAPTER 31

Woe to those who run to Egypt for help, trusting their mighty cavalry and chariots instead of looking to the Holy One of Israel and consulting Him.

2  In His wisdom, He will send great evil on His people and will not change His mind. He will rise against them for the evil they have done, and crush their allies too.

3  For these Egyptians are mere men, not God!

Their horses are puny flesh, not mighty spirits! When the Lord clenches His fist against them, they will stumble and fall among those they are trying to help. All will fail together.

*     *     *     *     *

4, 5   But the Lord has told me this: When a lion, even a young one, kills a sheep, he pays no attention to the shepherd's shouts and noise. He goes right on and eats. In such manner the Lord will come and fight upon Mount Zion. He will not be frightened away! He, the Lord of Hosts, will hover over Jerusalem as birds hover round their nests, and He will defend the city and deliver it.

6   Therefore, O my people, though you are such wicked rebels, come, return to God.

7   I know the glorious day will come when every one of you will throw away his golden idols and silver images—which in your sinfulness you have made.

8   And the Assyrians will be destroyed, but not by swords of men. The "sword of God" will smite them. They will panic and flee, and the strong young Assyrians will be taken away as slaves.

9   Even their generals will quake with terror and flee when they see the battle flags of Israel, says the Lord. For the flame of God burns brightly in Jerusalem.

## CHAPTER 32

Look, a righteous king is coming, with honest princes!
2   He will shelter Israel from the storm and wind. He will refresh her as a river in the desert and

as the cooling shadow of a mighty rock within a hot and weary land.

3     Then at last the eyes of Israel will open wide to God; His people will listen to His voice.

4     Even the hotheads among them will be full of sense and understanding, and those who stammer in uncertainty will speak out plainly.

5     In those days the ungodly, the atheists, will not be heroes! Wealthy cheaters will not be spoken of as generous, outstanding men!

6     Everyone will recognize an evil man when he sees him, and hypocrites will fool no one at all. Their lies about God and their cheating of the hungry will be plain for all to see.

7     The smooth tricks of evil men will be exposed, as will all the lies they use to oppress the poor in the courts.

8     But good men will be generous to others and will be blessed of God for all they do.

9     Listen, you women who loll around in lazy ease; listen to me and I will tell you your reward:

10    In a short time—in just a little more than a year—suddenly you'll care, O careless ones. For the crops of fruit will fail; the harvest will not take place.

11    Tremble, O women of ease; throw off your unconcern. Strip off your pretty clothes—wear sackcloth for your grief.

12    Beat your breasts in sorrow for those bountiful farms of yours that will soon be gone, and for those fruitful vines of other years.

13  For your lands will thrive with thorns and briers; your joyous homes and happy cities will be gone.

14  Palaces and mansions will all be deserted, the crowded cities empty. Wild herds of donkeys and goats will graze upon the mountains where the watchtowers are,

15  Until at last the Spirit is poured down on us from heaven. Then once again enormous crops will come.

16  Then justice will rule through all the land,

17  And out of justice, peace. Quietness and confidence will reign forever more.

18  My people will live in safety, quietly at home.

19  But the Assyrians[6] will be destroyed and their cities laid low.

20  And God will greatly bless His people. Wherever they plant, bountiful crops will spring up, and their flocks and herds will graze in green pastures.

## CHAPTER 33

Woe to you, Assyrians,[7] who have destroyed everything around you but have never felt destruction for yourselves. You expect others to respect their promises to you, while you betray them! Now you, too, will be betrayed and destroyed.

2  But to us, O Lord, be merciful, for we have

---

[6]Implied.
[7]Implied.

waited for You. Be our strength each day and our salvation in the time of trouble.

3 The enemy runs at the sound of Your voice. When You stand up, the nations flee.

4 Just as locusts strip the fields and vines, so Jerusalem will strip the fallen army of Assyria![8]

5 The Lord is very great, and lives in heaven. He will make Jerusalem the home of justice and goodness and righteousness.

6 An abundance of salvation is stored up for Judah in a safe place, along with wisdom and knowledge and reverence for God.

7 But now your ambassadors weep in bitter disappointment, for Assyria has refused their cry for peace.

8 Your roads lie in ruins; travelers detour on back roads. The Assyrians have broken their peace pact[9] and care nothing for the promises they made in the presence of witnesses—they have no respect for anyone.

9 All the land of Israel is in trouble; Lebanon has been destroyed; Sharon has become a wilderness; Bashan and Carmel are plundered.

10 But the Lord says, I will stand up and show My power and might.

11 You Assyrians will gain nothing by all your efforts. Your own breath will turn to fire and kill you.

12 Your armies will be burned to lime, like thorns cut down and tossed in the fire.

---

[8] 2 Kings 19:35.
[9] 2 Kings 18:14-17.

13 Listen to what I have done, O nations far away! And you that are near, acknowledge My might!

14 The sinners among My people shake with fear. "Which one of us," they cry, "can live here in the presence of this all-consuming, Everlasting Fire?"

15 I will tell you who can live here: All who are honest and fair, who reject making profit by fraud, who hold back their hands from taking bribes, who refuse to listen to those who plot murder, who shut their eyes to all enticement to do wrong.

16 Such as these shall dwell on high. The rocks of the mountains will be their fortress of safety; food will be supplied to them and they will have all the water they need.

17 Your eyes will see the King in His beauty, and the highlands of heaven far away.

18 Your mind will think back to this time of terror when the Assyrian officers outside your walls are counting your towers and estimating how much they will get from your fallen city.

19 But soon they will all be gone. These fierce, violent people, with a strange, jabbering language you can't understand, will disappear.

20 Instead you will see Jerusalem at peace, a place where God is worshiped, a city quiet and unmoved.

21 The glorious Lord will be to us as a wide river of protection, and no enemy can cross.

22 For the Lord is our Judge, our Lawgiver and our King; He will care for us and save us.

23 The enemies' sails hang loose on broken masts

with useless tackle. Their treasure will be divided by the people of God; even the lame will win their share.

24 The people of Israel will no longer say, "We are sick and helpless," for the Lord will forgive them their sins and bless them.

## CHAPTER 34

Come here and listen, O nations of the earth; let the world and everything in it hear my words.

2 For the Lord is enraged against the nations; His fury is against their armies. He will utterly destroy them and deliver them to slaughter.

3 Their dead will be left unburied, and the stench of rotting bodies will fill the land, and the mountains will flow with their blood.

4 At that time the heavens above will melt away and disappear just like a rolled up scroll, and the stars will fall as leaves, as ripe fruit from the trees.

5 And when My sword has finished its work in the heavens, then watch, for it will fall upon Edom, the people I have doomed.

6 The sword of the Lord is sated with blood; it is gorged with flesh as though used for slaying lambs and goats for sacrifice. For the Lord will slay a great sacrifice in Edom and make a mighty slaughter there.

7 The strongest will perish, young boys and veterans too. The land will be soaked with blood, and the soil made rich with fat.

8　For it is the day of vengeance, the year of recompense for what Edom has done to Israel.

9　The streams of Edom will be filled with burning pitch, and the ground will be covered with fire.

10　This judgment on Edom will never end. Its smoke will rise up forever. The land will lie deserted from generation to generation; no one will live there any more.

11　There the hawks and porcupines will live, and owls and ravens. For God will observe that land and find it worthy of destruction. He will test its nobles and find them worthy of death.

12　It will be called "The Land of Nothing," and its princes soon will all be gone.

13　Thorns will overrun the palaces, and nettles will grow in its forts; and it will become the haunt of jackals and a home for ostriches.

14　The wild animals of the desert will mingle there with wolves and hyenas. Their howls will fill the night. There the night-monsters will scream at each other, and the demons will come there to rest.

15　There the owl will make her nest and lay her eggs and hatch her young and nestle them beneath her wings; and the kites will come, each one with its mate.

16　Search the Book of the Lord and see all that He will do; not one detail will He miss; not one kite will be there without a mate, for the Lord has said it, and His Spirit will make it all come true.

17　He has surveyed and subdivided the land and deeded it to those doleful creatures; they shall possess it forever, from generation to generation.

## CHAPTER 35

Even the wilderness and desert will rejoice in those days; the desert will blossom with flowers.

2 Yes, there will be an abundance of flowers and singing and joy! The deserts will become as green as the Lebanon mountains, as lovely as Mount Carmel's pastures and Sharon's meadows; for the Lord will display His glory there, the excellency of our God.

3 With this news bring cheer to all discouraged ones.

4 Encourage those who are afraid. Tell them, "Be strong, fear not, for your God is coming to destroy your enemies. He is coming to save you."

5 And when He comes, He will open the eyes of the blind, and unstop the ears of the deaf.

6 The lame man will leap up like a deer, and those who could not speak will shout and sing! Springs will burst forth in the wilderness, and streams in the desert.

7 The parched ground will become a pool, with springs of water in the thirsty land. Where desert jackals lived, there will be reeds and rushes!

8 And a main road will go through that once-deserted land; it will be named "The Holy Highway." No evil-hearted men may walk upon it. God will walk there with you; even the most stupid cannot miss the way.

9 No lion will lurk along its course, nor will there

be any other dangers; only the redeemed will travel there.

10   These, the ransomed of the Lord, will go home along that road to Zion, singing the songs of everlasting joy. For them all sorrow and all sighing will be gone forever; only joy and gladness will be there.

## CHAPTER 36

So in the fourteenth year of King Hezekiah's reign, Sennacherib, king of Assyria, came to fight against the walled cities of Judah and conquered them.

2   Then he sent his personal representative with a great army from Lachish to confer with King Hezekiah in Jerusalem. He camped near the outlet of the upper pool, along the road going past the field where cloth is bleached.

3   Then Eliakim, Hilkiah's son, who was the prime minister of Israel, and Shebna, the king's scribe, and Joah (Asaph's son), the royal secretary, formed a truce team and went out of the city to meet with him.

4   The Assyrian ambassador told them to go and say to Hezekiah, "The mighty king of Assyria says you are a fool to think that the king of Egypt will help you.

5   What are the Pharaoh's promises worth? Mere words won't substitute for strength, yet you rely on him for help, and have rebelled against Me!

6   Egypt is a dangerous ally. She is a sharpened stick that will pierce your hand if you lean on it. That is

the experience of everyone who has ever looked to her for help.

7 But perhaps you say, 'We are trusting in the Lord our God!' Oh? Isn't He the one your king insulted, tearing down His temples and altars in the hills and making everyone in Judah worship only at the altars here in Jerusalem?

8, 9 My master, the king of Assyria, wants to make a little bet with you!—that you don't have 2000 men left in your entire army! If you do, he will give you 2000 horses for them to ride on! With that tiny army, how can you think of proceeding against even the smallest and worst contingent of my master's troops? For you'll get no help from Egypt.

10 What's more, do you think I have come here without the Lord's telling me to take this land? The Lord said to me, 'Go and destroy it!' "

11 Then Eliakim and Shebna and Joah said to him, "Please talk to us in Aramaic[a] for we understand it quite well. Don't speak in Hebrew, for the people on the wall will hear."

12 But he replied, "My master wants everyone in Jerusalem to hear this, not just you. He wants them to know that if you don't surrender, this city will be put under siege until everyone is so hungry and thirsty that he will eat his own dung and drink his own urine."

13 Then he shouted in Hebrew to the Jews listening on the wall, "Hear the words of the great king, the king of Assyria:

---

[a]Aramaic was the language used in international diplomacy at this time.

14 Don't let Hezekiah fool you—nothing he can do will save you.

15 Don't let him talk you into trusting in the Lord by telling you the Lord won't let you be conquered by the king of Assyria.

16 Don't listen to Hezekiah, for here is the king of Assyria's offer to you: Give me a present as a token of surrender; open the gates and come out, and I will let you each have your own farm and garden and water,

17 Until I can arrange to take you to a country very similar to this one—a country where there are bountiful harvests of grain and grapes, a land of plenty.

18 Don't let Hezekiah deprive you of all this by saying the Lord will deliver you from my armies. Has any other nation's gods ever gained victory over the armies of the King of Assyria?

19 Don't you remember what I did to Hamath and Arpad? Did their gods save them? And what about Sepharvaim and Samaria? Where are their gods now?

20 Of all the gods of these lands, which one has ever delivered their people from my power? Name just one! And do you think this God of yours can deliver Jerusalem from me? Don't be ridiculous!"

21 But the people were silent and answered not a word, for Hezekiah had told them to say nothing in reply.

22 Then Eliakim (son of Hilkiah), the prime minister, and Shebna, the royal scribe, and Joah (son of Asaph), the royal secretary, went back to Hezekiah with clothes ripped to shreds as a sign of their despair and told him all that had happened.

# CHAPTER 37

When King Hezekiah heard the results of the meeting, he tore his robes and wound himself in coarse cloth used for making sacks, as a sign of humility and mourning, and went over to the Temple to pray.

2 Meanwhile he sent Eliakim his prime minister, and Shebna his royal scribe, and the older priests—all dressed in sackcloth—to Isaiah the prophet, son of Amoz.

3 They brought him this message from Hezekiah: "This is a day of trouble and frustration and blasphemy; it is a serious time, as when a woman is in heavy labor trying to give birth, and the child does not come.

4 But perhaps the Lord your God heard the blasphemy of the king of Assyria's representative as he scoffed at the Living God. Surely God won't let him get away with this! Surely God will rebuke him for those words! Oh, Isaiah, pray for us who are left!"

5 So they took the king's message to Isaiah.

6 Then Isaiah replied, "Tell King Hezekiah that the Lord says, Don't be disturbed by this speech from the servant of the king of Assyria, and his blasphemy.

7 For a report from Assyria will reach the king that he is needed at home at once, and he will return to his own land, where I will have him killed."

8, 9 Now the Assyrian envoy left Jerusalem and went to consult his king, who had left Lachish and was besieging Libnah. But at this point the Assyrian king received word that Tirhakah, crown prince of Ethiopia, was leading an army against him (from the south).[4] Upon hearing this, he sent messengers back to Jerusalem to Hezekiah with this message:

10   "Don't let this God you trust in fool you by promising that Jerusalem will not be captured by the King of Assyria!

11   Just remember what has happened wherever the kings of Assyria have gone, for they have crushed everyone who has opposed them. Do you think you will be any different?

12   Did their gods save the cities of Gozan, Haran, or Rezeph, or the people of Eden in Telassar? No, the Assyrian kings completely destroyed them!

13   And don't forget what happened to the king of Hamath, to the king of Arpad, and to the kings of the cities of Sepharavaim, Hena, and Ivvah."

14   As soon as King Hezekiah had read this letter, he went over to the Temple and spread it out before the Lord,

15   And prayed, saying,

16, 17   "O Lord of Hosts, God of Israel enthroned above the cherubim, YOU ALONE are God of all the kingdoms of the earth. You alone made heaven and earth. Listen as I plead; see me as I pray; look at this letter from King Sennacherib, for he has mocked the Living God.

18   It is true, O Lord, that the kings of Assyria have destroyed all those nations, just as the letter says,

---

[4]Implied.

19 And thrown their gods into the fire; for they weren't gods at all, but merely idols, carved by men from wood and stone. Of course the Assyrians could destroy them.

20 O Lord our God, save us so that all the kingdoms of the earth will know that You are God, and You alone."

21 Then Isaiah, the son of Amoz, sent this message to King Hezekiah: "The Lord God of Israel says, This is My answer to your prayer against Sennacherib, Assyria's king.

22 The Lord says to him: My people—the helpless virgin daughter of Zion—laughs at you and scoffs and shakes her head at you in scorn.

23 Who is it you scoffed against and mocked? Whom did you revile? At whom did you direct your violence and pride? It was against the Holy One of Israel!

24 You have sent your messengers to mock the Lord. You boast, 'I came with my mighty army against the nations of the west. I cut down the tallest cedars and choicest cypress trees. I conquered their highest mountains and destroyed their thickest forests.'

25 You boast of wells you've dug in many a conquered land, and Egypt with all its armies is no obstacle to you!

26 But do you not yet know that it was I who decided all this long ago? That it was I who gave you all this power from ancient times? I have caused all this to happen as I planned—that you should crush walled cities into ruined heaps.

27   That's why their people had so little power, and were such easy prey for you. They were as helpless as the grass, as tender plants you trample down beneath your feet, as grass upon the housetops, burnt yellow by the sun.

28   But I know you well—your comings and goings and all you do—and the way you have raged against Me.

29   Because of your anger against the Lord—and I heard it all!—I have put a hook in your nose and a bit in your mouth and led you back to your own land by the same road you came."

30   Then God said to Hezekiah, "Here is the proof that I am the One who is delivering this city from the king of Assyria: This year[5] he will abandon his siege. Although it is too late now to plant your crops, and you will have only volunteer grain this fall, still it will give you enough seed for a small harvest next year, and two years from now[6] you will be living in luxury again.

31   And you who are left in Judah will take root again in your own soil and flourish and multiply.

32   For a remnant shall go out from Jerusalem to repopulate the land; the power of the Lord of Hosts will cause all this to come to pass.

33   As for the king of Assyria, his armies shall not enter Jerusalem, nor shoot their arrows there, nor march outside its gates, nor build up an earthen bank against its walls.

---

[5]Implied.
[6]The third harvest from then would yield a bumper crop.

34   He will return to his own country by the road he came on, and will not enter this city, says the Lord.

35   For My own honor I will defend it, and in memory of My servant David."

36   That night the Angel of the Lord went out to the camp of the Assyrians and killed 185,000 soldiers; when the living wakened the next morning, all these lay dead before them.

37   Then Sennacherib, king of Assyria, returned to his own country, to Nineveh.

38   And one day while he was worshiping in the temple of Nisroch his god, his sons Adrammelech and Sharezer killed him with their swords; then they escaped into the land of Ararat, and Essarhaddon his son became king.

## CHAPTER 38

It was just before all this that Hezekiah became deathly sick and Isaiah the prophet (Amoz' son) went to visit him and gave him this message from the Lord: "Set your affairs in order, for you are going to die; you will not recover from this illness."

2   When Hezekiah heard this, he turned his face to the wall and prayed:

3   "O Lord, don't You remember how true I've been to You and how I've always tried to obey You in everything You said?" Then he broke down with great sobs.

4   So the Lord sent another message to Isaiah:

5   "Go and tell Hezekiah that the Lord God of your forefather David hears you praying and sees your tears and will let you live 15 more years.

6   He will deliver you and this city from the king of Assyria. I will defend you, says the Lord,

7   And here is My guarantee:

8   I will send the sun backwards ten degrees as measured on Ahaz' sun dial!" So the sun retraced ten degrees that it had gone down!

9   When King Hezekiah was well again, he wrote this poem about his experience:

10   "My life is but half done and I must leave it all. I am robbed of my normal years, and now I must enter the gates of Sheol.

11   Never again will I see the Lord in the land of the living. Never again will I see my friends in this world.

12   My life is blown away like a shepherd's tent; it is cut short as when a weaver stops his working at the loom. In one short day my life hangs by a thread.

13   All night I moaned; it was like being torn apart by lions.

14   Delirious, I chattered like a swallow and mourned like a dove; my eyes grew weary of looking up for help. 'O God,' I cried, 'I am in trouble—help me.'

15   But what can I say? For He Himself has sent this sickness. All my sleep has fled because of my soul's bitterness.

16   O Lord, Your discipline is good and leads to life and health. Oh, heal me and make me live!

17   Yes, now I see it all—it was good for me to undergo this bitterness, for You have lovingly delivered me from death; You have forgiven all my sins.

18   For dead men cannot praise You.[7] They cannot be filled with hope and joy.

19   The living, only the living, can praise You as I do today. One generation makes known Your faithfulness to the next.

20   Think of it! The Lord healed me! Every day of my life from now on I will sing my songs of praise in the Temple, accompanied by the orchestra."

21   (For Isaiah had told Hezekiah's servants, "Make an ointment of figs and spread it over the boil, and he will get well again."

22   And then Hezekiah had asked, "What sign will the Lord give me to prove that He will heal me?")

## CHAPTER 39

S oon afterwards, the king of Babylon (Merodachbaladan, the son of Baladan) sent Hezekiah a present and his best wishes,[8] for he had heard that Hezekiah had been very sick and now was well again.

2   Hezekiah appreciated this and took the envoys from Babylon on a tour of the palace, showing them his

---

[7]The meaning is unclear. Perhaps Hezekiah was unaware of the blessedness of the future life for those who trust in God (Isaiah 57:1,2). Or perhaps his meaning is that "Dead bodies cannot praise You."
[8]Merodach-baladan was at this time planning a revolt in the east against Sennacherib, so he was especially interested in Hezekiah's activities in the west.

treasure house full of silver, gold, spices and perfumes. He took them into his jewel rooms, too, and opened to them all his treasures—everything.

3    Then Isaiah the prophet came to the king and said, "What did they say? Where are they from?" "From far away in Babylon," Hezekiah replied.

4    "How much have they seen?" asked Isaiah. And Hezekiah replied, "I showed them everything I own, all my priceless treasures."

5    Then Isaiah said to him, "Listen to this message from the Lord of Hosts:

6    The time is coming when everything you have— all the treasures stored up by your fathers—will be carried off to Babylon. Nothing will be left.

7    And some of your own sons will become slaves, yes, eunuchs, in the palace of the king of Babylon."

8    "All right," Hezekiah replied. "Whatever the Lord says is good. At least there will be peace during my lifetime!"

## CHAPTER 40

Comfort, oh, comfort My people, says your God.

2    Speak tenderly to Jerusalem and tell her that her sad days are gone. Her sins are pardoned, and the Lord will give her twice as many blessings as He gave her punishment before.

3    Listen! I hear the voice of someone shouting, "Make a road for the Lord through the wilderness; make Him a straight, smooth road through the desert.

4  Fill the valleys; level the hills; straighten out the crooked paths and smooth off the rough spots in the road.

5  The glory of the Lord will be seen by all mankind together." The Lord has spoken—it shall be.

6  The voice says, "Shout!"

"What shall I shout?" I asked.

"Shout that man is like the grass that dies away, and all his beauty fades like dying flowers.

7  The grass withers, the flower fades beneath the breath of God. And so it is with fragile man.

8  The grass withers, the flowers fade, but the Word of our God shall stand forever."

9  O Crier of Good News, shout to Jerusalem from the mountain tops! Shout louder—don't be afraid —tell the cities of Judah, "Your God is coming!"

10  Yes, the Lord God is coming with mighty power; He will rule with awesome strength. See, His reward is with Him, to each as he has done.

11  He will feed His flock like a shepherd; He will carry the lambs in His arms and gently lead the ewes with young.

12  Who else has held the oceans in His hands and measured off the heavens with His ruler? Who else knows the weight of all the earth and weighs the mountains and the hills?

13  Who can advise the Spirit of the Lord or be His teacher or give Him counsel?

14  Has He ever needed anyone's advice? Did He need instruction as to what is right and best?

15 No, for all the peoples of the world are nothing in comparison with Him—they are but a drop in the bucket, dust on the scales. He picks up the islands as though they had no weight at all.

16 All of Lebanon's forests do not contain sufficient fuel to consume a sacrifice large enough to honor Him, nor are all its animals enough to offer to our God.

17 All the nations are as nothing to Him; in His eyes they are less than nothing—mere emptiness and froth.

18 How can we describe God? With what can we compare Him?

19 With an idol? An idol, made from a mold, overlaid with gold, and with silver chains around its neck?

20 The man too poor to buy expensive gods like that will find a tree free from rot and hire a man to carve a face on it, and that's his god—a god that cannot even move!

21 Are you so ignorant? Are you so deaf to the words of God—the words He gave before the worlds began? Have you never heard nor understood?

22 It is God who sits above the circle of the earth. (The people below must seem to Him like grasshoppers!) He is the One who stretches out the heavens like a curtain and makes His tent from them.

23 He dooms the great men of the world and brings them all to naught.

24 They hardly get started, barely take root, when He blows on them and their work withers and the wind carries them off like straw.

25 "With whom will you compare Me? Who is My equal?" asks the Holy One.

26 Look up into the heavens! Who created all these stars? As a shepherd[9] leads his sheep, calling each by its pet name, and counts them to see that none are lost or strayed, so God does with stars and planets!

27 O Jacob, O Israel, how can you say that the Lord doesn't see your troubles and isn't being fair?

28 Don't you yet understand? Don't you know by now that the everlasting God, the Creator of the farthest parts of the earth, never grows faint or weary? No one can fathom the depths of His understanding.

29 He gives power to the tired and worn out, and strength to the weak.

30 Even the youths shall be exhausted, and the young men will all give up.

31 But they that wait upon the Lord shall renew their strength; they shall mount up with wings like eagles; they shall run and not be weary; they shall walk and not faint.

## CHAPTER 41

Listen in silence before Me, O lands beyond the sea. Bring your strongest arguments. Come now and speak. The court is ready for your case.

2 Who has stirred up this one from the east,[1] whom victory meets at every step? Who, indeed, but the Lord? God has given him victory over many nations

9Implied.
1Doubtless Cyrus the Great of Persia. See Isaiah 44:28.

and permitted him to trample kings underfoot and to put entire armies to the sword.

3     He chases them away and goes on safely, though the paths he treads are new.

4     Who has done such mighty deeds, directing the affairs of generations of mankind as they march by? It is I, the Lord, the First and Last; I alone am He.

5     The lands beyond the sea watch in fear and wait for word of Cyrus' new campaigns. Remote lands tremble and mobilize for war.

6     Each man encourages his neighbor and says, "Don't worry. He won't win."

7     But they rush to make a new idol; the carver hurries the goldsmith, and the molder helps at the anvil. "Good," they say. "It's coming along fine. Now we can solder on the arms." Carefully they join the parts together, and then fasten the thing in place so it won't fall over!

8     But as for you, O Israel, you are Mine, My chosen ones; for you are Abraham's family, and he was My friend.

9     I have called you back from the ends of the earth and said that you must serve but Me alone, for I have chosen you and will not throw you away.

10     Fear not, for I am with you. Do not be dismayed. I am your God. I will strengthen you; I will help you; I will uphold you with My victorious right hand.[2]

11     See, all your angry enemies lie confused and shattered. Anyone opposing you will die.

---

[2]Or, "with the right hand of My righteousness."

12  You will look for them in vain—they will all be gone.

13  I am holding you by your right hand—I, the Lord your God—and I say to you, Don't be afraid; I am here to help you.

14  Despised though you are, fear not, O Israel; for I will help you. I am the Lord, your Redeemer; I am the Holy One of Israel.

15  You shall be a new and sharp-toothed threshing instrument to tear all enemies apart, making chaff of mountains.

16  You shall toss them in the air; the wind shall blow them all away; whirlwinds shall scatter them. And the joy of the Lord shall fill you full; you shall glory in the God of Israel.

17  When the poor and needy seek water and there is none and their tongues are parched from thirst, then I will answer when they cry to Me. I, Israel's God, will not ever forsake them.

18  I will open up rivers for them on high plateaus! I will give them fountains of water in the valleys! In the deserts will be pools of water, and rivers fed by springs shall flow across the dry, parched ground.

19  I will plant trees—cedars, myrtle, olive trees, the cypress, fir and pine—on barren land.

20  Everyone will see this miracle and understand that it is God who did it, Israel's Holy One.

21  Can your idols make such claims as these? Let them come and show what they can do! says God, the King of Israel.

22   Let them try to tell us what occurred in years gone by, or what the future holds.

23   Yes, that's it! If you are gods, tell what will happen in the days ahead! Or do some mighty miracle that makes us stare, amazed.

24   But no! You are less than nothing, and can do nothing at all. Anyone who chooses you needs to have his head examined!

25   But I have stirred up (Cyrus) from the north and east; he will come against the nations and call on My name, and I will give him victory over kings and princes. He will tread them as a potter tramples clay.

26   Who but I have told you this would happen? Who else predicted this, making you admit that he was right? No one else! None other said one word!

27   I was the first to tell Jerusalem, "Look! Look! Help is on the way!"

28   Not one of your idols told you this. Not one gave any answer when I asked.

29   See, they are all foolish, worthless things; your idols are all as empty as the wind.


## CHAPTER 42

See My Servant,[3] whom I uphold; My Chosen One, in whom I delight. I have put My Spirit upon Him; He will reveal justice to the nations of the world.

2   He will be gentle—He will not shout nor quarrel in the streets.

---

[3]Not Cyrus, as in Chapter 41, but Christ.

3   He will not break the bruised reed, nor quench the dimly burning flame. He will encourage the faint-hearted, those tempted to despair. He will see full justice given to all who have been wronged.

4   He won't be satisfied[4] until truth and righteousness prevail throughout the earth, nor until even distant lands beyond the seas have put their trust in Him.

5   The Lord God who created the heavens and stretched them out and created the earth and everything in it, and gives life and breath and spirit to everyone in all the world, He is the One who says (to His servant, the Messiah)[5],

6   "I the Lord have called You to demonstrate My righteousness. I will guard and support You, for I have given You to My people as the personal confirmation of My covenant with them.[6] You shall also be a light to guide the nations unto Me.

7   You will open the eyes of the blind, and release those who sit in prison darkness and despair.

8   I am the Lord! That is My name, and I will not give My glory to anyone else; I will not share My praise with carved idols.

9   Everything I prophesied came true, and now I will prophesy again. I will tell you the future before it happens."

10   Sing a new song to the Lord; sing His praises, all you who live in earth's remotest corners! Sing, O sea! Sing, all you who live in distant lands beyond the sea!

---

[4]Literally, "He will not burn dimly or be bruised until . . ."
[5]Implied.
[6]Or, "You will be My covenant with all the people . . ."

11   Join in the chorus, you desert cities—Kedar and Sela! And you, too, dwellers in the mountain tops.

12   Let the western coastlands glorify the Lord and sing His mighty power.

13   The Lord will be a mighty warrior, full of fury toward His foes. He will give a great shout and prevail.

14   Long has He been silent; He has restrained Himself. But now He will give full vent to His wrath; He will groan and cry like a woman delivering her child.

15   He will level the mountains and hills and blight their greenery. He will dry up the rivers and pools.

16   He will bring blind Israel along a path they have not seen before. He will make the darkness bright before them and smooth and straighten out the road ahead. He will not forsake them.

17   But those who trust in idols and call them gods will be greatly disappointed; they will be turned away.

18   Oh, how blind and deaf you are towards God! Why won't you listen? Why won't you see?

19   Who in all the world is as blind as My own people,[7] who are designed to be My messengers of truth? Who is so blind as My "dedicated one," the "servant of the Lord"?

20   You see and understand what is right but won't heed nor do it; you hear but you won't listen.

21   The Lord has magnified His Law and made it truly glorious. Through it He had planned to show the world that He is righteous.

22   But what a sight His people are—these who

---

[7]Literally, "as My servant."

were to demonstrate to all the world the glory of His Law;[8] for they are robbed, enslaved, imprisoned, trapped, fair game for all, with no one to protect them.

23    Won't even one of you apply these lessons from the past and see the ruin that awaits you up ahead?

24    Who let Israel be robbed and hurt? Did not the Lord? It is the Lord they sinned against, for they would not go where He sent them nor listen to His laws.

25    That is why God poured out such fury and wrath on His people and destroyed them in battle. Yet, though set on fire and burned, they will not understand the reason why—that it is God, wanting them to repent.[9]

## CHAPTER 43

**B**ut now the Lord who created you, O Israel, says, Don't be afraid, for I have ransomed you; I have called you by name; you are Mine.

2    When you go through deep waters and great trouble, I will be with you. When you go through rivers of difficulty, you will not drown! When you walk through the fire of oppression, you will not be burned up—the flames will not consume you.

3    For I am the Lord your God, your Savior, the Holy One of Israel. I gave Egypt and Ethiopia and Seba (to Cyrus[9]) in exchange for your freedom, as your ransom.

4    Others died that you might live; I traded their

---

[8]Implied from previous verse.
[9]Implied.

lives for yours because you are precious to Me and honored, and I love you.

5 Don't be afraid, for I am with you. I will gather you from east and west,

6 From north and south. I will bring My sons and daughters back to Israel from the farthest corners of the earth.

7 All who claim Me as their God will come, for I have made them for My glory; I created them.

8 Bring them back to Me—blind as they are and deaf when I call (although they see and hear!)

9 Gather the nations together! Which of all their idols ever has foretold such things? Which can predict a single day ahead? Where are the witnesses of anything they said? If there are no witnesses, then they must confess that only God can prophesy.

10 But I have witnesses, O Israel, says the Lord! You are My witnesses and My servants, chosen to know and to believe Me and to understand that I alone am God. There is no other God; there never was and never will be.

11 I am the Lord, and there is no other Savior.

12 Whenever you have thrown away your idols, I have shown you My power. With one word I have saved you. You have seen Me do it; you are My witnesses that it is true.

13 From eternity to eternity I am God. No one can oppose what I do.

14 The Lord, your Redeemer, the Holy One of Israel, says, For your sakes I will send an invading

army against Babylon, that will walk in almost un-scathed. The boasts of the Babylonians will turn to cries of fear.

15 I am the Lord, your holy One, Israel's Creator and King.

16 I am the Lord, who opens a way through the waters, making a path right through the sea.

17 I called forth the mighty army of Egypt with all its chariots and horses, to lie beneath the waves, dead, their lives snuffed out like candlewicks.

18 But forget all that—it is nothing compared to what I'm going to do!

19 For I'm going to do a brand new thing. See, I have already begun! Don't you see it? I will make a road through the wilderness of the world for My people to go home, and create rivers for them in the desert!

20 The wild animals in the fields will thank Me, the jackals and ostriches too, for giving them water in the wilderness, yes, springs in the desert, so that My people, My chosen ones, can be refreshed.

21 I have made Israel for Myself, and these My people will some day honor Me before the world.

22 But O My people, you won't ask My help; you have grown tired of Me!

23 You have not brought Me the lambs for burnt offerings; you have not honored Me with sacrifices. Yet My requests for offerings and incense have been very few! I have not treated you as slaves.

24 You have brought Me no sweet-smelling in-cense nor pleased Me with the sacrificial fat. No, you

have presented Me only with sins, and wearied Me with all your faults.

25 I, yes, I alone am He who blots away your sins for My own sake and will never think of them again.

26 Oh, remind Me of this promise of forgiveness, for we must talk about your sins. Plead your case for My forgiving you.

27 From the very first your ancestors sinned against Me—all your forebears transgressed My law.

28 That is why I have deposed your priests and destroyed Israel, leaving her to shame.

## CHAPTER 44

Listen to Me, O My servant Israel, O My chosen ones:

2 The Lord who made you, who will help you, says, O servant of Mine, don't be afraid. O Jerusalem, My chosen ones, don't be afraid.

3 For I will give you abundant water for your thirst and for your parched fields. And I will pour out My Spirit and My blessings on your children.

4 They shall thrive like watered grass, like willows on a river bank.

5 "I am the Lord's," they'll proudly* say, or "I am a Jew," and tattoo upon their hands the name of God or the honored name of Israel.

6 The Lord, the King of Israel, says—yes, it is

*Implied.

Israel's Redeemer, the Lord of Hosts who says it—I am the First and Last; there is no other God.

7 Who else can tell you what is going to happen in the days ahead? Let them tell you if they can, and prove their power. Let them do as I have done since ancient times.

8 Don't, don't be afraid. Haven't I proclaimed from ages past (that I would save you[1])? You are My witnesses—is there any other God? No! None that I know about! There is no other Rock!

9 What fools they are who manufacture idols for their gods. Their hopes remain unanswered. They themselves are witnesses that this is so, for their idols neither see nor know. No wonder those who worship them are so ashamed.

10 Who but a fool would make his own god—an idol that can help him not one whit!

11 All that worship these will stand before the Lord in shame, along with all these carpenters—mere men—who claim that they have made a god. Together they will stand in terror.

12 The metalsmith stands at his forge to make an axe, pounding on it with all his might. He grows hungry and thirsty, weak and faint.

13 Then the woodcarver takes the axe and uses it to make an idol. He measures and marks out a block of wood and carves the figure of a man. Now he has a wonderful idol that can't so much as move from where it is placed.

---

[1] Implied.

14  He cuts down cedars, he selects the cypress and the oak, he plants the ash in the forest to be nourished by the rain.

15  And after his care, he uses part of the wood to make a fire to warm himself and bake his bread, and then—he really does—he takes the rest of it and makes himself a god—a god for men to worship! An idol to fall down before and praise!

16  Part of the tree he burns to roast his meat and to keep him warm and fed and well-content,

17  And with what's left he makes his god: a carved idol! He falls down before it and worships it and prays to it. "Deliver me," he says. "You are my god!"

18  Such stupidity and ignorance! God has shut their eyes so that they cannot see, and closed their minds from understanding.

19  The man never stops to think or figure out, "Why, it's just a block of wood! I've burned it for heat and used it to bake my bread and roast my meat. How can the rest of it be a god? Should I fall down before a chunk of wood?"

20  The poor, deluded fool feeds on ashes; he is trusting what can never give him any help at all. Yet he cannot bring himself to ask, "Is this thing, this idol that I'm holding in my hand, a lie?"

21  Pay attention, Israel, for you are My servant; I made you, and I will not forget to help you.

22  I've blotted out your sins; they are gone like morning mist at noon! Oh, return to Me, for I have paid the price to set you free.

23   Sing, O heavens, for the Lord has done this
wondrous thing. Shout, O earth; break forth into song,
O mountains and forests, yes, and every tree; for the
Lord redeemed Jacob and is glorified in Israel!

24   The Lord, your Redeemer who made you, says,
All things were made by Me; I alone stretched out the
heavens. By Myself I made the earth and everything in
it.

25   I am the One who shows what liars all false
prophets are, by causing something else to happen than
the things they say. I make wise men give opposite
advice to what they should, and make them into fools.

26   But what My prophets say, I do; when they say
Jerusalem will be delivered and the cities of Judah lived
in once again—it shall be done!

27   When I speak to the rivers and say, "Be dry!"
they shall be dry.

28   When I say of Cyrus,[2] "He is My shepherd," he
will certainly do as I say; and Jerusalem will be rebuilt
and the Temple restored, for I have spoken it.


## CHAPTER 45


This is the Lord's message to Cyrus,[2] God's anointed,
whom He has chosen to conquer many lands. God
shall empower his right hand and he shall crush the
strength of mighty kings. God shall open the gates of

---

[2]This was written many years before Cyrus began his meteoric rise to
power.

Babylon to him; the gates shall not be shut against him any more.

2    I will go before you, Cyrus, and level the mountains and smash down the city gates of brass and iron bars.

3    And I will give you treasures hidden in the darkness, secret riches; and you will know that I am doing this—I, the Lord, the God of Israel, the One Who calls you by your name.

4    And why have I named you for this work? For the sake of Jacob, My servant—Israel, My chosen. I called you by name when you didn't know Me.

5    I am the Lord; there is no other God. I will strengthen you and send you out to victory even though you don't know Me,

6    And all the world from east to west will know there is no other God. I am the Lord and there is no one else. I alone am God.

7    I form the light and make the dark. I send good times and bad. I, the Lord, am He Who does these things.

8    Open up, O heavens. Let the skies pour out their righteousness. Let salvation and righteousness sprout up together from the earth. I, the Lord, created them.

9    Woe to the man who fights with his Creator. Does the pot argue with its maker? Does the clay dispute with him who forms it, saying, "Stop, you're doing it wrong!" or the pot exclaim, "How clumsy can you be!"?

10    Woe to the baby just being born who squalls to

his father and mother, "Why have you produced me? Can't you do anything right at all?"

11 The Lord, the Holy One of Israel, Israel's Creator, says: What right have you to question what I do? Who are you to command Me concerning the work of My hands?

12 I have made the earth and created man upon it. With My hands I have stretched out the heavens and commanded all the vast myriads of stars.

13 I have raised up Cyrus[3] to fulfill My righteous purpose, and I will direct all his paths. He shall restore My city and free My captive people—and not for a reward!

14 The Lord says: The Egyptians, Ethiopians and Sabeans shall be subject to you. They shall come to you with all their merchandise and it shall all be yours. They shall follow you as prisoners in chains, and fall down on their knees before you and say, "The only god there is, is your God!"

15 Truly, O God of Israel, Savior, You work in strange, mysterious ways.

16 All who worship idols shall be disappointed and ashamed.

17 But Israel shall be saved by the Lord with eternal salvation; they shall never be disappointed in their God through all eternity.

18 For the Lord created the heavens and earth and

[3]Literally, "I have raised up him . . ." The reference probably is also to Christ in the more distant future, as well as to Cyrus.

put everything in place, and He made the world to be lived in, not to be an empty chaos. I am the Lord, He says, and there is no other!

19 I publicly proclaim bold promises; I do not whisper obscurities in some dark corner so that no one can know what I mean. And I didn't tell Israel to ask Me for what I didn't plan to give! No, for I, the Lord, speak only truth and righteousness.

20 Gather together and come, you nations that escape from Cyrus' hand. What fools they are who carry around the wooden idols and pray to gods that cannot save!

21 Consult together, argue your case and state your proofs that idol-worship pays! Who but God has said that these things concerning Cyrus would come true? What idol ever told you they would happen? For there is no other God than Me—a just God and a Saviour—no, not one!

22 Let all the world look to Me for salvation! For I am God; there is no other.

23 I have sworn by Myself and I will never go back on my word, for it is true—that every knee in all the world shall bow to Me, and every tongue shall swear allegiance to My Name.

24 "In the Lord is all my righteousness and strength," the people shall declare. And all who were angry with Him shall come to Him and be ashamed.

25 In the Lord all the generations of Israel shall be justified, triumphant.

# CHAPTER 46

The idols of Babylon, Bel and Nebo,[4] are being hauled away on ox carts! But look! The beasts are stumbling! The cart is turning over! The gods are falling out onto the ground! Is that the best that they can do? If they cannot even save themselves from such a fall, how can they save their worshipers from Cyrus?

3 Listen to Me, all Israel who are left; I have created you and cared for you since you were born.

4 I will be your God through all your lifetime, yes, even when your hair is white with age. I made you and I will care for you. I will carry you along and be your Savior.

5 With what in all of heaven and earth do I compare? Whom can you find who equals Me?

6 Will you compare Me with an idol made lavishly with silver and with gold? They hire a goldsmith to take your wealth and make a god from it! Then they fall down and worship it!

7 They carry it around on their shoulders, and when they set it down it stays there, for it cannot move! And when someone prays to it there is no answer, for it cannot get him out of his trouble.

8 Don't forget this, O guilty ones.

9 And don't forget the many times I clearly told you what was going to happen in the future. For I am God—I only—and there is no other like Me

---

[4] Names of Marduk and Nabu, the two principal gods in the Babylonian pantheon.

10   Who can tell you what is going to happen. All I say will come to pass, for I do whatever I wish.

11   I will call that swift bird of prey from the east —that man Cyrus from far away. And he will come and do My bidding. I have said I would do it and I will.

12   Listen to Me, you stubborn, evil men!

13   For I am offering you My deliverance; not in the distant future, but right now! I am ready to save you; and I will restore Jerusalem, and Israel, who is My glory."

## CHAPTER 47

O Babylon, the unconquered, come sit in the dust; for your days of glory, pomp and honor are ended. O daughter of Chaldea, never again will you be the lovely princess, tender and delicate.

2   Take heavy millstones and grind the corn; remove your veil;[5] strip off your robe; expose yourself to public view.

3   You shall be in nakedness and shame. I will take vengeance upon you and will not repent."

4   So speaks our Redeemer, who will save Israel from Babylon's mighty power; the Lord of Hosts is His Name, the Holy One of Israel.

5   Sit in darkness and silence, O Babylon; never again will you be called "The Queen of Kingdoms."

6   For I was angry with My people Israel and began

---

[5]In ancient Babylonia (and in many eastern lands today) only harlots were permitted to go without veils.

to punish them a little by letting them fall into your hands, O Babylon. But you showed them no mercy. You have made even the old folks carry heavy burdens.

7 You thought your reign would never end, Queen Kingdom of the world. You didn't care a whit about My people or think about the fate of those who do them harm.

8 O pleasure-mad kingdom, living at ease, bragging as the greatest in the world—listen to the sentence of My court upon your sins. You say, "I'll never be a widow; I'll never lose my children."

9 Well, those two things shall come upon you in one moment, in full measure in one day: widowhood and the loss of your children, despite all your witchcraft and magic.

10 You felt secure in all your wickedness. "No one sees me," you said. Your "wisdom" and "knowledge" have caused you to turn away from God and claim greatness above anyone in all the world.

11 That is why disaster shall overtake you suddenly—so suddenly that you won't know where it comes from. And there will be no atonement then to cleanse away your sins.

12 Call out the demon hordes you've worshiped all these years. Call on them to help you strike deep terror into many hearts again.

13 You have advisors by the ton—your astrologers and stargazers, who try to tell you what the future holds.

14 But they are as useless as dried grass burning in

the fire. They cannot even deliver themselves! You'll get no help from them at all. Theirs is no fire to sit beside to make you warm!

15    And all your friends of childhood days shall slip away and disappear, unable to help.


## CHAPTER 48


Hear Me, My people: you swear allegiance to the Lord without meaning a word of it, when you boast of living in the Holy City and brag about depending on the God of Israel.

3    Time and again I told you what was going to happen in the future. My words were scarcely spoken when suddenly I did just what I said.

4    I knew how hard and obstinate you are. Your necks are as unbending as iron; you are as hardheaded as brass.

5    That is why I told you ahead of time what I was going to do, so that you could never say, "My idol did it; my carved image commanded it to happen!"

6    You have heard My predictions and seen them fulfilled, but you refuse to agree it is so. Now I will tell you new things I haven't mentioned before, secrets you haven't heard.

7    Then you can't say, "We knew that all the time!"

8    Yes, I'll tell you things entirely new, for I know so well what traitors you are, rebels from earliest childhood, rotten through and through.

9   Yet for My own sake and for the honor of My Name I will hold back My anger and not wipe you out.

10   I refined you in the furnace of affliction, but found no silver there. You are worthless, with nothing good in you at all.

11   Yet for My own sake—yes, *for My own sake*— I will save you from My anger and not destroy you lest the heathen say their gods have conquered Me. I will not let them have My glory.

12   Listen to Me, My people, My chosen ones! I alone am God. I am the First; I am the Last.

13   It was My hand that laid the foundations of the earth; the palm of My right hand spread out the heavens above; I spoke and they came into being.

14   Come, all of you, and listen. Among all your idols, which one has ever told you this: "The Lord loves Cyrus. He will use him to put an end to the empire of Babylonia. He will utterly rout the armies of the Chaldeans"?

15   But I am saying it. I have called Cyrus; I have sent him on this errand and I will prosper him.

16   Come closer and listen. I have always told you plainly what would happen, so that you could clearly understand. And now the Lord God and His spirit have sent Me (with this message):

17   The Lord, your Redeemer, the Holy One of Israel, says, I am the Lord your God, who punishes you for your own good and leads you along the paths that you should follow.

18   Oh, that you had listened to My laws! Then you

would have had peace flowing like a gentle river, and great waves of righteousness.

19 Then you would have become as numerous as the sands along the seashores of the world, too many to count, and there would have been no need for your destruction.

20 Yet even now, be free from your captivity! Leave Babylon, singing as you go; shout to the ends of the earth that the Lord has redeemed His servants, the Jews.

21 They were not thirsty when He led them through the deserts; He divided the rock, and water gushed out for them to drink.

22 But there is no peace, says the Lord, for the wicked.

## CHAPTER 49

Listen to Me, all of you in far off lands: The Lord called Me before My birth. From within the womb He called Me by My name.

2 God will make My words of judgment sharp as swords. He has hidden Me in the shadow of His hand; I am like a sharp arrow in His quiver.

3 He said to Me: "You are My servant, a Prince of Power⁶ with God, and You shall bring Me glory."

4 I replied, "But My work for them seems all in vain; I have spent My strength for them without response. Yet I leave it all with God for My reward."

---

⁶Or, "Israel."

5 "And now," said the Lord—the Lord who formed Me from My mother's womb to serve Him who commissioned Me to restore to Him His people Israel, who has given Me the strength to perform this task and honored Me for doing it!—

6 "You shall do more than restore Israel to Me. I will make You a Light to the nations of the world to bring My salvation to them too."

7 The Lord, the Redeemer and Holy One of Israel, says to the One who is despised, rejected by mankind, and kept beneath the heel of earthly rulers: "Kings shall stand at attention when You pass by; princes shall bow low because the Lord has chosen You; He, the faithful Lord, the Holy One of Israel, chooses You."

8, 9 The Lord says, "Your request has come at a favorable time. I will keep You from premature[7] harm and give You as a token and pledge to Israel, proof that I will reestablish the land of Israel and reassign it to its own people again. Through You I am saying to the prisoners of darkness, 'Come out! I am giving you your freedom!' They will be My sheep, grazing in green pastures and on the grassy hills.

10 They shall neither hunger nor thirst; the searing sun and scorching desert winds will not reach them any more. For the Lord in His mercy will lead them beside the cool waters.

11 And I will make My mountains into level paths for them; the highways shall be raised above the valleys.

---

[7] Implied.

12 See, My people shall return from far away, from north and west and south."

13 Sing for joy, O heavens; shout, O earth; break forth with song, O mountains; for the Lord has comforted His people, and will have compassion upon them in their sorrow.

14 Yet they say, "My Lord deserted us; He has forgotten us."

15 "Never! Can a mother forget her little child and not have love for her own son? Yet even if that should be, I will not forget you.

16 See, I have tatooed your name upon My palm and ever before Me is a picture of Jerusalem's walls in ruins.

17 Soon your rebuilders shall come and chase away all those destroying you.

18 Look and see, for the Lord has vowed that all your enemies shall come and be your slaves. They will be as jewels to display, as bridal ornaments.

19 Even the most desolate parts of your abandoned land shall soon be crowded with your people, and your enemies who enslaved you shall be far away.

20 The generations born in exile shall return and say, 'We need more room! It's crowded here!'

21 Then you will think to yourself, 'Who has given me all these? For most of my children were killed and the rest were carried away into exile, leaving me here alone. Who bore these? Who raised them for me?' "

22 The Lord God says, "See, I will give a signal to the Gentiles and they shall carry your little sons back to

you in their arms, and your daughters on their shoulders.

23 Kings and queens shall serve you; they shall care for all your needs. They shall bow to the earth before you, and lick the dust from off your feet; then you shall know I am the Lord. Those who wait for Me shall never be ashamed."

24 Who can snatch the prey from the hands of a mighty man? Who can demand that a tyrant let his captives go?

25 But the Lord says, "Even the captives of the most mighty and most terrible shall all be freed; for I will fight those who fight you, and I will save your children.

26 I will feed your enemies with their own flesh and they shall be drunk with rivers of their own blood. All the world shall know that I, the Lord, am your Savior and Redeemer, the Mighty One of Israel."

## CHAPTER 50

The Lord asks, Did I sell you to My creditors? Is that why you aren't here? Is your mother gone because I divorced her and sent her away? No, you sold yourselves for your sins. And your mother was taken in payment for your debts.

2 Was I too weak to save you? Is that why the house is silent and empty when I come home? Have I no longer power to deliver? No, that is not the reason!

For I can rebuke the sea and make it dry! I can turn the rivers into deserts, covered with dying fish.

3 I am the One who sends the darkness out across the skies.

4 The Lord God has given Me His words of wisdom so that I may know what I should say to all these weary ones. Morning by Morning He wakens Me and opens My understanding to His will.

5 The Lord God has spoken to Me and I have listened; I do not rebel nor turn away.

6 I give My back to the whip, and My cheeks to those who pull out the beard. I do not hide from shame —they spit in My face.

7 Because the Lord God helps Me, I will not be dismayed; therefore, I have set My face like flint to do His will, and I know that I will triumph.

8 He who gives Me justice is near. Who will dare to fight against Me now? Where are My enemies? Let them appear!

9 See, the Lord God is for Me! Who shall declare Me guilty? All My enemies shall be destroyed like old clothes eaten up by moths!

10 Who among you fears the Lord and obeys His Servant? If such men walk in darkness, without one ray of light, let them trust the Lord, let them rely upon their God.

11 But see here, you who live in your own light, and warm yourselves from your own fires and not from God's; you will live among sorrows.

# CHAPTER 51

Listen to Me, all who hope for deliverance, who seek the Lord! Consider the quarry from which you were mined, the rock from which you were cut! Yes, think about your ancestors Abraham and Sarah, from whom you came. You worry at being so small and few, but Abraham was only *one* when I called him. But when I blessed him, he became a great nation.

3 And the Lord shall bless Israel again, and make her deserts blossom; her barren wilderness shall become as beautiful as the Garden of Eden. Joy and gladness shall be found there, thanksgiving and lovely songs.

4 Listen to Me, My people; listen, O Israel, for I will see that right prevails.

5 My mercy and justice are coming soon; your salvation is on the way. I will rule the nations; they shall wait for Me and long for Me to come.

6 Look high in the skies and watch the earth beneath, for the skies shall disappear like smoke, the earth shall wear out like a garment, and the people of the earth shall die like flies. But My salvation lasts forever; My righteous rule will never die nor end.

7 Listen to Me, you who know the right from wrong and cherish My laws in your hearts: don't be afraid of people's scorn or their slanderous talk.

8 For the moth shall destroy them like garments; the worm shall eat them like wool; but My justice and

mercy shall last forever, and My salvation from generation to generation.

9 Awake, O Lord! Rise up and robe Yourself with strength. Rouse Yourself as in the days of old when You slew Egypt, the dragon of the Nile.[8]

10 Are You not the same today, the mighty God Who dried up the sea, making a path right through it for Your ransomed ones?

11 The time will come when God's redeemed will all come home again. They shall come with singing to Jerusalem, filled with joy and everlasting gladness; sorrow and mourning will all disappear.

12 "I, even I, am He who comforts you and gives you all this joy. So what right have you to fear mere mortal men, who wither like the grass and disappear?

13 And yet you have no fear of God, your Maker —you have forgotten Him, the One who spread the stars throughout the skies and made the earth. Will you be in constant dread of men's oppression, and fear their anger all day long?

14 Soon, soon you slaves shall be released; dungeon, starvation and death are not your fate.

15 For I am the Lord your God, the Lord of Hosts, who dried a path for you right through the sea, between the roaring waves.

16 And I have put My words in your mouth and hidden you safe within My hand. I planted the stars in place and molded all the earth. I am the One who says to Israel, 'You are Mine.' "

---

[8]Literally, "Rahab, the dragon."

17   Wake up, wake up, Jerusalem! You have drunk enough from the cup of the fury of the Lord. You have drunk to the dregs the cup of terror and squeezed out the last drops.

18   Not one of her sons is left alive to help or tell her what to do.

19   These two things have been your lot: desolation and destruction. Yes, famine and the sword. And who is left to sympathize? Who is left to comfort you?

20   For your sons have fainted and lie in the streets, helpless as wild goats caught in a net. The Lord has poured out His fury and rebuke upon them.

21   But listen now to this, afflicted ones—full of troubles and in a stupor (but not from being drunk)—

22   This is what the Lord says, the Lord your God Who cares for His people: See, I take from your hands the terrible cup; you shall drink no more of My fury; it is gone at last.

23   But I will put that terrible cup into the hands of those who tormented you and trampled your souls to the dust and walked upon your backs."

## CHAPTER 52

Wake up, wake up, Jerusalem, and clothe yourselves with strength (from God[9]). Put on your beautiful clothes, O Zion, Holy City; for sinners—those who turn from God—will no longer enter your gates.

---

[9]Implied.

2 Rise from the dust, Jerusalem; take off the slave bands from your neck, O captive daughter of Zion.

3 For the Lord says, When I sold you into exile I asked no fee from your oppressors; now I can take you back again and owe them not a cent!

4 My people were tyrannized without cause by Egypt and Assyria, and I delivered them.

5 And now, what is this? asks the Lord. Why are My people enslaved again, and oppressed without excuse? Those who rule them shout in exultation, and My name is constantly blasphemed, day by day.

6 Therefore I will reveal My name to My people and they shall know the power in that name. Then at last they will recognize that it is I, yes, I, who speaks to them.

7 How beautiful upon the mountains are the feet of those who bring the happy news of peace and salvation, the news that the God of Israel reigns.

8 The watchmen shout and sing with joy, for right before their eyes they see the Lord God bring His people home again.

9 Let the ruins of Jerusalem break into joyous song, for the Lord has comforted His people; He has redeemed Jerusalem.

10 The Lord has bared His holy arm before the eyes of all the nations; the ends of the earth shall see the salvation of our God.

11 Go now, leave your bonds and slavery. Put Babylon and all it represents far behind you—it is unclean to you. You are the holy people of the Lord;

purify yourselves, all you who carry home the vessels of the Lord.

12 You shall not leave in haste, running for your lives; for the Lord will go ahead of you, and He, the God of Israel, will protect you from behind.

13 See, My Servant[1] shall prosper; He shall be highly exalted.

14, 15 Yet many shall be amazed when they see Him—yes, even far-off foreign nations and their kings; they shall stand dumbfounded, speechless in His presence. For they shall see and understand what they had not been told before. They shall see My Servant beaten and bloodied, so disfigured one would scarcely know it was a person standing there. So shall He cleanse[2] many nations.

## CHAPTER 53

But, oh, how few believe it! Who will listen? To whom will God reveal His saving power?

2 In God's eyes[3] He was like a tender green shoot, sprouting from a root in dry and sterile ground. But in our eyes there was no attractiveness at all, nothing to make us want Him.

3 We despised Him and rejected Him—a man of sorrows, acquainted with bitterest grief. We turned our

---

[1] The Servant of the Lord, as the term is used here, is the Messiah, our Lord Jesus. This was the interpretation of this passage by Christ, Himself, and the writers of the New Testament and orthodox Christianity ever since.
[2] Or, "So shall He startle many nations." The meaning of the Hebrew word is uncertain.
[3] Literally, "before Him."

backs on Him and looked the other way when He went by. He was despised and we didn't care.

4 Yet it was *our* grief He bore, *our* sorrows that weighed Him down. And we thought His troubles were a punishment from God, for His *own* sins!

5 But He was wounded and bruised for *our* sins. He was chastised that we might have peace; He was lashed—and we were healed!

6 *We* are the ones who strayed away like sheep! *We*, who left God's paths to follow our own. Yet God laid on *Him* the guilt and sins of every one of us!

7 He was oppressed and He was afflicted, yet He never said a word. He was brought as a lamb to the slaughter; and as a sheep before her shearers is dumb, so He stood silent before the ones condemning Him.

8 From prison and trial they led Him away to His death. But who among the people of that day realized it was their sins that He was dying for—that he was suffering their punishment?

9 He was buried like a criminal in a rich man's grave; but He had done no wrong, and had never spoken an evil word.

10 Yet it was the Lord's good plan to bruise Him and fill Him with grief. But when His soul has been made an offering for sin, then He shall have a multitude of children, many heirs. He shall live again[4] and God's program shall prosper in His hands.

11 And when He sees all that is accomplished by the anguish of His soul, He shall be satisfied; and be-

[4]Literally, "He shall prolong His days."

cause of what He has experienced, My righteous Servant shall make many to be counted righteous before God, for He shall bear all their sins.

12　Therefore I will give Him the honors of one who is mighty and great, because He has poured out His soul unto death. He was counted as a sinner, and He bore the sins of many, and he pled with God for sinners.

## CHAPTER 54

Sing, O childless woman! Break out into loud and joyful song, Jerusalem,[5] for she who was abandoned has more blessings[6] now than she whose husband stayed!

2　Enlarge your house; build on additions; spread out your home!

3　For you will soon be bursting at the seams! And your descendants will possess the cities left behind during the exile, and rule the nations that took their lands.

4　Fear not; you will no longer live in shame. The shame of your youth and the sorrows of widowhood will be remembered no more,

5　For your Creator will be your "husband." The Lord of Hosts is His name; He is your Redeemer, the Holy One of Israel, the God of all the earth.

6　For the Lord has called you back from your grief—a young wife abandoned by her husband.

7　For a brief moment I abandoned you. But with great compassion I will gather you.

---

[5] Implied.
[6] Literally, "children."

8 In a moment of anger I turned My face a little while; but with everlasting love I will have pity on you, says the Lord, your Redeemer.

9 Just as in the time of Noah I swore that I would never again permit the waters of a flood to cover the earth and destroy its life, so now I swear that I will never again pour out My anger on you as I have during this exile.

10 For the mountains may depart and the hills disappear, but My kindness shall not leave you. My promise of peace for you will never be broken, says the Lord Who has mercy upon you.

11 O My afflicted people, tempest-tossed and troubled, I will rebuild you on a foundation of sapphires and make the walls of your houses from precious jewels.

12 I will make your towers of sparkling agate, and your gates and walls of shining gems.

13 And all your citizens shall be taught by Me, and their prosperity shall be great.

14 You will live under a government that is just and fair. Your enemies will stay far away; you will live in peace. Terror shall not come near.

15 If any nation comes to fight you, it will not be sent by me to punish you. Therefore it will be routed, for I am on your side.[7]

16 I have created the smith who blows the coals beneath the forge and makes the weapons of destruction. And I have created the armies that destroy.

---

[7]Literally, "because of you."

17 But in that coming day, no weapon turned against you shall succeed, and you will have justice against every courtroom lie. This is the heritage of the servants of the Lord. This is the blessing I have given you, says the Lord.

## CHAPTER 55

Say there! Is anyone thirsty? Come and drink—even if you have no money! Come, take your choice of wine and milk—it's all free!

2 Why spend your money on foodstuffs that don't give you strength? Why pay for groceries that don't do you any good? Listen and I'll tell you where to get good food that fattens up the soul!

3 Come to me with your ears wide open. Listen, for the life of your soul is at stake. I am ready to make an everlasting covenant with you, to give you all the unfailing mercies and love that I had for King David.[8]

4 He proved My power by conquering foreign nations.[9]

5 You also will command the nations and they will come running to obey, not because of your own power or virtue but because I, the Lord your God, have glorified you.

6 Seek the Lord while you can find Him. Call upon Him now while He is near.

---

[8] See II Samuel 7 for the terms of God's covenant with David, here remembered.
[9] Implied.

7 Let men cast off their wicked deeds; let them banish from their minds the very thought of doing wrong! Let them turn to the Lord that He may have mercy upon them, and to our God, for He will abundantly pardon!

8 This plan of Mine is not what you would work out, neither are My thoughts the same as yours!

9 For just as the heavens are higher than the earth, so are My ways higher than yours, and My thoughts than yours.

10 As the rain and snow come down from heaven and stay upon the ground to water the earth, and cause the grain to grow and to produce seed for the farmer and bread for the hungry,

11 So also is My Word. I send it out and it always produces fruit. It shall accomplish all I want it to, and prosper everywhere I send it.

12 You will live in joy and peace. The mountains and hills, the trees of the field—all the world around you—will rejoice.

13 Where once were thorns, fir trees will grow; where briers grew, the myrtle trees will sprout up. This miracle will make the Lord's Name very great and be an everlasting sign (of God's power and love).[1]

## CHAPTER 56

Be just and fair to all, the Lord God says. Do what's right and good, for I am coming soon to rescue you.

[1] Implied.

2   Blessed is the man who refuses to work during My sabbath days of rest, but honors them; and blessed is the man who checks himself from doing wrong.

3   And My blessings are for Gentiles, too, when they accept the Lord; don't let them think that I will make them second class citizens. And this is for the eunuchs too. They can be as much Mine as anyone.

4   For I say this to the eunuchs who keep His sabbaths holy and choose the things that please Him, and come to grips with His laws:

5   I will give them—in My house, within My walls —a name far greater than the honor they would receive from having sons and daughters. For the name that I will give them is an everlasting one; it will never disappear.

6   As for the Gentiles, the outsiders who join the people of the Lord and serve Him and love His Name, and are His servants and don't desecrate the Sabbath, and have accepted His covenant and promises,

7   I will bring them also to My holy mountain of Jerusalem, and make them full of joy within My House of Prayer. I will accept their sacrifices and offerings, for My Temple shall be called "A House of Prayer for All People"!

8   For the Lord God who brings back the outcasts of Israel says, I will bring others too besides My people Israel.

9   Come, wild animals of the field; come, tear apart the sheep; come, wild animals of the forest, devour My people.[2]

---

[2]Implied.

10   For the leaders of My people—the Lord's watchmen, His shepherds—are all blind to every danger. They are feather-brained and give no warning when danger comes. They love to lie there, love to sleep, to dream.

11   And they are as greedy as dogs, never satisfied; they are stupid shepherds who only look after their own interest, each trying to get as much as he can for himself from every possible source.

12   "Come," they say. "We'll get some wine and have a party; let's all get drunk. This is really living; let it go on and on, and tomorrow will be better yet!

## CHAPTER 57

The good men perish; the godly die before their time, and no one seems to care or wonder why. No one seems to realize that God is taking them away from evil days ahead.

2   For the godly who die shall rest in peace.

3   But you—come here, you witches' sons, you offspring of adulterers and harlots!

4   Who is it you mock, making faces and sticking out your tongues? You children of sinners and liars!

5   You worship your idols with great zeal beneath the shade of every tree, and slay your children as human sacrifices down in the valleys, under overhanging rocks.

6   Your gods are the smooth stones in the valleys.

You worship them and they, not I, are your inheritance. Does all this make Me happy?

7, 8   You have committed adultery on the tops of the mountains, for you worship idols there, deserting Me. Behind closed doors you set your idols up and worship someone other than Me. This is adultery, for you are giving these idols your love, instead of loving Me.

9   You have taken pleasant incense and perfume to Molech as your gift. You have traveled far, even to hell itself, to find new gods to love.

10   You grew weary in your search, but you never gave up. You strengthened yourself and went on.

11   Why were you more afraid of them than of Me? How is it that you gave not even a second thought to Me? Is it because I've been too gentle, that you have no fear of Me?

12   And then there is your "righteousness" and your "good works"—none of which will save you.

13   Let's see if the whole collection of your idols can help you when you cry to them to save you! They are so weak that the wind can carry them off! A breath can puff them away. But he who trusts in Me shall possess the land and inherit My Holy Mountain.

14   I will say, Rebuild the road! Clear away the rocks and stones. Prepare a glorious highway for My people's return from captivity."

15   The high and lofty One who inhabits eternity, the Holy One, says this: I live in that high and holy place where those with contrite, humble spirits dwell;

and I refresh the humble and give new courage to those with repentant hearts.

16 For I will not fight against you forever, nor always show My wrath; if I did, all mankind would perish—the very souls that I have made.

17 I was angry and smote these greedy men. But they went right on sinning, doing everything their evil hearts desired.

18 I have seen what they do, but I will heal them anyway! I will lead them and comfort them, helping them to mourn and to confess their sins.

19 Peace, peace to them, both near and far, for I will heal them all.

20 But those who still reject Me[3] are like the restless sea, which is never still, but always churns up mire and dirt.

21 There is no peace, says my God, for them!

## CHAPTER 58

Shout with the voice of a trumpet blast; tell My people of their sins!

2 Yet they act so pious! They come to the Temple every day and are so delighted to hear the reading of My laws—just as though they would obey them—just as though they don't despise the commandments of their God! How anxious they are to worship correctly; oh, how they love the Temple services!

---

[3]Literally, "the wicked."

3 'We have fasted before You,' they say. 'Why aren't You impressed? Why don't You see our sacrifices? Why don't You hear our prayers? We have done much penance, and You don't even notice it!' I'll tell you why! Because you are living in evil pleasure even while you are fasting, and you keep right on oppressing your workers.

4 Look, what good is fasting when you keep on fighting and quarreling? This kind of fasting will never get you anywhere with Me.

5 Is this what I want—this doing of penance and bowing like reeds in the wind and putting on sackcloth and covering yourselves with ashes? Is this what you call fasting?

6 No, the kind of fast I want is that you stop oppressing those who work for you and treat them fairly and give them what they earn.

7 I want you to share your food with the hungry and bring right into your own homes those who are helpless, poor and destitute. Clothe those who are cold and don't hide from relatives who need your help.

8 If you do these things, God will shed His own glorious light upon you. He will heal you; your godliness will lead you forward; and goodness will be a shield before you, and the glory of the Lord will protect you from behind.

9 Then, when you call, the Lord will answer. "Yes, I am here," He will quickly reply. All you need to do is to stop oppressing the weak, and to stop making false accusations and spreading vicious rumors!

10 Feed the hungry! Help those in trouble! Then

your light will shine out from the darkness, and the darkness around you shall be as bright as day.

11    And the Lord will guide you continually, and satisfy you with all good things, and keep you healthy too; and you will be like a well-watered garden, like an everflowing spring.

12    Your sons will rebuild the long-deserted ruins of your cities, and you will be known as "The People Who Rebuild Their Walls and Cities."

13    If you keep the Sabbath holy, not having your own fun and business on that day, but enjoying the Sabbath and speaking of it with delight as the Lord's holy day, and honoring the Lord in what you do, not following your own desires and pleasure, nor talking idly—

14    Then the Lord will be your delight, and I will see to it that you ride high, and get your full share of the blessings I promised to Jacob, your father. The Lord has spoken.

## CHAPTER 59

Listen now! The Lord isn't too weak to save you! And He isn't getting deaf! He can hear you when you call!

2    But the trouble is that your sins have cut you off from God. Because of sin He has turned His face away from you and will not listen anymore.

3    For your hands are those of murderers and your

fingers are filthy with sin. You lie and grumble and oppose the good.

4 No one cares about being fair and true. Your lawsuits are based on lies; you spend your time plotting evil deeds and doing them.

5 You spend your time and energy in spinning evil plans which end up in deadly actions.

6 You cheat and shortchange everyone. Everything you do is filled with sin; violence is your trademark.

7 Your feet run to do evil and rush to murder; your thoughts are only of sinning, and wherever you go you leave behind a trail of misery and death.

8 You don't know what true peace is, nor what it means to be just and good; you continually do wrong and those who follow you won't experience any peace, either.

9 It is because of all this evil that you aren't finding God's blessings; that's why He doesn't punish those who injure you. No wonder you are in darkness when you expected light. No wonder you are walking in the gloom.

10 No wonder you grope like blind men and stumble along in broad daylight, yes, even at brightest noontime, as though it were the darkest night! No wonder you are like corpses when compared with vigorous young men!

11 You roar like hungry bears; you moan with mournful cries like doves. You look for God to keep you, but He doesn't. He has turned away.

12   For your sins keep piling up before the righteous God, and testify against you.

Yes, we know what sinners we are.

13   We know our disobedience; we have denied the Lord our God. We know what rebels we are and how unfair we are, for we carefully plan our lies.

14   Our courts oppose the righteous man; fairness is unknown. Truth falls dead in the streets, and justice is outlawed.

15   Yes, truth is gone, and anyone who tries a better life is soon attacked. The Lord saw all the evil and was displeased to find no steps taken against sin.

16   He saw no one was helping you, and wondered that no one intervened. Therefore He Himself stepped in to save you through His mighty power and justice.

17   He put on righteousness as armor, and the helmet of salvation on His head. He clothed Himself with robes of vengeance and of godly fury.

18   He will repay His enemies for their evil deeds—fury for His foes in distant lands.

19   Then at last they will reverence and glorify the name of God from west to east. For He will come like a flood-tide driven by Jehovah's breath.

20   He will come as a Redeemer to those in Zion who have turned away from sin.

21   "As for Me, this is My promise to them," says the Lord: "My Holy Spirit shall not leave them, and they shall want the good and hate the wrong—they and their children and their children's children forever."

# CHAPTER 60

A rise, My people! Let your light shine for all the nations to see! For the glory of the Lord is streaming from you.

2 Darkness as black as night shall cover all the peoples of the earth, but the glory of the Lord will shine from you.

3 All nations will come to your light; mighty kings will come to see the glory of the Lord upon you.

4 Lift up your eyes and see! For your sons and daughters are coming home to you from distant lands.

5 Your eyes will shine with joy, your hearts will thrill, for merchants from around the world will flow to you, bringing you the wealth of many lands.

6 Vast droves of camels will converge upon you, dromedaries from Midian and Sheba and Ephah, too, bringing gold and incense to add to the praise of God.

7 The flocks of Kedar shall be given you, and the rams of Nabaioth for My altars, and I will glorify My glorious Temple in that day.

8 And who are these who fly like a cloud to Israel, like doves to their nests?

9 I have reserved the ships of many lands, the very best,[4] to bring the sons of Israel home again from far away, bringing their wealth with them. For the Holy One of Israel, known around the world, has glorified you in the eyes of all.

---

[4] Literally, "the ships of Tarshish."

10   Foreigners will come and build your cities. Presidents and kings will send you aid. For though I destroyed you in My anger, I will have mercy on you through My grace.

11   Your gates will stay wide open around the clock to receive the wealth of many lands. The kings of the world will cater to you.

12   For the nations refusing to be your allies⁵ will perish; they shall be destroyed.

13   The glory of Lebanon will be yours—the forests of firs and pines, and box trees—to beautify My sanctuary. My Temple will be glorious.

14   The sons of anti-Semites will come and bow before you! They will kiss your feet! They will call Jerusalem "The City of the Lord" and "The Glorious Mountain of the Holy One of Israel."

15   Though once despised and hated and rebuffed by all, you will be beautiful forever, a joy for all the generations of the world; for I will make you so.

16   Powerful kings and mighty nations shall provide you with the choicest of their goods to satisfy your every need, and you will know at last and really understand that I, the Lord, am your Savior and Redeemer, the Mighty One of Israel.

17   I will exchange your brass for gold, your iron for silver, your wood for brass, your stones for iron. Peace and righteousness shall be your taskmasters!

18   Violence will disappear out of your land—all war will end. Your walls will be "Salvation" and your gates "Praise."

---

⁵Literally, "that will not serve you."

19   No longer will you need the sun or moon to give you light, for the Lord your God will be your everlasting light, and He will be your glory.

20   Your sun shall never set; the moon shall not go down—for the Lord will be your everlasting light; your days of mourning all will end.

21   All your people will be good. They will possess their land forever, for I will plant them there with My own hands; this will bring Me glory.

22   The smallest family shall multiply into a clan; the tiny group shall be a mighty nation.  I, the Lord, will bring it all to pass when it is time.

## CHAPTER 61

The Spirit of the Lord God is upon Me, because the Lord has anointed Me to bring good news to the suffering and afflicted. He has sent Me to comfort the broken-hearted, to announce liberty to captives and to open the eyes of the blind.

2   He has sent Me to tell those who mourn that the time of God's favor to them has come, and the day of His wrath to their enemies.

3   To all who mourn in Israel He will give:
> Beauty for ashes;
> Joy instead of mourning;
> Praise instead of heaviness.

For God has planted them like strong and graceful oaks for His own glory.

4 And they shall rebuild the ancient ruins, repairing cities long ago destroyed, reviving them though they have lain there many generations.

5 Foreigners shall be your servants; they shall feed your flocks and plow your fields and tend your vineyards.

6 You shall be called priests of the Lord, ministers of our God. You shall be fed with the treasures of the nations and shall glory in their riches.

7 Instead of shame and dishonor, you shall have a double portion of prosperity and everlasting joy.

8 For I, the Lord, love justice; I hate robbery and wrong. I will faithfully reward My people for their suffering and make an everlasting covenant with them.

9 Their descendants shall be known and honored among the nations; all shall realize that they are a people God has blessed.

10 Let me tell you how happy God has made me! For He has clothed me with garments of salvation and draped about Me the robe of righteousness. I am like a bridegroom in his wedding suit or a bride with her jewels.

11 The Lord will show the nations of the world His justice; all will praise Him. His righteousness shall be like a budding tree, or like a garden in early spring, full of young plants springing up everywhere.

## CHAPTER 62

Because I love Zion, because my heart yearns for Jerusalem, I will not cease to pray for her or to cry out to God on her behalf until she shines forth in His righteousness and is glorious in His salvation.

2    The nations shall see your righteousness. Kings shall be blinded by your glory; and God will confer on you a new name.

3    He will hold you aloft in His hands for all to see—a splendid crown for the King of kings.

4    Never again shall you be called "The God-forsaken Land" or the "Land that God Forgot." Your new name will be "The Land of God's Delight" and "The Bride," for the Lord delights in you and will claim you as His own.

5    Your children will care for you, O Jerusalem, with joy like that of a young man who marries a virgin; and God will rejoice over you as a bridegroom with his bride.

6, 7    O Jerusalem, I have set intercessors[6] on your walls who shall cry to God all day and all night for the fulfillment of His promises. Take no rest, all you who pray, and give God no rest until He establishes Jerusalem and makes her respected and admired throughout the earth.

8    The Lord has sworn to Jerusalem with all His integrity: "I will never again give you to your enemies; never again shall foreign soldiers come and take away your grain and wine.

9    You raised it; you shall keep it, praising God. Within the Temple courts you yourselves shall drink the wine you pressed.

10    Go out! Go out! Prepare the roadway for My

---

[6]Literally, "watchmen."

people to return! Build the roads, pull out the boulders, raise the flag of Israel."

11    See, the Lord has sent His messengers to every land and said, "Tell My people, I, the Lord your God, am coming to save you and will bring you many gifts."

12    And they shall be called "The Holy People" and "The Lord's Redeemed," and Jerusalem shall be called "The Land of Desire" and "The City God Has Blessed."

## CHAPTER 63

Who is this who comes from Edom, from the city of Bozrah, with His magnificent garments of crimson? Who is this in kingly robes, marching in the greatness of His strength? "It is I, the Lord, announcing your salvation; I, the Lord, the One who is mighty to save!"

2    "Why are Your clothes so red, as from treading out the grapes?"

3    "I have trodden the wine press alone. No one was there to help Me. In My wrath I have trodden My enemies like grapes. In My fury I trampled My foes. It is their blood you see upon My clothes.

4    For the time has come for Me to avenge My people, to redeem them from the hands of their oppressors.

5    I looked but no one came to help them; I was amazed and appalled. So I executed vengeance alone; unaided, I meted out judgment.

6    I crushed the heathen nations in My anger and made them stagger and fall to the ground."

7    I will tell of the lovingkindnesses of God. I will praise Him for all He has done; I will rejoice in His great goodness to Israel, which He has granted in accordance with His mercy and love.

8    He said, "They are My very own; surely they will not be false again." And He became their Savior.

9    In all their affliction He was afflicted, and He personally[7] saved them. In His love and pity He redeemed them and lifted them up and carried them through all the years.

10    But they rebelled against Him and grieved His Holy Spirit. That is why He became their enemy and personally fought against them.

11    Then they remembered those days of old when Moses, God's servant, led His people out of Egypt and they cried out, "Where is the One who brought Israel through the sea, with Moses as their shepherd? Where is the God who sent His Holy Spirit to be among His people?

12    Where is He whose mighty power divided the sea before them when Moses lifted up his hand, and established His reputation forever?

13    Who led them through the bottom of the sea? Like fine stallions racing through the desert, they never stumbled.

14    Like cattle grazing in the valleys, so the Spirit of the Lord gave them rest. Thus He gave Himself a magnificent reputation.

---

[7]Or, "The Angel of His Presence saved them out of their affliction."

15   O Lord, look down from heaven and see us from Your holy, glorious home; where is the love for us You used to show—Your power, Your mercy and Your compassion? Where are they now?

16   Surely You are still our Father! Even if Abraham and Jacob would disown us, still You would be our Father, our Redeemer from ages past.

17   O Lord, why have You hardened our hearts and made us sin and turn against You? Return and help us, for we who belong to You need you so.[8]

18   How briefly we possessed Jerusalem! And now our enemies have destroyed her.

19   O God, why do You treat us as though we weren't Your people, as though we were a heathen nation that never called You "Lord"?

## CHAPTER 64

Oh, that You would burst forth from the skies and come down! How the mountains would quake in Your presence!

2   The consuming fire of Your glory would burn down the forests and boil the oceans dry. The nations would tremble before You; then Your enemies would learn the reason for Your fame!

3   So it was before when You came down, for You did awesome things beyond our highest expectations, and how the mountains quaked!

_____
[8]Literally, "for Your servants' sake."

4 For since the world began no one has seen or heard of such a God as ours, who works for those who wait for Him!

5 You welcome those who cheerfully do good, who follow godly ways. But we are not godly; we are constant sinners and have been all our lives. Therefore Your wrath is heavy on us. How can such as we be saved?

6 We are all infected and impure with sin. When we put on our prized robes of righteousness we find they are but filthy rags.[1] Like autumn leaves we fade, wither and fall. And our sins, like the wind, sweep us away.

7 Yet no one calls upon Your name or pleads with You for mercy. Therefore You have turned away from us and turned us over to our sins.

8 And yet, O Lord, You are our Father. We are the clay and You are the Potter. We are all formed by Your hand.

9 Oh, be not so angry with us, Lord, nor forever remember our sins. Oh, look and see that we are all Your people.

10 Your holy cities are destroyed; Jerusalem is a desolate wilderness.

11 Our holy, beautiful Temple where our fathers praised You is burned down, and all the things of beauty are destroyed.

12 After all of this, must You still refuse to help us, Lord? Will You stand silent and still punish us?

---

[1]Literally, "filthy as a menstruating woman's rags."

## CHAPTER 65

The Lord says, People[2] who never before inquired about Me are now seeking Me out. Nations[2] who never before searched for Me are finding Me.

2   But My own people—though I have been spreading out My arms to welcome them all day long—have rebelled; they follow their own evil paths and thoughts.

3   All day long they insult Me to My face by worshiping idols in many gardens and burning incense on the rooftops of their homes.

4   At night they go out among the graves and caves to worship evil spirits, and they eat pork and other forbidden foods.

5   Yet they say to one another, "Don't come too close, you'll defile me! For I am holier than you!" They stifle Me. Day in and day out they infuriate Me.

6   See, here is My decree all written out before Me: *I will not stand silent; I will repay. Yes, I will repay them—*

7   Not only for their own sins but for those of their fathers too, says the Lord, for they also burned incense on the mountains and insulted Me upon the hills. I will pay them back in full.

8   But I will not destroy them all, says the Lord; for just as good grapes are found among a cluster of bad ones (and someone will say, "Don't throw them

---

[2]Literally, "those." Some believe this verse as well as the next applies to Israelites rather than to the nations. But see Romans 10:20-21.

all away—there are some good grapes there!") so I will not destroy all Israel, for I have true servants there.

9 I will preserve a remnant of My people to possess the land of Israel; those I select will inherit it and serve Me there.

10 As for My people who have sought Me, the plains of Sharon shall again be filled with flocks, and the valley of Achor shall be a place to pasture herds.

11 But because the rest of you have forsaken the Lord and His Temple and worship gods of "Fate" and "Destiny,"

12 Therefore I will "destine" you to the sword, and your "fate" shall be a dark one; for when I called, you didn't answer; when I spoke, you wouldn't listen. You deliberately sinned before My very eyes, choosing to do what you know I despise.

13 Therefore the Lord God says, You shall starve, but My servants shall eat; you shall be thirsty while they drink; you shall be sad and ashamed, but they shall rejoice.

14 You shall cry in sorrow and vexation and despair, while they sing for joy.

15 Your name shall be a curse word among My people, for the Lord God will slay you and call His true servants by another name.[3]

16 And yet, the days will come[4] when all who invoke a blessing or take an oath shall swear by the God of Truth; for I will put aside My anger and forget the evil that you did.

---

[3] i.e., "Christians?" See Acts 11:26.
[4] Implied.

17 For see, I am creating new heavens and a new earth—so wonderful that no one will even think about the old ones anymore.

18 Be glad; rejoice forever in My creation. Look! I will recreate Jerusalem as a place of happiness, and her people shall be a joy!

19 And I will rejoice in Jerusalem, and in My people; and the voice of weeping and crying shall not be heard there any more.

20 No longer will babies die when only a few days old; no longer will men be considered old at 100! Only sinners will die that young!

21, 22 In those days, when a man builds a house, he will keep on living in it—it will not be destroyed by invading armies as in the past. My people will plant vineyards and eat the fruit themselves—their enemies will not confiscate it. For My people will live as long as trees and will long enjoy their hard won gains.

23 Their harvests will not be eaten by their enemies; their children will not be born as cannon fodder; for they are the children of those the Lord has blessed; and their children, too, shall be blessed.

24 I will answer them before they even call to Me. While they are still talking to Me about their needs, I will go ahead and answer their prayers!

25 The wolf and lamb shall feed together, the lion shall eat straw as the ox does, and poisonous snakes shall strike[5] no more! In those days nothing and no one shall be hurt or destroyed in all My holy mountain, says the Lord.

---

[5]Literally, "dust (i.e. not men!) shall be the serpent's food."

## CHAPTER 66

**H**eaven is My throne and the earth is My footstool: What Temple can you build for Me as good as that?

2 My hand has made both earth and skies, and they are Mine. Yet I will look with pity on the man who has a humble and a contrite heart, who trembles at My word.

3 But those who choose their own ways, delighting in their sins, are cursed. God will not accept their offerings. When such men sacrifice an ox on the altar of God, it is no more acceptable to Him than human sacrifice. If they sacrifice a lamb, or bring an offering of grain, it is as loathsome to God as putting a dog or the blood of a swine on His altar! When they burn incense to Him, He counts it the same as though they blessed an idol.

4 I will send great troubles upon them—all the things they feared; for when I called them, they refused to answer, and when I spoke to them, they would not hear. Instead, they did wrong before My eyes, and chose what they knew I despised.

5 Hear the words of God, all you who fear Him, and tremble at His words: Your brethren hate you and cast you out for being loyal to My name. "Glory to God," they scoff. "Be happy in the Lord!" But they shall be put to shame.

6 What is all the commotion in the city? What is

that terrible noise from the Temple? It is the voice of the Lord taking vengeance upon His enemies.

7, 8 Who has heard or seen anything as strange as this? For in one day, suddenly, a nation, Israel, shall be born, even before the birth pains come. In a moment, just as Israel's anguish starts, the baby is born; the nation begins.

9 Shall I bring to the point of birth and then not deliver? asks the Lord your God. No! Never!

10 Rejoice with Jerusalem; be glad with her, all you who love her, you who mourned for her.

11 Delight in Jerusalem; drink deep of her glory even as an infant at a mother's generous breasts.

12 Prosperity shall overflow Jerusalem like a river, says the Lord, for I will send it; the riches of the Gentiles will flow to her. Her children shall be nursed at her breasts, carried on her hips and dandled on her knees.

13 I will comfort you there as a little one is comforted by its mother.

14 When you see Jerusalem, your heart will rejoice; vigorous health will be yours. All the world will see the good hand of God upon His people, and His wrath upon His enemies.

15 For see, the Lord will come with fire and with swift chariots of doom to pour out the fury of His anger and His hot rebuke with flames of fire.

16 For the Lord will punish the world by fire and by His sword, and the slain of the Lord shall be many!

17 Those who worship idols that are hidden behind a tree in the garden, feasting there on pork and mouse

and all forbidden meat—they will come to an evil end, says Jehovah.

18 I see full well what they are doing; I know what they are thinking; so I will gather together all nations and people against Jerusalem, where they shall see My glory.

19 I will perform a mighty miracle against them; and I will send those[6] who escape, as missionaries to the nations—to Tarshish, Put, Lud, Mesech, Rosh, Tubal, Javan, and to the lands beyond the sea that have not heard My fame nor seen My glory. There they shall declare My glory to the Gentiles.

20 And they shall bring back all your brethren from every nation as a gift to the Lord, transporting them gently[7] on horses and in chariots, and in litters, and on mules and camels, to My holy mountain, to Jerusalem, says the Lord. It will be like offerings flowing into the Temple of the Lord at harvest time, carried in vessels consecrated to the Lord.

21 And I will appoint some of those returning to be My priests and Levites, says the Lord.

22 "As surely as My new heavens and earth shall remain, so surely shall you always be My people, with a name that shall never disappear.

23 All mankind shall come to worship Me from week to week and month to month.

24 And they shall go out and look at the dead

---

[6]It is not clear from the Hebrew whether "those who escape" means survivors of the armies of the nations, or survivors of the Jews in Israel. The context seems to favor the former. Put and Lud were in North Africa; Meshech, Rosh and Tubal were in Asia Minor and Armenia.
[7]Implied.

bodies of those who have rebelled against Me, for their worm shall never die; their fire shall not be quenched, and they shall be a disgusting sight to all mankind."

# Jeremiah

## CHAPTER 1

These are God's messages to Jeremiah the priest (the son of Hilkiah) who lived in the town of Anathoth in the land of Benjamin. The first of these messages came to him in the thirteenth year of the reign of Amon's son Josiah, king of Judah.

3 Others came during the reign of Josiah's son Jehoiakim, king of Judah, and at various other times until July of the eleventh year of the reign of Josiah's son Zedekiah, king of Judah, when Jerusalem was captured and the people were taken away as slaves.

\*     \*     \*     \*     \*

4 The Lord said to me:

5 "I knew you before you were formed within your mother's womb; before you were born I sanctified you and appointed you as My spokesman to the world."

6 "O Lord God," I said. "I can't do that! I'm far too young! I'm only a youth!"

7 "Don't say that," He replied, "for you will go wherever I send you and speak whatever I tell you to.

8 And don't be afraid of the people, for I, the Lord, will be with you and see you through."

9 Then He touched my mouth and said, "See, I have put My words in your mouth!

10 Today your work begins, to warn the nations and the kingdoms of the world. In accord with My words spoken through your mouth I will tear down some and destroy them, and plant others and nurture them and make them strong and great."

11 Then the Lord said to me, "Look, Jeremiah! What do you see?" And I replied, "I see a whip made from the branch of an almond tree."

12 And the Lord replied, "That's right, and it means that I will surely carry out My threats of punishment[1]."

13 Then the Lord asked me, "What do you see now?" And I replied, "I see a pot of boiling water, tipping southward, spilling over Judah[2]."

14 "Yes," He said, "for terror from the north will boil out upon all the people of this land.

15 I am calling the armies of the kingdoms of the north to come to Jerusalem and set their thrones at the gates of the city and all along its walls, and in all the other cities of Judah.

16 This is the way I will punish My people for deserting Me and for worshiping other gods—yes, idols they themselves have made!

17 Get up and dress and go out and tell them

---

[1]There is word play here between *shaqedh* (almond) in verse 11 and *shoqedh* (watching) in verse 12: "For I am watching over My word to perform it."
[2]Implied.

whatever I tell you to say. Don't be afraid of them, or else I will make a fool of you in front of them.

18   For see, today I have made you impervious to their attacks. They cannot harm you. You are strong like a fortified city that cannot be captured, like an iron pillar and heavy gates of brass. All the kings of Judah and its officers and priests and people will not be able to prevail against you.

19   They will try, but they will fail. For I am with you," says the Lord. "I will deliver you."

## CHAPTER 2

Again the Lord spoke to me and said:

2   "Go and shout this in Jerusalem's streets: The Lord says, I remember how eager you were to please Me as a young bride long ago and how you loved Me and followed Me even through the barren deserts.

3   In those days Israel was a holy people, the first of My children.[3] All who harmed them were counted deeply guilty, and great evil fell on anyone who touched them.

4, 5   O Israel, says the Lord, Why did your fathers desert Me? What sin did they find in Me that turned them away and changed them into fools who worship idols?

6   They ignore the fact that it was I, the Lord, who brought them safely out of Egypt and led them through

_____

[3]Literally, "the firstfruits of His harvest."

the barren wilderness, a land of deserts and rocks, of drought and death, where no one lives or even travels.

7   And I brought them into a fruitful land, to eat of its bounty and goodness, but they made it into a land of sin and corruption and turned My inheritance into an evil thing.

8   Even their priests cared nothing for the Lord, and their judges ignored Me; their rulers turned against Me, and their prophets worshiped Baal and wasted their time on nonsense.

9   But I will not give you up—I will plead for you to return to me, and will keep on pleading; yes, even with your children's children in the years to come!

10, 11   Look around you and see if you can find another nation anywhere that has traded in its old gods for new ones—even though their gods are nothing. Send to the west to the island of Cyprus; send to the east to the deserts of Kedar. See if anyone there has ever heard so strange a thing as this. And yet My people have given up their glorious God for silly idols!

12   The heavens are shocked at such a thing and shrink back in horror and dismay.

13   For My people have done two evil things: They have forsaken Me, the Fountain of Life-giving Water; and they have built for themselves broken cisterns that can't hold water!

14   Why has Israel become a nation of slaves? Why is she captured and led far away?

15   I see great armies marching on Jerusalem with

mighty shouts[4] to destroy her and leave her cities in ruins, burned and desolate.

16 I see the armies of Egypt rising against her, marching from their cities of Memphis and Tahpanhes to utterly destroy Israel's glory and power.

17 And you have brought this on yourselves by rebelling against the Lord your God when He wanted to lead you and show you the way!

18 What have you gained by your alliances with Egypt and with Assyria?

19 Your own wickedness will punish you. You will see what an evil, bitter thing it is to rebel against the Lord your God, fearlessly forsaking Him, says the Lord, the God of Hosts.

20 Long ago you shook off My yoke and broke away from my ties. Defiant, you would not obey Me. On every hill and under every tree you've bowed low before idols.

21 How could this happen? How could this be? For when I planted you, I chose My seed so carefully—the very best. Why have you become this degenerate race of evil men?

22 No amount of soap or lye can make you clean. You are stained with guilt that cannot ever be washed away. I see it always before me, the Lord God says.

23 You say it isn't so, that you haven't worshiped idols? How can you say a thing like that? Go and look in any valley in the land! Face the awful sins that you have done, O restless female camel, seeking for a male!

[4]Literally, "The lions have roared against him."

24  You are a wild donkey, sniffing the wind at mating time. (Who can restrain your lust?) Any jack wanting you need not search, for you come running to him!

25  Why don't you turn from all this weary running after other gods? But you say, 'Don't waste Your breath. I've fallen in love with these strangers and I can't stop loving them now!'

26, 27  Like a thief, the only shame that Israel knows is getting caught. Kings, princes, priests and prophets—all are alike in this. They call a carved-up wooden post their father, and for their mother they have an idol chiseled out from stone. Yet in time of trouble they cry to Me to save them!

28  Why don't you call on these gods you have made? When danger comes, let *them* go out and save you if they can! For you have as many gods as there are cities in Judah.

29  Don't come to Me—you are all rebels, says the Lord.

30  I have punished your children but it did them no good; they still will not obey. And you yourselves have killed my prophets as a lion kills its prey.

31  O My people, listen to the words of God: Have I been unjust to Israel? Have I been to them a land of darkness and of evil? Why then do My people say, 'At last we are free from God; we won't have anything to do with Him again!'

32  How can you disown your God like that?⁵ Can

─────────

⁵Implied.

a girl forget her jewels? What bride will seek to hide her wedding dress? Yet for years on end My people have forgotten Me—the most precious of their treasures.[5]

33   How you plot and scheme to win your lovers. The most experienced harlot could learn a lot from you!

34   Your clothing is stained with the blood of the innocent and the poor. Brazenly you murder without a cause.

35   And yet you say, 'I haven't done a thing to anger God. I'm sure He isn't angry!'[5] I will punish you severely because you say, 'I haven't sinned!'

36   First here, then there, you flit about, going from one ally to another for their help; but it's all no good— your new friends in Egypt will forsake you as Assyria did before.

37   You will be left in despair, and cover your face with your hands, for the Lord has rejected the ones that you trust. You will not succeed despite their aid."

## CHAPTER 3

There is a law[6] that if a man divorces a woman who then remarries, he is not to take her back again, for she has become corrupted. But though you have left Me and married many lovers, yet I have invited you to come to Me again, the Lord says.

---

[5]Implied.
[6]Deuteronomy 24:1-4.

2  Is there a single spot in all the land where you haven't been defiled by your adulteries—your worshiping these other gods?[7] You sit like a harlot beside the road waiting for a client!  You sit alone like a Bedouin in the desert.  You have polluted the land with your vile harlotry.

3  That is why even the springtime rains have failed. For you are a harlot, and completely unashamed.

4, 5  And yet you say to Me, 'O Father, You have always been my Friend; surely You won't be angry about such a little thing! Surely You will just forget it?' So you talk, and keep right on doing all the evil that you can."

*    *    *    *    *

6  This message from the Lord came to me during the reign of King Josiah:

"Have you seen what Israel does? Like a wanton wife who gives herself to other men at every chance, so Israel has worshiped other gods on every hill, beneath every shady tree.

7  I thought that someday she would return to Me and once again be Mine; but she didn't come back. And her faithless sister Judah saw the continued rebellion of Israel.

8  Yet she took no heed, even though she saw that I divorced faithless Israel. But now Judah too has left Me and given herself to harlotry, for she has gone to other gods to worship them.

9  She treated it all so lightly—to her it was nothing

[7]Implied.

at all that she should worship idols made of wood and stone. And so the land was greatly polluted and defiled.

10    Then, afterwards, this faithless one 'returned' to Me, but her 'sorrow' was only faked, the Lord God says.

11    In fact, faithless Israel is less guilty than treacherous Judah!

12    Therefore go and say to Israel, 'O Israel, My sinful people, come home to Me again, for I am merciful; I will not be forever angry with you.

13    Only acknowledge your guilt; admit that you rebelled against the Lord your God and committed adultery against Him by worshiping idols under every tree; confess that you refused to follow Me.

14    O sinful children, come home, for I am your Master and I will bring you again to the land of Israel —one from here and two from there, wherever you are scattered.

15    And I will give you leaders after My own heart, who will guide you with wisdom and understanding.

16    Then, when your land is once more filled with people, says the Lord, you will no longer wish for 'the good old days of long ago' when you possessed the Ark of God's covenant. Those days will not be missed or even thought about, and the Ark will not be reconstructed,

17    For the Lord Himself will be among you, and the whole city of Jerusalem will be known as the throne of the Lord, and all nations will come to Him there and no longer stubbornly follow their evil desires.

18 At that time the people of Judah and of Israel will return together from their exile in the north, to the land I gave their fathers as an inheritance forever.

19 And I thought how wonderful it would be for you to be here among My children. I planned to give you part of this beautiful land, the finest in the world. I looked forward to your calling me 'Father,' and thought that you would never turn away from Me again.

20 But you have betrayed Me; you have gone off and given yourself to a host of foreign gods; you have been like a faithless wife who leaves her husband.

21 I hear voices high upon the windswept mountains crying, crying. It is the sons of Israel who have turned their backs on God and wandered far away.

22 O My rebellious children, come back to Me again and I will heal you from your sins."

And they reply, "Yes, we will come; for You are the Lord our God.

23 We are weary of worshiping idols on the hills and of having orgies on the mountains. It is all a farce. Only in the Lord our God can Israel ever find her help and her salvation.

24 From our childhood we have seen everything our fathers had—flocks and herds and sons and daughters—squandered on priests and idols.

25 We lie in shame and in dishonor, for we and our fathers have sinned from childhood against the Lord our God; we have not obeyed Him."

## CHAPTER 4

O Israel, if you will truly return to Me and absolutely discard your idols,

2 And if you will swear by Me alone, the living God, and begin to live good, honest, clean lives, then you will be a testimony to the nations of the world and they will come to Me and glorify My Name.

3 The Lord is saying to the men of Judah and Jerusalem, Plow up the hardness of your hearts; otherwise the good seed will be wasted among the thorns.

4 Cleanse[8] your minds and hearts, not just your bodies, or else My anger will burn you to a crisp because of all your sins. And no one will be able to put the fire out.

5 Shout to Jerusalem and to all Judea, telling them to sound the alarm throughout the land. 'Run for your lives! Flee to the fortified cities!'

6 Send a signal from Jerusalem: 'Flee now, don't delay!' For I the Lord am bringing vast destruction on you from the north.[9]

7 A lion—a destroyer of nations—stalks from his lair; and he is headed for your land. Your cities will lie in ruin without inhabitant.

8 Put on clothes of mourning and weep with broken hearts, for the fierce anger of the Lord has not stopped yet.

---

[8]Literally, "Circumcise yourselves . . . remove the foreskin of your hearts."
[9]i.e., from Babylon. Nabopolasser and Nebuchadnezzar II soon attacked.

9 In that day, says the Lord, the king and the princes will tremble in fear; and the priests and the prophets will be stricken with horror."

10 (Then I said, "But Lord, the people have been deceived by what You said, for You promised great blessings on Jerusalem. Yet the sword is even now poised to strike them dead!")

11, 12 At that time He will send a burning wind from the desert upon them—not in little gusts but in a roaring blast—and He will pronounce their doom.

13 The enemy shall roll down upon us like a storm wind; his chariots are like a whirlwind; his steeds are swifter than eagles. Woe, woe upon us, for we are doomed.

14 O Jerusalem, cleanse your hearts while there is time. You can yet be saved by casting out your evil thoughts.

15 From Dan and from Mount Ephraim your doom has been announced.

16 Warn the other nations that the enemy is coming from a distant land and they shout against Jerusalem and the cities of Judah.

17 They surround Jerusalem like shepherds moving in on some wild animal! For My people have rebelled against Me, says the Lord.

18 Your ways have brought this down upon you; it is a bitter dose of your own medicine, striking deep within your hearts.

19 My heart, my heart—I writhe in pain; my heart pounds within me. I cannot be still because I have

heard, O my soul, the blast of the enemies' trumpets and the enemies' battle cries.

20 Wave upon wave of destruction rolls over the land, until it lies in utter ruin; suddenly, in a moment, every house is crushed.

21 How long must this go on? How long must I see war and death surrounding me?

22 "Until My people leave their foolishness, for they refuse to listen to Me; they are dull, retarded children who have no understanding. They are smart enough at doing wrong, but for doing right they have no talent, none at all."

23 I looked down upon their land and as far as I could see in all directions everything was ruins. And all the heavens were dark.

24 I looked at the mountains and saw that they trembled and shook.

25 I looked, and mankind was gone and the birds of the heavens had fled.

26 The fertile valleys were wilderness and all the cities were broken down before the presence of the Lord, and crushed by His fierce anger.

27 The Lord's decree of desolation covers all the land, "Yet," He says, "there will be a little remnant of My people left.

28 The earth shall mourn, the heavens shall be draped with black, because of My decree against My people, but I have made up My mind and I will not change it."

29 All the cities flee in terror at the noise of

marching armies coming near. The people hide in the bushes and flee to the mountains. All the cities are abandoned—all have fled in terror.

30 Why do you put on your most beautiful clothing and jewelry and brighten your eyes with mascara? It will do you no good! Your allies despise you and will kill you.

31 I have heard great crying like that of a woman giving birth to her child; it is the cry of my people gasping for breath, pleading for help, prostrate before their murderers.

## CHAPTER 5

Run up and down through every street in all Jerusalem; search high and low and see if you can find one fair and honest man! Search every square, and if you find just one, I'll not destroy the city!

2 Even under oath, they lie."

3 O Lord, You will take naught but truth. You have tried to get them to be honest, for You have punished them, but they won't change! You have destroyed them but they refuse to turn from their sins. They are determined, with faces hard as rock, not to repent.

4 Then I said, "But what can we expect from the poor and ignorant? They don't know the ways of God. How can they obey Him?"

5 I will go now to their leaders, the men of importance, and speak to them, for they know the ways of the

Lord and the judgment that follows sin. But they too had utterly rejected their God.

6 "So I will send upon them the wild fury of the 'lion from the forest;' the 'desert wolves' shall pounce upon them, and a 'leopard' shall lurk around their cities so that all who go out shall be torn apart; for their sins are very many; their rebellion against Me is great.

7 How can I pardon you? For even your children have turned away, and worship gods that are not gods at all. I fed My people until they were fully satisfied, and their thanks was to commit adultery wholesale and to gang up at the cities' brothels.

8 They are well-fed, lusty stallions, each neighing for his neighbor's mate.

9 Shall I not punish them for this? Shall I not send My vengeance on such a nation as this?

10 Go down the rows of the vineyards and destroy them! But leave a scattered few to live. Strip the branches from each vine, for they are not the Lord's.

11 For the people of Israel and Judah are full of treachery against Me, says the Lord.

12 They have lied and said, 'He won't bother us! No evil will come upon us! There will be neither famine nor war!'

13 'God's prophets,' they say, 'are windbags full of words with no divine authority. Their claims of doom will fall upon themselves, not us!'

14 Therefore this is what the Lord God of Hosts says to His prophets: Because of talk like this I'll take

your words and prophecies and turn them into raging fire and burn up these people like kindling wood.

15    See, I will bring a distant nation against you, O Israel, says the Lord; a mighty nation, an ancient[1] nation whose language you don't understand.

16    Their weapons are deadly; the men are all mighty.

17    And they shall eat your harvest and your children's bread, and your flocks of sheep and herds of cattle, yes, and your grapes and figs; and they shall sack your walled cities that you think are safe.

18    But I will not completely blot you out. So says the Lord.

19    And when your people ask, 'Why is it that the Lord is doing this to us?' then you shall say, 'You rejected Him and gave yourselves to other gods while in your land; now you must be slaves to foreigners in their lands.'

20    Make this announcement to Judah and to Israel:

21    Listen, O foolish, senseless people—you with the eyes that do not see and the ears that do not listen—

22    Have you no respect at all for Me? the Lord God asks. How can it be that you don't even tremble in My presence? I set the shorelines of the world by perpetual decrees, so that the oceans, though they toss and

[1]The kingdom of Babylonia, being revived in Jeremiah's time (around 626 B.C.) had a long and illustrious history. The Old Babylonian Empire lasted from about 1900 B.C. to 1550 B.C. (the days of the Hebrew patriarchs), and earlier kingdoms had ruled on Babylonian soil as early as 3000 B.C.

roar, can never pass those bounds. Isn't such a God to be feared and worshiped?

23, 24 But My people have rebellious hearts; they have turned against Me and gone off into idolatry. Though I am the One who gives them rain each year in spring and fall and sends the harvest times, yet they have no respect or fear for Me.

25 And so I have taken away these wondrous blessings from them. This sin has robbed them of all of these good things.

26 Among my people are wicked men who lurk for victims like a hunter hiding in a blind. They set their traps for men.

27 Like a coop full of chickens their homes are full of evil plots. And the result? Now they are great and rich,

28 And well-fed and well-groomed, and there is no limit to their wicked deeds. They refuse justice to orphans and the rights of the poor.

29 Should I sit back and act as though nothing is going on? the Lord God asks. Shouldn't I punish a nation such as this?

30 A horrible thing has happened in this land—

31 The prophets say only what the priests have told them to, and My people like it so! But your doom is certain."

## CHAPTER 6

Run, people of Benjamin, run for your lives! Flee from Jerusalem! Sound the alarm in Tekoa; send up a smoke signal at Beth-haccerem; warn everyone that a powerful army is on the way from the north, coming to destroy this nation!

2 Helpless as a girl, you are beautiful and delicate—and doomed.

3 Evil shepherds shall surround you. They shall set up camp around the city, and divide your pastures for their flocks.

4 See them prepare for battle. At noon it has begun. All afternoon it rages, until the evening shadows fall.

5 'Come,' they say. 'Let us attack by night and destroy her palaces!'

6 For the Lord of Hosts has said to them, cut down her trees for battering rams; smash down the walls of Jerusalem. This is the city to be punished, for she is vile through and through.

7 She spouts evil like a fountain! Her streets echo with the sounds of violence; her sickness and wounds are ever before Me.

8 This is your last warning, O Jerusalem. If you don't listen, I will empty the land.

9 Disaster on disaster shall befall you. Even the few who remain in Israel shall be gleaned again, the Lord of Hosts has said; for as a grape-gatherer checks each vine to pick what he has missed, so the remnant of My people shall be destroyed again.

10 But who will listen when I warn them? Their ears are closed and they refuse to hear. The word of God has angered them; they don't want it at all.

11 For all this I am full of the wrath of God against them. I am weary of holding it in. I will pour it out over Jerusalem, even upon the children playing in the streets, upon the gatherings of young men, and on husbands and wives and grandparents.

12 Their enemies shall live in their homes and take their fields and wives. For I will lift My fist against the people of this land, the Lord has said.

13 They are swindlers and liars, from the least of them right to the top! Yes, even My prophets and priests!

14 You can't heal a wound by saying it's not there! Yet the priests and prophets give assurances of peace when all is war.

15 Were My people ashamed when they worshiped idols? No, not at all—they didn't even blush. Therefore they shall lie among the slain. They shall die beneath My anger.

16 Yet the Lord pleads with you still: Ask where the good road is, the godly paths you used to walk in, in the days of long ago. Travel there, and you will find rest for your souls. But you reply, 'No, that is not the road we want!'

17 I set watchmen over you who warned you: 'Listen for the sound of the trumpet! It will let you know when trouble comes.' But you said, 'No! We won't pay any attention!'

18 This, then, is My decree against My people: (Listen to it, distant lands; listen to it, O My people in Jerusalem;

19 Listen to it, all the earth!) I will bring evil upon this people; it will be the fruit of their own sin, because they will not listen to Me. They reject My law.

20 There is no use now in burning sweet incense from Sheba before Me! Keep your expensive perfumes! I cannot accept your offerings; they have no sweet fragrance for Me.

21 I will make an obstacle course of the pathway of My people; fathers and sons shall be frustrated; neighbors and friends shall collapse together.

22 The Lord God says, See the armies marching from the north—a great nation is rising against you.

23 They are a cruel, merciless people, fully armed, mounted for war. The noise of their army is like a roaring sea."

24 We have heard the fame of their armies and we are weak with fright. Fright and pain have gripped us like that of women in travail.

25 Don't go out to the fields! Don't travel the roads! For the enemy is everywhere, ready to kill; we are terrorized at every turn.

26 "O Jerusalem, pride of My people, put on mourning-clothes and sit in ashes and weep bitterly as for an only son. For suddenly the destroying armies will be upon you.

27 Jeremiah, I have made you an assayer of metals, that you may test this My people and determine their value. Listen to what they are saying and watch what they are doing.

28 Are they not the worst of rebels, full of evil talk

against the Lord? They are insolent as brass, hard and cruel as iron.

29   The bellows blow fiercely; the refining fire grows hotter, but it can never cleanse them, for there is no pureness in them to bring out. Why continue the process longer? All is dross. No matter how hot the fire, they continue in their wicked ways.

30   I must label them 'Impure, Rejected Silver,' and I have discarded them."

## CHAPTER 7

Then the Lord said to Jeremiah:

2   "Go over to the entrance of the Temple of the Lord and give this message to the people: O Judah, listen to this message from God. Listen to it, all of you who worship here.

3   The Lord of Hosts, the God of Israel says: Even yet, if you quit your evil ways I will let you stay in your own land.

4   But don't be fooled by those who lie to you and say that since the Temple of the Lord is here, God will never let Jerusalem be destroyed.

5   You may remain under these conditions only: If you stop your wicked thoughts and deeds, and are fair to others;

6   And stop exploiting orphans, widows and foreigners. And stop your murdering. And stop worshiping idols as you do now to your hurt.

7   Then, and only then, will I let you stay in this land that I gave to your fathers to keep forever.

8   You think that because the Temple is here, you will never suffer? Don't fool yourselves!

9   Do you really think that you can steal, murder, commit adultery, lie, and worship Baal and all of those new gods of yours,

10   And then come here and stand before Me in My Temple and chant "God will save us!"—only to go right back to all these evil things again?

11   Is My Temple but a den of robbers in your eyes? For I see all the evil going on in there.

12   Go to Shiloh, the city I first honored with My name, and see what I did to her because of all the wickedness of My people Israel.

13, 14   And now, says the Lord, I will do the same thing here because of all this evil you have done. Again and again I spoke to you about it, rising up early and calling, but you refused to hear or answer. Yes, I will destroy this Temple, as I did in Shiloh—this Temple called by My name, which you trust for help, and this place I gave to you and to your fathers.

15   And I will send you into exile, just as I did your brothers, the people of Ephraim.

16   Pray no more for these people, Jeremiah. Neither weep for them nor pray nor beg that I should help them, for I will not listen.

17   Don't you see what they are doing throughout the cities of Judah and in the streets of Jerusalem?

18   No wonder My anger is great! Watch how the

children gather wood and the fathers build fires, and the women knead dough and make cakes to offer to 'The Queen of Heaven'[1] and to their other idol-gods!

19 Am I the One that they are hurting? asks the Lord. Most of all they hurt themselves, to their own shame.

20 So the Lord God says, I will pour out My anger, yes, My fury on this place—people, animals, trees and plants will be consumed by the unquenchable fire of My anger.

21 The Lord of Hosts, the God of Israel says, Away with your offerings and sacrifices!

22 It wasn't offerings and sacrifices I wanted from your fathers when I led them out of Egypt. That was not the point of My command.

23 But what I told them was: *Obey* Me and I will be your God and you shall be My people; only do as I say and all shall be well!

24 But they wouldn't listen; they kept on doing whatever they wanted to, following their own stubborn, evil thoughts. They went backwards instead of forwards.

25 Ever since the day your fathers left Egypt until now I have kept on sending them My prophets, day after day.

26 But they wouldn't listen to them or even try to

[1] A name by which Ishtar, the Mesopotamian goddess of love and war was called. After the fall of Jerusalem the refugees who fled to Egypt continued to worship her (chapter 44). A papyrus dating from the 5th century B.C., found at Hermopolis in Egypt, mentions the "Queen of Heaven" among the gods honored by the Jewish community.

hear. They are hard and stubborn and rebellious—worse even than their fathers were.

27 Tell them everything that I will do to them, but don't expect them to listen. Cry out your warnings, but don't expect them to respond.

28 Say to them: This is the nation that refuses to obey the Lord their God, and refuses to be taught. She continues to live a lie.

29 O Jerusalem, shave your head in shame and weep alone upon the mountains; for the Lord has rejected and forsaken this people of His wrath.

30 For the people of Judah have sinned before My very eyes, says the Lord. They have set up their idols right in My own Temple, polluting it.

31 They have built the altar called Topheth in the Valley of Ben-Hinnom; and there they burn to death their little sons and daughters as sacrifices to their gods—a deed so horrible I've never even thought of it, let alone commanded it to be done.

32 The time is coming, says the Lord, when that valley's name will be changed from 'Topheth,' or the 'Valley of Ben-Hinnom,' to the 'Valley of Slaughter'; for there will be so many slain to bury that there won't be room enough for all the graves and they will dump the bodies in that valley.

33 The bodies of My people shall be food for the birds and animals, and no one shall be left to scare them away.

34 I will end the happy singing and laughter in the streets of Jerusalem and in the cities of Judah, and the

joyous voices of the bridegrooms and brides. For the
land shall lie in desolation."

## CHAPTER 8

"Then," says the Lord, "the enemy shall break open
the graves of the kings of Judah and of the princes
and priests and prophets and people,

2    And dig out their bones and spread them out on
the ground before the sun and moon and stars—the
gods of My people!—whom they have loved and worshiped. Their bones shall not be gathered up again nor
buried but shall be scattered like dung upon the ground.

3    And those of this evil nation who are still left
alive shall long to die, rather than live where I will
scatter them," says the Lord of Hosts.

4, 5    Once again give them this message from the
Lord: "When a person falls, he jumps up again; when
he is on the wrong road and discovers his mistake, he
goes back to the fork where he made the wrong turn.
But these people keep on along their evil path, even
though I warn them.

6    I listen to their conversation and what do I hear?
Is anyone sorry for sin? Does anyone say, 'What a
terrible thing I have done?' No, all are rushing pell-
mell down the path of sin as swiftly as a horse rushing
to the battle!

7    The stork knows the time of her migration, as
does the turtledove, and the crane, and the swallow.

They all return at God's appointed time each year; but not My people! They don't accept the laws of God.

8 How can you say, 'We understand His laws,' when your teachers have twisted them up to mean a thing I never said?

9 These wise teachers of yours will be shamed by exile for this sin; for they have rejected the word of the Lord. Are they then so wise?

10 I will give their wives and their farms to others; for all of them, great and small, prophet and priest, have one purpose in mind—to get what isn't theirs.

11 They give useless medicine for My people's grievous wounds, for they assure them all is well when that isn't so at all!

12 Are they ashamed because they worship idols? No, not in the least; they don't even know how to blush! That is why I will see to it that they lie among the fallen. I will visit them with death.

13 Their figs and grapes will disappear, their fruit trees will die, and all the good things I prepared for them will soon be gone.

14 Then the people will say, 'Why should we wait here to die? Come, let us go to the walled cities and perish there. For the Lord our God has decreed our doom and given us a cup of poison to drink because of all our sins.

15 We expected peace, but no peace came; we looked for health but there was only terror.'

16 The noise of war resounds from the northern

border.[2] The whole land trembles at the approach of the terrible army, for the enemy is coming, and is devouring the land and everything in it—the cities and people alike.

17   For I will send these enemy troops among you like poisonous snakes which you cannot charm. No matter what you do, they shall bite you and you will die."

\*     \*     \*     \*     \*

18   My grief is beyond healing; my heart is broken.

19   Listen to the weeping of my people all across the land. "Where is the Lord?" they ask. "Has God deserted us?"

"Oh, why have they angered Me with their carved idols and strange evil rites?" the Lord replies.

20   "The harvest is finished; the summer is over and we are not saved."

21   I weep for the hurt of my people; I stand amazed, silent, dumb with grief.

22   Is there no medicine in Gilead? Is there no physician there? Why doesn't God do something? Why doesn't He help?

## CHAPTER 9

Oh, that my eyes were a fountain of tears; I would weep forever; I would sob day and night for the slain of my people!

[2]Literally, "The snorting of their war horses can be heard all the way from Dan in the north."

2   Oh, that I could go away and forget them and live in some wayside shack in the desert, for they are all adulterous, treacherous men.

3   "They bend their tongues like bows to shoot their arrows of untruth. They care nothing for right and go from bad to worse; they care nothing for Me," says the Lord.

4   Beware of your neighbor! Beware of your brother! All take advantage of one another and spread their slanderous lies.

5   With practiced tongues they fool and defraud each other; they wear themselves out with all their sinning.

6   "They pile evil upon evil, lie upon lie, and utterly refuse to come to Me," says the Lord.

7   Therefore the Lord of Hosts says this: "See, I will melt them in a crucible of affliction. I will refine them and test them like metal. What else can I do with them?

8   For their tongues aim lies like poisoned spears. They speak cleverly to their neighbors while planning to kill them.

9   Should not I punish them for such things as this? asks the Lord. Shall not My soul be avenged on such a nation as this?"

10   Sobbing and weeping, I point to their mountains and pastures, for now they are desolate, without a living soul. Gone is the lowing of cattle, gone the birds and wild animals. All have fled.

11   "And I will turn Jerusalem into heaps of ruined

houses where only jackals have their dens. The cities of Judah shall be ghost towns, with no one living in them."

12 Who is wise enough to understand all this? Where is the Lord's messenger to explain it? Why is the land a wilderness so that no one dares even to travel through?

13 "Because," the Lord replies, "My people have forsaken My commandments and not obeyed My laws.

14 Instead they have done whatever they pleased and worshiped the idols of Baal, as their fathers told them to.

15 Therefore this is what the Lord of Hosts, the God of Israel, says: Lo, I will feed them with bitterness and give them poison to drink.

16 I will scatter them around the world, to be strangers in distant lands; and even there the sword of destruction shall chase them until I have utterly destroyed them.

17, 18 The Lord of Hosts says: Send for the mourners! Quick! Begin your crying! Let the tears flow from your eyes.

19 Hear Jerusalem weeping in despair. 'We are ruined! Disaster has befallen us! We must leave our land and homes!' "

20 Listen to the words of God, O women who wail. Teach your daughters to wail and your neighbors too.

21 For death has crept in through your windows into your homes. He has killed off the flower of your

youth. Children no longer play in the streets; the young men gather no more in the squares.

22    Tell them this, says the Lord: Bodies shall be scattered across the fields like manure, like sheaves after the mower, and no one will bury them.

23    The Lord says: Let not the wise man bask in his wisdom, nor the mighty man in his might, nor the rich man in his riches.

24    Let them boast in this alone: That they truly know Me, and understand that I am the Lord, loyal, kind and good to everyone, and that I love to be this way to My people.

25, 26    A time is coming, says the Lord, when I will punish all those who are circumcised in body but not in spirit—the Egyptians, Edomites, Ammonites, Moabites, Arabs, and yes, even you people of Judah. For all these pagan nations also circumcise themselves. Unless you circumcise your hearts by loving Me, your circumcision is only a heathen rite like theirs, and nothing more.

## CHAPTER 10

Hear the word of the Lord, O Israel:

2, 3    Don't act like the people who make horoscopes and try to read their fate and future in the stars! Don't be frightened by predictions such as theirs, for it is all a pack of lies. Their ways are futile and foolish. They cut down a tree and carve an idol,

4    And decorate it with gold and silver and fasten it

securely in place with hammer and nails, so that it won't fall over,

5    And there stands their god! Like a helpless scarecrow in a garden. It cannot speak, and it must be carried, for it cannot walk. Don't be afraid of such a god for it can neither harm nor help, nor do you any good.

6    O Lord, there is no other God like You. For You are great and Your name is full of power.

7    Who would not fear You, O King of nations? (And that title belongs to You alone!) Among all the wise men of the earth and in all the kingdoms of the world there isn't anyone like You.

8    The wisest of men who worship idols are altogether stupid and foolish.

9    They bring beaten sheets of silver from Tarshish and gold from Uphaz, and give them to skillful goldsmiths who make their idols; then they clothe these gods in kingly purple robes that expert tailors make.

10    But the Lord is the only true God, the living God, the everlasting King. The whole earth shall tremble at His anger; the world shall hide before His displeasure.

11    Say this to those who worship other gods: Your so-called gods, who have not made the heavens and earth, shall vanish from the earth,

12    But our God formed the earth by His power and wisdom, and by His intelligence He hung the stars in space and stretched out the heavens.

13    It is His voice that echoes in the thunder of the

storm clouds. He causes mist to rise upon the earth; He sends the lightning and brings the rain; and from His treasuries He brings the wind.

14 But foolish men without knowledge of God bow before their idols. It is a shameful business that these men are in, for what they make are frauds, gods without life or power in them.

15 All are worthless, silly; they will be crushed when their makers perish.

16 But the God of Jacob is not like these foolish idols. He is the Creator of all, and Israel is His chosen nation. The Lord of Hosts is His name.

17 Pack your bags, He says. Get ready now to leave; the siege will soon begin.

18 For suddenly I'll fling you from this land and pour great troubles down; at last you shall feel My wrath.

19 *Desperate is my wound. My grief is great. My sickness is incurable, but I must bear it.*

20 *My home is gone; my children have been taken away and I will never see them again. There is no one left to help me rebuild my home.*

21 The shepherds of my people have lost their senses; they no longer follow God nor ask His will. Therefore they perish and their flocks are scattered.

22 Listen! Hear the terrible sound of great armies coming from the north. The cities of Judah shall become dens of jackals.

23 O Lord, I know it is not within the power of man to map his life and plan his course—

24　So You correct me, Lord; but please be gentle. Don't do it in Your anger for I would die.

25　Pour out Your fury on the nations who don't obey the Lord, for they have destroyed Israel and made a wasteland of this entire country.

## CHAPTER 11

Then the Lord spoke to Jeremiah once again and said:

Remind the men of Judah and all the people of Jerusalem that I made a contract with their fathers— and cursed is the man who does not heed it!

4　For I told them at the time I brought them out of slavery in Egypt that if they would obey Me and do whatever I commanded them, then they and all their children would be Mine and I would be their God.

5　And now, Israel, obey Me, says the Lord, so that I can do for you the wonderful things I swore I would if you obeyed. I want to give you a land that "flows with milk and honey," as it is today. Then I replied, "So be it, Lord!"

6　Then the Lord said: Broadcast this message in Jerusalem's streets—go from city to city throughout the land and say, Remember this agreement that your fathers made with God, and do all the things they promised Him they would.

7　For I solemnly said to your fathers when I brought them out of Egypt—and have kept on saying it over and over again until this day: Obey My every command!

8 But your fathers didn't do it. They wouldn't even listen. Each followed his own stubborn will and his proud heart. Because they refused to obey, I did to them all the evils stated in the contract.

9 Again the Lord spoke to me and said: I have discovered a conspiracy against Me among the men of Judah and Jerusalem.

10 They have returned to the sins of their fathers, refusing to listen to Me and worshiping idols. The agreement I made with their fathers is broken and canceled.

11 Therefore, the Lord says, I am going to bring calamity down upon them and they shall not escape. Though they cry for mercy, I will not listen to their pleas.

12 Then they will pray to their idols and burn incense before them, but that cannot save them from their time of anguish and despair.

13 O My people, you have as many gods as there are cities, and your altars of shame (your altars to burn incense to Baal) are along every street in Jerusalem.

14 Therefore, Jeremiah, pray no longer for this people, neither weep nor plead for them; for I will not listen to them when they are finally desperate enough to beg Me for help.

15 What right do My beloved people have to come any more to My Temple? For you have been unfaithful

and worshiped other gods. Can promises and sacrifices now avert your doom and give you life and joy again?

16 The Lord used to call you His green olive tree, beautiful to see and full of good fruit; but now He has sent the fury of your enemies to burn you up and leave you broken and charred.

17 It is because of the wickedness of Israel and Judah in offering incense to Baal that the Lord of Hosts who planted the tree has ordered it destroyed.

18 Then the Lord told me all about their plans and showed me their evil plots.

19 I had been as unsuspecting as a lamb or ox on the way to slaughter. I didn't know that they were planning to kill me! "Let's destroy this man and all his messages," they said. "Let's kill him so that his name will be forever forgotten."

20 O Lord of Hosts, You are just. See the hearts and motives of these men. Repay them for all that they have planned! I look to You for justice.

21, 22 And the Lord replied, The men of the city of Anathoth shall be punished for planning to kill you. They will tell you not to prophesy in God's name on pain of death. And so their young men shall die in battle; their boys and girls shall starve.

23 Not one of these plotters of Anathoth shall survive, for I will bring a great disaster upon them. Their time has come.

## CHAPTER 12

O Lord, You always give me justice when I bring a case before You to decide. Now let me bring You this complaint: Why are the wicked so prosperous? Why are evil men so happy?

2   You plant them. They take root and their business grows. Their profits multiply, and they are rich. They say, 'Thank God!' But in their hearts they give no credit to You.

3   But as for me—Lord, You know my heart—You know how much it longs for You. (And I am poor,[3] O Lord!) Lord, drag them off like helpless sheep to the slaughter. Judge them, O God!"

4   How long must this land of Yours put up with all their goings on? Even the grass of the field groans and weeps over their wicked deeds! The wild animals and birds have moved away, leaving the land deserted. Yet the people say, "God won't bring judgment on us. We're perfectly safe!"

5   The Lord replied to me: If racing with mere men—these men of Anathoth[4]—has wearied you, how will you race against horses, against the king, his court and all his evil priests?[4] If you stumble and fall on open ground, what will you do in Jordan's jungles?

6   Even your own brothers, your own family, have turned against you. They have plotted to call for a mob to lynch you. Don't trust them, no matter how pleasantly they speak. Don't believe them.

7   Then the Lord said: I have abandoned My people, My inheritance; I have surrendered My dearest ones to their enemies.

---

[3]Implied.
[4]Implied.

8   My people have roared at Me like a lion of the forest, so I have treated them as though I hated them.

9   My people have fallen. I will bring upon them swarms of vultures and wild animals to pick the flesh from their corpses.

10   Many foreign rulers have ravaged My vineyard, trampling down the vines, and turning all its beauty into barren wilderness.

11   They have made it desolate; I hear its mournful cry. The whole land is desolate and no one cares.

12   Destroying armies plunder the land; the sword of the Lord devours from one end of the nation to the other; nothing shall escape.

13   My people have sown wheat but reaped thorns; they have worked hard but it does them no good; they shall harvest a crop of shame, for the fierce anger of the Lord is upon them.

14   And now the Lord says this to the evil nations, the nations surrounding the land God gave His people Israel: See, I will force you from your land just as Judah will be forced from hers;

15   But afterwards I will return and have compassion on all of you, and will bring you home to your own land again, each man to his inheritance.

16   And if these heathen nations quickly learn My people's ways and claim Me as their God instead of Baal (whom they taught My people to worship), then they shall be strong among My people.

17   But any nation refusing to obey Me will be expelled again and finished, says the Lord.

## CHAPTER 13

The Lord said to me, Go and buy a linen loincloth and wear it, but don't wash it—don't put it in water at all.

2 So I bought the loincloth and put it on.

3 Then the Lord's message came to me again. This time He said:

4 Take the loincloth out to the Euphrates River and hide it in a hole in the rocks.

5 So I did; I hid it as the Lord had told me to.

6 Then, a long time afterwards, the Lord said: Go out to the river again and get the loincloth.

7 And I did; I dug it out of the hole where I had hidden it. But now it was mildewed and falling apart. It was utterly useless!

8, 9 Then the Lord said: This illustrates the way that I will rot the pride of Judah and Jerusalem.

10 This evil nation refuses to listen to Me, and follows its own evil desires and worships idols; therefore it shall become as this loincloth—good for nothing.

11 Even as a loincloth clings to a man's loins, so I made Judah and Israel to cling to Me, says the Lord. They were My people, an honor to My name. But then they turned away.

12 Tell them this: The Lord God of Israel says,

All your jugs will be full of wine. And they will reply, Of course, you don't need to tell us how prosperous we will be!⁵

13   Then tell them: You're getting the wrong impression.* I will fill everyone living in this land with helpless bewilderment—from the king sitting on David's throne, and the priests and the prophets right on down to all the people.

14   And I will smash fathers and sons against each other, says the Lord. I will not let pity nor mercy spare them from utter destruction.

15   Oh, that you were not so proud and stubborn! Then you would listen to the Lord, for He has spoken.

16   Give glory to the Lord your God before it is too late, before He causes deep, impenetrable darkness to fall upon you so that you stumble and fall upon the dark mountains; then, when you look for light, you will find only terrible darkness.

17   Do you still refuse to listen? Then in loneliness my breaking heart shall mourn because of your pride. My eyes will overflow with tears because the Lord's flock shall be carried away as slaves.

18   Say to the king and queen-mother,⁶ Come down from your thrones and sit in the dust, for your glorious crowns are removed from your heads. They are no longer yours.

19   The cities of the Negeb to the south of Jeru-

---

⁵Literally, "that every bottle shall be filled with wine."
*Implied.
⁶King Jehoiachin and his mother Nehashta.

salem have closed their gates against the enemy. They must defend themselves, for Jerusalem cannot help;[7] and all Judah shall be taken away as slaves.

20   See the armies marching from the north! Where is your flock, Jerusalem,[8] your beautiful flock I gave you to take care of?

21   How will you feel when I set your allies over you as your rulers? You will writhe in pain like a woman having a child.

22   And if you ask yourself, Why is all this happening to me? It is because of the grossness of your sins; that is why you have been raped and destroyed by the invading army.

23   Can the Ethiopian Negro change the color of his skin? or a leopard take away his spots? Nor can you who are so used to doing evil now start being good.

24, 25   Because you have put Me out of your mind and put your trust in false gods, I will scatter you as chaff is scattered by the fierce winds off the desert. This then is your allotment, that which is due you, which I have measured out especially for you.

26   I Myself will expose you to utter shame.

27   I am keenly aware of your apostasy, your faithlessness to Me, and your abominable idol worship in the fields and on the hills. Woe upon you, O Jerusalem! How long before you will be pure?

---

[7] Literally, "the cities are closed and none can open them." Perhaps the meaning is that they are permanently abandoned.
[8] Implied.

## CHAPTER 14

This message came to Jeremiah from the Lord explaining why He was holding back the rain:

2   Judah mourns; business has ground to a halt; all the people prostrate themselves to the earth and a great cry rises from Jerusalem.

3   The nobles send servants for water from the wells, but the wells are dry. The servants return, baffled and desperate, and cover their heads in grief.

4   The ground is parched and cracked for lack of rain; the farmers are afraid.

5   The deer deserts her fawn because there is no grass.

6   The wild donkeys stand upon the bare hills panting like thirsty jackals. They strain their eyes looking for grass to eat, but there is none to be found.

\*      \*      \*      \*      \*

7   O Lord, we have sinned against You grievously, yet help us for the sake of Your own reputation!

8   O Hope of Israel, our Savior in times of trouble, why are You as a stranger to us, as one passing through the land who is merely stopping for the night?

9   Are You also baffled? Are You helpless to save us? O Lord, You are right here among us, and we carry Your name; we are known as Your people. O Lord, don't desert us now!

10   But the Lord replies: You have loved to wander

far from Me and have not tried to follow in My paths; and now I will no longer accept you as My people; now I will remember all the evil you have done and punish your sins.

11 The Lord told me again: Don't ask Me any more to bless this people. Don't pray for them any more.

12 When they fast, I will not pay any attention; when they present their offerings and sacrifices to me, I will not accept them. What I will give them in return is war and famine and disease.

13 Then I said, O Lord God, their prophets are telling them that all is well—that no war or famine will come. They tell the people You will surely send them peace, that You will bless them.

14 Then the Lord said: The prophets are telling lies in My name. I didn't send them or tell them to speak or give them any message. They prophesy of visions and revelations they have never seen nor heard; they speak foolishness concocted out of their own lying hearts.

15 Therefore, the Lord says, I will punish these lying prophets who have spoken in My name though I did not send them, who say no war shall come nor famine. By war and famine they themselves shall die!

16 And the people to whom they prophesy—their bodies shall be thrown out into the streets of Jerusalem, victims of famine and war; there shall be no one to bury them. Husbands, wives, sons and daughters—all will be gone. For I will pour out terrible punishment upon them for their sins.

17   Therefore, tell them this: Night and day My eyes shall overflow with tears; I cannot stop My crying, for My people have been run through with a sword and lie mortally wounded on the ground.

18   If I go out in the fields, there lie the bodies of those the sword has killed; and if I walk in the streets, there lie those dead from starvation and disease. And yet the prophets and priests alike have made it their business to travel through the whole country reassuring everyone that all was well, speaking of things they knew nothing about.

19   "O Lord," the people will cry, "have You completely rejected Judah? Do You abhor Jerusalem? Even after punishment, will there be no peace? We thought, Now at last He will heal us and bind our wounds. But no peace has come and there is only trouble and terror everywhere.

20   O Lord, we confess our wickedness, and that of our fathers too.

21   Do not hate us, Lord; for the sake of Your own name. Do not disgrace Yourself and the throne of Your glory by forsaking Your promise to bless us!

22   What heathen god can give us rain? Who but You alone, O Lord our God, can do such things as this? Therefore we will wait for You to help us."

## CHAPTER 15

Then the Lord said to me, Even if Moses and Samuel stood before Me pleading for these people, even then I wouldn't help them—away with them! Get them out of My sight!

2   And if they say to you, But where can we go? tell them the Lord says: Those who are destined for death, to death; those who must die by the sword, to the sword; those doomed to starvation, to famine; and those for captivity, to captivity.

3   I will appoint over them four kinds of destroyers, says the Lord—the sword to kill, the dogs to tear, and the vultures and wild animals to finish up what's left.

4   Because of the wicked things that Manasseh, son of Hezekiah, king of Judah, did in Jerusalem, I will punish you so severely that your fate will horrify the peoples of the world.

5   Who will feel sorry for you, Jerusalem? Who will weep for you? Who will even bother to ask how you are?

6   You have forsaken Me and turned your backs upon Me. Therefore I will clench My fists against you to destroy you. I am tired of always giving you another chance.

7   I will sift you at the gates of your cities and take from you all that you hold dear, and I will destroy My own people because they refuse to turn back to Me from all their evil ways.

8   There shall be countless widows; at noon time I will bring death to the young men and sorrow to their mothers. I will cause anguish and terror to fall upon them suddenly.

9   The mother of seven sickens and faints, for all her

sons are dead. Her sun is gone down while it is yet day. She sits childless now, disgraced; for all her children have been killed.

10    Then Jeremiah said, "What sadness is mine, my mother; oh, that I had died at birth. For I am hated everywhere I go. I am neither a creditor soon to fore-close nor a debtor refusing to pay—yet they all curse me.

11    Well, let them curse! Lord, You know how I have pled with You on their behalf—how I have begged You to spare these enemies of mine."

\*     \*     \*     \*     \*

12, 13    Can a man break bars of northern iron or bronze? This people's stubborn will can't be broken either. So, because of all your sins against Me, I will deliver your wealth and treasures as spoil to the enemy.

14    I will have your enemies take you as slaves to a land where you have never been before; for My anger burns like fire, and it shall consume you.

\*     \*     \*     \*     \*

15    Then Jeremiah replied, "Lord, You know it is for Your sake that I am suffering. They are persecuting me because I have proclaimed Your word to them. Don't let them kill me! Rescue me from their clutches, and give them what they deserve!

16    Your words are what sustain me; they are food to my hungry soul. They bring joy to my sorrowing heart and delight me. How proud I am to bear Your name, O Lord.

17, 18    I have not joined the people in their merry feasts. I sit alone beneath the hand of God. I burst with indignation at their sins. Yet You have failed me in my time of need! You have let them keep right on with all their persecutions. Will they never stop hurting me? Your help is as uncertain as a seasonal mountain brook—sometimes a flood, sometimes as dry as a bone."

19 The Lord replied: "Stop this foolishness and talk some sense! Only if you return to trusting Me will I let you continue as My spokesman. You are to influence *them,* not let them influence *you!*

20 They will fight against you like a besieging army against a high city wall. But they will not conquer you for I am with you to protect and deliver you, says the Lord.

21 Yes, I will certainly deliver you from these wicked men and rescue you from their ruthless hands."

## CHAPTER 16

On yet another occasion God spoke to me, and said: 2 You must not marry and have children here.

3 For the children born in this city and their mothers and fathers

4 Shall die from terrible diseases. No one shall mourn for them or bury them, but their bodies shall lie on the ground to rot and fertilize the soil. They shall die from war and famine, and their bodies shall be picked apart by vultures and wild animals.

5 Do not mourn or weep for them, for I have

removed My protection and My peace from them—taken away My lovingkindness and My mercies.

6   Both great and small shall die in this land, unburied and unmourned, and their friends shall not cut themselves nor shave their heads as signs of sorrow (as is their heathen custom).

7   No one shall comfort the mourners with a meal, or send them a cup of wine expressing grief for their parents' death.

8   As a sign to them of these sad days ahead,[9] don't you join them any more in their feasts and parties—don't even eat a meal with them.

9   For the Lord of Hosts, the God of Israel, says: In your own lifetime, before your very eyes, I will end all laughter in this land—the happy songs, the marriage feasts, the songs of bridegrooms and of brides.

10   And when you tell the people all these things and they ask, "Why has the Lord decreed such terrible things against us? What have we done to merit such treatment? What is our sin against the Lord our God?"

11   Tell them the Lord's reply is this: Because your fathers forsook Me. They worshiped other gods and served them; they did not keep My laws,

12   *And you have been worse than your fathers were!* You follow evil to your hearts' content and refuse to listen to Me.

13   Therefore I will throw you out of this land and chase you into a foreign land where neither you nor your fathers have been before and there you can go

---

[9]Implied.

ahead and worship your idols all you like—and I will grant you no favors!

*     *     *     *     *

14, 15   But there will come a glorious day, says the Lord, when the whole topic of conversation will be that God is bringing His people home from the countries of the north, where He had sent them as slaves for punishment.   You will look back no longer to the time I brought you out from slavery in Egypt. That mighty miracle will scarcely be mentioned any more.  Yes, I will bring you back again, says the Lord, to this same land I gave your fathers.

*     *     *     *     *

16   Now I am sending for many fishermen to fish you from the deeps where you are hiding from My wrath. I am sending for hunters to chase you down like deer in the forests or mountain goats on inaccessible crags. Wherever you run to escape My judgment, I will find you and punish you.

17   For I am closely watching you and I see every sin. You cannot hope to hide from Me.

18   And I will punish you doubly for all your sins because you have defiled My land with your detestable idols, and filled it up with all your evil deeds.

19   O Lord, my Strength and Fortress, my Refuge in the day of trouble, nations from around the world will come to You saying, "Our fathers have been foolish, for they have worshiped worthless idols!

20   Can men make God? The gods they made are not real gods at all."

21   And when they come in that spirit, I will show

them[1] My power and might and make them understand at last that I alone am God.

## CHAPTER 17

My people sin as though commanded to, as though their evil were laws chiseled with an iron pen or diamond point upon their stony hearts or on the corners of their altars.

2, 3   Their youths do not forget to sin, worshiping idols beneath each tree, high in the mountains or in the open country down below. And so I will give all your treasures to your enemies as the price that you must pay for all your sins.

4   And the wonderful heritage I reserved for you will slip out of your hand; and I will send you away as slaves to your enemies in distant lands. For you have kindled a fire of My anger that shall burn forever.

5   The Lord says: Cursed is the man who puts his trust in mortal man and turns his heart away from God.

6   He is like a stunted shrub in the desert, with no hope for the future; he lives on the salt-encrusted plains in the barren wilderness; good times pass him by forever.

7   But blessed is the man who trusts in the Lord and has made the Lord his hope and confidence.

8   He is like a tree planted along a riverbank, with its roots reaching deep into the water—a tree not both-

---

[1]Literally, "Therefore, behold, I will cause them to know . . ."

ered by the heat nor worried by long months of drought. Its leaves stay green and it goes right on producing all its luscious fruit.

9 The heart is the most deceitful thing there is, and desperately wicked. No one can really know how bad it is!

10 Only the Lord knows! He searches all hearts and examines deepest motives so He can give to each person his right reward, according to his deeds—how he has lived.

11 Like a partridge filling her nest with young she has not hatched and which will soon desert her and fly away, so is the man who gets his wealth by unjust means. Sooner or later he will lose his riches and at the end of his life become a poor old fool.

12 But our refuge is Your throne, eternal, high and glorious.

13 O Lord, the Hope of Israel, all who turn away from You shall be disgraced and shamed; they are registered for earth and not for glory, for they have forsaken the Lord, the Fountain of living waters.

14 Lord, You alone can heal me, You alone can save, and my praises are for You alone.

15 Men scoff at me and say, "What is this word of the Lord you keep talking about? If these threats of yours are really from God, why don't they come true?"

16 Lord, I don't want the people crushed by terrible calamity. The plan is Yours, not mine. It is *Your* message I've given them, not my own. *I* don't want them doomed!

17 Lord, don't desert me now! You alone are my hope.

18 Bring confusion and trouble on all who persecute me; but give me peace. Yes, bring double destruction upon them!

19 Then the Lord said to me, Go and stand in the gates of Jerusalem, first at the gate where the king goes out, and then at each of the other gates,

20 And say to all the people: Hear the word of the Lord, kings of Judah and all the people of this nation, and all you citizens of Jerusalem;

21, 22 The Lord says: Take warning and live; do no unnecessary[2] work on the Sabbath day but make it a holy day. I gave this commandment to your fathers,

23 But they didn't listen or obey. They stubbornly refused to pay attention and be taught.

24 But if you obey Me, says the Lord, and refuse to work upon the Sabbath day and keep it separate, special and holy,

25 Then this nation shall continue forever. There shall always be descendants of David sitting on the throne here in Jerusalem; there shall always be kings and princes riding in pomp and splendor among the people; and this city shall remain forever.

26 And from all around Jerusalem and from the cities of Judah and Benjamin, and from the Negeb and from the lowlands west of Judah, the people shall come with their burnt offerings and grain offerings and in-

---

[2]Implied.

cense, bringing their sacrifices to praise the Lord in His Temple.

27 But if you will not listen to Me, if you refuse to keep the Sabbath holy, if on the Sabbath you bring in loads of merchandise through these gates of Jerusalem, just as on other days, then I will set fire to these gates and the fire shall spread to the palaces and utterly destroy them, and no one shall be able to put out the raging flames.

## CHAPTER 18

Here is another message to Jeremiah from the Lord: 2 Go down to the shop where clay pots and jars are made and I will talk to you there.

3 I did as He told me, and found the potter working at his wheel.

4 But the jar that he was forming didn't turn out as he wished, so he kneaded it into a lump and started again.

5 Then the Lord said:

6 O Israel, can't I do to you as this potter has done to his clay? As the clay is in the potter's hand, so are you in My hand.

7 Whenever I announce that a certain nation or kingdom is to be taken up and destroyed,

8 Then if that nation renounces its evil ways, I will not destroy it as I had planned.

9 And if I announce that I will make a certain nation strong and great,

10   But then that nation changes its mind and turns to evil and refuses to obey Me, then I too will change My mind and not bless that nation as I had said I would.

11   Therefore go and warn all Judah and Jerusalem, saying: Hear the word of the Lord, I am planning evil against you now instead of good; turn back from your evil paths and do what is right.

12   But they replied, "Don't waste your breath. We have no intention whatever of doing what God says. We will continue to live as we want to, free from any restraint, full of stubbornness and wickedness!"

13   Then the Lord said: Even among the heathen, no one has ever heard of such a thing! My people have done something too horrible to understand.

14   The snow never melts high up in the Lebanon mountains. The cold flowing streams from the crags of Mount Hermon never run dry.

15   These can be counted on. But not My people! For they have deserted Me and turned to foolish idols. They have turned away from the ancient highways of good, and walk the muddy paths of sin.

16   Therefore their land shall become desolate, so that all who pass by will gasp and shake their heads in amazement at its utter desolation.

17   I will scatter My people before their enemies as the east wind scatters dust; and in all their trouble I will turn My back on them and refuse to notice their distress.

18   Then the people said, "Come, let's get rid of

Jeremiah. We have our own priests and wise men and prophets—we don't need his advice. Let's silence him that he may speak no more against us, nor bother us again."

19 *O Lord, help me! See what they are planning to do to me!*

20 Should they repay evil for good? They have set a trap to kill me, yet I spoke well of them to You and tried to defend them from Your anger.

21 Now, Lord, let their children starve to death and let the sword pour out their blood! Let their wives be widows and be bereft of all their children! Let their men die in epidemics and their youths die in battle!

22 Let screaming be heard from their homes as troops of soldiers come suddenly upon them, for they have dug a pit for me to fall in, and they have hidden traps along my path.

23 Lord, You know all their murderous plots against me. Don't forgive them, don't blot out their sin, but let them perish before You; deal with them in Your anger.

## CHAPTER 19

The Lord said, Buy a clay jar and take it out into the valley of Ben-Hinnom by the east gate of the city. Take some of the elders of the people and some of the older priests with you, and speak to them whatever words I give you.

3 Then the Lord spoke to them and said: Listen to

the word of the Lord, kings of Judah and citizens of Jerusalem! The Lord of Hosts, the God of Israel, says, I will bring terrible evil upon this place, so terrible that the ears of those who hear it will prickle.

4    For Israel has forsaken Me and turned this valley into a place of shame and wickedness. The people burn incense to idols—idols that neither this generation nor their forefathers nor the kings of Judah have worshiped before—and they have filled this place with the blood of innocent children.

5    They have built high altars to Baal and there they burn their sons in sacrifice—a thing I never commanded them nor even thought of!

6    The day is coming, says the Lord, when this valley shall no longer be called "Topheth" or "Ben-Hinnom Valley," but "The Valley of Slaughter."

7    For I will upset the battle plans of Judah and Jerusalem and I will let invading armies kill you here and leave your dead bodies for vultures and wild animals to feed upon.

8    And I will wipe Jerusalem off the earth, so that everyone going by will gasp with astonishment at all that I have done to her.

9    I will see to it that your enemies lay siege to the city until all food is gone, and those trapped inside begin to eat their own children and friends.

10    And now, Jeremiah, as these men watch, smash the jar you brought with you.

11    And say to them, This is the message to you from the Lord of Hosts: As this jar lies shattered, so I

will shatter the people of Jerusalem; and as this jar cannot be mended, neither can they. The slaughter shall be so great that there won't be room enough for decent burial anywhere, and their bodies shall be heaped in this valley.

12    And as it will be in this valley, so it will be in Jerusalem. For I will fill Jerusalem with dead bodies too.

13    And I will defile all the homes in Jerusalem including the palace of the kings of Judah—wherever incense has been burned upon the roofs to your star-gods, and libations poured out to them.

14    As Jeremiah returned from Topheth where he had delivered this message, he stopped in front of the Temple of the Lord and said to all the people,

15    The Lord of Hosts, the God of Israel, says: I will bring upon this city and her surrounding towns all the evil I have promised, because you have stubbornly refused to listen to the Lord.

# CHAPTER 20

Now when Pashhur (son of Immer), the priest in charge of the Temple of the Lord, heard what Jeremiah was saying,

2    He arrested Jeremiah and had him whipped and put in the stocks at Benjamin Gate near the Temple.

3    He left him there all night. The next day when Pashhur finally released him, Jeremiah said, "Pashhur,

the Lord has changed your name. He says from now on to call you 'The Man Who Lives in Terror.'

4    For the Lord will send terror on you and all your friends, and you will see them die by the swords of their enemies. I will hand over Judah to the king of Babylon, says the Lord, and he shall take away these people as slaves to Babylon and kill them.

5    And I will let your enemies loot Jerusalem. All the famed treasures of the city, with the precious jewels and gold and silver of your kings, shall be carried off to Babylon.

6    And as for you, Pashhur, you and all your family and household shall become slaves in Babylon and die there—you and those to whom you lied when you prophesied that everything would be all right."

7    Then I said, O Lord, You deceived me when You promised me Your help. I have to give them Your messages because You are stronger than I am, but now I am the laughingstock of the city, mocked by all.

8    You have never once let me speak a word of kindness to them; always it is disaster and horror and destruction. No wonder they scoff and mock and make my name a household joke.

9    And I can't quit! For if I say I'll never again mention the Lord—never more speak in His Name— then His word in my heart is like fire that burns in my bones, and I can't hold it in any longer.

10    Yet on every side I hear their whispered threats, and am afraid. "We will report you," they say. Even those who were my friends are watching me, waiting for

a fatal slip. "He will trap himself," they say, "and then we will get our revenge on him."

11    But the Lord stands beside me like a great warrior, and before Him, the Mighty, Terrible One, they shall stumble. They cannot defeat me; they shall be shamed and thoroughly humiliated, and they shall have a stigma upon them forever.

12    O Lord of Hosts, who knows those who are righteous and examines the deepest thoughts of hearts and minds, let me see Your vengeance on them. For I have committed my cause to You.

13    Therefore I will sing out in thanks to the Lord! Praise Him! For He has delivered me, poor and needy, from my oppressors.

14    Yet, cursed be the day that I was born!

15    Cursed be the man who brought my father the news that a son was born.

16    Let that messenger be destroyed like the cities of old which God overthrew without mercy. Terrify him all day long with battle shouts,

17    Because he did not kill me at my birth! Oh, that I had died within my mother's womb, that it had been my grave!

18    Why was I ever born? For my life has been but trouble and sorrow and shame.

## CHAPTER 21

Then King Zedekiah sent Pashhur (son of Malchiah) and Zephaniah the priest (son of Maaseiah) to Jeremiah, and begged, "Ask the Lord to help us, for Nebuchadnezzar, king of Babylon, has declared war on us! Perhaps the Lord will be gracious to us and do a mighty miracle as in olden times[3] and force Nebuchadnezzar to withdraw his forces."

3, 4   Jeremiah replied, "Go back to King Zedekiah and tell him the Lord God of Israel says; I will make all your weapons useless against the king of Babylon and the Chaldeans besieging you. In fact, I will bring your enemies right into the heart of this city,

5   And I Myself will fight against you, for I am very angry.

6   And I will send a terrible plague on this city, and both men and animals shall die.

7   And finally I will deliver King Zedekiah himself and all the remnant left in the city into the hands of King Nebuchadnezzar of Babylon, to slaughter them without pity or mercy.

8   Tell these people, the Lord says: Take your choice of life or death!

9   Stay here in Jerusalem and die—slaughtered by your enemies, killed by starvation and disease—or go out and surrender to the Chaldean army and live.

10   For I have set My face against this city; I will be its enemy and not its friend, says the Lord. It shall be captured by the king of Babylon and he shall reduce it to ashes.

11   And to the king of Judah, the Lord says:

---

[3] King Zedekiah doubtless had in mind God's deliverance of Jerusalem from Sennacherib, king of Assyria, in the days of Hezekiah (Isaiah 36-37.) But Zedekiah's hopes were dashed. He was Judah's last ruler before the exile of 597 B.C.

12   I am ready to judge you because of all the evil you are doing. Quick! Give justice to these you judge! Begin doing what is right before My burning fury flashes out upon you like a fire no man can quench.

13   I will fight against this city of Jerusalem, which boasts, 'We are safe; no one can touch us here!'

14   And I Myself will destroy you for your sinfulness, says the Lord. I will light a fire in the forests that will burn up everything in its path."

## CHAPTER 22

Then the Lord said to me: Go over and speak directly to the king of Judah and say,

2   Listen to this message from God, O king of Judah, sitting on David's throne; and let your servants and your people listen too.

3   The Lord says: Be fair-minded. Do what is right! Help those in need of justice! Quit your evil deeds! Protect the rights of aliens and immigrants, orphans and widows; stop murdering the innocent!

4   If you put an end to all these terrible deeds you are doing, then I will deliver this nation and once more give kings to sit on David's throne, and there shall be prosperity for all.

5   But if you refuse to pay attention to this warning, I swear by My own name, says the Lord, that this palace shall become a shambles.

6   For this is the Lord's message concerning the

palace: You are as beloved to Me as fruitful Gilead and the green forests of Lebanon; but I will destroy you and leave you deserted and uninhabited.

7    I will call for a wrecking crew to bring out its tools to dismantle you. They will tear out all of your fine cedar beams and throw them on the fire.

8    Men from many nations will pass by the ruins of this city and say to one another, "Why did the Lord do it? Why did He destroy such a great city?"

9    And the answer will be, "Because the people living here forgot the Lord their God and violated His agreement with them, for they worshiped idols."

10    Don't weep for the dead! Instead weep for the captives led away! For they will never return to see their native land again.

11    For the Lord says this about Jehoahaz who succeeded[4] his father King Josiah, and who was taken away as a captive:

12    He shall die in a distant land[5] and never again see his own country.

13    And woe to you, King Jehoiakim,[6] for you are building your great palace with forced labor. By not paying wages you are building injustice into its walls and oppression into its doorframes and ceilings.

14    You say, "I will build a magnificent palace with huge rooms and many windows, panelled throughout with fragrant cedar and painted a lovely red."

---

[4]Jehoahaz, or Shallum, reigned for 3 brief months in the year 609 B.C.
[5]Egypt.
[6]Implied. See verse 18. He was chosen by the Egyptians to replace Jehoahaz whom they took back to Egypt with them. He ruled from 609-598 B.C.

15    But a beautiful palace does not make a great king! Why did your father Josiah reign so long? Because he was just and fair in all his dealings. That is why God blessed him.

16    He saw to it that justice and help was given the poor and the needy and all went well for him. This is how a man lives close to God.

17    But you! You are full of selfish greed and all dishonesty! You murder the innocent, oppress the poor and reign with ruthlessness.

18    Therefore this is God's decree of punishment against King Jehoiakim, who succeeded his father Josiah on the throne: His family will not weep for him when he dies. His subjects will not even care that he is dead.

19    He shall be buried like a dead donkey—dragged out of Jerusalem and thrown on the garbage dump beyond the gate!

20    Weep, for your allies are gone. Search for them in Lebanon; shout for them at Bashan; seek them at the fording points of Jordan. See, they are all destroyed. Not one is left to help you!

21    When you were prosperous I warned you, but you replied, "Don't bother me." Since childhood you have been that way—you just won't listen!

22    And now all your allies have disappeared with a puff of wind; all your friends are taken off as slaves. Surely at last you will see your wickedness and be ashamed.

23    It's very nice to live graciously in a beautiful

palace among the cedars of Lebanon; but soon you will cry and groan in anguish—anguish as of a woman in travail.

24, 25 And as for you, Coniah,[7] son of Jehoiachim king of Judah—even if you were the signet ring on My right hand, I would pull you off and give you to those who seek to kill you, of whom you are so desperately afraid, to Nebuchadnezzar, king of Babylon, and his mighty army.

26 I will throw you and your mother out of this country, and you shall die in a foreign land.

27 You will never again return to the land of your desire.

28 This man Coniah is like a discarded, broken dish. He and his children will be exiled to distant lands.

29 O earth, earth, earth! Hear the word of the Lord!

30 The Lord says: Record this man Coniah as childless; for none of his children shall ever sit upon the throne of David or rule in Judah.[8] His life will amount to nothing.

## CHAPTER 23

The Lord declares: I will send disaster upon the leaders of My people—the shepherds of My sheep

---

[7]Coniah is an abbreviation—perhaps a disparaging nickname—for Jeconiah and Jehoiachin, his other names. His name means "The Lord will establish my throne!"
[8]This man Coniah's grandson, Zerubbabel, was briefly governor, but not king.

—for they have destroyed and scattered the very ones they were to care for.

2    Instead of leading My flock to safety, you have deserted them and driven them to destruction. And now I will pour out judgment upon you for the evil you have done to them.

3    And I will gather together the remnant of My flock from all the countries I have sent them, and bring them back into their own fold, and they shall be fruitful and increase.

4    And I will appoint responsible shepherds to care for them; and they shall not need to be afraid again; and all of them shall be accounted for continually.

5, 6    For the time is coming, says the Lord, when I will place a righteous Branch upon King David's throne. He shall be a King who shall rule with wisdom and justice and cause righteousness to prevail everywhere throughout the earth.[9] And this is His Name: THE LORD OUR RIGHTEOUSNESS. At that time Judah will be saved and Israel will live in peace.

7    In that day people will no longer say when taking an oath, "As the Lord lives who rescued the people of Israel from the land of Egypt,"

8    But they will say, "As the Lord lives who brought the Jews back from the countries to which He had exiled them to their own land of Israel."

9    My heart is broken for the false prophets, full of deceit. I awake with fear and stagger as a drunkard does from wine, because of the awful fate awaiting

---

[9]Or, "throughout the land."

them,[2] for God has decreed holy words of judgment against them.

10　For the land is full of adultery and the curse of God is on it. The land itself is mourning—the pastures are dried up—for the prophets do evil and their power is used wrongly.

11　And the priests are like the prophets, all ungodly, wicked men. I have seen their despicable acts right here in My own Temple, says the Lord.

12　Therefore their paths will be dark and slippery; they will be chased down dark and treacherous trails, and fall. For I will bring evil upon them and see to it, when their time has come, that they pay their penalty in full for all their sins.

13　I knew the prophets of Samaria were unbelievably evil, for they prophesied by Baal and led My people Israel into sin;

14　But the prophets of Jerusalem are even worse! The things they do are horrible; they commit adultery and love dishonesty. They encourage and compliment those who are doing evil, instead of turning them back from their sins. These prophets are as thoroughly depraved as the men of Sodom and Gomorrah were.

15　Therefore the Lord of Hosts says: I will feed them with bitterness and give them poison to drink. For it is because of them that wickedness fills this land.

16　This is My warning to My people, says the Lord of Hosts. Don't listen to these false prophets when they prophesy to you, filling you with futile hopes. They are

---

[2]Implied.

making up everything they say. They do not speak for Me!

17 They keep saying to these rebels who despise Me, "Don't worry! All is well"; and to those who live the way they want to, "The Lord has said you shall have peace!"

18 But can you name even one of these prophets who lives close enough to God to hear what He is saying? Has even one of them cared enough to listen?

19 See, the Lord is sending a furious whirlwind to sweep away these wicked men.

20 The terrible anger of the Lord will not abate until it has carried out the full penalty He decrees against them. Later, when Jerusalem has fallen,[3] you will see what I mean.

21 I have not sent these prophets, yet they claim to speak for Me; I gave them no message, yet they say their words are Mine.

22 If they were Mine, they would try to turn My people from their evil ways.

23 Am I a God who is only in one place and cannot see what they are doing?

24 Can anyone hide from Me? Am I not every-where in all of heaven and earth?

25 "Listen to the dream I had from God last night," they say. And then they proceed to lie in My name.

26 How long will this continue? If they are

_____
[3] Literally, "in the latter days."

"prophets," they are prophets of deceit, inventing everything they say.

27   By telling these false dreams they are trying to get My people to forget Me in the same way as their fathers did, who turned away to the idols of Baal.

28   Let these false prophets tell their dreams and let My true messengers faithfully proclaim My every word. There is a difference between chaff and wheat!

29   Does not My word burn like fire? asks the Lord. Is it not like a mighty hammer that smashed the rock to pieces?

30, 31   So I stand against these "prophets" who get their messages from each other—these smooth-tongued prophets who say, "This message is from God!"

32   Their made-up dreams are flippant lies that lead My people into sin. I did not send them and they have no message at all for My people, says the Lord.

33   When one of the people or one of their "prophets" or priests asks you, "Well, Jeremiah, what is the sad news from the Lord today?" you shall reply, "What sad news? You are the sad news, for the Lord has cast you away!"

34   And as for the false prophets and priests and people who joke about "today's sad news from God," I will punish them and their families for saying this.

35   You can ask each other, "What is God's message? What is He saying?"

36   But stop using this term, "God's sad news." For what is sad is you and your lying. You are twisting My

words and inventing "messages from God" that I didn't speak.

37  You may respectfully ask Jeremiah, "What is the Lord's message? What has He said to you?"

38, 39  But if you ask him about "today's sad news from God," when I have warned you not to mock like that, then I, the Lord God, will unburden Myself of the burden[4] you are to Me. I will cast you out of My presence, you and this city I gave to you and your fathers.

40  And I will bring reproach upon you and your name shall be infamous through the ages.

## CHAPTER 24

After Nebuchadnezzar, king of Babylon, had captured and enslaved Jeconiah (son of Jehoiakim), king of Judah, and exiled him to Babylon along with the princes of Judah and the skilled tradesmen—the carpenters and blacksmiths—the Lord gave me this vision.

2  I saw two baskets of figs placed in front of the Temple in Jerusalem. In one basket there were fresh, just-ripened figs, but in the other the figs were spoiled and moldy—too rotten to eat.

3  Then the Lord said to me, what do you see, Jeremiah? I replied, "Figs, some very good and some very bad."

---

[4]Literally, either "the *burden* of the Lord" or "the *message* of the Lord." This is a Hebrew pun.

4, 5    Then the Lord said: The good figs represent the exiles sent to Babylon. I have done it for their good.

6    I will see that they are well-treated and I will bring them back here again. I will help them and not hurt them; I will plant them and not pull them up.

7    I will give them hearts that respond to Me. They shall be My people and I will be their God, for they shall return to Me with great joy.

8    But the rotten figs represent Zedekiah, king of Judah, his officials and all the others of Jerusalem left here in this land; those too who live in Egypt. I will treat them like spoiled figs, too bad to use.

9    I will make them repulsive to every nation of the earth, and they shall be mocked and taunted and cursed wherever I compel them to go.

10    And I will send massacre and famine and disease among them until they are destroyed from the land of Israel, which I gave to them and to their fathers.

## CHAPTER 25

This message for all the people of Judah came from the Lord to Jeremiah during the fourth year of the reign of King Jehoiakim of Judah (son of Josiah). This was the year Nebuchadnezzar, king of Babylon, began his reign.

2, 3    "For the past twenty-three years," Jeremiah said, "from the thirteenth year of the reign of Josiah (son of Amon) king of Judah, until now, God has been sending me His messages. I have faithfully passed them on to you, but you haven't listened.

4   Again and again down through the years, God has sent you His prophets, but you have refused to hear.

5   Each time the message was this: Turn from the evil road you are traveling and from the evil things you are doing. Only then can you continue to live here in this land which the Lord gave to you and to your ancestors forever.

6   *Don't anger Me by worshiping idols; but if you are true to me, then I'll not harm you.*

7   But you won't listen; you have gone ahead and made Me furious with your idols. So you have brought upon yourselves all the evil that has come your way.

8, 9   And now the Lord God of Hosts says, Because you have not listened to Me, I will gather together all the armies of the north under Nebuchadnezzar, king of Babylon (I have appointed him as My deputy), and I will bring them all against this land and its people and against the other nations near you, and I will utterly destroy you and make you a byword of contempt forever.

10   I will take away your joy, your gladness and your wedding feasts; your businesses shall fail and all your homes shall lie in silent darkness.

11   This entire land shall become a desolate wasteland; all the world will be shocked at the disaster that befalls you. Israel and her neighboring lands shall serve the king of Babylon for seventy years.

12    Then, after these years[6] of slavery are ended, I will punish the king of Babylon[7] and his people for their sins; I will make the land of Chaldea an everlasting waste.

13    I will bring upon them all the terrors I have promised in this Book—all the penalties announced by Jeremiah against the nations.

14    For many nations and great kings shall enslave the Chaldeans, just as they enslaved My people; I will punish them in proportion to their treatment of My people.

15    For the Lord God said to me: "Take from My hand this wine cup filled to the brim with My fury, and make all the nations to whom I send you drink from it.

16    They shall drink from it and reel, crazed by the death blows I rain upon them."

17    So I took the cup of fury from the Lord and made all the nations drink from it—every nation God had sent me to:

18    I went to Jerusalem and to the cities of Judah, and their kings and princes drank of the cup so that from that day until this they have been desolate, hated and cursed, just as they are today.

19, 20    I went to Egypt, and Pharaoh and his servants, the princes and the people—they too drank from that terrible cup, along with all the foreign population living in his land. So did all the kings of the land

---

[6]Literally, "the seventy years."
[7]This event is further described in Daniel 5. The troops of Cyrus the Great entered Babylon in 539 B.C. and killed Belshazzar, the last Babylonian ruler.

of Uz and the kings of the Philistine cities: Ashkelon, Gaza, Ekron, and what remains of Ashdod,

21  And I visited the nations of Edom, Moab and Ammon;

22  And all the kings of Tyre and Sidon, and the kings of the regions across the sea;

23  Dedan and Tema and Buz, and the other heathen there;

24  And all the kings of Arabia and of the nomadic tribes of the desert;

25  And all the kings of Zimri, Elam and Media;

26  And all the kings of the northern countries, far and near, one after the other; and all the kingdoms of the world. And finally, the king of Babylon himself drank from this cup of God's wrath.

27  Tell them, "The Lord of Hosts, the God of Israel, says, Drink from this cup of My wrath until you are drunk and vomit and fall and rise no more, for I am sending terrible wars upon you."

28  And if they refuse to accept the cup, tell them: "The Lord of Hosts says you *must* drink it! You cannot escape!

29  I have begun to punish My own people, so should you go free? No, you shall not evade punishment. I will call for war against all the peoples of the earth."

30  Therefore prophesy against them. Tell them the Lord will shout against His own from His holy temple in heaven, and against all those living on the earth. He

will shout as the harvesters do who tread the juice from the grapes.

31 That cry of judgment will reach the farthest ends of the earth, for the Lord has a case against all the nations—all mankind. He will slaughter all the wicked.

32 See, declares the Lord of Hosts, the punishment shall go from nation to nation—a great whirlwind of wrath shall rise against the farthest corners of the earth.

33 On that day those the Lord has slain shall fill the earth from one end to the other. No one shall mourn for them nor gather up the bodies to bury them; they shall fertilize the earth.

34 Weep and moan, O evil shepherds; let the leaders of mankind beat their heads upon the stones, for their time has come to be slaughtered and scattered; they shall fall like fragile women.

35 And you will find no place to hide, no way to escape.

36 Listen to the frantic cries of the shepherds and to the leaders shouting in despair, for the Lord has spoiled their pastures.

37 People now living undisturbed will be cut down by the fierceness of the anger of the Lord.

38 He has left His lair like a lion seeking prey; their land has been laid waste by warring armies—because of the fierce anger of the Lord.

## CHAPTER 26

This message came to Jeremiah from the Lord during the first year of the reign of Jehoiakim (son of Josiah), king of Judah:

2    Stand out in front of the Temple of the Lord and make an announcement to all the people who have come there to worship from many parts of Judah. Give them the entire message; don't leave out one word of all I have for them to hear.

3    For perhaps they will listen and turn from their evil ways, and then I can withhold all the punishment I am ready to pour out upon them because of their evil deeds.

4    Tell them the Lord says: If you will not listen to Me and obey the laws I have given you,

5    And if you will not listen to My servants, the prophets—for I sent them again and again to warn you, but you would not listen to them—

6    Then I will destroy this Temple as I destroyed the tabernacle at Shiloh, and I will make Jerusalem a curse-word in every nation of the earth.

*     *     *     *     *

7, 8    When Jeremiah had finished his message, saying everything the Lord had told him to, the priests and false prophets and all the people in the Temple mobbed him, shouting, "Kill him! Kill him!"

9    "What right do you have to say the Lord will destroy this Temple like the one at Shiloh?" they yelled. "What do you mean—Jerusalem destroyed and not one survivor?"

10    When the high officials of Judah heard what was going on, they rushed over from the palace and sat down at the door of the Temple to hold court.

11　Then the priests and the false prophets presented their accusations to the officials and the people. "This man should die!" they said. "You have heard with your own ears what a traitor he is, for he has prophesied against this city."

12　Then Jeremiah spoke in his defense, "The Lord sent me," he said, "to prophesy against this Temple and this city. He gave me every word of all that I have spoken.

13　But if you stop your sinning and begin obeying the Lord your God, He will cancel all the punishment He has announced against you.

14　As for me, I am helpless and in your power— do with me as you think best.

15　But there is one thing sure, if you kill me, you will be killing an innocent man and the responsibility will lie upon you and upon this city and upon every person living in it; for it is absolutely true that the Lord sent me to speak every word that you have heard from me."

16　Then the officials and people said to the priests and false prophets, "This man does not deserve the death sentence, for he has spoken to us in the name of the Lord our God."

17　Then some of the wise old men stood and spoke to all the people standing around and said:

18　"The decision is right; for back in the days when Micah the Morasthite prophesied in the days of King Hezekiah of Judah, he told the people that God said: 'This hill shall be plowed like an open field and this city of Jerusalem razed into heaps of stone, and a forest shall grow at the top where the great Temple now stands!'

19 But did King Hezekiah and the people kill him for saying this? No, they turned from their wickedness and worshiped the Lord and begged the Lord to have mercy upon them; and the Lord held back the terrible punishment He had pronounced against them. If we kill Jeremiah for giving us the messages of God, who knows what God will do to us!"

20 Another true prophet of the Lord, Urijah (son of Shemaiah) from Kiriathjearim, was also denouncing the city and the nation at the same time as Jeremiah was.

21 But when King Jehoiakim and the army officers and officials heard what he was saying, the king sent to kill him. Urijah heard about it and fled to Egypt.

22 Then King Jehoiakim sent Elnathan (son of Achbor) to Egypt along with several other men to capture Urijah.

23 They took him prisoner and brought him back to King Jehoiakim, who butchered him with a sword and had him buried in an unmarked grave.

24 But Ahikam (son of Shaphan) the royal secretary,[9] stood with Jeremiah and persuaded the court not to turn him over to the mob to kill him.

[9]Implied. See 2 Kings 22:12.

## CHAPTER 27

This message came to Jeremiah from the Lord at the beginning of the reign of Jehoiakim[1] (son of Josiah), king of Judah:

2   Make a yoke and fasten it on your neck with leather thongs as you would strap a yoke on a plow-ox.

3   Then send messages to the kings of Edom, Moab, Ammon, Tyre and Sidon, through their ambassadors in Jerusalem,

4   Saying, Tell your masters that the Lord of Hosts, the God of Israel, sends you this message:

5   "By My great power I have made the earth and all mankind and every animal; and I give these things of Mine to anyone I want to.

6   So now I have given all your countries to King Nebuchadnezzar of Babylon, who is My deputy. And I have handed over to him all your cattle for his use.

7   All the nations shall serve him and his son and his grandson, until his time is up; and then many nations and great kings shall conquer Babylon and make him their slave.

8   Submit to him and serve him—put your neck under Babylon's yoke! I will punish any nation refusing to be his slave; I will send war, famine and disease upon that nation until he has conquered it.

9   Do not listen to your false prophets, fortune tel-

[1] Some versions read "Zedekiah."

lers, dreamers, mediums and magicians who say the king of Babylon will not enslave you.

10   For they are all liars, and if you follow their advice and refuse to submit to the king of Babylon, I will drive you out of your land and send you far away to perish.

11   But the people of any nation submitting to the king of Babylon will be permitted to stay in their own country and farm the land as usual."

12   A few years later,[2] Jeremiah repeated all these prophecies to Zedekiah, king of Judah. "If you want to live, submit to the king of Babylon," he said.

13   "Why do you insist on dying—you and your people? Why should you choose war and famine and disease, which the Lord has promised to every nation that will not submit to Babylon's king?

14   Don't listen to the false prophets who keep telling you the king of Babylon will not conquer you, for they are liars.

15   I have not sent them, says the Lord, and they are telling you lies in My name. If you insist on heeding them, I must drive you from this land to die—you and all these 'prophets' too."

16   I spoke again and again to the priests and all the people and told them: "The Lord says, Don't listen to your prophets who are telling you that soon the golden dishes taken from the Temple will be returned from Babylon. It is all a lie.

17   Don't listen to them. Surrender to the king of

---

[2]Implied.

Babylon and live, for otherwise this whole city will be destroyed.

18　If they are really God's prophets, then let them pray to the Lord of Hosts that the golden dishes still here in the Temple, left from before, and that those in the palace of the king of Judah and in the palaces in Jerusalem will not be carried away with you to Babylon!

19, 20, 21　For the Lord of Hosts says, The pillars of bronze standing before the Temple, and the great bronze basin in the Temple court, and the metal stands and all the other ceremonial articles left here by Nebuchadnezzar, king of Babylon, when he exiled all the important people of Judah and Jerusalem to Babylon, along with Jeconiah (son of Jehoiakim), king of Judah,

22　Will all yet be carried away to Babylon and will stay here until I send for them. Then I will bring them all back to Jerusalem again."

## CHAPTER 28

On a December day in that same year—the fourth year of the reign of Zedekiah, king of Judah— Hananiah (son of Azzur), a false prophet from Gibeon, addressed me publicly in the Temple while all the priests and people listened. He said:

2　"The Lord of Hosts, the God of Israel, declares: I have removed the yoke of the king of Babylon from your necks.

3   Within two years I will bring back all the temple treasures that Nebuchadnezzar carried off to Babylon,

4   And I will bring back King Jeconiah,[3] son of Jehoiakim, king of Judah, and all the other captives exiled to Babylon, says the Lord. I will surely remove the yoke put on your necks by the king of Babylon."

5   Then Jeremiah said to Hananiah, in front of all the priests and people,

6   "Amen! May your prophecies come true! I hope the Lord will do everything you say and bring back from Babylon the treasures of this Temple, with all our loved ones.

7   But listen now to the solemn words I speak to you in the presence of all these people.

8   The ancient prophets who preceded you and me spoke against many nations, always warning of *war, famine* and *plague.*

9   So a prophet who foretells *peace* has the burden of proof on him to prove that God has really sent him. Only when his message comes true can it be known that he really is from God."

10   Then Hananiah, the false prophet, took the yoke off Jeremiah's neck and broke it.

11   And Hananiah said again to the crowd that had gathered, "The Lord has promised that within two years He will release all the nations now in slavery to King Nebuchadnezzar of Babylon." At that point Jeremiah walked out.

---

[3]Or, "Jehoiachin," as he is also called.

12   Soon afterwards, the Lord gave this message to Jeremiah:

13   Go and tell Hananiah that the Lord says, You have broken a wooden yoke but these people have yokes of iron on their necks.

14   The Lord of Hosts, the God of Israel, says: I have put a yoke of iron on the necks of all these nations, forcing them into slavery to Nebuchadnezzar, king of Babylon. And nothing will change this decree, for I have even given him all your flocks and herds.

15   Then Jeremiah said to Hananiah, the false prophet, "Listen, Hananiah, the Lord has not sent you, and the people are believing your lies.

16   Therefore the Lord says you must die. This very year your life will end because you have rebelled against the Lord."

17   And sure enough, two months later Hananiah died.

## CHAPTER 29

After Jeconiah the king, and the queen-mother, and the court officials, and the tribal officers and craftsmen had been deported to Babylon by Nebuchadnezzar, Jeremiah wrote them a letter from Jerusalem, addressing it to the Jewish elders and priests and prophets, and to all the people.

3   He sent the letter with Elasah (son of Shaphan) and Gemariah (son of Hilkiah) when they went to

Babylon as King Zedekiah's ambassadors to Nebuchad-nezzar. And this is what the letter said:

4 The Lord of Hosts, the God of Israel, sends this message to all the captives He has exiled to Babylon from Jerusalem:

5 Build homes and plan to stay; plant vineyards, for you will be there many years.

6 Marry and have children, and then find mates for them and have many grandchildren. Multiply! Don't dwindle away!

7 And work for the peace and prosperity of Baby-lon. Pray for her, for if Babylon has peace, so will you.

8 The Lord of Hosts, the God of Israel, says: Don't let the false prophets and mediums who are there among you fool you. Don't listen to the dreams that they invent,

9 For they prophesy lies in My name. I have not sent them, says the Lord.

10 The truth is this: You will be in Babylon for a lifetime.[4] But then I will come and do for you all the good things I have promised, and bring you home again.

11 For I know the plans I have for you, says the Lord. They are plans for good and not for evil, to give you a future and a hope.

12 In those days when you pray, I will listen.

13 You will find Me when you seek Me, if you look for Me in earnest.

14 Yes, says the Lord, I will be found by you, and

---

[4] Literally, "for seventy years."

I will end your slavery and restore your fortunes, and gather you out of the nations where I sent you and bring you back home again to your own land.

15 But now, because you accept the false prophets among you and say the Lord has sent them,

16, 17 I will send war, famine and plague upon the people left here in Jerusalem—on your relatives who were not exiled to Babylon, and on the king who sits on David's throne—and make them like rotting figs, too bad to eat.

18 And I will scatter them around the world. And in every nation where I place them they will be cursed and hissed and mocked,

19 For they refuse to listen to Me though through My prophets I spoke to them again and again.

20 Therefore listen to the word of God, all you Jewish captives over there in Babylon.

21 The Lord of Hosts, the God of Israel, says this about your false prophets, Ahab (son of Kolaiah) and Zedekiah (son of Maaseiah), who are declaring lies to you in My name: Look, I am turning them over to Nebuchadnezzar to execute publicly.

22 Their fate shall become proverbial of all evil, so that whenever anyone wants to curse someone he will say, "The Lord make you like Zedekiah and Ahab whom the king of Babylon burned alive!"

23 For these men have done a terrible thing among My people. They have committed adultery with their neighbors' wives and have lied in My name. I know, for I have seen everything they do, says the Lord.

24    And say this to Shemaiah the Dreamer:[5]

25    The Lord of Hosts, the God of Israel, says: You have written a letter to Zephaniah (son of Maaseiah) the priest, and sent copies to all the other priests and to everyone in Jerusalem.

26    And in this letter you have said to Zephaniah, "The Lord has appointed you to replace Jehoiada as priest in Jerusalem. And it is your responsibility to arrest any madman who claims to be a prophet, and to put him in the stocks and collar.

27    Why haven't you done something about this false prophet Jeremiah of Anathoth?

28    For he has written to us here in Babylon saying that our captivity will be long, and that we should build permanent homes and plan to stay many years, that we should plant fruit trees, for we will be here to eat the fruit from them for a long time to come."

29    Zephaniah took the letter over to Jeremiah and read it to him!

30    Then the Lord gave this message to Jeremiah:

31    Send an open letter to all the exiles in Babylon and tell them this: The Lord says that because Shemaiah the Nehelamite has "prophesied" to you when I didn't send him, and has fooled you into believing his lies,

32    I will punish him and his family. None of his descendants shall see the good I have waiting for My people, for he has taught you to rebel against the Lord.

---

[5]Literally, "the Nehelamite." Nehelam was Shemaiah's home town, the name of which means "Dreamer." This seems to be another of the frequent puns in the prophetic books.

# CHAPTER 30

This is another of the Lord's messages to Jeremiah: 2 The Lord God of Israel says, write down for the record all that I have said to you.

3 For the time is coming when I will restore the fortunes of My people, Israel and Judah, and I will bring them home to this land that I gave to their fathers; they shall possess it and live here again.

4 And write this also concerning Israel and Judah:

5 "Where shall we find peace?" they cry. "There is only fear and trembling.

6 Do men give birth? Then why do they stand there, ashen-faced, hands pressed against their sides like women in labor?"

7 Alas, in all history when has there ever been a time of terror such as in that coming day? It is a time of trouble for my people—for Jacob—such as they have never known before. Yet God will rescue them!

8 For on that day, says the Lord of Hosts, I will break the yoke from their necks and snap their chains, and foreigners shall no longer be their masters!

9 For they shall serve the Lord their God, and David their King,[6] whom I will raise up for them, says the Lord.

10 So don't be afraid, oh, Jacob My servant; don't be dismayed, oh, Israel; for I will bring you home again

---

[6] The Messiah, David's greater Son, whom God has raised up for them.

from distant lands, and your children from their exile. They shall have rest and quiet in their own land, and no one shall make them afraid.

11 For I am with you and I will save you, says the Lord. Even if I utterly destroy the nations where I scatter you, I will not exterminate you; I will punish you, yes—you will not go unpunished.

12 For your sin is an incurable bruise, a terrible wound.

13 There is no one to help you or to bind up your wound and no medicine does any good.

14 All your lovers have left you and don't care anything about you any more; for I have wounded you cruelly, as though I were your enemy; mercilessly, as though I were an implacable foe; for your sins are so many, your guilt is so great.

15 Why do you protest your punishment? Your sin is so scandalous that your sorrow should never end! It is because your guilt is great that I have had to punish you so much.

16 But in that coming day, all who are destroying you shall be destroyed; and all your enemies shall be slaves; those who rob you shall be robbed; and those attacking you shall be attacked.

17 I will give you back your health again and heal your wounds. Now you are called "The Outcast" and "Jerusalem, the Place Nobody Wants."

18 But, says the Lord, when I bring you home again from your captivity and restore your fortunes,

Jerusalem will be rebuilt upon her ruins; the palace will be reconstructed as it was before.

19    The cities will be filled with joy and great thanksgiving, and I will multiply My people and make of them a great and honored nation.

20    Their children shall prosper as in David's reign; their nation shall be established before Me, and I will punish anyone who hurts them.

21    They will have their own ruler again.[7] He will not be a foreigner. And I will invite him to be a priest at My altars, and he shall approach Me, for who would dare to come unless invited.

22    And You shall be My people and I will be your God.

23    Suddenly the devastating whirlwind of the Lord roars with fury; it shall burst upon the heads of the wicked.

24    The Lord will not call off the fierceness of His wrath until it has finished all the terrible destruction He has planned. Later on[8] you will understand what I am telling you.


# CHAPTER 31


At that time, says the Lord, all the families of Israel shall recognize Me as the Lord; they shall act like My people.

---

[7]This verse probably refers to the restoration after the Babylonian captivity (the rulers of the Maccabean period were priests as well as kings) as well as to the final restoration under Christ.
[8]Literally, "in the latter days."

2   I will care for them as I did those who escaped from Egypt, to whom I showed My mercies in the wilderness, when Israel sought for rest.

3   For long ago the Lord had said to Israel: I have loved you, O My people, with an everlasting love; with lovingkindness I have drawn you to Me.

4   I will rebuild your nation, O virgin of Israel. You will again be happy and dance merrily with the timbrels.

5   Again you will plant your vineyards upon the mountains of Samaria and eat from your own gardens there.

6   The day shall come when watchmen on the hills of Ephraim will call out and say, "Arise, and let us go up to Zion to the Lord our God."

7   For the Lord says, Sing with joy for all that I will do for Israel, the greatest of the nations! Shout out with praise and joy: "The Lord has saved His people, the remnant of Israel."

8   For I will bring them from the north and from earth's farthest ends, not forgetting their blind and lame, young mothers with their little ones, those ready to give birth. It will be a great company who comes.

9   Tears of joy shall stream down their faces, and I will lead them home with great care. They shall walk beside the quiet streams and not stumble. For I am a Father to Israel, and Ephraim is My oldest child.

10   Listen to this message from the Lord, you nations of the world, and publish it abroad: The Lord who scattered His people will gather them back to-

gether again and watch over them as a shepherd does his flock.

11  He will save Israel from those who are too strong for them!

12  They shall come home and sing songs of joy upon the hills of Zion, and shall be radiant over the goodness of the Lord—the good crops, the wheat and the wine and the oil, and the healthy flocks and herds. Their life shall be like a watered garden, and all their sorrows shall be gone.

13  The young girls will dance for joy, and men folk—old and young—will take their part in all the fun; for I will turn their mourning into joy and I will comfort them and make them rejoice, for their captivity with all its sorrows will be behind them.

14  I will feast the priests with the abundance of offerings brought to them at the Temple; I will satisfy My people with My bounty, says the Lord.

15  The Lord spoke to me again, saying: In Ramah there is bitter weeping, Rachel[9] is weeping for her children and she cannot be comforted, for they are gone.

16  But the Lord says: Don't cry any longer; for I have heard your prayers[1] and you will see them again; they will come back to you from the distant land of the enemy.

17  There is hope for your future, says the Lord, and your children will come again to their own land.

---

[9]Symbolic mother of the northern tribes, who were taken away by the Assyrians as slaves.
[1]Literally, "for your work shall be rewarded."

18 I have heard Ephraim's groans: "You have punished me greatly; but I needed it all, as a calf must be trained for the yoke. Turn me again to You and restore me, for You alone are the Lord, my God.

19 I turned away from God but I was sorry afterwards. I kicked myself for My stupidity. I was thoroughly ashamed of all I did in younger days."

20 And the Lord replies: Ephraim is still My son, My darling child. I had to punish him, but I still love him. I long for him and surely will have mercy on him.

21 As you travel into exile, set up road signs pointing back to Israel. Mark your pathway well. For you shall return again, O virgin Israel, to your cities here.

22 How long will you vacillate, O wayward daughter? For the Lord will cause something new and different to happen—Israel shall seek Him!²

23 The Lord of Hosts, the God of Israel, says: When I bring them back again they shall say in Judah and her cities, "The Lord bless you, O center of righteousness, O holy hill!"

24 And city dwellers and farmers and shepherds alike shall live together in peace and happiness.

25 For I have given rest to the weary and joy to all the sorrowing.

26 (Then Jeremiah wakened. "Such sleep is very sweet!" he said.)

27 The Lord says: The time will come when I will

---

²Literally, "a woman shall court a suitor," or, "a woman shall encompass a man."

greatly increase the population and multiply the number of cattle here in Israel.

28 In the past I painstakingly destroyed the nation but now I will carefully build it up.

29 The p e o p l e shall no longer quote this proverb—"Children pay for their fathers' sins."[3]

30 For everyone shall die for his own sins—the person eating sour grapes is the one whose teeth are set on edge.

31 The day will come, says the Lord, when I will make a new contract with the people of Israel and Judah.

32 It won't be like the one I made with their fathers when I took them by the hand to bring them out of the land of Egypt—a contract they broke, forcing me to reject them,[4] says the Lord.

33 But this is the new contract I will make with them: I will inscribe My laws upon their hearts,[5] so that they shall want to honor Me;[6] then they shall truly be My people and I will be their God.

34 At that time it will no longer be necessary to admonish one another to know the Lord. For everyone, both great and small, shall really know Me then, says the Lord, and I will forgive and forget their sins.

35 The Lord who gives us sunlight in the daytime

---

[3]Literally, "The fathers eat the sour grapes and the children's teeth are set on edge."

[4]Some versions read, "a covenant they broke, even though I cared for them as a husband does his wife."
See Hebrews 8:9b.

[5]i.e., rather than upon tablets of stone, as were the Ten Commandments.

[6]In Jeremiah 17:1 their sin was inscribed on their hearts, so that they wanted above all to disobey. This change seems to describe an experience very much like, if not the same as, the new birth.

and the moon and stars to light the night, and who stirs the sea to make the roaring waves—His name is Lord of Hosts—says this:

36 I am as likely to reject My people Israel as I am to do away with these laws of nature!

37 Not until the heavens can be measured and the foundations of the earth explored, will I consider casting them away forever for their sins!

38, 39 For the time is coming, says the Lord, when all Jerusalem shall be rebuilt for the Lord, from the Tower of Hananel at the northeast corner,[7] to the Corner Gate at the northwest;[7] and from the Hill of Gareb at the southwest,[7] across to Goah on the southeast.[7]

40 And the entire city including the graveyard and ash dump in the valley shall be holy to the Lord, and so shall all the fields out to the brook of Kidron, and from there to the Horse Gate on the east side of the city; it shall never again be captured or destroyed.

## CHAPTER 32

The following message came to Jeremiah from the Lord in the tenth year of the reign of Zedekiah, king of Judah (which was the eighteenth year of Nebuchadnezzar's reign).

2 At this time Jeremiah was imprisoned in the

---

[7]Implied.

dungeon beneath[8] the palace, while the Babylonian army was besieging Jerusalem.

3 King Zedekiah had put him there for continuing to prophesy that the city would be conquered by the king of Babylon;

4 And that King Zedekiah would be caught and taken as a prisoner before the king of Babylon for trial and sentencing.

5 "He shall take you to Babylon and imprison you there for many years until you die. Why fight the facts? You can't win! Surrender now!" Jeremiah had told him again and again.

6, 7 Then this message from the Lord came to Jeremiah: Your cousin Hanamel (son of Shallum) will soon arrive to ask you to buy the farm he owns in Anathoth; for by law you have a chance to buy before it is offered to anyone else.

8 So Hanamel came, as the Lord had said he would, and visited me in the prison. "Buy my field in Anathoth, in the land of Benjamin," he said, "for the law gives you the first right to purchase it." Then I knew for sure that the message I had heard was really from the Lord.

9 So I bought the field, paying Hanamel seventeen shekels of silver.

10 I signed and sealed the deed of purchase before witnesses, and weighed out the silver and paid him.

11 Then I took the sealed deed containing the terms and conditions, and also the unsealed copy,

---

[8]Literally, "in the court of the prison in the palace."

12   And publicly, in the presence of my cousin Hanamel and the witnesses who had signed the deed, and as the prison guards watched, I handed the papers to Baruch (son of Neriah, who was the son of Mahseiah).

13   And I said to him as they all listened:

14   "The Lord of Hosts, God of Israel, says: Take both this sealed deed and the copy and put them into a pottery jar to preserve them for a long time.

15   For the Lord of Hosts, God of Israel, says, In the future these papers will be valuable.[9] Someday people will again own property here in this country and will be buying and selling houses and vineyards and fields."

16   Then after I had given the papers to Baruch I prayed:

17   "O Lord God! You have made the heavens and earth by Your great power; nothing is too hard for You!

18   You are loving and kind to thousands, yet children suffer for their fathers' sins; You are the great and mighty God, the Lord of Hosts.

19   You have all wisdom and do great and mighty miracles; for Your eyes are open to all the ways of men, and You reward everyone according to his life and deeds.

20   You have done incredible things in the land of Egypt—things still remembered to this day. And You have continued to do great miracles in Israel and all

---

[9]Implied.

around the world. You have made Your name very great, as it is today.

21   You brought Israel out of Egypt with mighty miracles and great power and terror.

22   You gave Israel this land that You promised their fathers long ago—a wonderful land that 'flows with milk and honey.'

23   Our fathers came and conquered it and lived in it, but they refused to obey You or to follow Your laws; they have hardly done one thing You told them to. That is why You have sent all this terrible evil upon them.

24   See how the siege mounds have been built against the city walls; and the Babylonians shall conquer the city by sword, famine and disease. Everything has happened just as You said—as You determined it should!

25   And yet You say to buy the field—paying good money for it before these witnesses—even though the city will belong to our enemies."

26   Then this message came to Jeremiah:

27   I am the Lord, the God of all mankind; is there anything too hard for Me?

28   Yes, I will give this city to the Babylonians and to Nebuchadnezzar, king of Babylon; he shall conquer it.

29   And the Babylonians outside the walls shall come in and set fire to the city and burn down all these houses where the roofs have been used to offer incense to Baal, and to pour out libations to other gods, causing My fury to rise!

30   For Israel and Judah have done nothing but

wrong since their earliest days; they have infuriated Me with all their evil deeds.

31　From the time this city was built until now it has done nothing but anger Me; so I am determined to be rid of it.

32　The sins of Israel and Judah—the sins of the people, of their kings, officers, priests and prophets—stir Me up.

33　They have turned their backs upon Me and refused to return; day after day, year after year, I taught them right from wrong, but they would not listen or obey.

34　They have even defiled My own Temple by worshiping their abominable idols there.

35　And they have built high altars to Baal in the Valley of Hinnom. There they have burnt their children as sacrifices to Molech—something I never commanded, and cannot imagine suggesting. What an incredible evil causing Judah to sin so greatly.

36　Now therefore the Lord God of Israel says concerning this city, it will fall to the king of Babylon through warfare, famine and disease;

37　But I will bring My people back again from all the countries where in My fury I will scatter them. I will bring them back to this very city, and make them live in peace and safety.

38　And they shall be My people and I will be their God.

39　And I will give them one heart and mind to

worship Me forever, for their own good and for the good of all their descendants.

40　And I will make an everlasting covenant with them, promising never again to desert them, but only to do them good. I will put a desire into their hearts to worship Me, and they shall never leave Me.

41　I will rejoice to do them good and will replant them in this land, with great joy.

42　Just as I have sent all these terrors and evils upon them, so will I do all the good I have promised them.

43　Fields will again be bought and sold in this land, now ravaged by the Babylonians, where men and animals alike have disappeared.

44　Yes, fields shall once again be bought and sold —deeds signed and sealed and witnessed—in the country of Benjamin and here in Jerusalem, in the cities of Judah and in the hill country, in the Philistine plain and in the Negeb too, for some day I will restore prosperity to them.

## CHAPTER 33

While Jeremiah was still in jail, the Lord sent him this second message:

2　The Lord, the Maker of heaven and earth—Jehovah is His name—says this:

3　Ask Me and I will tell you some remarkable secrets about what is going to happen here.

4　For though you have torn down the houses of

this city, and the king's palace too, for materials to strengthen the walls against the siege guns of the enemy,

5   Yet the Babylonians will enter, and the men of this city are already as good as dead, for I have determined to destroy them in My furious anger. I have abandoned them because of all their wickedness, and I will not pity them when they cry for help.

6   Nevertheless the time will come when I will heal Jerusalem's damage and give her prosperity and peace.

7   I will rebuild the cities of both Judah and Israel and restore their fortunes.

8   And I will cleanse away all their sins against Me, and pardon them.

9   Then this city will be an honor to Me, and it will give Me joy and be a source of praise and glory to Me before all the nations of the earth! The people of the world will see the good I do for My people and will tremble with awe!

10, 11   The Lord declares that the happy voices of bridegrooms and of brides, and the joyous song of those bringing thanksgiving offerings to the Lord will be heard again in this doomed land. The people will sing: "Praise the Lord! For He is good and His mercy endures forever!" For I will make this land happier and more prosperous than it has ever been before.

12   This land—though every man and animal and city is doomed—will once more see shepherds leading sheep and lambs.

13   Once again their flocks will prosper in the

mountain villages and in the cities east of the Philistine plain, in all the cities of the Negeb, in the land of Benjamin, in the vicinity of Jerusalem and in all the cities of Judah.

14 Yes, the day will come, says the Lord, when I will do for Israel and Judah all the good I promised them.

15 At that time I will bring to the throne the true Son[1] of David, and He shall rule justly.

16 In that day the people of Judah and Jerusalem shall live in safety and their motto will be, "The Lord is our righteousness!"

17 For the Lord declares that from then on, David shall forever have an heir sitting on the throne of Israel.

18 And there shall always be Levites to offer burnt offerings and meal offerings and sacrifices to the Lord.

19 Then this message came to Jeremiah from the Lord:

20, 21 If you can break My covenant with the day and with the night so that day and night don't come on their usual schedule, only then will My covenant with David, My servant, be broken so that he shall not have a son to reign upon his throne; and My covenant with the Levite priests My ministers is non-cancellable.

22 And as the stars cannot be counted nor the sand upon the seashores measured, so the descendants of David My servant and the line of the Levites who minister to Me will be multiplied.

---

[1]Or, "the true vine from the roots of David." Christ was the true vine, the only true expression of David, the man after God's own heart.

23   The Lord spoke to Jeremiah again and said:

24   Have you heard what people are saying?—that the Lord chose Judah and Israel and then abandoned them! They are sneering and saying that Israel isn't worthy to be counted as a nation.

25, 26   But this is the Lord's reply: I would no more reject My people than I would change My laws of night and day, of earth and sky. I will never abandon the Jews, or David My servant, or change the plan that his Child will someday rule these descendants of Abraham, Isaac and Jacob. Instead I will restore their prosperity and have mercy on them.

## CHAPTER 34

This is the message that came to Jeremiah from the Lord when Nebuchadnezzar, king of Babylon, and all his armies from all the kingdoms he ruled, came and fought against Jerusalem and the cities of Judah:

2   Go tell Zedekiah, king of Judah, that the Lord says this: I will give this city to the king of Babylon and he shall burn it.

3   You shall not escape; you shall be captured and taken before the king of Babylon and he shall pronounce sentence against you and you shall be exiled to Babylon.

4   But listen to this, O Zedekiah, king of Judah: God says you won't be killed in war and carnage,

5   But that you will die quietly among your people, and they will burn incense in your memory, just as they did for your fathers. They will weep for you and say, "Alas, our king is dead!" This I have decreed, says the Lord.

6   So Jeremiah delivered the message to King Zedekiah.

7   At this time the Babylonian army was besieging Jerusalem, Lachish and Azekah—the only walled cities of Judah still standing.

8   This is the message that came to Jeremiah from the Lord after King Zedekiah of Judah had freed all the slaves in Jerusalem—

9   (For King Zedekiah had ordered everyone to free his Hebrew slaves, both men and women. He had said that no Jew should be the master of another Jew for all were brothers.

10   The princes and all the people had obeyed the king's command and freed their slaves, but the action was only temporary.

11   They changed their minds and made their servants slaves again.[2]

12   That is why the Lord gave the following message to Jerusalem.)

13   The Lord, the God of Israel, says: I made a covenant with your fathers long ago when I brought them from their slavery in Egypt.

---

[2]When the siege was temporarily lifted (Jer. 37:6-11) they became bold and returned to their sins.

14   I told them that every Hebrew slave must be freed after serving six years. But this was not done.

15   Recently you began doing what was right, as I commanded you, and freed your slaves. You had solemnly promised Me in My Temple that you would do it.

16   But now you refuse and have defiled My name by shrugging off your oath and have made them slaves again.

17   Therefore, says the Lord, because you will not listen to Me and release them, I will release you to the power of death by war and famine and disease. And I will scatter you over all the world as exiles.

18, 19   Because you have refused the terms of our contract I will cut you apart like you cut apart the calf when you walked between its halves to solemnize your vows. Yes, I will butcher you, whether you are princes, court officials, priests or people—for you have broken your oath.

20   I will give you to your enemies and they shall kill you. I will feed your dead bodies to the vultures and wild animals.

21   And I will surrender Zedekiah, king of Judah, and his officials to the army of the king of Babylon, though he has departed from the city for a little while.

22   I will summon the Babylonian armies back again and they will fight against it and capture this city and burn it. And I will see to it that the cities of Judah are completely destroyed and left desolate without a living soul.

## CHAPTER 35

This is the message the Lord gave Jeremiah when Jehoiakim (son of Josiah) was the king of Judah:[3]

2   Go to the settlement where the families of the Rechabites live and invite them to the Temple. Take them into one of the inner rooms and offer them a drink of wine.

3   So I went over to see Jaazaniah (son of Jeremiah, who was the son of Habazziniah), and brought him and all his brothers and sons—representing all the Rechab families—

4   To the Temple, into the room assigned for the use of the sons of Hanan the prophet (the son of Igdaliah). This room was located next to the one used by the palace official, directly above the room of Maaseiah (son of Shallum), who was the temple doorman.

5   I set cups and jugs of wine before them and invited them to have a drink,

6   But they refused. "No," they said. "We don't drink, for Jonadab our father (son of Rechab) commanded that none of us should ever drink, neither we nor our children forever.

7   He also told us not to build houses or plant crops or vineyards and not to own farms, but always to live in tents; and that if we obeyed we would live long, good lives in our own land.

[3]This is apparently an early message to Jeremiah, and is not here in its chronological order with the other messages.

8　And we have obeyed him in all these things. We have never had a drink of wine since then, nor our wives or our sons or daughters either.

9　We haven't built houses or owned farms or planted crops.

10　We have lived in tents and have fully obeyed everything that Jonadab our father commanded us.

11　But when Nebuchadnezzar, king of Babylon, arrived in this country, we were afraid and decided to move to Jerusalem. That's why we are here."

12　Then the Lord gave this message to Jeremiah:

13　The Lord of Hosts, the God of Israel, says: Go and say to Judah and Jerusalem, Won't you learn a lesson from the families of Rechab?

14　They don't drink because their father told them not to. But I have spoken to you again and again and you won't listen or obey.

15　I have sent you prophet after prophet to tell you to turn back from your wicked ways and to stop worshiping other gods and that if you obeyed, then I would let you live in peace here in the land I gave to you and your fathers. But you wouldn't listen or obey.

16　The families of Rechab have obeyed their father completely, but you have refused to listen to Me.

17　Therefore the Lord God of Hosts, the God of Israel, says: Because you refuse to listen or answer when I call, I will send upon Judah and Jerusalem all the evil I have ever threatened.

18, 19　Then Jeremiah turned to the Rechabites and said: "The Lord of Hosts, the God of Israel, says that because you have obeyed your father in every respect, he shall always have descendants who will worship me."

## CHAPTER 36

In the fourth year⁴ of the reign of King Jehoiakim of Judah (son of Josiah) the Lord gave this message to Jeremiah:

2  "Get a scroll and write down all My messages against Israel, Judah and the other nations. Begin with the first message back in the days of Josiah, and write down every one of them.

3  Perhaps when the people of Judah see in writing all the terrible things I will do to them, they will repent. And then I can forgive them."

4  So Jeremiah sent for Baruch (son of Neriah), and as Jeremiah dictated, Baruch wrote down all the prophecies.

5  When all was finished, Jeremiah said to Baruch, "Since I am a prisoner here,

6  You read the scroll in the Temple on the next Day of Fasting, for on that day people will be there from all over Judah.

7  Perhaps even yet they will turn from their evil ways and ask the Lord to forgive them before it is too late, even though these curses of God have been pronounced upon them."

⁴Probably in the summer of 605 B.C., shortly after Nebuchadnezzar's victory over the Egyptian army at Carchemish.

8　Baruch did as Jeremiah told him to, and read all these messages to the people at the Temple.

9　This occurred on the Day of Fasting held in December of the fifth year of the reign of King Jehoiakim (son of Josiah). People came from all over Judah to attend the services at the Temple that day.

10　Baruch went to the office of Gemariah the Scribe (son of Shaphan) to read the scroll. (This room was just off the upper assembly hall of the Temple, near the door of the New Gate.)

11　When Micaiah (son of Gemariah, son of Shaphan) heard the messages from God,

12　He went down to the palace to the conference room where the administrative officials were meeting. Elishama (the Scribe) was there, as well as Delaiah (son of Shamaiah), Elnathan (son of Achbor), Gemariah (son of Shaphan), Zedekiah (son of Hananiah), and all the others with similar responsibilities.

13　When Micaiah told them about the messages Baruch was reading to the people,

14, 15　The officials sent Jehudi (son of Nethaniah, son of Shelemiah, son of Cushi) to ask Baruch to come and read the messages to them too, and Baruch did.

16　By the time he finished they were badly frightened. "We must tell the king," they said.

17　"But first, tell us how you got these messages. Did Jeremiah himself dictate them to you?"

18　So Baruch explained that Jeremiah had dictated them to him word by word, and he had written them down in ink upon the scroll.

19 "You and Jeremiah both hide," the officials said to Baruch. "Don't tell a soul where you are!"

20 Then the officials hid the scroll in the room of Elishama the Scribe and went to tell the king.

21 The king sent Jehudi to get the scroll. Jehudi brought it from Elishama the Scribe and read it to the king as all his officials stood by.

22 The king was in a winterized part of the palace at the time, sitting in front of a fireplace,⁵ for it was December, and cold.

23 And whenever Jehudi finished reading three or four columns, the king would take his knife, and slit off the section and throw it into the fire, until the whole scroll was destroyed.

24, 25 And no one protested except Elnathan, Delaiah and Germariah. They pled with the king not to burn the scroll, but he wouldn't listen to them. Not another of the king's officials showed any signs of fear or anger at what he had done.

26 Then the king commanded Jerahmeel ( a member of the royal family⁶) and Seraiah (son of Azriel) and Shelemiah (son of Abdeel) to arrest Baruch and Jeremiah. But the Lord hid them!

27 After the king had burned the scroll, the Lord said to Jeremiah:

28 Get another scroll and write everything again just as you did before,

---

⁵More literally, "a large brazier in which a fire was burning."
⁶"A son of the king."

29 And say this to the king: "The Lord says, You burned the scroll because it said the king of Babylon would destroy this country and everything in it.

30 And now the Lord adds this concerning you, Jehoiakim, king of Judah: He shall have no one to sit⁷ upon the throne of David. His dead body shall be thrown out to the hot sun and frosty nights,

31 And I will punish him and his family and his officials because of their sins. I will pour out upon them all the evil I promised—upon them and upon all the people of Judah and Jerusalem, for they wouldn't listen to My warnings."

32 Then Jeremiah took another scroll and dictated again to Baruch all he had written before, only this time the Lord added a lot more!

## CHAPTER 37

Nebuchadnezzar, king of Babylon, did not appoint Coniah (King Jehoiakim's son) to be the new king of Judah.⁸ Instead he chose Zedekiah (son of Josiah).

2 But neither King Zedekiah nor his officials nor the people who were left in the land listened to what the Lord said through Jeremiah.

3 Nevertheless, King Zedekiah sent Jehucal (son

⁷A three month inter-regnum by his son Jehoiachin (also called Coniah and Jeconiah) evidently did not qualify as "sitting on the throne" under the meaning of permanence in the Hebrew expression used here.
⁸The people of Jerusalem who had assassinated King Jehoiakim appointed his son Coniah as ruler before Nebuchadnezzar captured the city. The Babylonians took Coniah to Babylon as a political hostage.

of Shelemiah) and Zephaniah the priest (son of Maaseiah) to ask Jeremiah to pray for them.

4    (Jeremiah had not been imprisoned yet, so he could go and come as he pleased.)

5    When the army of Pharaoh Hophra of Egypt appeared at the southern border of Judah to relieve the besieged city of Jerusalem, the Babylonian army withdrew from Jerusalem to fight the Egyptians.

6    Then the Lord sent this message to Jeremiah:

7    "The Lord, the God of Israel, says: Tell the king of Judah who sent you to ask Me what is going to happen that Pharaoh's army, though it came here to help you, is about to return in flight to Egypt! The Babylonians shall defeat them and send them scurrying home.

8    These Babylonians shall capture this city and burn it to the ground.

9    Don't fool yourselves that the Babylonians are gone for good. They aren't!

10    Even if you destroyed the entire Babylonian army until there were only a handful of survivors and they lay wounded in their tents, yet they would stagger out and defeat you and put this city to the torch!"

11    When the Babylonian army set out from Jerusalem to engage Pharaoh's army in battle,

12    Jeremiah started to leave the city to go to the land of Benjamin, to see the property he had bought.[9]

13    But as he was walking through the Benjamin Gate, a sentry arrested him as a traitor, claiming he was

---

[9]See chapter 32:6-15.

defecting to the Babylonians. The guard making the arrest was Irijah (son of Shelemiah, grandson of Hannaniah).

14   "That's not true," Jeremiah said. "I have no intention whatever of doing any such thing!" But Irijah wouldn't listen; he took Jeremiah before the city officials.

15, 16   They were incensed with Jeremiah and had him flogged and put into the dungeon under the house of Jonathan the Scribe, which had been converted into a prison. Jeremiah was kept there for several days,

17   But eventually King Zedekiah sent for him to come to the palace secretly. The king asked him if there was any recent message from the Lord. "Yes," said Jeremiah, "there is! You shall be defeated by the king of Babylon!"

18   Then Jeremiah broached the subject of his imprisonment. "What have I ever done to deserve this?" he asked the king. "What crime have I committed? Tell me what I have done against you or your officials or the people?

19   Where are those prophets now who told you that the king of Babylon would not come?

20   Listen, O my lord the king: I beg you, don't send me back to that dungeon, for I'll die there."

21   Then King Zedekiah commanded that Jeremiah not be returned to the dungeon, but be placed in the palace prison instead, and that he be given a small loaf of fresh bread every day as long as there was any left in the city. So Jeremiah was kept in the palace prison.[1]

----
[1]Literally, "the court of the guard."

## CHAPTER 38

But when Shephatiah (son of Mattan) and Gedaliah (son of Pashur) and Jucal (son of Shelemiah) and Pashur (son of Malchiah) heard what Jeremiah had been telling the people—

2  That everyone remaining in Jerusalem would die by sword, starvation or disease, but anyone surrendering to the Babylonians would live;

3  And that the city of Jerusalem would surely be captured by the king of Babylon—

4  They went to the king and said: "Sir, this fellow must die. That kind of talk will undermine the morale of the few soldiers we have left, and of all the people too. This man is a traitor."

5  So King Zedekiah agreed. "All right," he said. "Do as you like—I can't stop you."

6  They took Jeremiah from his cell and lowered him by ropes into an empty cistern in the prison yard. (It belonged to Malchiah, a member of the royal family.) There was no water in it, but there was a thick layer of mire at the bottom, and Jeremiah sank down into it.

7  When Ebedmelech the Ethiopian, an important palace official, heard that Jeremiah was in the cistern,

8  He rushed out to the Gate of Benjamin where the king was holding court,

9  "My lord the king," he said, "these men have

done a very evil thing in putting Jeremiah into the cistern. He will die of hunger, for almost all the bread in the city is gone."

10 Then the king commanded Ebedmelech to take thirty men with him and pull Jeremiah out before he died.

11 So Ebedmelech took thirty men and went to a discarded supply depot in the palace where used clothing was kept. There he found some old rags and discarded garments which he took to the cistern and lowered to Jeremiah on a rope.

12 Ebedmelech called down to Jeremiah, "Use these rags under your armpits to protect you from the ropes." Then, when Jeremiah was ready,

13 They pulled him out and returned him to the palace prison, where he remained.

14 One day King Zedekiah sent for Jeremiah to meet him at the side entrance of the Temple. "I want to ask you something," the king said, "and don't try to hide the truth."

15 Jeremiah said, "If I tell you the truth, you will kill me. And you won't listen to me anyway."

16 So King Zedekiah swore before Almighty God his Creator that he would not kill Jeremiah or give him to the men who were after his life.

17 Then Jeremiah said to Zedekiah, "The Lord, the God of Hosts, the God of Israel, says: If you will surrender to Babylon, you and your family shall live and the city will not be burned.

18   If you refuse to surrender, this city shall be set afire by the Babylonian army and you will not escape."

19   "But I am afraid to surrender," the king said, "for the Babylonians will hand me over to the Jews who have defected to them, and who knows what they will do to me?"

20   Jeremiah replied, "You won't get into their hands if only you will obey the Lord; your life will be spared and all will go well for you.

21, 22   But if you refuse to surrender, the Lord has said that all the women left in your palace will be brought out and given to the officers of the Babylonian army; and these women will taunt you with bitterness. 'Fine friends you have,' they'll say, 'those Egyptians. They have betrayed you and left you to your fate!'

23   All your wives and children will be led out to the Babylonians, and you will not escape. You will be seized by the king of Babylon, and this city will be burned."

24   Then Zedekiah said to Jeremiah, "On pain of death, don't tell anyone you told me this!

25   And if my officials hear that I talked with you and they threaten you with death unless you tell them what we discussed,

26   Just say that you begged me not to send you back to the dungeon in Jonathan's house, for you would die there."

27   And sure enough, it wasn't long before all the city officials came to Jeremiah and asked him why the king had called for him. So he said what the king had

told him to, and they left without finding out the truth, for the conversation had not been overheard by anyone.

28 And Jeremiah remained confined to the prison yard until the day that Jerusalem was retaken by the Babylonians.

## CHAPTER 39

It was in January of the ninth year of the reign of King Zedekiah of Judah, that King Nebuchadnezzar and all his army came against Jerusalem again and besieged it.

2 Two years later, in the month of July, they breached the wall, and the city fell,

3 And all the officers of the Babylonian army came in and sat in triumph at the middle gate. Nergal-sharezer was there, and Samgarnebo and Sarsechim and Nergal-sharezer the king's chief assistant, and many others.

4 When King Zedekiah and his soldiers realized that the city was lost, they fled during the night, going out through the gate between the two walls back of the palace garden and across the fields toward the Jordan valley.

5 But the Babylonians chased the king and caught him on the plains of Jericho and brought him to Nebuchadnezzar, king of Babylon who was at Riblah, in the land of Hamath, where he pronounced judgment upon him.

6 The king of Babylon made Zedekiah watch as they killed his children and all the nobles of Judah.

7 Then he gouged out Zedekiah's eyes and bound him in chains to send him away to Babylon as a slave.

8 Meanwhile the army burned Jerusalem, including the palace, and tore down the walls of the city.

9 Then Nebuzaradan, the captain of the guard, and his men sent the remnant of the population and all those who had defected to him to Babylon.

10 But throughout the land of Judah he left a few people, the very poor, and gave them fields and vineyards.

11, 12 Meanwhile King Nebuchadnezzar had told Nebuzaradan to find Jeremiah. "See that he isn't hurt," he said. "Look after him well and give him anything he wants."

13 So Nebuzaradan, the captain of the guard, and Nebushazban, the chief of the eunuchs, and Nergal-sharezer, the king's advisor and all the officials took steps to do as the king had commanded.

14 They sent soldiers to bring Jeremiah out of the prison, and put him into the care of Gedaliah (son of Ahikam, son of Shaphan), to take him back to his home. And Jeremiah lived there among his people who were left in the land.

15 The Lord gave the following message to Jeremiah before the Babylonians arrived, while he was still in prison.

16 "Send this word to Ebedmelech the Ethiopian: The Lord of Hosts, the God of Israel, says: I will do to this city everything I threatened; I will destroy it before your eyes,

17 But I will deliver you. You shall not be killed by those you fear so much.

18 As a reward for trusting Me I will preserve your life and keep you safe."

## CHAPTER 40

Nebuzaradan, captain of the guard, took Jeremiah to Ramah along with all the exiled people of Jerusalem and Judah who were being sent to Babylon, but then released him.

2, 3 The captain called for Jeremiah and said, "The Lord your God has brought this disaster on this land, just as He said He would. For these people have sinned against the Lord. That is why it happened.

4 Now I am going to take off your chains and let you go. If you want to come with me to Babylon, fine; I will see that you are well cared for. But if you don't want to come, don't. The world is before you—go where you like.

5 If you decide to stay, then return to Gedaliah, who has been appointed as governor of Judah by the king of Babylon, and stay with the remnant he rules. But it's up to you; go where you like." Then Nebuzaradan gave Jeremiah some food and money and let him go.

6 So Jeremiah returned to Gedaliah and lived in Judah with the people left in the land.

7 Now when the leaders of the Jewish guerilla

bands in the countryside heard that the king of Babylon had appointed Gedaliah as governor over the poor of the land who were left behind, and had not exiled everyone to Babylon,

8   They came to see Gedaliah at Mizpah, where his headquarters were. These are the names of the leaders who came: Ishmael (son of Nethaniah), Johanan and Jonathan (sons of Kareah), Seraiah (son of Tanhumeth), the sons of Ephai (the Netophathite), Jezaniah (son of a Maacathite), and their men.

9   And Gedaliah assured them that it would be safe to surrender to the Babylonians. "Stay here and serve the king of Babylon," he said, " and all will go well for you.

10   As for me, I will stay at Mizpah and intercede for you with the Babylonians who will come here to oversee my administration. Settle in any city you wish and live off the land. Harvest the grapes and summer fruits and olives and store them away."

11   When the Jews in Moab and among the Ammonites and in Edom and the other nearby countries heard that a few people were still left in Judah, and that the king of Babylon had not taken them all away, and that Gedaliah was the governor,

12   They all began to return to Judah from the many places to which they had fled. They stopped at Mizpah to discuss their plans with Gedaliah and then went out to the deserted farms and gathered a great harvest of wine-grapes and other crops.

13, 14   But soon afterwards Johanan (son of Kareah) and the other guerilla leaders came to Mizpah to warn Gedaliah that Baalis, king of the Ammonites, had sent Ishmael (son of Nethaniah) to assassinate him. But Gedaliah wouldn't believe them.

15   Then Johanan had a private conference with Gedaliah. Johanan volunteered to kill Ishmael secretly. "Why should we let him come and murder you?" Johanan asked. "What will happen then to the Jews who have returned? Why should this remnant be scattered and lost?"

16   But Gedaliah said, "I forbid you from doing any such thing, for you are lying about Ishmael."

## CHAPTER 41

But in October, Ishmael (son of Nethaniah, son of Elishama), who was a member of the royal family and one of the king's top officials, arrived in Mizpah accompanied by ten men. Gedaliah invited them to dinner.

2   While they were eating, Ishmael and the ten men in league with him suddenly jumped up, pulled out their swords and killed Gedaliah.

3   Then they went out and slaughtered all the Jewish officials and Babylonian soldiers who were in Mizpah with Gedaliah.

4   The next day, before the outside world knew what had happened,

5   Eighty men approached Mizpah from Shechem, Shiloh and Samaria, to worship at the Temple of the

Lord. They had shaved off their beards, torn their clothes and cut themselves, and were bringing offerings and incense.

6 Ishmael went out from the city to meet them, crying as he went. When he faced them he said, "Oh, come and see what has happened to Gedaliah!"

7 Then, when they were all inside the city, Ishmael and his men killed all but ten of them and threw their bodies into a cistern.

8 The ten had talked Ishmael into letting them go by promising to bring him their treasures of wheat, barley, oil and honey they had hidden away.

9 The cistern where Ishmael dumped the bodies of the men he murdered was the large one constructed by King Asa when he fortified Mizpah to protect himself against Baasha, king of Israel.[3]

10 Ishmael made captives of the king's daughters and of all the people who had been left under Gedaliah's care in Mizpah by Nebuzaradan, captain of the guard. Soon after he took them with him when he headed toward the country of the Ammonites.

11 But when Johanan (son of Kareah) and the rest of the guerilla leaders heard what Ishmael had done,

12 They took all their men and set out to stop him. They caught up with him at the pool near Gibeon.

13, 14 The people with Ishmael shouted for joy when they saw Johanan and his men, and ran to meet them.

---

[3]See I Kings 15:22. Fifty-three cisterns have been uncovered by excavators at the site of ancient Mizpah.

15 Meanwhile Ishmael escaped with eight of his men into the land of the Ammonites.

16, 17 Then Johanan and his men went to the village of Geruth Chimham, near Bethlehem, taking with them all those they had rescued—soldiers, women, children and eunuchs, to prepare to leave for Egypt.

18 For they were afraid of what the Babylonians would do when the news reached them that Ishmael had killed Gedaliah the governor, for he had been chosen and appointed by the Babylonian emperor.

## CHAPTER 42

Then Johanan and the army captains and all the people, great and small, came to Jeremiah

2 And said, "Please pray for us to the Lord your God, for as you know so well, we are only a tiny remnant of what we were before.

3 Beg the Lord your God to show us what to do and where to go."

4 "All right," Jeremiah replied. "I will ask Him and I will tell you what He says. I will hide nothing from you."

5 Then they said to Jeremiah, "May the curse of God be on us if we refuse to obey whatever He says we should do!

6 Whether we like it or not, we will obey the Lord our God, to whom we send you with our plea. For if we obey Him, everything will turn out well for us."

7   Ten days later the Lord gave His reply to Jeremiah.

8   So he called for Johanan and the captains of his forces, and for all the people, great and small,

9   And said to them: "You sent me to the Lord, the God of Israel, with your request, and this is His reply:

10   Stay here in this land. If you do, I will bless you and no one will harm you. For I am sorry for all the punishment I have had to give to you.

11   Don't fear the King of Babylon any more, for I am with you to save you and to deliver you from his hand.

12   And I will be merciful to you by making him kind so that he will not kill you or make slaves of you but will let you stay here in your land.

13, 14   But if you refuse to obey the Lord and say, 'We will not stay here,'—and insist on going to Egypt where you think you will be free from war and hunger and alarms,

15   Then this is what the Lord replies, O remnant of Judah: The Lord of Hosts, the God of Israel, says: If you insist on going to Egypt,

16   The war and famine you fear will follow close behind you and you will perish there.

17   That is the fate awaiting every one of you who insists on going to live in Egypt. Yes, you will die from sword, famine and disease. None of you will escape from the evil I will bring upon you there.

18   For the Lord of Hosts, the God of Israel, says: Just as My anger and fury were poured out upon the

people of Jerusalem, so it will be poured out on you when you enter Egypt. You will be received with disgust and with hatred—you will be cursed and reviled. And you will never again see your own land.

19 For the Lord has said: O remnant of Judah, do not go to Egypt!" Jeremiah concluded: "Never forget the warning I have given you today.

20 If you go, it will be at the cost of your lives. For you were deceitful when you sent me to pray for you and said, 'Just tell us what God says and we will do it!'

21 And today I have told you exactly what He said, but you will not obey any more now than you did the other times.

22 Therefore know for a certainty that you will die by sword, famine and disease in Egypt, where you insist on going."

## CHAPTER 43

When Jeremiah had finished giving this message from God to all the people,

2, 3 Azariah (son of Hoshaiah) and Johanan (son of Kareah) and all the other proud men, said to Jeremiah, "You lie! The Lord our God hasn't told you to tell us not to go to Egypt! Baruch (son of Neriah) has plotted against us and told you to say this so that we will stay here and be killed by the Babylonians or carried off to Babylon as slaves."

4 So Johanan and all the guerilla leaders and all the people refused to obey the Lord to stay in Judah.

5 All of them, including all those who had returned from the nearby countries where they had fled, now started off for Egypt with Johanan and the other captains in command.

6 In the crowd were men, women and children, the king's daughters and all those whom Nebuzaradan, the captain of the guard, had left with Gedaliah. They even forced Jeremiah and Baruch to go with them too.

7 And so they arrived in Egypt at the city of Tahpanhes; for they would not obey the Lord.

8 Then at Tahpanhes, the Lord spoke to Jeremiah again and said:

9 "Call together the men of Judah and, as they watch you, bury large rocks between the pavement stones at the entrance of Pharaoh's palace here in Tahpanhes,

10 And tell the men of Judah this: The Lord of Hosts, the God of Israel, says: I will surely bring Nebuchadnezzar, king of Babylon, here to Egypt, for he is My servant. I will set his throne upon these stones that I have hidden. He shall spread his royal canopy over them.

11 And when he comes he shall destroy the land of Egypt, killing all those I want killed, and capturing those I want captured; and many shall die of plague.

12 He will set fire to the temples of the gods of Egypt and burn the idols and carry off the people as his captives. And he shall plunder the land of Egypt as a shepherd picks fleas from his cloak! And he himself shall leave unharmed.

13   And he shall break down the obelisks standing in the city of Heliopolis, and burn down the temples of the gods of Egypt."

## CHAPTER 44

This is the message God gave to Jeremiah concerning all the Jews who were living in the north of Egypt in the cities of Migdol, Tahpanhes and Memphis, and throughout southern Egypt as well:

2, 3   "The Lord of Hosts, the God of Israel, says: You saw what I did to Jerusalem and to all the cities of Judah. Because of all their wickedness they lie in heaps and ashes, without a living soul. For My anger rose high against them for worshiping other gods—'gods' that neither they nor you nor any of your fathers have ever known.

4   I sent My servants, the prophets, to protest over and over again and to plead with them not to do this horrible thing I hate,

5   But they wouldn't listen and wouldn't turn back from their wicked ways; they have kept right on with their sacrifices to these 'gods.'

6   And so My fury and anger boiled forth and fell as fire upon the cities of Judah and into the streets of Jerusalem; and there is desolation until this day.

7   And now the Lord, the God of Hosts, the God of Israel, asks you: Why are you destroying yourselves? For not one of you shall live—not a man, woman or child among you who has come here from Judah, not even the babies in arms.

8   For you are rousing My anger with the idols you have made and worshiped here in Egypt, burning incense to them, and causing Me to destroy you completely and to make you a curse and a stench in the nostrils of all the nations of the earth.

9   Have you forgotten the sins of your fathers, and the sins of the kings and queens of Judah, and your own sins, and the sins of your wives in Judah and Jerusalem?

10   And even until this very hour there has been no apology; no one has wanted to return to Me, or follow the laws I gave you and your fathers before you.

11   Therefore the Lord of Hosts, the God of Israel, says: There is fury in My face and I will destroy every one of you!

12   I will take this remnant of Judah that insisted on coming here to Egypt and I will consume them. They shall fall here in Egypt, killed by famine and sword; all shall die, from the least to the greatest. They shall be despised and loathed, cursed and hated.

13   I will punish them in Egypt just as I punished them in Jerusalem, by sword, famine and disease.

14   Not one of them shall escape from My wrath except those who repent of their coming and escape from the others by returning again to their own land."

15   Then all the women present and all the men who knew that their wives had burned incense to idols, (it was a great crowd of all the Jews in Southern Egypt), answered Jeremiah:

16   "We will not listen to your false 'Messages from God'!

17　We will do whatever we want to. We will burn incense to the 'Queen of Heaven'[4] and sacrifice to her just as much as we like—just as we and our fathers before us, and our kings and princes have always done in the cities of Judah and in the streets of Jerusalem; for in those days we had plenty to eat and we were well off and happy!

18　But ever since we quit burning incense to the 'Queen of Heaven' and stopped worshiping her we have been in great trouble and have been destroyed by sword and famine."

19　"And," the women added, "do you suppose that we were worshiping the 'Queen of Heaven' and pouring out our libations to her and making cakes for her with her image on them, without our husbands knowing it and helping us? Of course not!"

20　Then Jeremiah said to all of them, men and women alike, who had given him that answer:

21　"Do you think the Lord didn't know that you and your fathers and your kings and princes and all the people were burning incense to idols in the cities of Judah and in the streets of Jerusalem?

22　It was because He could no longer bear all the evil things you were doing that He made your land desolate, an incredible ruin, cursed, without an inhabitant, as it is today.

23　The very reason all these terrible things have befallen you is because you have burned incense and sinned against the Lord and refused to obey Him."

[4]"Queen of Heaven"; see note on Chapter 7, verse 18.

24 Then Jeremiah said to them all, including the women: "Listen to the word of the Lord, all you citizens of Judah who are here in Egypt!

25 The Lord of Hosts, the God of Israel, says: Both you and your wives have said that you will never give up your devotion and sacrifices to the 'Queen of Heaven,' and you have proved it by your actions. Then go ahead and carry out your promises and vows to her!

26 But listen to the word of the Lord, all you Jews who are living in the land of Egypt: I have sworn by My great name, says the Lord, that it will do you no good to seek my help and blessing any more, saying, 'O Lord our God, help us!'

27 For I will watch over you, but *not* for good! I will see to it that evil befalls you, and you shall be destroyed by war and famine until all of you are dead.

28 Only those who return to Judah (it will be but a tiny remnant) shall escape My wrath, but all who refuse to go back—who insist on living in Egypt—shall find out who tells the truth, I or they!

29 And this is the proof I give you that all I have threatened will happen to you, and that I will punish you here:

30 I will turn Pharaoh Hophra,[5] king of Egypt, over to those[6] who seek his life, just as I turned Zedekiah, king of Judah, over to Nebuchadnezzar, king of Babylon."

---

[5]Hophra, or Apries, ruled Egypt from 588 to 568 B.C.
[6]Pharaoh Hophra was killed by Amasis, one of his generals who had revolted and who was then crowned in his place.

## CHAPTER 45

This is the message[7] Jeremiah gave to Baruch in the fourth year of the reign of King Jehoiakim (son of Josiah), after Baruch had written down all God's messages as Jeremiah was dictating them to him:

2 O Baruch, the Lord God of Israel says this to you:

3 You have said, 'Woe is me! Don't I have troubles enough already? And now the Lord has added more! I am weary of my own sighing and I find no rest.'

4 But tell Baruch this, The Lord says: I will destroy this nation that I built; I will wipe out what I established.

5 Are you seeking great things for yourself? Don't do it! For though I will bring great evil upon all these people, I will protect you wherever you go, as your reward.

## CHAPTER 46

Here are the messages given to Jeremiah concerning foreign nations.

### The Egyptians

2 This message was given against Egypt at the occasion of the battle of Carchemish when Pharaoh Necho, king of Egypt, and his army were defeated beside the

[7]This message, in point of time, follows Chapter 36.

Euphrates River by Nebuchadnezzar, king of Babylon, in the fourth year of the reign of Jehoiakim (son of Josiah), king of Judah:

3 Buckle on your armor, you Egyptians and advance to battle!

4 Harness the horses and prepare to mount them—don your helmets, sharpen your spears, put on your armor.

5 But look! The Egyptian army flees in terror; the mightiest of its soldiers run without a backward glance. Yes, terror shall surround them on every side, says the Lord.

6 The swift will not escape, nor the mightiest of warriors. In the north, by the river Euphrates, they have stumbled and fallen.

7 What is this mighty army, rising like the Nile at flood time, overflowing all the land?

8 It is the Egyptian army, boasting that it will cover the earth like a flood, destroying every foe.

9 Then come, O horses and chariots and mighty soldiers of Egypt! Come, all of you from Cush and Put and Lud who handle the shield and bend the bow!

10 For this is the day of the Lord God of Hosts, a day of vengeance upon His enemies. The sword shall devour until it is sated; yes, drunk with your blood; for the Lord God of Hosts will receive a sacrifice today in the north country beside the river Euphrates!

11 Go up to Gilead for medicine, O virgin daughter of Egypt! Yet there is no cure for your wounds. Though you have used many medicines, there is no healing for you.

12 The nations have heard of your shame. The earth is filled with your cry of despair and defeat; your mightiest soldiers will stumble across each other and fall together.

13 Then God gave Jeremiah this message concerning the coming of Nebuchadnezzar, king of Babylon, to attack Egypt:

14 Shout it out in Egypt; publish it in the cities of Migdol, Memphis and Tahpanhes! Mobilize for battle, for the sword of destruction shall devour all around you.

15 Why has Apis, your bull god, fled in terror? Because the Lord knocked him down before your enemies.

16 Vast multitudes fall in heaps. (Then the remnant of the Jews will say, "Come, let us return again to Judah where we were born and get away from all this slaughter here!")

17 Rename Pharaoh Hophra and call him "The Man with No Power but with Plenty of Noise!"

18 As I live, says the King, the Lord of Hosts, one is coming against Egypt who is as tall as Mount Tabor or Mount Carmel by the sea!

19 Pack up; get ready to leave for exile, you citizens of Egypt, for the city of Memphis shall be utterly destroyed, and left without a soul alive.

20, 21 Egypt is sleek as a heifer, but a gadfly sends her running—a gadfly from the north! Even her famed mercenaries have become like frightened calves. They turn and run, for it is the day of great calamity for Egypt, a time of great punishment.

22, 23 Silent as a serpent gliding away, Egypt flees; the invading army marches in. The numberless soldiers cut down your people like woodsmen who clear a forest of its trees.

24 Egypt is as helpless as a girl before these men from the north.

25 The Lord of Hosts, the God of Israel, says: I will punish Amon, god of Thebes, and all the other gods of Egypt. I will punish Pharaoh too, and all who trust in him.

26 I will deliver them into the hands of those who want them killed—into the hands of Nebuchadnezzar, king of Babylon, and his army. But afterwards the land shall recover from the ravages of war.

27 But don't you be afraid, O My people who return to your own land; don't be dismayed; for I will save you from far away and bring your children from a distant land. Yes, Israel shall return and be at rest and nothing shall make her afraid.

28 Fear not, O Jacob, My servant, says the Lord, for I am with you. I will destroy all the nations to which I have exiled you, but I will not destroy you. I will punish you, but only enough to correct you.

## CHAPTER 47

### The Philistines

This is God's message to Jeremiah concerning the Philistines of Gaza, before the city was captured[8] by the Egyptian army.

---

[8]In 609 B.C., the year King Josiah died.

2　The Lord says: A flood is coming from the north to overflow the land of the Philistines; it will destroy their cities and everything in them. Strong men will scream in terror and all the land will weep.

3　Hear the clattering hoofs and rumbling wheels as the chariots go rushing by: fathers flee without a backward glance at their helpless children,

4　For the time has come when all the Philistines and their allies from Tyre and Sidon will be destroyed. For the Lord is destroying the Philistines, those colonists from Caphtor.

5　The cities of Gaza and Ashdod will be razed to the ground and lie in ruins. O descendants of the Anakim, how you will lament and mourn!

6　O sword of the Lord, when will you be at rest again? Go back into your scabbard; rest and be still!

7　But how can it be still when the Lord has sent it on an errand? For the city of Ashkelon and those living along the sea must be destroyed.

## CHAPTER 48

### The Moabites

This is the message of the Lord of Hosts, the God of Israel, against Moab: Woe to the city of Nebo, for it shall lie in ruins. The city of Kiriathaim and its forts are overwhelmed and captured.

2, 3, 4　No one will ever brag of Moab any more, for there is a plot against her life. In Heshbon, plans have been completed to destroy her. "Come," they say,

"We will cut her off from being a nation." In Madmen all is silent. And then the roar of battle will surge against Horonaim, for all Moab is being destroyed. Her crying will be heard as far away as Zoar.

5 Her refugees will climb the hills of Luhith, weeping bitterly, while cries of terror rise from the city below.

6 Flee for your lives; hide in the wilderness!

7 For you trusted in your wealth and skill; therefore you shall perish. Your god Chemosh, with his priests and princes, shall be taken away to distant lands!

8 All the villages and cities, whether they be on the plateaus or in the valleys, shall be destroyed, for the Lord has said it.

9 Oh, for wings for Moab that she could fly away; for her cities shall be left without a living soul.

10 Cursed be those withholding their swords from your blood, refusing to do the work that God has given them!

11 From her earliest history Moab has lived there undisturbed from all invasions. She is like wine that has not been poured from flask to flask, and is fragrant and smooth. But now she shall have the pouring out of exile!

12 The time is coming soon, the Lord has said, when He will send troublers to spill her out from jar to jar and then shatter the jars!

13 Then at last Moab shall be ashamed of her idol Chemosh, as Israel was of her calf-idol at Bethel.

14 Do you remember that boast of yours: "We are heroes, mighty men of war?"

15 But now Moab is to be destroyed; her destroyer is on the way; her choicest youth are doomed to slaughter, says the King, the Lord of Hosts.

16 Calamity is coming fast to Moab.

17 O friends of Moab, weep for her and cry! See how the strong, the beautiful is shattered!

18 Come down from your glory and sit in the dust, O people of Dibon; for those destroying Moab shall shatter Dibon too, and tear down all her towers.

19 Those in Aroer stand anxiously beside the road to watch, and shout to those who flee from Moab, "What has happened there?"

20 And they reply, "Moab lies in ruins; weep and wail. Tell it by the banks of the Arnon, that Moab is destroyed.

21 All the cities of the tableland lie in ruins too, for God's judgment has been poured out upon them all—on Holon and Jahzah and Mephaath,

22 And Dibon and Nebo and Beth-diblathaim,

23 And Kiriathaim and Beth-gamul and Bethmeon,

24 And Kerioth and Bozrah—and all the cities of the land of Moab, far and near.

25 The strength of Moab is ended—her horns are cut off; her arms are broken.

26 Let her stagger and fall like a drunkard, for she has rebelled against the Lord. Moab shall wallow in her vomit, scorned by all.

27 For you scorned Israel and robbed her, and were happy at her fall.

28　O people of Moab, flee from your cities and live in the caves like doves that nest in the clefts of the rocks.

29　We have all heard of the pride of Moab, for it is very great. We know your loftiness, your arrogance and your haughty heart.

30　I know her insolence, the Lord has said, but her boasts are false—her helplessness is great.

31　Yes, I wail for Moab, my heart is broken for the men of Kir-heres.

32　O men of Sibmah, rich in vineyards, I weep for you even more than Jazer. For the destroyer has cut off your spreading tendrils and harvested your grapes and summer fruits. He has plucked you bare!

33　Joy and gladness is gone from fruitful Moab. The presses yield no wine; no one treads the grapes with shouts of joy. There is shouting, yes, but not the shouting of joy.

34　Instead the awful cries of terror and pain rise from all over the land—from Heshbon clear across to Elealeh and to Jahaz; from Zoar to Horonaim and to Eglath-shelishiyah. The pastures of Nimrim are deserted now.

35　For the Lord says: I have put a stop to Moab's worshiping false gods and burning incense to idols.

36　Sad sings My heart for Moab and Kir-heres, for all their wealth has disappeared.

37　They shave their heads and beards in anguish, and slash their hands and put on clothes of sackcloth.

38   Crying and sorrow will be in every Moabite home and on the streets; for I have smashed and shattered Moab like an old, unwanted bottle.

39   How it is broken! Hear the wails! See the shame of Moab! For she is a sign of horror and of scoffing to her neighbors now.

40   A vulture circles ominously above the land of Moab, says the Lord.

41   Her cities are fallen; her strongholds are seized. The hearts of her mightiest warriors fail with fear like women in the pains of giving birth.

42   Moab shall no longer be a nation, for she has boasted against the Lord.

43   Fear and traps and treachery shall be your lot, O Moab, says the Lord.

44   He who flees shall fall in a trap and he who escapes from the trap shall run into a snare. I will see to it that you do not get away, for the time of your judgment has come.

45   They flee to Heshbon, unable to go farther. But a fire comes from Heshbon—Sihon's ancestral home—and devours the land from end to end with all its rebellious people.

46   Woe to you, O Moab; the people of the god Chemosh are destroyed, and your sons and daughters are taken away as slaves.

47   But in the latter days, says the Lord, I will re-establish Moab.

(Here the prophecy concerning Moab ends.)

## CHAPTER 49

### The Ammonites

What is this you are doing? Why are you living in the cities of the Jews? Aren't the Jews enough to fill them up? Didn't they inherit them from Me? Why then have you, who worship Milcom, taken over Gad and all its cities?

2 I will punish you for this, the Lord declares, by destroying your city of Rabbah. It shall become a desolate heap, and the neighboring towns shall be burned. Then Israel shall come and take back her land from you again. She shall dispossess those who dispossessed her, says the Lord.

3 Cry out, O Heshbon, for Ai is destroyed! Weep, daughter of Rabbah! Put on garments of mourning; weep and wail, hiding in the hedges, for your god Milcom shall be exiled along with his princes and priests.

4 You are proud of your fertile valleys, but they will soon be ruined. O wicked daughter, you trusted in your wealth and thought no one could ever harm you.

5 But see, I will bring terror upon you, says the Lord God of Hosts. For all your neighbors shall drive you from your land and none shall help your exiles as they flee.

6 But afterward I will restore the fortunes of the Ammonites, says the Lord.

\*     \*     \*     \*     \*

## The Edomites

7  The Lord of Hosts says: Where are all your wise men of days gone by? Is there not one left in all of Teman?

8  Flee to the remotest parts of the desert, O people of Dedan[9]; for when I punish Edom, I will punish you!

9, 10  Those who gather grapes leave a few for the poor, and even thieves don't take everything, but I will strip bare the land of Esau, and there will be no place to hide. Her children, her brothers, her neighbors—all will be destroyed—and she herself will perish too.

11  (But I will preserve your fatherless children who remain; and let your widows depend upon Me.)

12  The Lord says to Edom: If the innocent must suffer, how much more must you! You shall not go unpunished! You must drink this cup of judgment!

13  For I have sworn by My own name, says the Lord, that Bozrah shall become heaps of ruins, cursed and mocked; and her cities shall be eternal wastes.

14  I have heard this message from the Lord: He has sent a messenger to call the nations to form a coalition against Edom and destroy her.

15  I will make her weak among the nations and despised by all, says the Lord.

16  You have been fooled by your fame and your pride, living there in the mountains of Petra, in the clefts of the rocks. But though you live among the peaks with the eagles, I will bring you down, says the Lord.

---

[9]Dedan was in Northern Arabia and was a flourishing caravan city at the time of Jeremiah and Ezekiel.

17   The fate of Edom will be horrible; all who go by will be appalled, and gasp at the sight.

18   Your cities will become as silent as Sodom and Gomorrah and their neighboring towns, says the Lord. No one will live there anymore.

19   I will send against them one who will come like a lion from the wilds of Jordan stalking the sheep in the fold. Suddenly Edom shall be destroyed, and I will appoint over the Edomites the person of My choice. For who is like Me and who can call Me to account?

20   What shepherd can defy Me? Take note: the Lord will certainly do this to Edom and also the people of Teman—even little children will be dragged away as slaves! It will be a shocking thing to see.

21   The earth shakes with the noise of Edom's fall; the cry of the people is heard as far away as the Red Sea.

22   The one who will come will fly as swift as a vulture and will spread his wings against Bozrah. Then the courage of the mightiest warriors will disappear like that of women in labor.

\*       \*       \*       \*       \*

## Damascus

23   The cities of Hamath and Arpad are stricken with fear, for they have heard the news of their doom. Their hearts are troubled like a wild sea in a raging storm.

24   Damascus has become feeble and all her people turn to flee. Fear, anguish and sorrow have gripped her as they do women in labor.

25  O famous city, city of joy, how you are forsaken now!

26  Your young men lie dead in the streets; your
entire army shall be destroyed in one day, says the
Lord of Hosts.

27  And I will start a fire at the edge of Damascus
that shall burn up the palaces of Benhadad.

\*　　\*　　\*　　\*　　\*

### Kedar and Hazor

28  This prophecy is about Kedar[1] and the kingdoms of Hazor, which are going to be destroyed by
Nebuchadnezzar, king of Babylon, for the Lord will
send him to destroy them.

29  Their flocks and their tents will be captured,
says the Lord, with all their household goods. Their
camels will be taken away, and all around will be the
shouts of panic, "We are surrounded and doomed!"

30  Flee for your lives, says the Lord. Go deep into
the deserts, O people of Hazor[2]; for Nebuchadnezzar,
king of Babylon, has plotted against you and is preparing to destroy you.

31  "Go," said the Lord to King Nebuchadnezzar.
"Attack those wealthy Bedouin tribes living alone in the
desert without a care in the world, boasting that they
are self-sufficient—that they need neither walls nor
gates.

32  Their camels and cattle shall all be yours, and I

---

[1] An Arab tribe living in the desert east of Palestine.
[2] Not the Hazor mentioned in Joshua and Judges—a great city north of
the Sea of Galilee; but rather, a group of Arab tribes.

will scatter these heathen[3] to the winds. From all directions I will bring calamity upon them."

33    Hazor shall be a home for wild animals of the desert. No one shall ever live there again. It shall be desolate forever.

\*        \*        \*        \*        \*

### Elam

34    God's message against Elam came to Jeremiah in the beginning of the reign of Zedekiah, king of Judah:

35    The Lord of Hosts says: I will destroy the army of Elam,

36    And I will scatter the people of Elam to the four winds; they shall be exiled to countries throughout the world.

37    My fierce anger will bring great evil upon Elam, says the Lord, and I will cause her enemies to wipe her out.

38    And I will set My throne in Elam, says the Lord. I will destroy her king and princes.

39    But in the latter days I will bring the people back, says the Lord.

## CHAPTER 50

### Babylon

This is the message from the Lord against Babylon and the Chaldeans, spoken by Jeremiah the prophet:

2    Tell all the world that Babylon will be destroyed; her god Marduk will be utterly disgraced!

---

[3]Literally, "those who cut the corners of their hair."

3 For a nation shall come down upon her from the north with such destruction that no one shall live in her again; all shall be gone—both men and animals shall flee.

4 Then the people of Israel and Judah shall join together, weeping and seeking the Lord their God.

5 They shall ask the way to Zion and start back home again. "Come," they will say, "let us be united to the Lord with an eternal pledge that will never be broken again."

6 My people have been lost sheep. Their shepherds led them astray and then turned them loose in the mountains. They lost their way and didn't remember how to get back to the fold.

7 All who found them devoured them and said, "We are permitted to attack them freely, for they have sinned against the Lord, the God of justice, the hope of their fathers."

8 But now, flee from Babylon, the land of the Chaldeans; lead My people home again,

9 For see, I am raising up an army of great nations from the north and I will bring them against Babylon to attack her, and she shall be destroyed. The enemies' arrows go straight to the mark; they do not miss!

10 And Babylon shall be sacked until everyone is sated with loot, says the Lord.

11 Though you were glad, O Chaldeans, plunderers of My people, and are fat as cows that feed in lush pastures, and neigh like stallions,

12 Yet your mother shall be overwhelmed with

shame, for you shall become the least of the nations—a wilderness, a dry and desert land.

13 Because of the anger of the Lord, Babylon shall become deserted wasteland, and all who pass by shall be appalled, and shall mock at her for all her wounds.

14 Yes, prepare to fight with Babylon, all you nations round about; let the archers shoot at her; spare no arrows, for she has sinned against the Lord.

15 Shout against her from every side. Look! She surrenders! Her walls have fallen. The Lord has taken vengeance. Do to her as she has done!

16 Let the migrant farm hands all depart. Let them rush back to their own lands as the enemies advance.

17 The Israelites are like sheep the lions chase. First the king of Assyria ate them up; then Nebuchadnezzar, the king of Babylon, crunched their bones.

18 Therefore the Lord of Hosts, the God of Israel, says: Now I will punish the king of Babylon and his land as I punished the king of Assyria.

19 And I will bring Israel home again to her own land, to feed in the fields of Carmel and Bashan and to be happy once more on Mount Ephraim and Mount Gilead.

20 In those days, says the Lord, no sin shall be found in Israel or in Judah, for I will pardon the remnant I preserve.

21 Go up, O My warriors, against the land of Merathaim[5] and against the people of Pekod.[6] Yes,

[5] In southern Babylonia.
[6] In eastern Babylonia.

march against Babylon, the land of rebels, a land that I will judge! Annihilate them, as I have commanded you.

22 Let there be the shout of battle in the land, a shout of great destruction.

23 Babylon, the mightiest hammer in all the earth, lies broken and shattered. Babylon is desolate among the nations!

24 O Babylon, I have set a trap for you and you are caught, for you have fought against the Lord.

25 The Lord has opened His armory and brought out weapons to explode His wrath upon His enemies. The terror that befalls Babylon will be the work of the Lord, the God of Hosts.

26 Yes, come against her from distant lands; break open her granaries; knock down her walls and houses into heaps of ruins and utterly destroy her; let nothing be left.

27 Not even her cattle—woe to them, too! Kill them all! For the time has come for Babylon to be devastated.

28 But My people will flee; they will escape back to their own country to tell how the Lord their God has broken forth in fury upon those who destroyed His Temple.

29 Send out a call for archers to come to Babylon; surround the city so that none can escape. Do to her as she has done to others, for she has haughtily defied the Lord, the Holy One of Israel.

30 Her young men will fall in the streets and die; her warriors will all be killed.

31 For see, I am against you, O people so proud; and now your day of reckoning has come.

32 Land of pride, you will stumble and fall and no one will raise you up, for the Lord will light a fire in the cities of Babylon that will burn everything around them.

33 The Lord of Hosts says: The people of Israel and Judah have been wronged. Their captors hold them and refuse to let them go.

34 But their Redeemer is strong. His name is the Lord of Hosts. He will plead for them and see that they are freed to live again in quietness in Israel. As for the people of Babylon—there is no rest for them!

35 The sword of destruction shall smite the Chaldeans, says the Lord. It shall smite the people of Babylon—her princes and wise men too.

36 All her wise counselors shall become fools! Panic shall sieze her mightiest warriors!

37 War shall devour her horses and chariots, and her allies from other lands shall become as weak as women. Her treasures shall all be robbed;

38 Even her water supply will fail. And why? Because the whole land is full of images and the people are madly in love with their idols.

39 Therefore this city of Babylon shall become inhabited by ostriches and jackals; it shall be a home for the wild animals of the desert. Never again shall it be lived in by human beings; it shall lie desolate forever.

40 The Lord declares that He will destroy Babylon

just as He destroyed Sodom and Gomorrah and their neighboring towns. No one has lived in them since, and no one will live again in Babylon.

41 See them coming! A great army from the north! It is accompanied by many kings called by God from many lands.

42 They are fully armed for slaughter; they are cruel and show no mercy; their battle cry roars like the surf against the shoreline. O Babylon, they ride against you fully ready for the battle.

43 When the king of Babylon received the dispatch his hands fell helpless at his sides; pangs of terror gripped him like the pangs of a woman in labor.

44 *I will send against them an invader who will come upon them suddenly, like a lion from the jungles of Jordan that leaps upon the grazing sheep. I will put her defenders to flight and appoint over them whomsoever I please. For who is like Me? What ruler can oppose My will? Who can call Me to account?*

45 *Listen to the plan of the Lord against Babylon, the land of the Chaldeans. For even little children shall be dragged away as slaves; oh, the horror; oh, the terror.*

46 The whole earth shall shake at Babylon's fall and her cry of despair shall be heard around the world.

## CHAPTER 51

The Lord says: I will stir up a destroyer against Babylon, against that whole land of the Chaldeans, and destroy it.

2   Winnowers shall come and winnow her and blow her away; they shall come from every side to rise against her in her day of trouble.

3   The arrows of the enemy shall strike down the bowmen of Babylon and pierce her warriors in their coats of mail. No one shall be spared; both young and old alike shall be destroyed.

4   They shall fall down slain in the land of the Chaldeans, slashed to death in her streets.

5   For the Lord of Hosts has not forsaken Israel and Judah. He is still their God; but the land of the Chaldeans⁷ is filled with sin against the Holy One of Israel.

6   Flee from Babylon! Save yourselves! Don't get trapped! If you stay, you will be destroyed when God takes His vengeance on all of Babylon's sins.

7   Babylon has been as a golden cup in the Lord's hands; a cup from which He made the whole earth drink and go mad.

8   But now, suddenly Babylon too has fallen; weep for her; give her medicine; perhaps she can yet be healed.

9   We would help her if we could, but nothing can save her now. Let her go. Abandon her and return to your own land, for God is judging her from heaven.

10   The Lord has vindicated us. Come, let us declare in Jerusalem all the Lord our God has done.

11   Sharpen the arrows! Lift up the shields! For the Lord has stirred up the spirit of the kings of the Medes

---

⁷Implied.

to march on Babylon and destroy her. This is His vengeance on those who wronged His people and desecrated His Temple.

12 Prepare your defenses, Babylon! Set many watchmen on your walls; send out an ambush; for the Lord will do all He has said He would concerning Babylon.

13 O wealthy port, great center of commerce, your end has come; the thread of your life is cut.

14 The Lord of Hosts has taken this vow, and sworn to it in His own Name: Your cities shall be filled with enemies, like fields filled with locusts in a plague; and they shall lift to the skies their mighty shouts of victory.

15 God made the earth by His power and wisdom. He stretched out the heavens by His understanding.

16 When He speaks there is thunder in the heavens and He causes the vapors to rise around the world; He brings the lightning with the rain and the winds from His treasuries.

17 Compared to Him, all men are stupid beasts. They have no wisdom—none at all! The silversmith is dulled by the images he makes, for in making them he lies; for he calls them gods, when there is not a breath of life in them at all!

18 Idols are nothing! They are lies! And the time is coming when God will come and see, and shall destroy them all.

19 But the God of Israel is no idol! For He made everything there is, and Israel is His nation; the Lord of Hosts is His name.

20    Cyrus[8] is God's battleaxe and sword. I will use you, says the Lord, to break nations in pieces and to destroy many kingdoms.

21    With you I will crush armies, destroying the horse and his rider, the chariot and the charioteer;

22    Yes, and the civilians too, both old and young, young men and maidens;

23    Shepherds and flocks; farmers and oxen; captains and rulers;

24    Before your eyes I will repay Babylon and all the Chaldeans for all the evil they have done to My people, says the Lord.

25    For see, I am against you, O mighty mountain, Babylon, destroyer of the earth! I will lift My hand against you and roll you down from your heights and leave you, a burnt out mountain.

26    You shall be desolate forever[9]; even your stones shall never be used for building again. You shall be completely wiped out.

27    Signal many nations to mobilize for war on Babylon. Sound the battle cry; bring out the armies of Ararat, Minni, and Ashkenaz. Appoint a leader; bring a multitude of horses!

28    Bring against her the armies of the kings of the Medes and their generals, and the armies of all the countries they rule.

29    Babylon trembles and writhes in pain, for all

[8]Literally, "you are . . ." Cyrus was used of God to conquer Babylon. See also, Isaiah 44:28; 45:1.
[9]This complete destruction of the city of Babylon was accomplished by later Persian kings. Jeremiah here sees the long range picture of the city's history, and does not confine himself to Cyrus.

that the Lord has planned against her stands unchanged. Babylon will be left desolate without a living soul.

30 Her mightiest soldiers no longer fight; they stay in their barracks; their courage is gone; they have become as women. The invaders have burned the houses and broken down the city gates.

31 Messengers from every side come running to the king to tell him all is lost!

32 All the escape routes are blocked; the fortifications are burning and the army is in panic.

33 For the Lord of Hosts, the God of Israel, says: Babylon is like the wheat upon a threshing floor; in just a little while the flailing will begin.

34, 35 The Jews in Babylon say, "Nebuchadnezzar, king of Babylon, has eaten and crushed us and emptied out our strength; he has swallowed us like a great monster and filled his belly with our riches and cast us out of our own country. May Babylon be repaid for all she did to us! May she be paid in full for all our blood she spilled!"

36 And the Lord replies: I will be your lawyer; I will plead your case; I will avenge you; I will dry up her river, her water supply,

37 And Babylon shall become a heap of ruins, haunted by jackals, a land horrible to see, incredible, without a living soul.

38 In their drunken feasts, the men of Babylon roar like lions.

39 And while they lie inflamed with all their wine, I will prepare a different kind of feast for them, and

make them drink until they fall unconscious to the floor, to sleep forever, never to waken again, says the Lord.

40 I will bring them like lambs to the slaughter, like rams and goats.

41 How Babylon is fallen—great Babylon, lauded by all the earth! The world can scarce believe its eyes at Babylon's fall!

42 The sea has risen upon Babylon; she is covered by its waves.

43 Her cities lie in ruins—she is a dry wilderness where no one lives nor even travelers pass by.

44 And I will punish Bel, the god of Babylon, and pull from his mouth what he has taken. The nations shall no longer come and worship him; the wall of Babylon has fallen.

45 O My people, flee from Babylon; save yourselves from the fierce anger of the Lord.

46 But don't panic when you hear the first rumor of approaching forces. For rumors will keep coming year by year. Then there will be a time of civil war as the governors of Babylon fight against each other.

47 For the time is surely coming when I will punish this great city and all her idols; her dead shall lie in the streets.

48 Heaven and earth shall rejoice, for out of the north shall come destroying armies against Babylon says the Lord.

49 Just as Babylon killed the people of Israel, so must she be killed.

50 Go, you who escaped the sword! Don't stand and watch—flee while you can! Remember the Lord and return to Jerusalem far away!

51 *"We are ashamed because the Temple of the Lord has been defiled by foreigners from Babylon."*

52 Yes, says the Lord. But the time is coming for the destruction of the idols of Babylon. All through the land will be heard the groans of the wounded.

53 Though Babylon be as powerful as heaven, though she increase her strength immeasurably, she shall die, says the Lord.

54 Listen! Hear the cry of great destruction out of Babylon, the land the Chaldeans rule!

55 For the Lord is destroying Babylon; her mighty voice is stilled as the waves roar in upon her.

56 Destroying armies come and slay her mighty men; all her weapons break in her hands; for the Lord God gives just punishment and is giving Babylon all her due.

57 I will make drunk her princes, wise men, rulers, captains, warriors. They shall sleep and not wake up again! So says the King, the Lord of Hosts.

58 For the wide walls of Babylon shall be leveled to the ground and her high gates shall be burned; the builders from many lands have worked in vain—their work shall be destroyed by fire!

\* \* \* \* \*

59 During the fourth year of Zedekiah's reign, this message came to Jeremiah to give to Seraiah (son of Neriah, son of Mahseiah), concerning Seraiah's cap-

ture[1] and exile to Babylon along with Zedekiah, king of Judah. (Seraiah was quartermaster of Zedekiah's army.)

60   Jeremiah wrote on a scroll all the terrible things God had scheduled against Babylon—all the words written above—

61, 62   And gave the scroll to Seraiah and said to him, "When you get to Babylon, read what I have written and say, 'Lord, You have said that You will destroy Babylon so that not a living creature will remain; and it will be abandoned forever.'

63   Then, when you have finished reading the scroll, tie a rock to it and throw it into the Euphrates river,

64   And say, 'So shall Babylon sink, never more to rise, because of the evil I am bringing upon her.'"

(This ends Jeremiah's messages.)

## CHAPTER 52

### (Events told about in Chapter 39.)

Zedekiah was twenty-one years old when he became king, and he reigned eleven years in Jerusalem. His mother's name was Hamutal (daughter of Jeremiah of Libnah).

2   But he was a wicked king, just as Jehoiakim had been.

3   Things became so bad at last that the Lord, in

---

[1]This event occurred six years after this prophecy.

His anger, saw to it that Zedekiah rebelled against the king of Babylon until he and the people of Israel were ejected from the Lord's presence in Jerusalem and Judah, and were taken away as captives to Babylon.

4 In the ninth year of Zedekiah's reign, on the tenth day of the tenth month, Nebuchadnezzar, king of Babylon, came with all his army against Jerusalem and built forts around it.

5 And laid siege to the city for two years.

6 Then finally, on the ninth day of the fourth month, when the famine in the city was very serious, with the last of the food entirely gone,

7 The people in the city tore a hole in the city wall and all the soldiers fled from the city during the night, going out by the gate between the two walls near the king's gardens (for the city was surrounded by the Chaldeans), and made a dash for it across the fields, toward Arabah.

8 But the Chaldean soldiers chased them and caught King Zedekiah in some fields near Jericho—for all his army was scattered from him.

9 They brought him to the king of Babylon who was staying in the city of Riblah in the kingdom of Hamath, and there judgment was passed upon him.

10 He made Zedekiah watch while his sons and all the princes of Judah were killed before his eyes,

11 And then his eyes were gouged out and he was taken in chains to Babylon and put in prison for the rest of his life.

12 On the tenth day of the fifth month during the

nineteenth year[2] of the reign of Nebuchadnezzar, king of Babylon, Nebuzaradan, captain of the guard, arrived in Jerusalem,

13   And burned the Temple and the palace and all the larger homes,

14   And set the Chaldean army to work tearing down the walls of the city.

15   Then he took to Babylon, as captives, some of the poorest of the people—along with those who survived the city's destruction, and those who had deserted Zedekiah and had come over to the Babylonian army, and the tradesmen who were left.

16   But he left some of the poorest people to care for the crops as vinedressers and plowmen.

17   The Babylonians dismantled the two large bronze pillars that stood at the entrance of the Temple, and the bronze laver and bronze bulls on which it stood, and carted them off to Babylon.

18   And he took along all the bronze pots and kettles, and ash shovels used at the altar, and the snuffers, spoons, bowls, and all the other items used in the Temple.

19   He also took the firepans and the solid gold and silver candlesticks and cups and bowls.

20   The weight of the two enormous pillars and the laver and twelve bulls was tremendous. They had no way of estimating it. (They had been made in the days of King Solomon.)

--------

[2]Late in July, 587 B.C.

21   For the pillars were each 27 feet high and 18 feet in circumference, hollow, with three-inch walls.

22   The top 7½ feet of each column had bronze carvings, a network of bronze pomegranates.

23   There were 96 pomegranates on the sides, and on the network round about there were 100 more.

24, 25   The captain of the guard took along with him, as his prisoners, Seraiah the chief priest, and Zephaniah his assistant, the three chief Temple guards, one of the commanding officers of the army, seven of the king's special counselors discovered in the city, and the secretary of the general-in-chief of the Jewish army (who was in charge of recruitment) and 60 other men of importance found hiding.

26   He took them to the king of Babylon at Riblah,

27   Where the king killed them all. So it was that Judah's exile was accomplished.

28   The number of captives taken to Babylon in the seventh year of Nebuchadnezzar's reign was 3,023.

29   Then, eleven years later, he took 832 more;

30   Five years after that he sent Nebuzaradan, his captain of the guard, and took 745—a total of 4,600 captives in all.

31   On February 25, of the 37th year of the imprisonment in Babylon of Jehoiachin, king of Judah, Evil-merodach, who became king of Babylon that year, was kind to King Jehoiachin and brought him out of prison,

32   And spoke pleasantly to him and gave him preference over all the other kings in Babylon,

33   And gave him new clothes and fed him from the king's kitchen as long as he lived.

34   And he was given a regular allowance to cover his daily needs until the day of his death.

# The Lamentations of Jeremiah

## CHAPTER 1

Jerusalem's streets, once thronged with people, are silent now. Like a widow broken with grief, she sits alone in her mourning. She, once queen of nations, is now a slave.

2    She sobs through the night; tears run down her cheeks. Among all her lovers,[1] there is none to help her. All her friends are now her enemies.

3    Why is Judah led away, a slave? Because of all the wrong she did to others, making them her slaves. Now she sits in exile far away. There is no rest, for those she persecuted have turned and conquered her.

4    The roads to Zion mourn, no longer filled with joyous throngs who come to celebrate the Temple feasts; the city gates are silent; her priests groan; her virgins have been dragged away. Bitterly she weeps.

5    Her enemies prosper, for the Lord has punished Jerusalem for all her many sins; her young children are captured and taken far away as slaves.

6    All her beauty and her majesty are gone; her princes are like starving deer that search for pasture—

---

[1] The reference is to Egypt and Israel's other former allies.

helpless game too weak to keep on running from their foes.

7　And now in the midst of all Jerusalem's sadness she remembers happy bygone days. She thinks of all the precious joys she had before her mocking enemy struck her down—and there was no one to give her aid.

8　For Jerusalem sinned so horribly; therefore she is tossed away like dirty rags. All who honored her despise her now, for they have seen her stripped naked and humiliated. She groans and hides her face.

9　She indulged herself in immorality, and refused to face the fact that punishment was sure to come. Now she lies in the gutter with no one left to lift her out. "O Lord," she cries, "see my plight. The enemy has triumphed."

10　Her enemies have plundered her completely, taking everything precious she owns. She has seen foreign nations violate her sacred Temple—foreigners You had forbidden even to enter.

11　Her people groan and cry for bread; they have sold all they have for food to give a little strength. "Look, O Lord," she prays, "and see how I'm despised."

12　Is it nothing to you, all you who pass by? Look and see if there is any sorrow like my sorrow, because of all the Lord has done to me in the day of His fierce wrath.

13　He has sent fire from heaven that burns within my bones; He has placed a pitfall in my path and turned me back. He has left me sick and desolate the whole day through.

14   He wove my sins into ropes to hitch me to a yoke of slavery. He sapped my strength and gave me to my enemies; I am helpless in their hands.

15   The Lord has trampled all my mighty men. A great army has come at His command to crush the noblest youth. The Lord has trampled His beloved city as grapes in a winepress.

16   For all these things I weep; tears flow down my cheeks. My Comforter is far away—He who alone could help me. My children have no future; we are a conquered land.

17   Jerusalem pleads for help but no one comforts her. For the Lord has spoken: "Let her neighbors be her foes! Let her be thrown out like filthy rags!"

18   And the Lord is right; for we rebelled. And yet, O people everywhere, behold and see my anguish and despair; for my sons and daughters are taken far away as slaves to distant lands.

19   I begged my allies[2] for their help. False hope— they could not help at all. Nor could my priests and elders—they were starving in the streets while searching through the garbage dumps for bread.

20   *See, O Lord, my anguish;* my heart is broken and my soul despairs; for I have terribly rebelled. In the streets the sword awaits me; at home, disease and death.

21   *Hear my groans!* And there is no one anywhere to help. All my enemies have heard my troubles and they are glad to see what You have done. And yet, O

---

[2]Literally, "lovers." The reference is probably to Egypt.

Lord, the time will surely come—for You have promised it—when You will do to them as You have done to me.

22   Look also on their sins, O Lord, and punish them as You have punished me; for my sighs are many and my heart is faint.

## CHAPTER 2

A cloud of anger from the Lord has overcast Jerusalem; the fairest city of Israel lies in the dust of the earth, cast from the heights of heaven at His command. In His day of awesome fury He has shown no mercy even to His Temple.[3]

2   The Lord without mercy has destroyed every home in Israel. In his wrath He has broken every fortress, every wall. He has brought the kingdom to dust, with all its rulers.

3   All the strength of Israel vanishes beneath His wrath. He has withdrawn His protection as the enemy attacks. God burns across the land of Israel like a raging fire.

4   He bends His bow against His people as though He were an enemy. His strength is used against them to kill their finest youth. His fury is poured out like fire upon them.

5   Yes, the Lord has vanquished Israel like an enemy. He has destroyed her forts and palaces. Sorrows and tears are His portion for Jerusalem.

---

[3]Literally, "footstool."

6  He has violently broken down His Temple as though it were a booth of leaves and branches in a garden! No longer can the people celebrate their holy feasts and sabbaths. Kings and priests together fall before His wrath.

7  The Lord has rejected His own altar, for He despises the false "worship" of His people; He has given their palaces to their enemies, who carouse in the Temple as Israel used to do on days of holy feasts!

8  The Lord determined to destroy Jerusalem. He laid out an unalterable line of destruction. Therefore the ramparts and walls fell down before Him.

9  Jerusalem's gates are useless. All their locks and bars are broken, for He has crushed them. Her kings and princes are enslaved in far-off lands, without a temple, without a divine law to govern them, or prophetic vision to guide them.

10  The elders of Jerusalem sit upon the ground in silence, clothed in sackcloth; they throw dust upon their heads in sorrow and despair. The virgins of Jerusalem hang their heads in shame.

11  I have cried until the tears no longer come; my heart is broken, my spirit poured out, as I see what has happened to my people; little children and tiny babies are fainting and dying in the streets.

12  "Mamma, Mamma, we want food," they cry, and then collapse upon their mothers' shrunken breasts. Their lives ebb away like those wounded in battle.

13  In all the world has there ever been such sorrow? O Jerusalem, what can I compare your anguish

to? How can I comfort you? For your wound is deep as the sea. Who can heal you?

14 Your "prophets" have said so many foolish things, false to the core. They have not tried to hold you back from slavery by pointing out your sins. They lied and said that all was well.

15 All who pass by scoff and shake their heads and say, "Is this the city called 'Most Beautiful in All the World,' and 'Joy of All the Earth'?"

16 All your enemies deride you. They hiss and grind their teeth and say, "We have destroyed her at last! Long have we waited for this hour and it is finally here! With our own eyes we've seen her fall."

17 But it is the Lord who did it, just as He had warned. He has fulfilled the promises of doom He made so long ago. He has destroyed Jerusalem without mercy and caused her enemies to rejoice over her and boast of their power.

18 Then the people wept before the Lord. O walls of Jerusalem, let tears fall down upon you like a river; give yourselves no rest from weeping day or night.

19 Rise in the night and cry to your God. Pour out your hearts like water to the Lord; lift up your hands to Him; plead for your children as they faint with hunger in the streets.

20 *O Lord, think! These are Your own people to whom You are doing this.* Shall mothers eat their little children, those they bounced upon their knees? Shall priests and prophets die within the Temple of the Lord?

21 See them lying in the streets—old and young,

boys and girls, killed by the enemies' swords. You have killed them, Lord, in Your anger, You have killed them without mercy.

22 You have deliberately called for this destruction; in the day of Your anger none escaped or remained. All my little children lie dead upon the streets before the enemy.

## CHAPTER 3

I am the man who has seen the afflictions that come from the rod of God's wrath.

2 He has brought me into deepest darkness, shutting out all light.

3 He has turned against me. Day and night His hand is heavy on me.

4 He has made me old and has broken my bones.

5 He has built forts against me and surrounded me with anguish and distress.

6 He buried me in dark places, like those long dead;

7 He has walled me in; I cannot escape; He has fastened me with heavy chains.

8 And though I cry and shout, He will not hear my prayers!

9 He has shut me into a place of high, smooth walls[4]; He has filled my path with detours.

10 He lurks like a bear, like a lion, waiting to attack me.

---

[4]Literally, "He has walled up my ways with hewn stone."

11   He has dragged me into the underbrush and torn me with His claws, and left me bleeding and desolate.

12   He has bent His bow and aimed it squarely at me,

13   And sent His arrows deep within my heart.

14   My own people laugh at me; all day long they sing their ribald songs.

15   He has filled me with bitterness, and given me a cup to drink of deepest sorrows.

16   He has made me eat gravel and broken my teeth; He has rolled me in ashes and dirt.

17   O Lord, all peace and all prosperity have long since gone, for You have taken them away. I have forgotten what enjoyment is.

18   All hope is gone; my strength has turned to water, for the Lord has left me.

19   Oh, remember the bitterness and suffering You have dealt to me!

20   For I can never forget these awful years; always my soul will live in utter shame.

21   *Yet there is one ray of hope:*

22   *His compassion never ends.* It is only the Lord's mercies that have kept us from complete destruction.

23   Great is His faithfulness; His lovingkindness begins afresh each day.

24   My soul claims the Lord as my inheritance; therefore I will hope in Him.

25   The Lord is wonderfully good to those who wait for Him, to those who seek for Him.

26  It is good both to hope and wait quietly for the salvation of the Lord.

27  It is good for a young man to be under discipline,

28  For it causes him to sit apart in silence beneath the Lord's demands,

29  To lie face downward in the dust; then at last there is hope for him.

30  Let him turn the other cheek to those who strike him, and accept their awful insults,

31  For the Lord will not abandon him forever.

32  Although God gives him grief, yet He will show compassion too, according to the greatness of His lovingkindness.

33  For He does not enjoy afflicting men and causing sorrow.

34, 35, 36  But you have trampled and crushed beneath your feet the lowly of the world, and deprived men of their God-given rights, and refused them justice. No wonder the Lord has had to deal with you!

37  For who can act against you without the Lord's permission?

38  It is the Lord who helps one and harms another.

39  Why then should we, mere humans as we are, murmur and complain when punished for our sins?

40  Let us examine ourselves instead, and repent and turn again to the Lord.

41  Let us lift our hearts and hands to Him in heaven,

42   For we have sinned; we have rebelled against the Lord, and He has not forgotten it.

43   You have engulfed us by Your anger, Lord, and slain us without mercy.

44   You have veiled Yourself as with a cloud so that our prayers do not reach through.

45   You have made us as refuse and garbage among the nations.

46   All our enemies have spoken out against us.

47   We are filled with fear, for we are trapped and desolate, destroyed.

48, 49   My eyes flow day and night with never-ending streams of tears because of the destruction of my people.

50   Oh, that the Lord might look down from heaven and respond to my cry!

51   My heart is breaking over what is happening to the young girls of Jerusalem.

52   My enemies, whom I have never harmed, chased me as though I were a bird.

53   They threw me in a well and capped it with a rock.

54   The water flowed above my head. I thought, This is the end!

55   But I called upon Your name, O Lord, from deep within the well,

56   And You heard me! You listened to my pleading; You heard my weeping!

57   Yes, You came at my despairing cry and told me not to fear.

58   O Lord, You are my lawyer! Plead my case! For You have redeemed my life.

59   You have seen the wrong they did to me; be my Judge, to prove me right.

60   You have seen the plots my foes have laid against me.

61   You have heard the vile names they have called me,

62   And all they say about me and their whispered plans.

63   See how they laugh and sing with glee, preparing my doom.

64   O Lord, repay them well for all the evil they have done.

65   Harden their hearts and curse them, Lord.

66   Go after them in fierce pursuit and wipe them off the earth, beneath the heavens of the Lord.

## CHAPTER 4

How the finest gold has lost its luster! For the inlaid[5] Temple walls are scattered in the streets!

2   The cream of our youth—the finest of the gold— are treated as earthenware pots.

3, 4   Even the jackals feed their young, but not my people, Israel. They are like cruel desert ostriches,

[5]Implied.

heedless of their babies' cries. The children's tongues stick to the roofs of their mouths for thirst, for there is not a drop of water left. Babies cry for bread but no one can give them any.

5 Those who used to eat fastidiously are begging in the streets for anything at all. Those brought up in palaces now scratch in garbage pits for food.

6 For the sin of my people is greater than that of Sodom, where utter disaster struck in a moment without the hand of man.

7 Our princes were lean and tanned,[6] the finest specimens of men;

8 But now their faces are as black as soot. No one can recognize them. Their skin sticks to their bones; it is dry and hard and withered.

9 Those killed by the sword are far better off than those who die of slow starvation.

10 Tender-hearted women have cooked and eaten their own children; thus they survived the siege.

11 But now at last the anger of the Lord is satisfied; His fiercest anger has been poured out. He started a fire in Jerusalem that burned it down to its foundations.

12 Not a king in all the earth—no one in all the world—would have believed an enemy could enter through Jerusalem's gates!

13 Yet God permitted it because of the sins of her prophets and priests, who defiled the city by shedding innocent blood.

---

[6]Literally, "were purer than snow, whiter than milk, more ruddy than rubies, polished like sapphires."

14    Now these same men are blindly staggering through the streets, covered with blood, defiling everything they touch.

15    "Get away!" the people shout at them. "You are defiled!" They flee to distant lands and wander there among the foreigners; but none will let them stay.

16    The Lord Himself has dealt with them; He no longer helps them; for they persecuted the priests and elders who stayed true to God.

17    We look for our allies[7] to come and save us, but we look in vain. The nation we expected most to help us makes no move at all.

18    We can't go into the streets without danger to our lives. Our end is near—our days are numbered. We are doomed.

19    Our enemies are swifter than the eagles; if we flee to the mountains they find us. If we hide in the wilderness, they are waiting for us there.

20    Our king—the life of our life, the Lord's anointed—was captured in their snares. Yes, even our mighty king, about whom we had boasted that under his protection we could hold our own against any nation on earth!

21    Do you rejoice, O people of Edom, in the land of Uz? But you too will feel the awful anger of the Lord.

22    Israel's exile for her sins will end at last, but Edom's never.

---

[7]The reference is probably to Egypt.

## CHAPTER 5

O Lord, remember all that has befallen us; see what sorrows we must bear!

2   Our homes, our nation, now are filled with foreigners.

3   We are orphans—our fathers dead, our mothers widowed.

4   We must even pay for water to drink; our fuel is sold to us at the highest of prices.

5   We bow our necks beneath the victors' feet; unending work is now our lot.

6   We beg for bread from Egypt, and Assyria too.

7   Our fathers sinned but died before the hand of judgment fell. We have borne the blow that they deserved!

8   Our former servants have become our masters; there is no one left to save us.

9   We went into the wilderness to hunt for food, risking death from enemies.

10   Our skin was black from famine.

11   They rape the women of Jerusalem and the girls in Judah's cities.

12   Our princes are hanged by their thumbs. Even aged men are treated with contempt.

13   They take away the young men to grind their grain and the little children stagger beneath their heavy loads.

14  The old men sit no longer in the city gates; the young no longer dance and sing.

15  The joy of our hearts has ended; our dance has turned to death.[8]

16  Our glory is gone. The crown is fallen from our head. Woe upon us for our sins.

17  Our hearts are faint and weary; our eyes grow dim.

18  Jerusalem and the Temple of the Lord are desolate, deserted by all but wild animals lurking in the ruins.

19  O Lord, forever You remain the same! Your throne continues from generation to generation.

20  Why do You forget us forever? Why do You forsake us for so long?

21  Turn us around and bring us back to You again! That is our only hope! Give us back the joys we used to have!

22  *Or have You utterly rejected us? Are You angry with us still?*

---

[8]Literally, "to mourning."

# Ezekiel

## CHAPTER 1

**E**zekiel *was a priest (the son of Buzi) who lived with the Jewish exiles beside the Chebar Canal in Babylon.*

One day late in June, when I was 30 years old,[1] the heavens were suddenly opened to me and I saw visions from God.

4  I saw, in this vision, a great storm coming towards me from the north, driving before it a huge cloud glowing with fire, with a mass of fire inside that flashed continually; and in the fire there was something that shone like polished brass.

5  Then from the center of the cloud, four strange forms appeared that looked like men,

6  Except that each had four faces and two pairs of wings!

7  Their legs were those of men, but their feet were cloven like calves' feet, and shone like burnished brass.

8  And beneath each of their wings I could see human hands.

9  The four living beings were joined wing to wing, and they flew straight forward without turning.

---

[1] Literally, "in the 30th year."
[2] Implied.

10    Each had the face of a man (in front),[2] with a lion's face on the right side (of his head),[2] and the face of an ox on his left side, and the face of an eagle at the back of his head!

11    Each had two pairs of wings spreading out from the middle of his back. One pair stretched out to attach to the wings of the living beings on each side; and the other pair covered his body.

12    Wherever their spirit[3] went they went, going straight forward without turning.

13    Going up and down among them were other forms that glowed like bright coals of fire or brilliant torches, and it was from these the lightning flashed.

14    The living beings darted to and fro swift as lightning.

15    As I stared at all of this, I saw four wheels on the ground beneath them, one wheel belonging to each.

16    The wheels looked like they were made of polished amber and each wheel was constructed with a second wheel crosswise inside.*

17    They could go in any of the four directions without having to face around.

18    The four wheels had rims and spokes, and the rims were filled with eyes around their edges.

19, 20, 21    When the four living beings flew forward, the wheels moved forward with them. When they flew upwards, the wheels went up too. When the living

---

[3]Literally, "the spirit."
*Literally, "a wheel within a wheel," perhaps as in a gyroscope.

beings stopped, the wheels stopped. For the spirit of the four living beings was in the wheels; so wherever their spirit went, the wheels and the living beings went there too.

22    The sky spreading out above them looked as though it were made of crystal; it was inexpressibly beautiful.

23    Each being's wings stretched straight out to touch the others' wings, and each had two wings covering his body.

24    And as they flew their wings roared like waves against the shore, or like the voice of God, or like the shouting of a mighty army. When they stopped they let down their wings.

25    And every time they stopped, there came a voice from the crystal sky[4] above them.

26    For high in the sky above them was what looked like a throne made of beautiful blue sapphire stones; and upon it sat Someone who appeared to be a Man.

27, 28    From His waist up, He seemed to be all glowing bronze, dazzling like fire; and from His waist down He seemed to be entirely flame; and there was a glowing halo like a rainbow all around Him. That was the way the glory of the Lord appeared to me. And when I saw it, I fell face downward on the ground, and heard the voice of Someone speaking to me:

---

[4]Literally, "from above the firmament, over their heads."

# CHAPTER 2

A nd He said to me: "Stand up, son of dust,[5] and I will talk to you."

2   And the Spirit entered into me as He spoke, and set me on my feet.

3   "Son of dust," He said, "I am sending you to the nation of Israel, to a nation rebelling against Me. They and their fathers have kept on sinning against Me until this very hour.

4   For they are a hard-hearted, stiff-necked people. But I am sending you to give them My messages—the messages of the Lord God.

5   And whether they listen or not (for remember, they are rebels), they will at least know they have had a prophet among them.

6   Son of dust, don't be afraid of them; don't be frightened even though their threats are sharp and barbed and sting like scorpions. Don't be dismayed by their dark scowls. For remember, they are rebels!

7   You must give them My messages whether they listen or not (but they won't,[6] for they are utter rebels).

8   Listen, son of dust, to what I say to you. Don't you be a rebel too! Open your mouth and eat what I give you."

[5]Or, "son of man". . . and so also 87 times throughout the book of Ezekiel. The connotation is "mortal man." In Daniel 7:13, the corresponding Aramaic expression is used for the Messiah as representative of the human race of which He is the head.
[6]Implied.

9, 10    Then I looked and saw a hand holding out to me a scroll, with writing on both sides. He unrolled it, and I saw that it was full of warnings and sorrows and pronouncements of doom.

# CHAPTER 3

And He said to me: "Son of dust, eat what I am giving you—eat this scroll! Then go and give its message to the people of Israel."

2    So I took the scroll.

3    "Eat it all," He said. And when I ate it, it tasted sweet as honey.

4    Then He said: "Son of dust, I am sending you to the people of Israel with My messages.

5    I am not sending you to some far-off foreign land where you can't understand the language—

6    No, not to tribes with strange, difficult tongues. (If I did, they would listen!)

7    I am sending you to the people of Israel, and they won't listen to you anymore than they listened to Me! For the whole lot of them are hard, impudent and stubborn.

8    But see, I have made you hard and stubborn too—as tough as they are.

9    I have made your forehead as hard as rock. So don't be afraid of them, or fear their sullen, angry looks, even though they are such rebels."

10    Then He added: "Son of dust, let all My words

sink deep into your own heart first; listen to them carefully for yourself.

11 Then, afterward, go to your people in exile, and whether or not they will listen, tell them: 'This is what the Lord God says!' "

12 Then the Spirit lifted me up and the glory of the Lord began to move away, accompanied by the sound of a great earthquake.[7]

13 It was the noise of the wings of the living beings as they touched against each other, and the sound of their wheels beside them.

14, 15 The Spirit lifted me up and took me away to Tel Abib, another colony of Jewish exiles beside the Chebar River. I went in bitterness and anger,[8] but the hand of the Lord was strong upon me. And I sat among them, overwhelmed, for seven days.

16 At the end of the seven days, the Lord said to me:

17 "Son of dust, I have appointed you as a watchman for Israel; whenever I send My people a warning, pass it on to them at once.

18 If you refuse to warn the wicked when I want you to tell them, "You are under the penalty of death, therefore repent and save your life"—they will die in their sins, but I will punish you. I will demand your blood for theirs.

19 But if you warn them and they keep on sinning,

---

[7]Literally, "I heard behind me the sound of a great earthquake."
[8]Literally, "I went in the heat of my spirit"—not necessarily anger, but indicated here by this reaction.

and refuse to repent, they will die in their sins, but you are blameless—you have done all you could.

20   And if a good man becomes bad, and you refuse to warn him of the consequences, and the Lord destroys him, his previous good deeds won't help him—he shall die in his sin. But I will hold you responsible for his death, and punish you.

21   But if you warn him and he repents, he shall live and you have saved your own life too."

22   I was helpless in the hand of God, and when He said to me, "Go out into the valley and I will talk to you there"—

23   I arose and went, and oh, I saw the glory of the Lord there, just as in my first vision! And I fell to the ground on my face.

24   Then the Spirit entered into me and set me on my feet. He talked to me and said: "Go, imprison yourself in your house;

25   And I will paralyze[9] you so you can't leave;

26   And I will make your tongue stick to the roof of your mouth so that you can't reprove them; for they are rebels.

27   But whenever I give you a message, then I will loosen your tongue and let you speak, and you shall say to them: "The Lord God says, Let anyone listen who wants to, and let anyone refuse who wants to, for they are rebels."

[9]Literally, "lay bands upon you."

# CHAPTER 4

And now, son of dust, take a large brick and lay it before you and draw a map of the city of Jerusalem on it. Draw a picture of siege mounds being built against the city, and enemy camps around it, and battering rams surrounding the walls.

3 And put an iron plate between you and the city, like a wall of iron. Demonstrate how an enemy army will capture Jerusalem!

There is special meaning in each detail of what I have told you to do. For it is a warning to the people of Israel.

4, 5 Now lie on your left side for 390[1] days, to show that Israel will be punished for 390 years by captivity and doom. Each day you lie there represents a year of punishment ahead for Israel.

6 Afterwards, turn over and lie on your right side for 40 days, to signify the years of Judah's punishment. Each day will represent one year.

7 Meanwhile continue your demonstration of the siege of Jerusalem; lie there with your arm bared (to signify great strength and power in the attack against her[2]). This will prophesy her doom.

8 And I will paralyze[3] you so that you can't turn over from one side to the other until you have completed all the days of your siege.

[1] Some versions read, "190 days."
[2] Implied.
[3] Literally, "I will lay bands upon you."

9    During the first 390 days eat bread made of flour mixed from wheat, barley, beans, lentils, and spelt. Mix the various kinds of flour together in a jar.

10    You are to ration this out to yourself at the rate of eight ounces at a time, one meal a day.

11    And use one quart of water a day; don't use more than that.

12    Each day take flour from the barrel and prepare it as you would barley cakes. While all the people are watching, bake it over a fire, using dried human dung as fuel, and eat it.

13    For the Lord declares, "Israel shall eat defiled bread in the Gentile lands to which I exile them!"

14    Then I said, "O Lord God, must I be defiled by using dung? For I have never been defiled before in all my life. From the time I was a child until now I have never eaten any animal that died of sickness or that I found injured or dead; and I have never eaten any of the kinds of animals our law forbids."[4]

15    Then the Lord said, "All right, you may use cow dung instead of human dung."

16    Then He told me, "Son of dust, bread will be tightly rationed in Jerusalem. It will be weighed out with great care and eaten fearfully. And the water will be portioned out in driblets, and the people will drink it with dismay.

17    I will cause the people to lack both bread and water, and to look at one another in frantic terror, and to waste away beneath their punishment."

[4] See the dietary laws Ezekiel here refers to, in Leviticus 11.

## CHAPTER 5

Son of dust, take a sharp sword and use it as a barber's razor to shave your head and beard; use balances to weigh the hair into three equal parts.

2   Place a third of it at the center of your map of Jerusalem. After your siege, burn it there. Scatter another third across your map and slash at it with a knife. Scatter the last third to the wind, for I will chase My people with the sword.

3   Keep just a bit of the hair and tie it up in your robe;

4   Then take a few hairs out and throw them into the fire, for a fire shall come from this remnant and destroy all Israel."

5, 6, 7   The Lord God says, "This illustrates what will happen to Jerusalem, for she has turned away from My laws and has been even more wicked than the nations surrounding her."

8   Therefore the Lord God says, "I, even I, am against you and will punish you publicly while all the nations watch.

9   Because of the terrible sins you have committed, I will punish you more terribly than I have ever done before or will ever do again.

10   Fathers will eat their own sons, and sons will eat their fathers; and those who survive will be scattered into all the world.

11 For I promise you: Because you have defiled My Temple with idols and evil sacrifices, therefore I will not spare you nor pity you at all.

12 One third of you will die from famine and disease; one third will be slaughtered by the enemy; and one third I will scatter to the winds, sending the sword of the enemy chasing after you.

13 Then at last My anger will be appeased. And all Israel will know that what I threaten, I do.

14 So I will make a public example of you before all the surrounding nations and before everyone traveling past the ruins of your land.

15 You will become a laughingstock to the world and an awesome example to everyone, for all to see what happens when the Lord turns against an entire nation in furious rebuke. I, the Lord, have spoken it!

16 I will shower you with deadly arrows of famine to destroy you. The famine will become more and more serious until every bit of bread is gone.

17 And not only famine will come, but wild animals will attack you and kill you and your families; disease and war will stalk your land, and the sword of the enemy will slay you; I, the Lord, have spoken it!"

## CHAPTER 6

Again a message came from the Lord:
2 Son of dust, look over toward the mountains of Israel and prophesy against them.

3 Say to them, "O mountains of Israel, hear the message of the Lord God against you and against the rivers and valleys. I, even I the Lord, will bring war upon you to destroy your idols.

4, 5, 6, 7 All your cities will be smashed and burned, and the idol altars abandoned; your gods will be shattered; the bones of their worshipers will lie scattered among the altars. Then at last you will know I am the Lord.

8 But I will let a few of My people escape—to be scattered among the nations of the world.

9 Then when they are exiled among the nations, they will remember Me, for I will take away their adulterous hearts—their love of idols—and I will blind their lecherous eyes that long for other gods. Then at last they will loathe themselves for all this wickedness.

10 They will realize that I alone am God, and that I wasn't fooling when I told them that all this would happen to them.

11 The Lord God says: Raise your hands in horror and shake your head* with deep remorse and say, 'Alas for all the evil we have done!' For you are going to perish from war and famine and disease.

12 Disease will strike down those in exile; war will destroy those in the land of Israel; and any who remain will die by famine and siege. So at last I will expend My fury on you.

13 When your slain lie scattered among your idols and altars on every hill and mountain and under every

---

*Literally, "clap your hands and stamp your feet."

green tree and great oak where they offered incense to their gods—you will realize that I alone am God.

14   I will crush you and make your cities desolate from the wilderness in the south to Riblah in the north. Then you will know I am the Lord."

## CHAPTER 7

This further message came to me from God:

2   "Tell Israel, Wherever you look—east, west, north or south—your land is finished.

3   No hope remains, for I will loose My anger on you for your worshiping of idols.

4   I will turn My eyes away and show no pity; I will repay you in full, and you shall know I am the Lord."

5, 6   The Lord God says: "With one blow after another I will finish you. The end has come; your final doom is waiting.

7   O Israel, the day of your damnation dawns; the time has come; the day of trouble nears. It is a day of shouts of anguish, not shouts of joy!

8, 9   Soon I will pour out My fury and let it finish its work of punishing you for all your evil deeds. I will not spare nor pity you; and you will know that I, the Lord, am doing it.

10, 11   The day of judgment has come; the morning dawns; for your wickedness and pride have run their course and reached their climax—none of these rich and wicked men of pride shall live. All your boasting will die away, and no one will be left to bewail your fate.

12 Yes, the time has come; the day draws near. There will be nothing to buy or sell, for the wrath of God is on the land.

13 And even if a merchant lives, his business will be gone, for God has spoken against all the people of Israel; all will be destroyed. Not one of those whose lives are filled with sin will recover.

14 'Mobilize' the trumpets shout to Israel's army; but no one listens, for My wrath is on them all.

15 If you go outside the walls, there stands the enemy to kill you. If you stay inside, famine and disease will devour you.

16 Any who escape will be lonely as mourning doves hiding on the mountains, each weeping for his sins.

17 All hands shall be feeble, and all knees as weak as water.

18 You shall clothe yourselves with sackcloth, and horror and shame shall cover you; you shall shave your heads in sorrow and remorse.

19 Throw away your money! Toss it out like worthless rubbish, for it will have no value in that day of wrath. It will neither satisfy nor feed you, for your love of money is the reason for your sin.

20 I gave you gold to use in decorating the Temple, and you used it instead to make idols! Therefore I will take it all away from you.

21   I will give it to foreigners and to wicked men as booty. They shall defile My Temple.

22   I will not look when they defile it, nor will I stop them. Like robbers, they will loot the treasures and leave the Temple in ruins.

23   Prepare chains for My people, for the land is full of bloody crimes. Jerusalem is filled with violence, so I will enslave her people.

24   I will crush your pride by bringing to Jerusalem the worst of the nations to occupy your homes, break down your fortifications you are so proud of, and defile your Temple.

25   For the time has come for the cutting off of Israel. You will sue for peace, but you won't get it.

26, 27   Calamity upon calamity will befall you; woe upon woe, disaster upon disaster! You will long for a prophet to guide you, but the priests and elders and the kings and princes will stand helpless, weeping in despair. The people will tremble with fear, for I will do to them the evil they have done, and give them all their just deserts. They shall learn that I am the Lord."

## CHAPTER 8

Then, late in August of the sixth year of King Jehoiachin's captivity,* as I was talking with the elders of Judah in my home, the power of the Lord God fell upon me.

*Implied.

2 I saw what appeared to be a Man; from His waist down, He was made of fire; from His waist up, He was all amber-colored brightness.

3 He put out what seemed to be a hand and took me by the hair. And the Spirit lifted me up into the sky and seemed to transport me to Jerusalem, to the entrance of the north gate, where the large idol was that had made the Lord so angry.

4 Suddenly the glory of the God of Israel was there, just as I had seen it before in the valley.

5 He said to me, "Son of dust, look toward the north." So I looked and, sure enough, north of the altar gate, in the entrance, stood the idol.

6 And He said: "Son of dust, do you see what they are doing? Do you see what great sins the people of Israel are doing here, to push Me from My Temple? But come, and I will show you greater sins than these!"

7 Then He brought me to the door of the Temple court; where I made out an opening in the wall.

8 "Now dig into the wall," He said. I did, and uncovered a door to a hidden room.

9 "Go on in," He said, "and see the wickedness going on in there!"

10 So I went in. The walls were covered with pictures of all kinds of snakes, lizards and hideous creatures, besides all the various idols worshiped by the people of Israel.

11 Seventy elders of Israel were standing there

along with Jaazaniah (son of Shaphan) worshiping the pictures. Each of them held a censer of burning incense, so there was a thick cloud of smoke above their heads.

12 Then the Lord said to me: "Son of dust, have you seen what the elders of Israel are doing in their minds? For they say, 'The Lord doesn't see us; He has gone away!'"

13 Then He added, "Come, and I will show you greater sins than these!"

14 He brought me to the north gate of the Temple, and there sat women weeping for Tammuz,[7] their god.

15 "Have you seen this?" He asked. "But I will show you greater evils than these!"

16 Then He brought me into the inner court of the Temple and there at the door, between the porch and the bronze altar, were about twenty-five men standing with their backs to the Temple of the Lord, facing east, worshiping the sun!

17 "Have you seen this?" He asked. "Is it nothing to the people of Judah that they commit these terrible sins, leading the whole nation into idolatry, thumbing their noses at Me and arousing My fury against them?

18 Therefore I will deal with them in fury. I will neither pity nor spare. And though they scream for mercy, I will not listen."

[7]The women wept for Tammuz, the god of fertility, because, according to Mesopotamian myths, he had been killed, and fertility had vanished with him.

# CHAPTER 9

Then He thundered, "Call those to whom I have given the city! Tell them to bring their weapons with them!"

2 Six men appeared at His call, coming from the upper north gate, each one with his sword. One of them wore linen clothing and carried a writer's case strapped to his side. They all went into the Temple and stood beside the bronze altar.

3 And the glory of the God of Israel rose from the cherubim where it had rested and stood above the entrance[8] to the Temple. And the Lord called to the man with the writer's case.

4 And said to him, "Walk through the streets of Jerusalem and put a mark on the foreheads of the men who weep and sigh because of all the sins they see around them."

5 Then I heard the Lord tell the other men: "Follow him through the city and kill everyone whose forehead isn't marked. Spare not nor pity them—

6 Kill them all—old and young, girls, women and little children; but don't touch anyone with the mark. And begin right here at the Temple." And so they began by killing the seventy elders.

7 And He said, "Defile the Temple! Fill its courts

---

[8]Literally, "above the threshold of . . ."

with the bodies of those you kill! Go!" And they went out through the city and did as they were told.

8   While they were fulfilling their orders, I was alone. I fell to the ground on my face and cried out: "O Lord God! Will Your fury against Jerusalem wipe out everyone left in Israel?"

9   But He said to me, "The sins of the people of Israel and Judah are very great and all the land is full of murder and injustice, for they say, 'The Lord doesn't see it! He has gone away!'

10   And so I will not spare them nor have any pity on them, and I will fully repay them for all that they have done."

11   Just then the man in linen clothing, carrying the writer's case, reported back and said, "I have finished the work You gave me to do."

## CHAPTER 10

Suddenly a throne of beautiful blue sapphire[9] appeared in the sky above the heads of the cherubim.

2   Then the Lord spoke to the man in linen clothing and said: "Go in between the whirling wheels beneath the cherubim and take a handful of glowing coals and scatter them over the city." He did so while I watched.

3   The cherubim were standing at the south end of

---

[9]Literally, "lapis lazuli."

the Temple when the man went in. And the cloud of glory filled the inner court.

4 Then the glory of the Lord rose from above the cherubim and went over to the door of the Temple; and the Temple was filled with the cloud of glory, and the court of the Temple was filled with the brightness of the glory of the Lord.

5 And the sound of the wings of the cherubim was as the voice of Almighty God when He speaks and could be heard clear out in the outer court.

6 When the Lord told the man in linen clothing to go between the cherubim and take some burning coals from between the wheels, the man went in and stood beside one of the wheels,

7, 8 And one of the cherubim reached out his hand (for each cherub had, beneath his wings, what looked like human hands) and took some live coals from the flames between the cherubim and put them into the hands of the man in linen clothes, who took them and went out.

9-13 Each of the four cherubim had a wheel beside him. "Whirling Wheels," as I heard them called, for each one had a second wheel crosswise within, sparkled like chrysolite, giving off a greenish-yellow glow.

Because of the construction of these wheels,[1] the cherubim could go straight forward in each of four directions; they did not turn when they changed direction but could go in any of the four ways their faces looked.

---

[1]Implied.

Each of the four wheels was covered with eyes, including the rims and spokes.

14    Each of the four cherubim had four faces—the first was that of an ox;[2] the second, a man's; the third, a lion's; and the fourth, an eagle's.

15, 16    These were the same beings I had seen beside the Chebar Canal, and when they rose into the air the wheels rose with them, and stayed beside them as they flew.

17    When the cherubim stood still, so did the wheels, for the spirit[3] of the cherubim was in the wheels.

18    Then the glory of the Lord moved from the door of the Temple and stood above the cherubim.

19    And as I watched, the cherubim flew with their wheels beside them to the east gate of the Temple. And the glory of the God of Israel was above them.

20    These were the living beings I had seen beneath the God of Israel beside the Chebar Canal. I knew they were the same,

21    For each had four faces and four wings, with what looked like human hands under their wings.

22    Their faces too were identical to the faces of those I had seen at the Canal, and they traveled straight ahead, just as the others did.

## CHAPTER 11

Then the Spirit lifted me and brought me over to the east gate of the Temple, where I saw twenty-

---

[2]Literally, "cherub's face." See. Ezek. 1:10.
[3]That is, the wheel was a living part of the bodies of the cherubim. Hence it could not be separated from the cherubim.

five of the most prominent men of the city, including two officers Jaazaniah (son of Azur) and Pelatiah (son of Benaiah).

Then the Spirit said to me, "Son of dust, these are the men who are responsible for all of the wicked counsel being given out in this city.

3 For they say to the people, 'It is time to rebuild Jerusalem, for our city is an iron shield and will protect us from all harm.[4]

4 Therefore, son of dust, prophesy against them loudly and clearly."

5 Then the Spirit of the Lord came upon me and told me to say: "The Lord says to the people of Israel; Is that what you are saying? Yes, I know it is, for I know everything you think—every thought that comes into your minds.

6 You have murdered endlessly and filled your streets with the dead.

7 Therefore the Lord God says: You think this city is an iron shield? No, it isn't! It will not protect you. Your slain will lie within it, but you will be dragged out and slaughtered.[5]

8 I will expose you to the war you have so greatly feared, says the Lord God,

9 And I will take you from Jerusalem and hand you over to foreigners who will carry out my judgments against you.

[4]Literally, "this city the caldron and we the flesh."
[5]Literally, "Your slain . . . are the flesh and this is the caldron; but you will be brought out from it."

10   You will be slaughtered all the way to the borders of Israel, and you will know I am the Lord.

11   No, this city will not be an iron shield for you, and you safe within. I will chase you even to the borders of Israel,

12   And you will know I am the Lord—you who have not obeyed Me, but rather have copied the nations all around you."

13   While I was still speaking and telling them this, Pelatiah (son of Benaiah) suddenly died. Then I fell to the ground on my face and cried out: "O Lord God, are You going to kill everyone in all Israel?"

14   Again a message came from the Lord.

15   "Son of dust, the remnant left in Jerusalem are saying about your brother exiles: 'It is because they were so wicked that the Lord has deported them. Now the Lord has given us their land!'

16   But tell the exiles that the Lord God says: Although I have scattered you in the countries of the world, yet I will be a sanctuary to you for the time that you are there,

17   And I will gather you back from the nations where you are scattered and give you the land of Israel again.

18   And when you return you will remove every trace of all this idol worship.

19   I will give you one heart and a new spirit; I will take from you your hearts of stone and give you tender hearts of love for God,

20 So that you can obey My laws and be My people, and I will be your God.

21 But as for those now in Jerusalem,[6] who long for idols, I will repay them fully for their sins," the Lord God says.

22 Then the cherubim lifted their wings and rose into the air with their wheels beside them; and the glory of the God of Israel stood above them.

23 Then the glory of the Lord rose from over the city and stood above the mountain on the east side.

24 Afterwards the Spirit of God carried me back again to Babylon, to the Jews in exile there. And so ended the vision of my visit to Jerusalem.

25 And I told the exiles everything the Lord had shown me.

## CHAPTER 12

Again a message came to me from the Lord:

2 "Son of dust, He said. "You live among rebels who could know the truth if they wanted to, but they don't want to; they could hear Me if they would listen, but they won't,

3 For they are rebels. So now put on a demonstration, to show them what being exiled will be like. Pack whatever you can carry on your back and leave your home—go somewhere else. Go in the daylight so they can see, for perhaps even yet they will consider what this means, even though they are such rebels.

[6]Implied.

4   Bring your baggage outside your house during
the daylight so they can watch. Then leave the house at
night, just as captives do when they begin their long
march to distant lands.

5   Dig a tunnel through the city wall while they are
observing and carry your possessions out through the
hole.

6   As they watch, lift your pack to your shoulders
and walk away into the night; muffle your face and
don't gaze around. All this is a sign to the people of
Israel of the evil that will come upon Jerusalem."

7   So I did as I was told. I brought my pack outside
in the daylight—all I could take into exile—and in the
evening I dug through the wall with my hands. I went
out into the darkness with my pack on my shoulder
while the people looked on.

8   The next morning this message came to me from
the Lord:

9   "Son of dust, these rebels, the people of Israel,
have asked what all this means.

10   Tell them the Lord God says it is a message to
King Zedekiah[7] in Jerusalem and to all the people of
Israel.

11   Explain that what you did was a demonstration
of what is going to happen to them; for they shall be
driven out of their homes and sent away into exile.

12   Even King Zedekiah shall go out at night
through a hole in the wall, taking only what he can

[7]Literally, "to the prince in Jerusalem."

carry with him, with muffled face, for he won't be able to see.[8]

13 I will capture him in My net and bring him to Babylon, the land of the Chaldeans; but he shall not see it,[8] and he shall die there.

14 I will scatter his servants and guards to the four winds and send the sword after them.

15 And when I scatter them among the nations, then they shall know I am the Lord.

16 But I will spare a few of them from death by war and famine and disease. I will save them to confess to the nations how wicked they have been, and they shall know I am the Lord."

\* \* \* \* \*

17 Then this message came to me from the Lord:

18 "Son of dust, tremble as you eat your meals; ration out your water as though it were your last,

19 And say to the people, the Lord God says that the people of Israel and Jerusalem shall ration their food with utmost care and sip their tiny portions of water in utter despair because of all their sins.

20 Your cities shall be destroyed and your farmlands deserted; and you shall know I am the Lord."

\* \* \* \* \*

21 Again a message came to me from the Lord:

22 "Son of dust, what is that proverb they quote in Israel—'The days as they pass make liars out of every prophet.'

---

[8]Literally, "that he may not see the land with his eyes." Apparently a reference to the fact that his eyes were put out before he was taken to Babylon, Jeremiah 52:11.

23　The Lord God says, I will put an end to this proverb and they will soon stop saying it. Give them this one instead: 'The time has come for all these prophecies to be fulfilled.'

24　Then you will see what becomes of all the false predictions of safety and security for Jerusalem.

25　For I am the Lord! What I threaten always happens. There will be no more delays, O rebels of Israel! I will do it in your own lifetime!" says the Lord God.

26　Then this message came:

27　"Son of dust, the people of Israel say, 'His visions won't come true for a long, long time.'

28　Therefore say to them: 'The Lord God says, All delay has ended! I will do it now!"

## CHAPTER 13

Then this message came to me:

2, 3　"Son of dust, prophesy against the false prophets of Israel who are inventing their own visions and claiming to have messages from Me when I have never told them anything at all. Woe upon them!

4　O Israel, these 'prophets' of yours are as useless as foxes for rebuilding your walls!

5　O evil prophets, what have you ever done to strengthen the walls of Israel against her enemies—by strengthening Israel in the Lord?

6　Instead you have lied when you said, 'My message is from God!' God did not send you. And yet you expect Him to fulfill your prophecies.

7 Can you deny that you have claimed to see 'visions' you never saw, and that you have said, 'This message is from God,' when I never spoke to you at all?

8 Therefore the Lord God says: I will destroy you for these 'visions' and lies.

9 My hand shall be against you, and you shall be cut off from among the leaders of Israel; I will blot out your names and you will never see your own country again. And you shall know I am the Lord.

10 For these evil men deceive My people by saying, 'God will send peace,' when that is not His plan at all! My people build a flimsy wall and these prophets praise them for it—and cover it with whitewash!

11 Tell these evil builders that their wall will fall. A heavy rainstorm will undermine it; great hailstones and mighty winds will knock it down.

12 And when the wall falls, the people will cry out, 'Why didn't you tell us that it wasn't good enough? Why did you whitewash it and cover up its faults?'

13 Yes, it will surely fall. The Lord God says: I will sweep it away with a storm of indignation and with a great flood of anger and with hailstones of wrath.

14 I will break down your whitewashed wall, and it will fall on you and crush you, and you shall know I am the Lord.

15 Then at last My wrath against the wall will be completed; and concerning those who praised it, I will say: The wall and its builders both are gone.

16 For they were lying prophets, claiming Jerusalem will have peace when there is no peace, says the Lord God."

\* \* \* \* \*

17 "Son of dust, speak out against the women prophets too who pretend the Lord has given them His messages.

18 Tell them the Lord God says: Woe to these women who are damning the souls of My people, of both young and old alike, by tying magic charms on their wrists and furnishing them with magic veils and selling them indulgences. They refuse to even offer help unless they get a profit from it.[9]

19 For the sake of a few paltry handfuls of barley or a piece of bread will you turn away My people from Me? You have led those to death who should not die! And you have promised life to those who should not live, by lying to My people—and how they love it!

20 And so the Lord says: I will crush you because you hunt My people's souls with all your magic charms. I will tear off the charms and set My people free like birds from cages.

21 I will tear off the magic veils and save My people from you; they will no longer be your victims; and you shall know I am the Lord.

22 Your lies have discouraged the righteous, when I didn't want it so. And you have encouraged the wicked by promising life, though they continue in their sins.

---

[9]Literally, "will you hunt the souls of my people and save your own souls alive?"

23   But you will lie no more; no longer will you talk of seeing 'visions' that you never saw, nor practice your magic; for I will deliver My people out of your hands by destroying you, and you shall know I am the Lord."

## CHAPTER 14

Then some of the elders of Israel visited me, to ask me for a message from the Lord,

2   And this is the message that came to me to give to them:

3   "Son of dust, these men worship idols in their hearts—should I let them ask me anything?

4   Tell them, the Lord God says: I the Lord will personally deal with anyone in Israel who worships idols and then comes to ask My help.

5   For I will punish the minds and hearts of those who turn from Me to idols.

6, 7   Therefore warn them that the Lord God says: Repent and destroy your idols, and stop worshiping them in your hearts. I the Lord will personally punish everyone, whether people of Israel or the foreigners living among you, who rejects Me for idols, and then comes to a prophet to ask for My help and advice.

8   I will turn upon him and make a terrible example of him, destroying him; and you shall know I am the Lord.

9   And if one of the false prophets gives him a

message anyway, it is a lie. His prophecy will not come true, and I will stand against that 'prophet' and destroy him from among My people Israel.

10 False prophets and hypocrites—evil people who say they want My words—all will be punished for their sins,

11 So that the people of Israel will learn not to desert Me and not to be polluted any longer with sin; but to be My people and I their God. So says the Lord."

12 Then this message of the Lord came to me:

13 "Son of dust, when the people of this land sin against Me, then I will crush them with My fist and break off their food supply and send famine to destroy both man and beast.

14 If Noah, Daniel and Job were all living today, they alone would be saved by their righteousness, and I would destroy the remainder of Israel, says the Lord God.

15 When I send an invasion of dangerous wild animals into the land to devastate the land,

16 Even if these three men were living, the Lord God swears that it would do no good—it would not save the people from their doom. Those three only would be saved, but the land would be devastated.

17 Or when I bring war against that land and tell the armies of the enemy to come and destroy everything,

18 Even if these three men were in the land, the Lord God declares that they alone would be saved.

19 And when I pour out My fury by sending an epidemic of disease into the land and the plague kills man and beast alike,

20 Though Noah, Daniel and Job were living there, the Lord God says that only they would be saved, because of their righteousness.

21 And the Lord says: Four great punishments await Jerusalem to destroy all life: war, famine, ferocious beasts, plague.

22 If there are survivors and they come here to join you as exiles in Babylon, you will see with your own eyes how wicked they are, and you will know it was right for Me to destroy Jerusalem.

23 You will agree, when you meet them, that it is not without cause that all these things are being done to Israel."

## CHAPTER 15

Then this message came to me from the Lord:

2 "Son of dust, what good are vines from the forest? Are they as useful as trees? Are they even as valuable as a single branch?

3 No, for vines can't be used even for making pegs to hang up pots and pans!

4 All they are good for is fuel—and even so, they burn but poorly!

5, 6 So they are useless both before and after being put in the fire! This is what I mean, the Lord God says: The people of Jerusalem are like the vines of the forest—useless before being burned and certainly useless afterwards!

7 And I will set Myself against them to see to it that if they escape from one fire, they will fall into another; and then you shall know I am the Lord.

8 And I will make the land desolate because they worship idols," says the Lord God.

## CHAPTER 16

Then again a message came to me from the Lord.

2 "Son of dust," He said, "speak to Jerusalem about her loathesome sins.

3 Tell her, the Lord God says: You are no better than the people of Canaan—your father must have been an Amorite and your mother a Hittite![1]

4 When you were born, no one cared for you. When I first saw you, your umbilical cord was uncut, and you had been neither washed nor rubbed with salt nor clothed.

5 No one had the slightest interest in you; no one pitied you or cared for you. On that day when you were born, you were dumped out into a field and left to die, unwanted.

6, 7 But I came by and saw you there, covered with your own blood, and I said, 'Live! Thrive like a plant in the field!' And you did! You grew up and

---

[1] The Amorites and Hittites were nations who turned their backs to all knowledge of God.

became tall, slender and supple, a jewel among jewels. And when you reached the age of maidenhood your breasts were full-formed and your pubic hair had grown; yet you were naked.

8 Later, when I passed by and saw you again, you were old enough for marriage; and I wrapped My cloak around you to legally declare My marriage vow. I signed a covenant with you, and you became Mine.

9, 10 Then, when the marriage had taken place, I gave you beautiful clothes of linens and silk, embroidered, and sandals made of dolphin hide.

11 I gave you lovely ornaments, bracelets and beautiful necklaces,

12 A ring for your nose and two more for your ears, and a lovely tiara for your head.

13 And so you were made beautiful with gold and silver; and your clothes were silk and linen and beautifully embroidered. You ate the finest foods and became more beautiful than ever. You looked like a queen, and so you were!

14 Your reputation was great among the nations for your beauty; it was perfect because of all the gifts I gave you, says the Lord God.

15 But you thought you could get along without Me—you trusted in your beauty instead; and you gave yourself as a harlot to every man who came along. Your beauty was his for the asking.

16 You used the lovely things I gave you for making idol shrines and to decorate your bed of harlotry.

Unbelievable! There has never been anything like it before!

17  You took the very jewels and gold and silver ornaments I gave to you and made statues of men and worshiped them, which is adultery against Me.

18  You used the beautifully embroidered clothes I gave you—to cover your idols! And used My oil and incense to worship *them!*

19  You set before them—imagine it—the fine flour and oil and honey I gave you; you used it as a lovely sacrifice to *them!*

20  And you took My sons and daughters you had borne to Me, and sacrificed them to your gods; and they are gone. Wasn't it enough that you should be a harlot?

21  Must you also slay My children in the fires of strange altars?

22  And in all these years of adultery and sin you have not thought of those days long ago when you were naked and covered with blood.

23  And then, in addition to all your other wickedness—woe, woe upon you, says the Lord God—

24  You built a spacious brothel for your lovers, and idol altars on every street,

25  And there you offered your beauty to every man who came by in an endless stream of prostitution.

26  And you added lustful Egypt to your harlotries by your alliance with her. My anger is great.

27  Therefore I have crushed you with My fist; I have reduced your boundaries and delivered you into

the hands of those who hate you—the Philistines—and even they are ashamed of you.

28 You have committed adultery with the Assyrians too (by making them your allies and worshiping their gods[2]); it seems that you can never find enough new gods. After your adultery there, you still weren't satisfied,

29 So you worshiped the gods of that great merchant land of Babylon—and you still weren't satisfied.

30 What a filthy heart you have, says the Lord God, to do such things as these; you are a brazen harlot

31 Building your idol altars, your brothels, on every street. You have been worse than a harlot, so eager for sin that you have not even charged for your love!

32 Yes, you are an adulterous wife who lives with other men instead of her own husband.

33, 34 Harlots charge for their services—men pay with many gifts. But not you, you give *them* gifts, bribing them to come to you! So you are different from other prostitutes. But you had to pay them, for no one wanted you.

35 O harlot, hear the word of the Lord:

36 The Lord God says: Because I see your filthy sins, your adultery with your lovers—your worshiping of idols—and the slaying of your children as sacrifices to your gods,

37 This is what I am going to do: I will gather together all your allies—these lovers of yours you have

---

[2] Implied.

sinned with, both those you loved and those you hated
—and I will make you naked before them, that they
may see you.

38  I will punish you as a murderess is punished
and as a woman breaking wedlock living with other
men.

39  I will give you to your lovers—these many nations—to destroy, and they will knock down your
brothels and idol altars, and strip you and take your
beautiful jewels and leave you naked and ashamed.

40, 41  They will burn your homes, punishing you
before the eyes of many women. And I will see to it that
you stop your adulteries with other gods and end your
payments to your allies for their love.

42  Then at last My fury against you will die away;
My jealousy against you will end, and I will be quiet
and not be angry with you anymore.

43  But first, because you have not remembered
your youth, but have angered Me by all these evil things
you do, I will fully repay you for all of your sins, says
the Lord. For you are thankless in addition to all your
other faults.

44  'Like mother, like daughter'—that is what
everyone will say of you.

45  For your mother loathed her husband and her
children; and you do too. And you are exactly like your
sisters, for they despised their husbands and their children. Truly, your mother must have been a Hittite and
your father an Amorite.

46  Your older sister is Samaria, living with her daughters north of you; your younger sister is Sodom and her daughters, in the south.

47  You have not merely sinned as they do—no, that was nothing to you; in a very short time you far surpassed them.

48  As I live, the Lord God says, Sodom and her daughters have never been as wicked as you and your daughters.

49  Your sister Sodom's sins were pride and laziness and too much food, while the poor and needy suffered outside her door.

50  She insolently worshiped many idols as I watched. Therefore I crushed her.

51  Even Samaria has not committed half your sins. You have worshiped idols far more than your sisters have; they seem almost righteous in comparison with you!

52  Don't be surprised then by the lighter punishment they get. For your sins are so awful that in comparison with you, your sisters seem innocent!

53  (But someday I will restore the fortunes of Sodom and Samaria again, and those of Judah too.)

54  Your terrible punishment will be a consolation to them, for it will be greater than theirs.

55  Yes, your sisters, Sodom and Samaria, and all their people will be restored again; and Judah too will prosper in that day.

56  In your proud days you held Sodom in unspeakable contempt.

57 But now your greater wickedness has been exposed to all the world, and you are the one who is scorned—by Edom and all her neighbors and by all the Philistines.

58 This is part of your punishment for all your sins, says the Lord.

59, 60 For the Lord God says: I will repay you for your broken promises. Nevertheless, you lightly broke your solemn vows to Me, yet I will keep the pledge I made to you when you were young. I will establish an everlasting covenant with you forever,

61 And you will remember with shame all the evil you have done; and you will be overcome by My favor when I take your sisters, Samaria and Sodom, and make them your daughters, for you to rule over. You will know you don't deserve this gracious act, for you did not keep My covenant.

62 I will reaffirm My covenant with you, and you will know I am the Lord.

63 Despite all you have done, I will be kind to you again; you will cover your mouth in silence and in shame when I forgive you all that you have done, says the Lord God."

## CHAPTER 17

Then this message came to me from the Lord:

2 "Son of dust, give this riddle to the people of Israel:

3, 4 A great eagle with broad wings full of many-colored feathers came to Lebanon and plucked off the shoot at the top of the tallest cedar tree and carried it into a city filled with merchants.

5  There he planted it[3] in fertile ground beside a broad river, where it would grow as quickly as a willow tree.

6  It took root and grew and became a low but spreading vine that turned toward the eagle and produced strong branches and luxuriant leaves.

7  But when another great, broad-winged, full-feathered eagle came along, this tree sent its roots and branches out toward him instead,

8  Even though it was already in good soil with plenty of water to become a splendid vine, producing leaves and fruit.

9  The Lord God asks: 'Shall I let this tree grow and prosper?' No! I will pull it out roots and all! I will cut off its branches and let its leaves wither and die. It will pull out easily enough—it won't take a big crew or a lot of equipment to do that.

10  Though the vine began so well, will it thrive? No, it will wither away completely when the east wind touches it, dying in the same choice soil where it had grown so well."

11  Then this message came to me from the Lord:

12, 13  "Ask these rebels of Israel: Don't you understand what this riddle of the eagles means? I will tell you. Nebuchadnezzar, king of Babylon (the first of the two eagles),[4] came to Jerusalem and took away her king

---
[3]Literally, "planted the seed of the land."

and princes (her topmost buds and shoots[4]) and
brought them to Babylon. Nebuchadnezzar made a
covenant with a member of the royal family (Zedekiah[4]), and made him take an oath of loyalty. He took
a seedling and planted it in fertile ground beside a broad
river and he exiled the top men of Israel's government,

14    So that Israel would not be strong again and
revolt. But by keeping her promises, Israel could be
respected and maintain her identity.

15    Nevertheless, Zedekiah rebelled against Babylon,
sending ambassadors to Egypt to seek for a great
army and many horses to fight against Nebuchadnezzar. But will Israel prosper after breaking all her
promises like that? Will she succeed?

16    No! For as I live, says the Lord, the king of
Israel shall die. (Nebuchadnezzar will pull out the tree,
roots and all!) Zedekiah[4] shall die in Babylon, where
the king lives who gave him his power, and whose
covenant he despised and broke.

17    Pharaoh and all his mighty army shall fail to
help Israel when the king of Babylon lays siege to
Jerusalem again and slaughters many lives.

18    For the king of Israel broke his promise after
swearing to obey; therefore he shall not escape.

19    The Lord God says: As I live, surely I will
punish him for despising the solemn oath he made in
My name.

20    I will throw My net over him and he shall be

---

[4]Implied.

captured in My snare, and I will bring him to Babylon and deal with him there for this treason against Me.

21    And all the best soldiers of Israel will be killed by the sword, and those remaining in the city will be scattered to the four winds. Then you will know that I, the Lord, have spoken these words.

22, 23    The Lord God says: I, Myself, will take the finest and most tender twig from the top of the highest cedar, and I, Myself, will plant it on the top of Israel's highest mountain. It shall become a noble cedar, bringing forth branches and bearing fruit. Animals of every sort will gather under it; its branches will shelter every kind of bird.

24    And everyone shall know that it is I, the Lord, who cuts down the high trees and exalts the low; that I make the green tree wither and the dry tree grow. I, the Lord, have said that I would do it, and I will."


# CHAPTER 18

Then the Lord's message came to me again.

2    "Why do people use this proverb about the land of Israel: The children are punished for their fathers' sins?[6]

3    As I live, says the Lord God, you will not use this proverb any more in Israel,

4    For all souls are Mine to judge—fathers and

---

[6]Literally, "the fathers have eaten sour grapes and the children's teeth are set on edge."

sons alike—and My rule is this: It is for a man's own sins that he will die.

5 But if a man is just and does what is lawful and right,

6 And has not gone out to the mountains to feast before the idols of Israel and worship them, and does not commit adultery, nor lie with any woman during the time of her menstruation,

7 And is a merciful creditor, not holding on to the items given to him in pledge by poor debtors, and is no robber, but gives food to the hungry and clothes to those in need,

8 And grants loans without interest,[7] and stays away from sin, and is honest and fair when judging others,

9 And obeys My laws—that man is just, says the Lord, and he shall surely live.

10 But if that man has a son who is a robber or murderer and who fulfills none of his responsibilities,

11 Who refuses to obey the laws of God, but worships idols on the mountains and commits adultery,

12 And oppresses the poor and needy, and robs his debtors by refusing to let them redeem what they have given him in pledge, and loves idols and worships them,

13 And loans out his money at interest[8]—shall that man live? No! He shall surely die, and it is his own fault.

14 But if this sinful man has, in turn, a son who

[7] Or, "without any usury."
[8] Or, "at usurious interest."

sees all his father's wickedness, so that he fears God and decides against that kind of life,

15 And doesn't go up on the mountains to feast before the idols and worship them, and does not commit adultery,

16 And is fair to those who borrow from him and doesn't rob them, but feeds the hungry and clothes the needy,

17 And helps the poor and does not loan money at interest,[8] and obeys My laws—he shall not die because of his father's sins; he shall surely live.

18 But his father shall die for his own sins because he is cruel and robs and does wrong.

19 'What?' you ask. 'Doesn't the son pay for his father's sins?' No! For if the son does what is right and keeps My laws, he shall surely live.

20 The one who sins is the one who dies. The son shall not be punished for his father's sins, nor the father for his son's. The righteous person will be rewarded for his own goodness and the wicked person for his wickedness.

21 But if a wicked person turns away from all his sins and begins to obey My laws and do what is just and right, he shall surely live and not die.

22 All his past sins will be forgotten; and he shall live because of his goodness.

23 Do you think I like to see the wicked die? asks the Lord. Of course not! I only want him to turn from his wicked ways and live.

24 However, if a righteous person turns to sinning

and acts like any other sinner, should he be allowed to live? No, of course not. All his previous goodness will be forgotten and he shall die for his sins.

25 Yet you say: 'The Lord isn't being fair!' Listen to Me, O people of Israel. Am I the One who is unfair, or is it you?

26 When a good man turns away from being good and begins sinning and dies in his sins, he dies for the evil he has done.

27 And if a wicked person turns away from his wickedness and obeys the law, and does right, he shall save his soul,

28 For he has thought it over and decided to turn from his sins and live a good life. He shall surely live— he shall not die.

29 And yet the people of Israel keep saying: 'The Lord is unfair!' O people of Israel, it is you who are unfair, not Me.

30 I will judge each of you, O Israel, and punish or reward each according to your own actions. Oh, turn from your sins while there is yet time.

31 Put them behind you and receive a new heart and a new spirit. For why will you die, O Israel?

32 I do not enjoy seeing you die, the Lord God says. Turn, turn and live!

## CHAPTER 19

Sing this death dirge for the leaders of Israel:

2 What a woman your mother was—like a lioness! Her children were like lion's cubs!

3 One of her cubs (King Jehoahaz⁹) grew into a strong young lion, and learned to catch prey and became a man-eater.

4 Then the nations called out their hunters and trapped him in a pit and brought him in chains to Egypt.

5 When Israel, the mother lion, saw that all her hopes for him were gone, she took another of her cubs (King Jehoiachin\*) and taught him to be 'king of the beasts.'

6 He became a leader among the lions and learned to catch prey; and he too became a man-eater.

7 He demolished the palaces of the surrounding nations and ruined their cities; their farms were desolated, their crops destroyed; everyone in the land shook with terror when they heard him roar.

8 Then the armies of the nations surrounded him, coming from every side, and trapped him in a pit and captured him.

9 They prodded him into a cage and brought him before the king of Babylon. He was held in captivity so that his voice could never again be heard upon the mountains of Israel.

10 Your mother was like a vine beside an irrigation ditch, with lush, green foliage because of all the water.

11 Its strongest branch became a ruler's scepter and it was very great, towering above the others and noticed from far away.

---

⁹Implied.

12 But the vine was uprooted in fury and thrown down to the ground. Its branches were broken and withered by a strong wind from the east; the fruit was destroyed by fire.

13 Now the vine is planted in the wilderness where the ground is hard and dry.

14 It is decaying from within;* no strong branch remains. The fulfillment of this sad prophecy has already begun, and there is more ahead."

## CHAPTER 20

Late in July, six[1] years after king Jeconiah was captured, some of the elders of Israel came to ask instructions from the Lord, and sat before me awaiting His reply.

2 Then the Lord gave me this message:

3 "Son of dust, say to the elders of Israel: The Lord God says: How dare you come to ask My help? I swear that I will tell you nothing.

4 Judge them, son of dust; condemn them; tell them of all the sins of this nation from the times of their fathers until now.

5, 6 Tell them the Lord God says: When I chose Israel and revealed Myself to her in Egypt, I swore to her and her descendants that I would bring them out of

---

[1]Literally, "in the seventh year of Jeconiah's captivity."
*Literally, "A fire is gone out of the rods of its branches and devoured its fruit."

Egypt to a land I had discovered and explored for them—a good land, flowing as it were with milk and honey, the best of all lands anywhere.

7 Then I said to them: Get rid of every idol; do not defile yourselves with the Egyptian gods, for I am the Lord your God.

8 But they rebelled against Me and would not listen. They didn't get rid of their idols, nor forsake the gods of Egypt. Then I thought, I will pour out My fury upon them and fulfill My anger against them while they are still in Egypt.

9, 10 But I didn't do it, for I acted to protect the honor of My name, lest the Egyptians laugh at Israel's God who couldn't keep them back from harm. So I brought My people out of Egypt right before the Egyptians' eyes, and led them into the wilderness.

11 There I gave them My laws so they could live by keeping them. If anyone keeps them, he shall live.

12 And I gave them the Sabbath—a day of rest every seventh day—as a symbol between them and Me, to remind them that it is I, the Lord, who sanctifies them; that they are truly My people.

13 But Israel rebelled against Me. There in the wilderness they refused My laws. They would not obey My rules even though obeying them means life. And they misused My Sabbaths. Then I thought, I will pour out My fury upon them and utterly consume them in the desert.

14 But again I refrained in order to protect the honor of My name, lest the nations who saw Me bring

them out of Egypt would say that it was because I couldn't care for them that I destroyed them.

15 But I swore to them in the wilderness that I would not bring them into the land I had given them, a land full of milk and honey, the choicest spot on earth,

16 Because they laughed at My laws, ignored My wishes, and violated My Sabbaths—their hearts were with their idols!

17 Nevertheless, I spared them. I didn't finish them off in the wilderness.

18 Then I spoke to their children and said: Don't follow your fathers' footsteps. Don't defile yourselves with their idols;

19 For I am the Lord your God. Follow My laws; keep My ordinances;

20 Hallow My Sabbaths; for they are a symbol of the contract between us to help you remember that I am the Lord your God.

21 But their children too rebelled against Me. They refused My laws—the laws that, if a person keeps them, he shall live. And they defiled My Sabbaths. So then I said: Now at last I will pour out My fury upon you in the wilderness.

22 Nevertheless, again I withdrew My judgment against them to protect My name among the nations who had seen My power in bringing them out of Egypt.

23, 24 But I took a solemn oath against them while they were in the wilderness that I would scatter them, dispersing them to the ends of the earth because they did not obey My laws but scorned them and violated My Sabbaths and longed for their fathers' idols.

25    I let them adopt[2] customs and laws which were worthless. Through the keeping of them they could not attain life.[3]

26    In the hope that they would draw back in horror, and know that I alone am God, I let them pollute themselves with the very gifts I gave them. They burnt their first-born children as offerings to their gods!

27, 28    Son of dust, tell them that the Lord God says: Your fathers continued to blaspheme and betray Me when I brought them into the land I promised them, for they offered sacrifices and incense on every high hill and under every tree! They roused My fury as they offered up their sacrifices to those 'gods.' They brought their perfumes and incense and poured out their drink offerings to them!

29    I said to them: 'What is this place of sacrifice[4] where you go?' And so it is still called 'The Place of Sacrifice'—that is how it got its name.

30    The Lord God wants to know whether you are going to pollute yourselves just as your fathers did, and keep on worshiping idols?

31    For when you offer gifts to them and give your little sons to be burned to ashes as you do even today, shall I listen to you or help you, Israel? As I live, the Lord God says, I will not give you any message, though you have come to Me to ask.

---

[2]Literally, "gave them."
[3]Literally, "ordinances by which they could not have life." Doubtless, the reference is to the pagan customs of verses 18 and 26. In contrast, see verse 11.
[4]Literally, "bamah"—a hilltop area where sacrifices were made to the gods.

32 What you have in mind will not be done—to be like the nations all around you, serving gods of wood and stone.

33 I will rule you with an iron fist and in great anger and with power.

34 With might and fury I will bring you out from the lands where you are scattered,

35, 36 And will bring you into My desert judgment hall.[5] I will judge you there, and get rid of the rebels, just as I did in the wilderness after I brought you out of Egypt.

37 I will count you carefully and let only a small quota return.

38 And the others—the rebels and all those who sin against Me—I will purge from among you. They shall not enter Israel, but I will bring them out of the countries where they are in exile. And when that happens, you will know I am the Lord.

39 O Israel, the Lord God says: If you insist on worshiping your idols, go right ahead, but then don't bring your gifts to Me as well! Such desecration of My holy name must stop!

40 For at Jerusalem in My holy mountain, says the Lord, all Israel shall worship Me. There I will accept you, and require you to bring Me your offerings and the finest of your gifts.

41 You will be to Me as an offering of perfumed

---

[5]Literally, "the wilderness of the people," meaning the Syro-Arabian deserts, peopled by nomadic tribes. This desert would be traversed in returning to Israel from Babylon.

incense when I bring you back from exile; and the nations will see the great change in your hearts.

42　　Then, when I have brought you home to the land I promised your fathers, you will know I am the Lord.

43　　Then you will look back at all your sins and loathe yourselves because of the evil you have done.

44　　And when I have honored My name by blessing you despite your wickedness, then, O Israel, you will know I am the Lord."

\*　　\*　　\*　　\*　　\*

45　　Then this message came to me from the Lord:

46　　"Son of dust, look towards Jerusalem and speak out against it and the forest lands of the Negeb.

47　　Prophesy to it and say: Hear the word of the Lord. I will set you on fire, O forest, and every tree will die, green and dry alike. The terrible flames will not be quenched and they will scorch the world.

48　　And all the world will see that I, the Lord, have set the fire. It shall not be put out."

49　　Then I said, O Lord God, they say of me, "He only talks in riddles!"

## CHAPTER 21

Then this message came to me from the Lord:
2　　"Son of dust, face toward Jerusalem and prophesy against Israel and against My Temple![6]

---

[6]Literally, "against the sanctuaries."

3  For the Lord says: I am against you, Israel. I will unsheath My sword and destroy your people, good and bad alike—

4  I will not spare even the righteous. I will make a clean sweep throughout the land from the Negeb to your northern borders.

5  All the world shall know that it is I, the Lord. His sword is in His hand, and it will not return to its sheath again until its work is finished.

6  Sigh and groan before the people, son of dust, in your bitter anguish; sigh with grief and broken heart.

7  When they ask you why, tell them: Because of the fearsome news that God has given me. When it comes true, the boldest heart will melt with fear; all strength will disappear; every spirit will faint; strong knees will tremble and become as weak as water. And the Lord God says: Your doom is on the way; my judgments will be fulfilled!"

\*          \*          \*          \*

8  Then again this message came to me from God:

9, 10, 11  "Son of dust, tell them this: A sword is being sharpened and polished for terrible slaughter. Now will you laugh? For those far stronger than you have perished beneath its power. It is ready now to hand to the executioner.

12  Son of dust, with sobbing, beat upon your thigh, for that sword shall slay My people and all their leaders. All alike shall die.

13  It will put them all to the test—and what chance do they have? the Lord God asks.

14  Prophesy to them in this way: Clap your hands vigorously, then take a sword and brandish it twice, thrice, to symbolize the great massacre they face!

15  Let their hearts melt with terror, for a sword glitters at every gate; it flashes like lightning; it is razor-edged for slaughter.

16  O sword, slash to the right and slash to the left, wherever you will, wherever you want.

17  And you have prophesied with clapping hands that I, the Lord, will smite Jerusalem and satisfy My fury."

18  Then this message came to me. The Lord said:

19, 20  "Son of dust, make a map and on it trace two routes for the king of Babylon to follow—one to Jerusalem and the other to Rabbah in Trans-Jordan.[7] And put a signpost at the fork in the road from Babylon.

21  For the king of Babylon stands at a fork uncertain whether to attack Jerusalem or Rabbah. He will call his magicians to use divination; they will cast lots by shaking arrows from the quiver; they will sacrifice to idols and inspect the liver[8] of their sacrifice.

22  They will decide to turn toward Jerusalem! With battering rams they will go against the gates, shouting for the kill; they will build siege towers and make a hill against the walls to reach the top.

23  Jerusalem won't understand this treachery; how could the diviners make this terrible mistake? For Babylon is Judah's ally and has sworn to defend Jeru-

---

[7] Literally, "Rabbah of the Ammonites."
[8] A very common type of divination by which ancients thought they could obtain information from the gods.

salem! But (the king of Babylon) will think only of the times the people rebelled. He will attack and defeat them.

24 The Lord God says: Again and again your guilt cries out against you, for your sins are open and unashamed. Wherever you go, whatever you do, all is filled with sin. And now the time of punishment has come.

25 O King Zedekiah,[1] evil prince of Israel, your final day of reckoning is here.

26 Take off your jeweled crown, the Lord God says. The old order changes. Now the poor are exalted, and the rich brought very low.

27 I will overturn, overturn, overturn, the kingdom, so that even the new order that emerges will not succeed until the Man appears who has a right to it. And I will give it all to Him.

28 Son of dust, prophesy to the Ammonites too, for they mocked My people in their woe. Tell them this: Against you also My glittering sword is drawn from its sheath; it is sharpened and polished and flashes like lightning.

29 Your magicians and false prophets have told you lies of safety and success—that your gods will save you from the king of Babylon. Thus they have caused your death along with all the other wicked; for when the day of final reckoning has come you will be wounded unto death.

---

[1] Implied.

30   Shall I return My sword to its sheath before I deal with you? No, I will destroy you in your own country where you were born.

31   I will pour out My fury upon you and blow upon the fire of My wrath until it becomes a roaring conflagration; and I will deliver you into the hands of cruel men skilled in destruction.

32   You are the fuel for the fire; your blood will be spilled in your own country and you will be utterly wiped out, your memory lost in history. For I, the Lord, have spoken it."

## CHAPTER 22

Now another message came from the Lord. He said:
2   "Son of dust, indict Jerusalem as the City of Murder. Publicly denounce her terrible deeds.

3   City of Murder, doomed and damned—City of Idols, filthy and foul—

4   You are guilty both of murder and idolatry. Now comes your day of doom. You have reached the limit of your years. I will make you a laughingstock and a reproach to all the nations of the world.

5   Near and far they will mock you, a city of infamous rebels.

6   Every leader in Israel who lives within your walls is bent on murder.

7 Fathers and mothers are contemptuously ignored; immigrants and visitors are forced to pay you for your "protection"; orphans and widows are wronged and oppressed.

8 The things of God are all despised; My Sabbaths are ignored.

9 Prisoners are falsely accused and sent to their death. Every mountain top is filled with idols; lewdness is everywhere.

10 There are men who commit adultery[2] with their fathers' wives and lie with menstruous women.

11 Adultery with a neighbor's wife, a daughter-in-law, a half-sister—this is common.

12 Hired murderers, loan racketeers and extortioners are everywhere. You never even think of Me and My commands, the Lord God says.

13 But now I snap My fingers and call a halt to your dishonest gain and bloodshed.

14 How strong and courageous will you be then, in My day of reckoning? For I, the Lord, have spoken, and I will do all that I have said.

15 I will scatter you throughout the world and burn out the wickedness within you.

16 You will be dishonored among the nations; and you shall know I am the Lord."

17 Then the Lord said this:

18, 19, 20 "Son of dust, the people of Israel are the worthless slag left when silver is smelted. They are

[2]Or, "You degrade yourselves through homosexual practices and through lying with women in their time of menstruation.

the dross, compounded from the brass, the tin, the iron and the lead. Therefore the Lord God says: Because you are worthless dross, I will bring you to My crucible in Jerusalem, to smelt you with the heat of my wrath.

21    I will blow the fire of My wrath upon you,

22    And you will melt like silver in fierce heat, and you will know that I, the Lord, have poured My wrath upon you."

23    Again the message of the Lord came to me saying:

24    "Son of dust, say to the people of Israel: In the day of My indignation you shall be like an uncleared wilderness, or a desert without rain.

25    Your 'prophets' have plotted against you like lions stalking prey. They devour many lives; they seize treasures and extort wealth; they multiply the widows in the land.

26    Your priests have violated My laws and defiled My Temple and My holiness. To them the things of God are no more important than any daily task. They have not taught My people the difference between right and wrong, and they disregard My Sabbaths, so My holy Name is greatly defiled among them.

27    Your leaders are like wolves, who tear apart their victims, and they destroy lives for profit.

28    Your 'prophets' describe false visions and speak false messages they claim are from God, when He hasn't spoken one word to them at all. Thus they repair the walls with whitewash!

29 Even the common people oppress and rob the poor and needy and cruelly extort the aliens.

30 I looked in vain for anyone who would build again the wall of righteousness that guards the land, who could stand in the gap and defend you from My just attacks; but I found not one.

31 And so the Lord God says: I will pour out My anger upon you; I will consume you with the fire of My wrath. I have heaped upon you the full penalty for all your sins."

## CHAPTER 23

The Lord's message came to me again saying:
2, 3 "Son of dust, there were two sisters who as young girls became prostitutes in Egypt.

4, 5 The older girl was named Oholah; her sister was Oholibah. (I am speaking of Samaria and Jerusalem!) I married them, and they bore Me sons and daughters. But then Oholah turned to other gods instead of Me, and gave her love to the Assyrians, her neighbors,

6 For they were all attractive young men, captains and commanders, in handsome blue, dashing about on their horses.

7 And so she sinned with them—the choicest men of Assyria—worshiping their idols, defiling herself.

8 For when she left Egypt, she did not leave her spirit of harlotry behind, but was still as lewd as in her

youth, when the Egyptians poured out their lusts upon her and robbed her of her virginity.

9　And so I delivered her into the evil clutches of the Assyrians whose gods she loved so much.

10　They stripped her and killed her and took away her children as their slaves. Her name was known to every woman in the land as a sinner who had received what she deserved.

11　But when Oholibah (Jerusalem) saw what had happened to her sister she went right ahead in the same way, and sinned even more than her sister.

12　She fawned over her Assyrian neighbors,[3] those handsome young men on fine steeds, those army officers in handsome uniforms—all of them desirable.

13　I saw the way she was going, following right along behind her older sister.

14, 15　She was in fact more debased than Samaria, for she fell in love with pictures she saw painted on a wall! They were pictures of Babylonian military officers, outfitted in striking red uniforms, with handsome belts, and flowing turbans on their heads.

16　When she saw these paintings she longed to give herself to the men pictured; so she sent messengers[4] to Chaldea to invite them to come to her.

17　And they came and committed adultery with her, defiling her in the bed of love; but afterwards she hated them and broke off all relations with them.[5]

---

[3]i.e., when Ahaz paid "protection money" to Tigleth-pilesen II (2 Kings 16:7, 8).
[4]This occurred when Hezekiah entertained the embassy from Babylon (Isaiah 38-39). Also during the reign of Manasseh.
[5]The anti-Babylonian party in Judah looked to Egypt for help during the reigns of the last two Judean kings, Jehoiakim and Zedekiah.

18  And I despised her just as I despised her sister, because she flaunted herself before them and gave herself to their lust.

19, 20  But that didn't bother her. She turned to even greater harlotry, sinning with the lustful men she remembered from her youth when she was a harlot in Egypt.*

21  And thus you celebrated those former days when as a young girl you gave your virginity to those from Egypt.

22  And now the Lord God says that He will raise against you, O Oholibah (Jerusalem), those very nations from which you turned away, disgusted.

23  For the Babylonians will come, and all the Chaldeans from Pekod and Shoa and Koa; and all the Assyrians with them—handsome young men of high rank, riding their steeds.

24  They will come against you from the north with chariots and wagons and a great army fully prepared for attack. They will surround you on every side with armored men and I will let them at you, to do with you as they wish.

25  And I will send My jealousy against you and deal furiously with you, and cut off your nose and ears; your survivors will be killed; your children will be taken away as slaves, and everything left will be burned.

---

*i.e., during the reign of Josiah.

26 They will strip you of your beautiful clothes and jewels.

27 And so I will put a stop to your lewdness and harlotry brought from the land of Egypt; you will no more long for Egypt and her gods.

28 For the Lord God says: I will surely deliver you over to your enemies, to those you loathe.

29 They will deal with you in hatred, and rob you of all that you own, leaving you naked and bare. And the shame of your harlotry shall be exposed to all the world.

30 You brought all this upon yourself by worshiping the gods of other nations, defiling yourself with all their idols.

31 You have followed in your sister's footsteps, so I will punish you with the same terrors that destroyed her.

32 Yes, the terrors that fell upon her will fall upon you—and the cup from which she drank was full and large. And all the world will mock you for your woe.

33 You will reel like a drunkard beneath the awful blows of sorrow and distress, just as your sister Samaria did.

34 In deep anguish you will drain that cup of terror to the very bottom and will lick the inside to get every drop. For I have spoken, says the Lord.

35 Because you have forgotten Me and turned your backs upon Me, therefore you must bear the consequence of all your sin.

36 Son of dust, you must accuse Jerusalem and Samaria of all their awful deeds.

37 For they have committed both adultery and murder; they have worshiped idols and murdered My children whom they bore to Me, burning them as sacrifices on their altars.

38 On the same day they defiled My Temple and ignored My Sabbaths,

39 For when they had murdered their children in front of their idols, then even that same day they actually came into My Temple to worship! That is how much regard they have for Me!

40 You even sent away to distant lands for priests to come with other gods for you to serve; and they have come and been welcomed! You bathed yourself, painted your eyelids, and put on your finest jewels for them.

41 You sat together on a beautifully embroidered bed and put My incense and My oil upon a table spread before you.

42 From your apartment came the sound of many men carousing—lewd men and drunkards from the wilderness, who put bracelets on your wrists and beautiful crowns upon your head.

43 Will they commit adultery with these who have become old harlot hags?

44 Yet that is what they did. They went in to them—to Samaria and Jerusalem, these shameless harlots—with all the zest of lustful men who visit prostitutes.

**45** But just persons everywhere will judge them for what they really are—adulteresses and murderers. They will mete out to them the sentences the law demands.

**46** The Lord God says: Bring an army against them and hand them out to be crushed and despised.

**47** For their enemies will stone them and kill them with swords; they will butcher their sons and daughters and burn their homes.

**48** Thus will I make lewdness and idolatry to cease from the land. My judgment will be a lesson against idolatry for all to see.

**49** For you will be fully repaid for all your harlotry, your worshiping of idols. You will suffer the full penalty; and you will know that I alone am God."

## CHAPTER 24

One day late in December of the ninth year (of King Jehoiachin's captivity), another message came to me from the Lord.

**2** "Son of dust," He said, "write down this date, for today the king of Babylon has attacked Jerusalem.

**3** And now give this parable to these rebels, Israel; tell them the Lord God says: Put a pot of water on the fire to boil.

**4** Fill it with choicest mutton, the rump and shoulder and all the most tender cuts.

**5** Use only the best sheep from the flock, and heap

fuel on the fire beneath the pot. Boil the meat well, until the flesh falls off the bones.

6 For the Lord God says: Woe to Jerusalem, City of Murderers; you are a pot that is pitted with rust and with wickedness. So take out the meat chunk by chunk in whatever order it comes—for none is better than any other.[6]

7 For her wickedness is evident to all—she boldly murders, leaving blood upon the rocks in open view for all to see; she does not even try to cover it.

8 And I have left it there, uncovered, to shout to Me against her and arouse My wrath and vengeance.

9 Woe to Jerusalem, City of Murderers. I will pile on the fuel beneath her.

10 Heap on the wood; let the fire roar and the pot boil. Cook the meat well and then empty the pot and burn the bones.

11 Now set it empty on the coals to scorch away the rust and corruption.

12 But all for naught—it all remains despite the hottest fire.

13 It is the rust and corruption of your filthy lewdness, of worshiping your idols. And now, because I wanted to cleanse you and you refused, remain filthy until My fury has accomplished all its terrors upon you!

14 I, the Lord, have spoken it; it shall come to pass and I will do it."

15 Again a message came to me from the Lord, saying:

---

[6]Literally, "no lot has fallen upon it."

16 "Son of dust, I am going to take away your lovely wife. Suddenly, she will die. Yet you must show no sorrow. Do not weep; let there be no tears.

17 You may sigh, but only quietly. Let there be no wailing at her grave; don't bare your head nor feet, and don't accept the food brought to you by consoling friends."

18 I proclaimed this to the people in the morning; and in the evening my wife died. The next morning I did all the Lord had told me to.

19 Then the people said: "What does all this mean? What are you trying to tell us?"

20, 21 And I answered, "The Lord told me to say to the people of Israel: I will destroy My lovely, beautiful Temple, the strength of your nation. And your sons and daughters in Judea will be slaughtered by the sword.

22 And you will do as I have done; you may not mourn in public or console yourself by eating the food brought to you by sympathetic friends.

23 Your head and feet shall not be bared; you shall not mourn or weep. But you will sorrow to one another for your sins, and mourn privately for all the evil you have done.

24 Ezekiel is an example to you, the Lord God says. You will do as he has done. And when that time comes, then you will know I am the Lord."

25 "Son of dust, on the day I finish taking from them in Jerusalem the joy of their hearts and their glory and joys—their wives and their sons and their daughters—

26 On that day a refugee from Jerusalem will start on a journey to come to you in Babylon to tell you what has happened.

27 And on the day of his arrival, your voice will suddenly return to you so that you can talk with him; and you will be a symbol for these people and they shall know I am the Lord."

## CHAPTER 25

Then the Lord's message came to me again. He said:

2 "Son of dust, look toward the land of Ammon and prophesy against its people.

3 Tell them: Listen to what the Lord God says. Because you scoffed when My Temple was destroyed, and mocked Israel in her anguish, and laughed at Judah when she was marched away captive,

4 Therefore I will let the Bedouins from the desert to the east of you overrun your land. They will set up their encampments among you. They will harvest all your fruit and steal your dairy cattle.

5 And I will turn the city of Rabbah into a pasture for camels and all the country of the Ammonites into a waste land where flocks of sheep can graze. Then you will know I am the Lord.

6 For the Lord God says: Because you clapped and stamped and cheered with glee at the destruction of My people,

7   Therefore I will lay My hand heavily upon you, delivering you to many nations for devastation. I will cut you off from being a nation any more. I will destroy you; then you shall know I am the Lord.

8   And the Lord God says: Because the Moabites have said that Judah is no better off than any other nation,

9, 10   Therefore I will open up the eastern flank of Moab, wiping out her frontier cities, the glory of the nation—Beth-jeshimoth, Baal-meon and Kiriathaim. And Bedouin tribes from the desert to the east will pour in upon her, just as they will upon Ammon. And Moab will no longer be counted among the nations.

11   Thus I will bring down My judgment upon the Moabites, and they shall know I am the Lord.

12   And the Lord God says: Because the people of Edom have sinned so greatly by avenging themselves upon the people of Judah,

13   I will smash Edom with My fist and wipe out her people, her cattle and her flocks. The sword will destroy everything from Teman to Dedan.

14   By the hand of My people, Israel, this shall be done. They will carry out My furious vengeance.

15   And the Lord God says: Because the Philistines have acted against Judah out of revenge and long-standing hatred,

16   I will shake My fist over the land of the Philistines, and I will wipe out the Cherithites and utterly destroy those along the sea coast.

17   I will execute terrible vengeance upon them to

rebuke them for what they have done. And when all this happens, then they shall know I am the Lord."

## CHAPTER 26

Another message came to me from the Lord on the first day of the month, in the eleventh year (after King Jehoiachin was taken away to captivity).

2 "Son of dust, Tyre has rejoiced over the fall of Jerusalem, saying, 'Ha! She who controlled the lucrative north-south trade routes along the coast and along the course of the Jordan River[7] has been broken, and I have fallen heir! Because she has been laid waste, I shall become wealthy!'

3 Therefore the Lord God says: I stand against you, Tyre, and I will bring nations against you like ocean waves.

4 They will destroy the walls of Tyre and tear down her towers. I will scrape away her soil and make her a bare rock!

5 Her island shall become uninhabited, a place for fishermen to spread their nets; for I have spoken it, says the Lord God. Tyre shall become the prey of many nations,

6 And her mainland city shall perish by the sword. Then they shall know I am the Lord.

7 For the Lord God says: I will bring Nebuchadnezzar, king of Babylon—the king of kings from the

7Literally, "The gate of the peoples."

north—against Tyre with a great army and cavalry and chariots.

8 First he will destroy your suburbs; then he will attack your mainland city by building a siege wall and raising a roof of shields against it.

9 He will set up battering rams against your walls and with sledge hammers demolish your forts.

10 The hoofs of his cavalry will choke the city with dust, and your walls will shake as the horses gallop through your broken gates, pulling chariots behind them.

11 Horsemen will occupy every street in the city; they will butcher your people, and your famous, huge pillars will topple.

12 They will plunder all your riches and merchandise and break down your walls. They will destroy your lovely homes and dump your stones and timber and even your dust into the sea.

13 I will stop the music of your songs. No more will there be the sound of harps among you.

14 I will make your island a bare rock,[8] a place for fishermen to spread their nets. You will never be rebuilt; for I, the Lord, have spoken it. So says the Lord.

15 The whole country will shake with your fall; the wounded will scream as the slaughter goes on.

16 Then all the seaport rulers shall come down from their thrones and lay aside their robes and beauti-

---

[8]Certain aspects of verses 12 and 14 exceed the actual damage done to Tyre by Nebuchadnezzar, and foreshadow what happened to the island settlement later as a result of the conquest by Alexander the Great.

ful garments and sit on the ground shaking with fear at what they have seen.

17 And they shall wail for you, singing this dirge: 'O mighty island city with your naval power that terrorized the mainland, how you have vanished from the seas!

18 How the islands tremble at your fall! They watch dismayed.'

19 For the Lord God says: I will destroy Tyre to the ground. You will sink beneath the terrible waves of enemy attack. Great seas shall swallow you.

20 I will send you to the pit of hell to lie there with those of long ago. Your city will lie in ruins, dead, like the bodies of those in the underworld who entered long ago the nether world of the dead. Never again will you be inhabited or be given beauty here in the land of those who live.

21 I will bring you to a dreadful end; no search will be enough to find you, says the Lord."


## CHAPTER 27

Then this message came to me from the Lord, he said:

2 "Son of dust, sing this sad dirge for Tyre:

3 O mighty seaport city, merchant center of the world, the Lord God speaks. You say, 'I am the most beautiful city in all the world.'

4 You have extended your boundaries out into the sea; your architects have made you glorious.

5   You are like a ship built of finest fir from Senir. They took a cedar from Lebanon to make a mast for you.

6   They made your oars from oaks of Bashan. The walls of your cabin are of cypress from the southern coast of Cyprus.

7   Your sails are made of Egypt's finest linens; you stand beneath awnings bright with purple and scarlet dyes from eastern Cyprus.

8   Your sailors come from Sidon and Arvad; your helmsmen are skilled men from Zemer.

9   Wise old craftsmen from Gebal do the calking. Ships come from every land with all their goods to barter for your trade.

10   Your army includes men from far off Paras, Lud and Put.[9] They serve you—it is a feather in your cap to have their shields hang upon your walls; it is the ultimate of honor.

11   Men from Arvad and from Helech[1] are the sentinels upon your walls; your towers are manned by men from Gamad. Their shields hang row on row upon the walls, perfecting your glory.

12   From Tarshish come all kinds of riches to your markets—silver, iron, tin and lead.

13   Merchants from Javan, Tubal and Meshech[2] bring slaves and bronze dishes,

14   While from Togarmah[2] come chariot horses, steeds and mules.

---

[9]These were three cities of ancient North Africa.
[1]A region in ancient Cilicia known from Assyrian records as Hilakku.
[2]Regions of Asia Minor, now in Turkey.

15 Merchants come to you from Rhodes; and many coastlands are your captive markets, giving payment in ebony and ivory.

16 Edom sends her traders to buy your many wares. They bring emeralds, purple dyes, embroidery, fine linen, and jewelry of coral and agate.

17 Judah and the cities in what was once the kingdom of Israel send merchants with wheat from Minnith and Pannag,[3] and with honey, oil and balm.

18 Damascus comes. She brings wines from Helbon, and white Syrian wool to trade for all the rich variety of goods you make.

19 Vedan and Javan bring Arabian yarn,[4] wrought iron, cassia and calamus,

20 While Dedan brings expensive saddleclothes for riding.

21 The Arabians, and Kedar's wealthy merchant princes bring you lambs and rams and goats.

22 The merchants of Sheba and Raamah come with all kinds of spices, jewels and gold.

23 Haran and Canneh, Eden, Asshur and Chilmad all send their wares.

24 They bring choice fabrics to trade—blue cloth, embroidery and many-colored carpets bound with cords and made secure.

25 The ships of Tarshish are your ocean caravans; your island warehouse is filled to the brim!

---

[3]Or, "with wheat, minnith and pannag. If these were commodities, their identification is uncertain.
[4]Or, probably better, "They exchanged wine from Uzal for your wares." The text here is uncertain.

26    But now your statesmen bring your ship of state into a hurricane! Your mighty vessel flounders in the heavy eastern gale,[5] and you are wrecked in the heart of the seas!

27    Everything is lost. Your riches and wares, your sailors and pilots, your shipwrights and merchants and soldiers and all the people sink into the sea on the day of your vast ruin.

28    The surrounding cities quake at the sound as your pilots scream with fright.

29    All your sailors out at sea come to land and watch upon the mainland shore,

30    Weeping bitterly and casting dust upon their heads and wallowing in ashes.

31    They shave their heads in grief and put on sackcloth and weep for you with bitterness of heart and deep mourning.

32    And this is the song of their sorrow: 'Where in all the world was there ever such a wondrous city as Tyre, destroyed in the midst of the sea?

33    Your merchandise satisfied the desires of many nations. Kings at the ends of the earth rejoiced in the riches you sent them.

34    Now you lie broken beneath the sea; all your merchandise and all your crew have perished with you.

35    All who live along the coastlands watch, incredulous. Their kings are horribly afraid and look on with twisted faces.

36    The merchants of the nations shake their heads, for your fate is dreadful; you have forever perished.' "

---

[5] i.e.—Nebuchadnezzar of Babylonia.

## CHAPTER 28

Here is another message given to me from the Lord: 2, 3 "Son of dust, say to the prince of Tyre: The Lord God says: You are so proud you think you are God, sitting on the throne of a god on your island home in the midst of the seas. But you are only a man, and not a god, though you boast yourself to be like God. You are wiser than Daniel, for no secret is hidden from you.

4 You have used your wisdom and understanding to get great wealth—gold and silver and many treasures.

5 Yes, your wisdom has made you very rich and very proud.

6 Therefore the Lord God says: Because you claim that you are as wise as God,

7 An enemy army, the terror of the nations, shall suddenly draw their swords against your marvelous wisdom and defile your splendor!

8 They will bring you to the pit of hell and you shall die as those pierced with many wounds, there on your island in the heart of the seas.

9 Then will you boast as a god? At least to these invaders you will be no god, but merely man!

10 You will die like an outcast at the hands of foreigners. For I have spoken it, the Lord God says."

\*    \*    \*    \*    \*

11    Then this further message came to me from the Lord:

12    "Son of dust, weep for the king of Tyre.[6] Tell him, the Lord God says: You were the perfection of wisdom and beauty.

13    You were in Eden, the garden of God; your clothing was bejeweled with every precious stone—ruby, topaz, diamond, chrysolite, onyx, jasper, sapphire, carbuncle, and emerald—all in beautiful settings of finest gold. They were given to you on the day you were created.

14    I appointed you to be the anointed guardian cherub. You had access to the holy mountain of God. You walked among the stones of fire.[7]

15    You were perfect in all you did from the day you were created until that time when wrong was found in you.

16    Your great wealth filled you with internal turmoil and you sinned. Therefore, I cast you out of the mountain of God like a common sinner. I destroyed you, O overshadowing cherub, from the midst of the stones of fire.[8]

17    Your heart was filled with pride because of all your beauty; you corrupted your wisdom for the sake of your splendor. Therefore I have cast you down to the ground and exposed you helpless before the curious gaze of kings.

---

[6]In this passage (verses 11-19) some descriptive phrases apply to a human king of Tyre, and some seem to apply to Satan. Great care must therefore be taken to apply these verses with discernment.
[7]Probably a symbol of the angels.
[8]Or, "and the guardian cherub drove you out from the midst of the stones of fire."

18   You defiled your holiness with lust for gain;[9] therefore I brought forth fire from your own actions[1] and let it burn you to ashes upon the earth in the sight of all those watching you.

19   All who know you are appalled at your fate; you are an example of horror; you are destroyed forever."

\*     \*     \*     \*     \*

20   Then another message came to me from the Lord.

21   "Son of dust, look toward the city of Sidon and prophesy against it. Say to it:

22   The Lord God says: I am your enemy, O Sidon, and I will reveal My power over you. When I destroy you and show forth My holiness upon you then all who see shall know I am the Lord.

23   I will send an epidemic of disease and an army to destroy; the wounded shall be slain in your streets by troops on every side. Then you will know I am the Lord.

24   No longer shall you and Israel's other neighbor nations prick and tear at Israel like thorns and briers, though they formerly despised her and treated her with great contempt.

25   The people of Israel will once more live in their own land, the land I gave their father Jacob. For I will gather them back again from distant lands where I have scattered them and I will show the nations of the world My holiness among My people.

---

[9]Literally, "in the unrighteousness of your trade."
[1]Literally, "I brought fire from the midst of you."

26    They will live safely in Israel, and build their homes and plant their vineyards. When I punish all the bordering nations that treated them with such contempt, then they shall know I am the Lord their God."

## CHAPTER 29

Late in December of the tenth year (of the imprisonment of King Jehoiachin), this message came to me from the Lord:

2    "Son of dust, face toward Egypt and prophesy against Pharaoh her king and all her people.

3    Tell them that the Lord God says: I am your enemy, Pharaoh, king of Egypt—mighty dragon lying in the middle of your rivers. For you have said, 'The Nile is mine; I have made it for myself!'

4    I will put hooks into your jaws and drag you out onto the land with fish sticking to your scales.

5    And I will leave you and all the fish stranded in the desert to die; and you won't be buried, for I have given you as food to the wild animals and birds.

6    Because of the way your might collapsed when Israel called on you for aid (instead of trusting Me),[2] all of you shall know I am the Lord.

7    Israel leaned on you but, like a cracked staff, you snapped beneath her hand and wrenched her shoulder out of joint and made her stagger with the pain.

8    Therefore the Lord God says: I will bring an

---

[2] Implied.

army against you, O Egypt, and destroy both men and herds.

9 The land of Egypt shall become a desolate wasteland, and the Egyptians will know that I, the Lord, have done it.

10 Because you said: "The Nile is mine! I made it!" Therefore I am against you and your river and I will utterly destroy the land of Egypt, from Migdol to Syene, as far south as the border of Ethiopia.

11 For forty years not a soul will pass that way, neither men nor animals. It will be completely uninhabited.

12 I will make Egypt desolate, surrounded by desolate nations, and her cities will lie as wastelands for forty years. I will exile the Egyptians to other lands.

13 But the Lord God says that at the end of the forty years He will bring the Egyptians home again from the nations to which they will be banished.

14 And I will restore the fortunes of Egypt and bring her people back to the land of Pathros in southern Egypt where they were born; but she will be an unimportant, minor kingdom.

15 She will be the lowliest of all the nations; never again will she raise herself above the other nations; never again will Egypt be great enough for that.

16 Israel will no longer expect any help from Egypt. Whenever she thinks of asking for it, then she will remember her sin in seeking it before. Then Israel will know that I alone am God.

\*     \*     \*     \*     \*

17 In the twenty-seventh year of King Jehoiachin's captivity,[3] around the middle of March, this message came to me from the Lord:

18 Son of dust, the army of King Nebuchadnezzar of Babylon fought hard against Tyre. The soldiers' heads were bald (from carrying heavy basketfuls of earth); their shoulders were raw and blistered (from burdens of stones for the siege). And Nebuchadnezzar received no compensation and could not pay the army for all this work.[4]

19 Therefore, the Lord God says, I will give the land of Egypt to Nebuchadnezzar, king of Babylon, and he will carry off her wealth, plundering everything she has, for his army.

20 Yes, I have given him the land of Egypt for his salary, because he was working for Me during those thirteen years at Tyre,[4] says the Lord.

21 And the day will come when I will cause the ancient glory of Israel to revive, and then at last her words will be respected, and Egypt shall know I am the Lord."

## CHAPTER 30

Another message from the Lord!

2, 3 "Son of dust, prophesy and say: The Lord God says, Weep, for the terrible day is almost here; the

---

[3] Implied.
[4] Tyre capitulated to Nebuchadnezzar at the end of a 13-year siege (587-574 B.C.). There was little left to pay the "salary" of Nebuchadnezzar, so the Lord was giving Egypt to him to make up for what he was "shortchanged" at Tyre.

day of the Lord; a day of clouds and gloom; a day of despair for the nations!

4  A sword shall fall on Egypt; the slain shall cover the ground. Her wealth is taken away, her foundations destroyed. The land of Cush has been ravished.

5  For Cush and Put and Lud, Arabia and Libya and all the countries leagued with them shall perish in that war.

6  For the Lord says: All Egypt's allies shall fall, and the pride of her power shall end. From Migdol to Syene they shall perish by the sword.

7  She shall be desolate, surrounded by desolate nations, and her cities shall be in ruins, surrounded by other ruined cities.

8  And they will know I am the Lord when I have set Egypt on fire and destroyed her allies.

9  At that time I will send swift messengers to bring panic to the Ethiopians; great terror shall befall them at that time of Egypt's doom. This will all come true.

10  For the Lord God says: Nebuchadnezzar, king of Babylon, will destroy the multitudes of Egypt.

11  He and his armies—the terror of the nations— are sent to demolish the land. They shall war against Egypt and cover the ground with the slain.

12  I will dry up the Nile and sell the whole land to wicked men. I will destroy Egypt and everything in it, using foreigners to do it. I, the Lord, have spoken it.

13  And I will smash the idols of Egypt and the images at Memphis, and there will be no king in Egypt; anarchy shall reign!

14 The cities of Pathros (along the upper Nile),[5] and Zoan and Thebes shall lie in ruins by My hand.

15 And I will pour out My fury upon Pelusium, the strongest fortress of Egypt, and I will stamp out the people of Thebes.

16 Yes, I will set fire to Egypt, Pelusium will be racked with pain, Thebes will be torn apart, Memphis will be in daily terror.

17 The young men of Heliopolis and Bubastis shall die by the sword and the women will be taken away as slaves.

18 When I come to break the power of Egypt it will be a dark day for Tahpanhes too; a dark cloud will cover her, and her daughters will be taken away as captives.

19 And so I will greatly punish Egypt and they shall know I am the Lord.

\*      \*      \*      \*      \*

20 A year later,[6] around the middle of March of the eleventh year of King Jehoiachin's captivity, this message came to me:

21 "Son of dust, I have broken the arm[7] of Pharaoh, king of Egypt, and it has not been set nor put into a cast to make it strong enough to hold a sword again.

22 For, the Lord God says, I am against Pharaoh, king of Egypt, and I will break both his arms—the

---

[5]Implied.
[6]587 B.C., the year Jerusalem fell to Nebuchadnezzar and was destroyed.
[7]When Pharaoh Hophra sent an army to relieve Jerusalem in 588, Nebuchadnezzar withdrew from the siege just long enough to defeat the Egyptian force. This is what Ezekiel means by the first "broken arm."

strong one and the one that was broken before, and I will make his sword clatter to the ground.

23   And I will banish the Egyptians to many lands.

24   And I will strengthen the arms of the king of Babylon and place My sword in his hand. But I will break the arms of Pharaoh, king of Egypt, and he shall groan before the king of Babylon as one who has been wounded unto death.

25   I will strengthen the hands of the king of Babylon, while the arms of Pharaoh fall useless to his sides. Yes, when I place My sword into the hand of the king of Babylon, and he swings it over the land of Egypt, Egypt shall know I am the Lord.

26   I will scatter the Egyptians among the nations; then they shall know I am the Lord."


# CHAPTER 31


In mid-May of the eleventh year of King Jehoiachin's captivity,[8] this message came to me from the Lord:

2, 3   "Son of dust, tell Pharaoh, king of Egypt, and all his people: You are as Assyria was—a great and mighty nation—like a cedar of Lebanon, full of thick branches and forest shade, with its head high up among the clouds.

4   Its roots went deep into the moist earth. It grew luxuriantly and gave streamlets of water to all the trees around.

---

[8]Implied.  It was the year 587 B.C., the year Jerusalem fell.

5    It towered above all the other trees. It prospered and grew long thick branches because of all the water at its roots.

6    The birds nested in its branches, and in its shade the flocks and herds gave birth to young. All the great nations of the world lived beneath its shadow.

7    It was strong and beautiful, for its roots went deep to water.

8    This tree was taller than any other in the garden of God; no cypress had branches equal to it; none had boughs to compare; none equalled it in beauty.

9    Because of the magnificence that I gave it, it was the envy of all the other trees of Eden.

10    But Egypt[9] has become proud and arrogant, the Lord God says. Therefore because she has set herself so high above the others, reaching to the clouds,

11    I will deliver her into the hands of a mighty nation, to destroy her as her wickedness deserves. I, Myself, will cut her down.

12    A foreign army (from Babylon)—the terror of the nations—will invade her land and cut her down and leave her fallen on the ground. Her branches will be scattered across the mountains and valleys and rivers of the land. All those who live beneath her shade will go away and leave her lying there.

13    The birds will pluck off her twigs and the wild animals will lie among her branches;

14    Let no other nation exult with pride for its own prosperity, though it be higher than the clouds; for all

[9]Implied.

are doomed and they will land in hell, along with all the proud men of the world.

15 The Lord God says: When she fell I made the oceans mourn for her and restrained their tides.[1] I clothed Lebanon in black and caused the trees of Lebanon to weep.

16 I made the nations shake with fear at the sound of her fall, for I threw her down to hell with all the others like her. And all the other proud trees of Eden, the choicest and the best of Lebanon, the ones whose roots went deep into the water, are comforted to find her there with them in hell.

17 Her allies too are all destroyed and perish with her. They went down with her to the nether world—those nations that had lived beneath her shade.

18 O Egypt, you are great and glorious among the trees of Eden—the nations of the world. And you will be brought down to the pit of hell with all these other nations. You will be among the nations you despise, killed by the sword. This is the fate of Pharaoh and all his teeming masses, says the Lord."

## CHAPTER 32

In mid-February of the twelfth year of King Jehoiachin's captivity, this message came to me from the Lord:

2 "Son of dust, mourn for Pharaoh, king of Egypt,

---

[1]Literally, "The great waters were held back."

and say to him: You think of yourself as a strong young lion among the nations, but you are merely a crocodile[2] along the banks of the Nile, making bubbles and muddying the stream.

3    The Lord God says: I will send a great army to catch you with My net. I will haul you out,

4    And leave you stranded on the land to die. And all the birds of the heavens will light upon you and the wild animals of the whole earth will devour you until they are glutted and full.

5    And I will cover the hills with your flesh and fill the valleys with your bones.

6    And I will drench the earth with your gushing blood, filling the ravines to the tops of the mountains.

7    I will blot you out, and I will veil the heavens and darken the stars. I will cover the sun with a cloud and the moon shall not give you her light.

8    Yes, darkness will be everywhere across your land—even the bright stars will be dark above you.

9    And when I destroy you,[3] grief will be in many hearts among the distant nations you have never seen.

10    Yes, terror shall strike in many lands, and their kings shall be terribly afraid because of all I do to you. They shall shudder with terror when I brandish My sword before them. They shall greatly tremble for their lives on the day of your fall.

11    For the Lord God says: The sword of the king of Babylon shall come upon you.

12    I will destroy you with Babylon's mighty army

---

[2]Or, "sea serpent."
[3]Or, "when I carry you captive among the nations."

—the terror of the nations. It will smash the pride of Egypt and all her people; all will perish.

13 I will destroy all your flocks and herds that graze beside the streams, and neither man nor animal will disturb those waters any more.

14 Therefore the waters of Egypt will be as clear and flow as smoothly as olive oil, the Lord God says.

15 And when I destroy Egypt and wipe out everything she has, then she shall know that I, the Lord, have done it.

16 Yes, cry for the sorrows of Egypt. Let all the nations weep for her and for her people, says the Lord."

\* \* \* \* \*

17 Two weeks later,[4] another message came to me from the Lord. He said:

18 "Son of dust, weep for the people of Egypt and for the other mighty nations. Send them down to the nether world among the denizens of death.

19 What nation is as beautiful as you, O Egypt? Yet your doom is the pit; you will be laid beside the people you despise.

20 The Egyptians will die with the multitudes slain by the sword, for the sword is drawn against the land of Egypt. She will be drawn down to judgment.

21 The mighty warriors in the nether world will welcome her as she arrives with all her friends, to lie there beside the nations she despised, all victims of the sword.

---

[4]Literally, "In the twelfth year, on the fifteenth day of the month."

22   The princes of Assyria lie there surrounded by the graves of all her people, those the sword has slain.

23   Their graves are in the depths of hell, surrounded by their allies. All these mighty men who once struck terror into the hearts of everyone are now dead at the hands of their foes.

24   Great kings of Elam lie there with their people. They scourged the nations while they lived, and now they lie undone in hell, their fate is the same as that of ordinary men.

25   They have a resting place among the slain, surrounded by the graves of all their people. Yes, they terrorized the nations while they lived, but now they lie in shame in the pit, slain by the sword.

26   The princes of Meshech and Tubal are there, surrounded by the graves of all their armies—all of them idolaters—who once struck terror to the hearts of all; now they lie dead.

27   They are buried in a common grave, and not as the fallen lords who are buried in great honor with their weapons beside them, with their shields covering them and[5] their swords beneath their heads. They were a terror to all while they lived.

28   Now you will lie crushed and broken among the idolaters, among those who are slain by the sword.

29   Edom is there with her kings and her princes; mighty as they were, they too lie among the others whom the sword has slain, with the idolaters who have gone down to the pit.

---

[5]Literally, "their iniquity (iniquities) upon their bones."

30 All the princes of the north are there, and the Sidonians, all slain. Once a terror, now they lie in shame; they lie in ignominy with all the other slain who go down to the pit.

31 When Pharaoh arrives, he will be comforted to find that he is not alone in having all his army slain, says the Lord God.

32 For I have caused My terror to fall upon all the living. And Pharaoh and his army shall lie among the idolaters who are slain by the sword."

## CHAPTER 33

Once again a message came to me from the Lord. He said:

2 "Son of dust, tell your people: When I bring an army against a country, and the people of that land choose a watchman,

3 And when he sees the army coming, and blows the alarm to warn them,

4 Then anyone who hears the alarm and refuses to heed it—well, if he dies the fault is his own.

5 For he heard the warning and wouldn't listen; the fault is his. If he had heeded the warning, he would have saved his life.

6 But if the watchman sees the enemy coming and doesn't sound the alarm and warn the people, he is responsible for their deaths. They will die in their sins, but I will charge the watchman with their deaths.

7 So with you, son of dust. I have appointed you as a watchman for the people of Israel; therefore listen to what I say and warn them for Me.

8 When I say to the wicked, 'O wicked man, you will die!' and you don't tell him what I say, so that he does not repent—that wicked person will die in his sins, but I will hold you responsible for his death.

9 But if you warn him to repent and he doesn't, he will die in his sin, and you will not be responsible.

10 O people of Israel, you are saying: 'Our sins are heavy upon us; we pine away with guilt. How can we live?'

11 Tell them: As I live, says the Lord God, I have no pleasure in the death of the wicked; *I desire that the wicked turn from his evil ways and live.* Turn, turn from your wickedness, for why will you die, O Israel?

12 For the good works of a righteous man will not save him if he turns to sin; and the sins of an evil man will not destroy him if he repents and turns from his sins.

13 I have said the good man will live. But if he sins, expecting his past goodness to save him, then none of his good deeds will be remembered. I will destroy him for his sins.

14 And when I tell the wicked he will die and then he turns from his sins and does what is fair and right—

15 If he gives back the borrower's pledge and returns what he has stolen and walks along the paths of right, not doing evil—he shall surely live. He shall not die.

16   None of his past sins shall be brought up against him, for he has turned to the good and shall surely live.

17   And yet your people are saying the Lord isn't fair. The trouble is *they* aren't fair.

18   For again I say, when the good man turns to evil, he shall die.

19   But if the wicked turns from his wickedness and does what's fair and just, he shall live.

20   Yet you are saying the Lord isn't fair. But I will judge each of you in accordance with his deeds."

\*     \*     \*     \*     \*

21   In the eleventh[6] year of our exile, late in December, one of those who escaped from Jerusalem arrived to tell me, "The city has fallen!"

22   Now the hand of the Lord had been upon me the previous evening, and He had healed me so that I could speak again by the time the man arrived.

23   Then this message came to me:

24   "Son of dust, the scattered remnants of Judah living among the ruined cities keep saying, 'Abraham was only one man and yet he got possession of the whole country! We are many, so we should certainly be able to get it back!'

25   But the Lord God says: You are powerless, for you do evil! You eat meat with the blood; you worship idols and murder. Do you suppose I'll let you have the land?

---

[6]Some manuscripts read, "In the twelfth year."

26 Murderers! Idolators! Adulterers! Should you possess the land?

27 Tell them: The Lord God says: As I live, surely those living in the ruins shall die by the sword. Those living in the open fields shall be eaten by wild animals, and those in the forts and caves shall die of disease.

28 I will desolate the land and her pride, and her power shall come to an end. And the mountain villages of Israel shall be so ruined that no one will even travel through them.

29 When I have ruined the land because of their sins, then they shall know I am the Lord.

30 Son of dust, your people are whispering behind your back. They talk about you in their houses and whisper about you at the doors saying 'Come on, let's have some fun! Let's go hear him tell us what the Lord is saying!'[7]

31 So they come as though they are sincere and sit before you listening. But they have no intention of doing what I tell them to; they talk very sweetly about loving the Lord, but with their hearts they are loving their money.

32 You are very entertaining to them, like someone who sings lovely songs with a beautiful voice or plays well on an instrument. They hear what you say but don't pay any attention to it!

33 But when all these terrible things happen to them—as they will—then they will know a prophet has been among them."

---

[7]Literally, "Come and let us hear what the word is that comes from the Lord!"

## CHAPTER 34

Then this message came to me from the Lord:

2 "Son of dust, prophesy against the shepherds, the leaders of Israel, and say to them: The Lord God says to you: Woe to the shepherds who feed themselves instead of their flocks. Shouldn't shepherds feed the sheep?

3 You eat the best food and wear the finest clothes, but you let your flocks starve.

4 You haven't taken care of the weak nor tended the sick nor bound up the broken bones nor gone looking for those who have wandered away and are lost. Instead you have ruled them with force and cruelty.

5 So they were scattered, without a shepherd. They have become a prey to every animal that comes along.

6 My sheep wandered through the mountains and hills and over the face of the earth, and there was no one to search for them or care about them.

7 Therefore, O shepherds, hear the word of the Lord:

8 As I live, says the Lord God, you abandoned My flock, leaving them to be attacked and destroyed, and you were no real shepherds at all, for you didn't search for them. You fed yourselves and let them starve,

9, 10 Therefore I am against the shepherds, and I will hold them responsible for what has happened to My flock. I will take away their right to feed the flock

—and take away their right to eat. I will save My flock from being taken for their food.

11 For the Lord God says: I will search and find My sheep.

12 I will be like a shepherd looking for his flock. I will find My sheep and rescue them from all the places they were scattered in that dark and cloudy day.

13 And I will bring them back from among the people and nations where they were, back home to their own land of Israel, and I will feed them upon the mountains of Israel and by the rivers where the land is fertile and good.

14 Yes, I will give them good pasture on the high hills of Israel. There they will lie down in peace and feed in luscious mountain pastures.

15, 16 I Myself will be the shepherd of My sheep, and cause them to lie down in peace, the Lord God says. I will seek My lost ones, those who strayed away, and bring them safely home again. I will put splints and bandages upon their broken limbs and heal the sick. And I will destroy the powerful, fat shepherds; I will feed them, yes—feed them punishment!

17 And as for you, O My flock—My people—the Lord God says, I will distinguish lambs from kids and rams from billy goats!

18 Is it a small thing to you, O evil shepherds, that you not only keep the best of the pastures for yourselves, but trample down the rest? That you take the best water for yourselves, and muddy the rest with your feet?

19   All that's left for My flock is what you've trampled down; all they have to drink is water that you've fouled.

20   Therefore the Lord God says: I will surely judge between these fat shepherds and their scrawny sheep.

21   For these shepherds push and butt and crowd My sick and hungry flock until they're scattered far away.

22   So I Myself will save My flock; no more will they be picked on and destroyed. And I will notice which is plump and which is thin, and why!

23   And I will set one Shepherd over all My people, even My servant, David. He shall feed them and be a shepherd to them.

24   And I, the Lord, will be their God, and My servant David shall be a Prince among My people. I, the Lord, have spoken it.

25   I will make a peace pact with them, and drive away the dangerous animals from the land so that My people can safely camp in the wildest places and sleep safely in the woods.

26   I will make My people and their homes around My hill a blessing. And there shall be showers, showers of blessing, for I will not shut off the rains but send them in their seasons.

27   Their fruit trees and fields will yield bumper crops, and everyone will live in safety. When I have broken off their chains of slavery and delivered them

from those who profiteered at their expense, they shall know I am the Lord.

28 No more will other nations conquer them nor wild animals attack. They shall live in safety and no one shall make them afraid.

29 And I will raise up a notable Vine (the Messiah)[8] in Israel so that My people will never again go hungry nor be shamed by heathen conquest.

30 In this way they will know that I, the Lord their God, am with them, and that they, the people of Israel, are My people, says the Lord God.

31 You are My flock, the sheep of My pasture. You are My men and I am your God, so says the Lord."

## CHAPTER 35

Again a message came from the Lord. He said:

2 "Son of dust, face towards Mount Seir and prophesy against the people saying:

3 The Lord God says: I am against you and I will smash you with My fist and utterly destroy you.

4, 5 Because you hate My people Israel, I will demolish your cities and make you desolate, and then you shall know I am the Lord. You butchered My people when they were helpless, when I had punished them for all their sins.

6 As I live, the Lord God says, since you enjoy

---

[8]Literally, "a plant of renown"; so perhaps the meaning is, "I will give them bumper crops." Either translation is permissable, but the word for "plant" is in the singular.

blood so much, I will give you a blood bath—your turn has come!

7  I will utterly wipe out the people of Mount Seir, killing off all those who try to escape and all those who return.

8  I will fill your mountains with the dead—your hills, your valleys and your rivers will be filled with those the sword has killed.

9  Never again will you revive. You will be abandoned forever; your cities will never be rebuilt. Then you shall know I am the Lord.

10  For you said, 'Both Israel and Judah shall be mine. We will take possession of them. What do we care that God is there!'

11  Therefore as I live, the Lord God says, I will pay back your angry deeds with Mine—I will punish you for all your acts of envy and of hate. And I will honor My name in Israel by what I do to you.

12  And you shall know that I have heard each evil word you spoke against the Lord, saying, 'His people are helpless; they are food for us to eat!'

13  Saying that, you boasted great words against the Lord. And I have heard them all!

14  The whole world will rejoice when I make you desolate.

15  You rejoiced at Israel's fearful fate. Now I will rejoice at yours! You will be wiped out, O people of Mount Seir and all who live in Edom! And then you will know I am the Lord!"

## CHAPTER 36

Son of dust, prophesy to Israel's mountains. Tell them: Listen to this message from the Lord.

2 Your enemies have sneered at you and claimed your ancient heights as theirs,

3 And destroyed you on every side and sent you away as slaves to many lands. You are mocked and slandered.

4 Therefore, O mountains of Israel, hear the word of the Lord God. He says to the hills and mountains, dales and valleys, and to the ruined farms and the long deserted cities, destroyed and mocked by heathen nations all around:

5 My anger is afire against these nations, especially Edom, for grabbing My land with relish, in utter contempt for Me, to take it for themselves.

6 Therefore prophesy and say to the hills and mountains, dales and valleys of Israel: The Lord God says, I am full of fury because you suffered shame before the surrounding nations.

7 Therefore I have sworn with hand held high, that those nations are going to have their turn of being covered with shame,

8 But for Israel, good times will return. There will be heavy crops of fruit to prepare for My people's return—and they will be coming home again soon!

9 See, I am for you, and I will come and help you as you prepare the ground and sow your crops.

10 I will greatly increase your population throughout all Israel, and the ruined cities will be rebuilt and filled with people.

11 Not only the people, but your flocks and herds will also greatly multiply. O mountains of Israel, again you will be filled with homes. I will do even more for you than I did before. Then you shall know I am the Lord.

12 My people will walk upon you once again, and you will belong to them again; and you will no longer be a place for burning their children on idol altars.

13 The Lord God says: Now the other nations taunt you, saying, 'Israel is a land that devours her people!'

14 But they will not say this any more. Your birth rate will rise and your infant mortality rate will drop off sharply, says the Lord.

15 No longer will those heathen nations sneer, for you will no longer be a nation of sinners, the Lord God says."

\* \* \* \* \*

16 Then this further word came to me from the Lord:

17 "Son of dust, when the people of Israel were living in their own country, they defiled it by their evil deeds; to Me their worship was as foul as filthy rags.[9]

18 They polluted the land with murder and with the worshiping of idols, so I poured out My fury upon them.

---

[9]Literally, "as a menstruous cloth."

19    And I exiled them to many lands; that is how I punished them for the evil way they lived.

20    But when they were scattered out among the nations, then they were a blight upon My holy Name because the nations said, 'These are the people of God and He couldn't protect them from harm!'

21    I am concerned about My reputation that was ruined by My people throughout the world.

22    Therefore say to the people of Israel: The Lord God says, I am bringing you back again, but not because you deserve it; I am doing it to protect My holy Name which you tarnished among the nations.

23    I will honor My great Name that you defiled, and the people of the world shall know I am the Lord. I will be honored before their eyes by delivering you from exile among them.[1]

24    For I will bring you back home again to the land of Israel.

25    Then it will be as though I had sprinkled clean water on you, for you will be clean—your filthiness will be washed away, your idol worship gone.

26    And I will give you a new heart—I will give you new and right desires—and put a new spirit within you. I will take out your stony hearts of sin and give you new hearts of love.[2]

27    And I will put My Spirit within you so that you will obey My laws and do whatever I command.

28    And you shall live in Israel, the land which I

---

[1] Implied.
[2] Literally, "hearts of flesh," in contrast to "hearts of stone."

gave your fathers long ago. And you shall be My people and I will be your God.

29    I will cleanse away your sins. I will abolish crop failures and famine.

30    I will give you huge harvests from your fruit trees and fields, and never again will the surrounding nations be able to scoff at your land for its famines.

31    Then you will remember your past sins and loathe yourselves for all the evils you did.

32    But always remember this: It is not for your own sakes that I will do this, but for Mine. O My people Israel, be utterly ashamed of all that you have done!

33    The Lord God says: When I cleanse you from your sins, I will bring you home again to Israel, and rebuild the ruins.

34    Acreage will be cultivated again that through the years of exile lay empty as a barren wilderness; all who passed by were shocked to see the extent of ruin in your land.

35    But when I bring you back they will say, 'This God-forsaken land has become like Eden's garden! The ruined cities are rebuilt and walled and filled with people!'

36    Then the nations all around—all those still left —will know that I, the Lord, rebuilt the ruins and planted lush crops in the wilderness. For I, the Lord, have promised it, and I will do it.

37, 38    The Lord God says: I am ready to hear Israel's prayers for these blessings, and to grant them their requests. Let them but ask and I will multiply them like the flocks that fill Jerusalem's streets at time of sacrifice. The ruined cities will be crowded once more, and everyone will know I am the Lord."

## CHAPTER 37

The power of the Lord was upon me and I was carried away by the Spirit of the Lord to a valley full of old, dry bones that were scattered everywhere across the ground. He led me around among them,

3   And then He said to me: "Son of dust, can these bones become people again?" I replied, "Lord, You alone know the answer to that."

4   Then He told me to speak to the bones and say: "O dry bones, listen to the words of God,

5   For the Lord God says, See! I am going to make you live and breathe again!

6   I will replace the flesh and muscles on you and cover you with skin. I will put breath into you, and you shall live and know I am the Lord."

7   So I spoke these words from God, just as He told me to; and suddenly there was a rattling noise from all across the valley, and the bones of each body came together and attached to each other as they used to be.

8   Then, as I watched, the muscles and flesh formed over the bones, and skin covered them, but the bodies had no breath.

9   Then He told me to call to the Wind and say:

"The Lord God says: Come from the four winds, O Spirit, and breathe upon these slain bodies, that they may live again."

10 So I spoke to the winds as He commanded me and the bodies began breathing; they lived, and stood up—a very great army.

11 Then He told me what the vision meant: "These bones," He said, "represent all the people of Israel. They say: 'We have become a heap of dried out bones—all hope is gone.'

12 But tell them, the Lord God says: My people, I will open your graves of exile and cause you to rise again and return to the land of Israel.

13 And, then at last, O My people, you will know I am the Lord.

14 I will put My Spirit into you, and you shall live and return home again to your own land. Then you will know that I, the Lord, have done just what I promised you."

15 Again a message from the Lord came to me, saying:

16 "Take a stick and carve on it these words: 'This stick represents Judah and her allied tribes.' Then take another stick and carve these words on it: 'This stick represents all the other tribes of Israel.'

17 Now hold them together in your hand as one stick.

18, 19, 20 Tell these people, (holding the sticks so they can see what you are doing), the Lord God says: I will take the tribes of Israel and join them to Judah and make them one stick in My hand.

21   For the Lord God says: I am gathering the people of Israel from among the nations, and bringing them home from around the world to their own land,

22   To unify them into one nation. One king shall be king of them all; no longer shall they be divided into two nations.

23   They shall stop polluting themselves with idols and their other sins; for I will save them from all this foulness. Then they shall truly be My people and I their God.

24   And David, My Servant—the Messiah—shall be their king, their only shepherd; and they shall obey My laws and all My wishes.

25   They shall live in the land of Israel where their fathers lived, the land I gave My servant Jacob. They and their children after them shall live there, and their grandchildren, for all generations. And My Servant David, their Messiah, shall be their Prince forever.

26   And I will make a covenant of peace with them, an everlasting pact. I will bless them and multiply them and put My Temple among them forever.

27   And I will make My home among them. Yes, I will be their God and they shall be My people.

28   And when My Temple remains among them, then the nations shall know that I, the Lord, have set Israel apart for special blessings."

## CHAPTER 38

H ere is another message to me from the Lord:
     2, 3   "Son of dust, face northward[3] toward the

---

[3]Implied.

land of Magog, and prophesy against Gog[4] king of
Meshech and Tubal. Tell him that the Lord God says: I
am against you, Gog,

4    I will put hooks into your jaws and pull you to
your doom. I will mobilize your troops and armored
cavalry, and make you a mighty host, all fully armed.

5    Peras, Cush and Put shall join you too with all
their weaponry;

6    And so shall Gomer and all his hordes and the
armies of Togarmah from the distant north, as well as
many others.

7    Be prepared! Stay mobilized. You are their
leader, Gog!

8    A long time from now you will be called to
action. In distant years you will swoop down onto the
land of Israel, that will be lying in peace after the
return of its people from many lands.

9    You and all your allies—a vast and awesome
army—will roll down upon them like a storm and cover
the land like a cloud.

10    For at that time an evil thought will have come
to your mind.

11    You will have said, 'Israel is an unprotected
land of unwalled villages! I will march against her and
destroy these people living in such confidence!'

[4]The names of Gog's confederates (Meshech, Tubal, Gomer, Beth-
togarmah) can be identified as Mushki, Tabal, Gimaraya, Tegerama,
peoples who lived in the mountainous area southeast of the Black Sea
and southwest of the Caspian, currently in central Turkey. It therefore
seems that Gog was, or is to be, the leader of one of these nations. But
from the context Gog seems to be a symbol rather than an historical
figure like Nebuchadnezzar. In any event, he represents the aggregate
military might of the forces opposed to God, especially in a mighty
battle of the end-times. See also Rev. 20:7-9.

12  I will go to those once-desolate cities that are now filled with people again—those who have returned from all the nations—and I will capture vast booty and many slaves. For the people are rich with cattle now, and the whole earth revolves around them!

13  But Sheba and Dedan[5] and the merchant princes of Tarshish with whom she trades[6] will ask, 'Who are you to rob them of silver and gold and drive away their cattle and seize their goods and make them poor?'

14  The Lord God says to Gog: When My people are living in peace in their land, then you will rouse yourself.

15, 16  You will come from all over the north with your vast host of cavalry and cover the land like a cloud. This will happen in the distant future—in the latter years of history.[7] I will bring you against My land, and My holiness will be vindicated in your terrible destruction before their eyes, so that all the nations will know that I am God.

17  The Lord God says: You are the one I spoke of long ago through the prophets of Israel, saying that after many years had passed, I would bring you against My people.

18  But when you come to destroy the land of Israel, My fury will rise!

19  For in My jealousy and blazing wrath, I promise a mighty shaking in the land of Israel on that day.

---

[5]Great trading centers in Arabia.
[6]Implied.
[7]Implied. Literally, "in the latter days," an expression which does not, in Hebrew usage, necessarily mean "the end times."

20    All living things shall quake in terror at My presence; mountains shall be thrown down; cliffs shall tumble; walls shall crumble to the earth.

21    I will summon every kind of terror against you, says the Lord God, and you will fight against yourselves in mortal combat!

22    I will fight you with sword, disease, torrential floods, great hailstones, fire and brimstone!

23    Thus will I show My greatness and bring honor upon My Name; and all the nations of the world will hear what I have done, and know that I am God!"


## CHAPTER 39


S on of dust, prophesy this also against Gog. Tell him: I stand against you, Gog, leader of Meshech and Tubal.

2    I will turn you and drive you towards the mountains of Israel, bringing you from the distant north. And I will destroy 85%[8] of your army in the mountains.

3    I will knock your weapons from your hands and leave you helpless.

4    You and all your vast armies will die upon the mountains. I will give you to the vultures and wild animals to devour you.

5    You will never reach the cities—you will fall upon the open fields; for I have spoken, the Lord God says.

---

[8]Literally, "leave one-sixth of you."

6   And I will rain down fire on Magog and on all your allies who live safely on the coasts, and they shall know I am the Lord.

7   Thus I will make known My holy Name among My people Israel; I will not let it be mocked at anymore. And the nations too shall know I am the Lord, the Holy One of Israel.

8   That day of judgment will come; everything will happen just as have I declared it.

9   The people of the cities of Israel will go out and pick up your shields and bucklers, bows and arrows, javelins and spears, to use for fuel—enough to last them seven years.

10   For seven years they will need nothing else for their fires. They won't cut wood from the fields or forests, for these weapons will give them all they need. They will use the possessions of those who abused them.

11   And I will make a vast graveyard for Gog and his armies in the Valley of the Travelers, east of the Dead Sea. It will block the path of the travelers. There Gog and all his armies will be buried. And they will change the name of the place to The Valley of Gog's Army.

12   It will take seven months for the people of Israel to bury the bodies.

13   Everyone in Israel will help, for it will be a glorious victory for Israel on that day when I demonstrate My glory, says the Lord.

14   At the end of the seven months, they will appoint

men to search the land systematically for any skeltons left and bury them, so that the land will be cleansed.

15, 16 Whenever anyone sees some bones, he will put up a marker beside them so that the buriers will see them and take them to the Valley of Gog's Army to bury them. A city named "Multitude" is there! And so the land will finally be cleansed.

17 And now, son of dust, call all the birds and animals and say to them: Gather together for a mighty sacrificial feast. Come from far and near to the mountains of Israel. Come, eat the flesh and drink the blood!

18 Eat the flesh of mighty men and drink the blood of princes—they are the rams, the lambs, the goats and the fat young bulls of Bashan for My feast!

19 Gorge yourselves with flesh until you are glutted, drink blood until you are drunk; this is the sacrificial feast I have prepared for you.

20 Feast at My banquet table—feast on horses, chariots and valiant warriors, says the Lord God.

21 Thus I will demonstrate My glory among the nations; all shall see the punishment of Gog and know that I have done it.

22 And from that time onward, the people of Israel will know I am the Lord their God.

23 And the nations will know why Israel was sent away to exile—it was punishment for sin; for they acted in treachery against their God. Therefore I turned My face away from them and let their enemies destroy them.

24 I turned My face away and punished them in proportion to the vileness of their sins.

25 But now, the Lord God says, I will end the captivity of My people and have mercy upon them and restore their fortunes, for I am concerned about My reputation!

26 Their time of treachery and shame will all be in the past; they will be home again, in peace and safety in their own land, with no one bothering them or making them afraid.

27 I will bring them home from the lands of their enemies—and My glory shall be evident to all the nations when I do it. Through them I will vindicate My holiness before the nations.

28 Then My people will know I am the Lord their God—responsible for sending them away to exile, and responsible for bringing them home. I will leave none of them remaining among the nations.

29 And I will never hide My face from them again, for I will pour out My Spirit upon them, says the Lord God."

## CHAPTER 40

Early in April of the twenty-fifth year of our exile —the fourteenth year after Jerusalem was captured—the hand of the Lord was upon me,

2 And in a vision He took me to the land of Israel and set me down on a high mountain where I saw what appeared to be a city opposite me.

3   Going nearer, I saw a man whose face shone like bronze standing beside the Temple gate,[9] holding in his hand a measuring tape and a measuring stick.

4   He said to me: "Son of dust, watch and listen and take to heart everything I show you, for you have been brought here so I can show you many things; and then you are to return to the people of Israel to tell them all you have seen.

5   The man began to measure the wall around the outside of the Temple area with his measuring stick, which was 10½ feet long. He told me, "This wall is 10½ feet high and 10½ feet wide."

6   Then he took me over to the passageway that goes through the eastern wall. We climbed the seven steps into the entrance and he measured the entry hall of the passage; it was 10½ feet wide.

7-12   Walking on through the passageway I saw that there were three guardrooms on each side; each of these rooms was 10½ feet square, with a distance of 8¾ feet along the wall between them. In front of these rooms was a low barrier 18 inches high and 18 inches wide.[1] Beyond the guardrooms was a 10½ foot doorway opening into a 14 foot hall with 3½ foot columns. Beyond this hall, at the inner end of the passageway was a vestibule 22¾ feet wide and 17½ feet long.

13   Then he measured the entire outside width of the passageway, measuring across the roof from the

[9]Implied.
[1]Or, an 18 inch pillar in front of (or between) the guardrooms, projecting out into the hallway.
[2]Implied.

WEST

VIEW OF EZEKIEL'S TEMPLE

## PLAN OF TEMPLE AREA

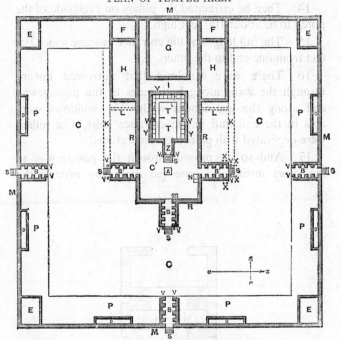

A, Altar.
B B B, Outer gate.
B' B' B', Inner gates.
C C, Outer court.
C', Inner court.
D D, Chambers in outer court.
E E, People's cooking-places.
F F, Priests' „
G, Building in separate place.
H H, Priests' chambers.
I, Space in separate place.
J, Chambers adjoining Temple.
K K, Walk.
L L, Screen walls.

M M, Wall of outer court.
N, Chambers in inner court for priests and singers.
O, Chamber for officiating priests.
P P, Pavement.
R R, Wall of inner court.
S S, Steps.
T, Temple.
T', Holy of Holies.
V V, Columns.
W W, Winding staircases.
X X, Places for killing sacrifices.
Y Y, Platform around chambers.
Z, Porch of Temple.

outside doors of the guardrooms; this distance was 43¾ feet.

14 Then he estimated the pillars on each side of the porch to be about 100 feet high.

15 The full length of the entrance passage was 87½ feet from one end to the other.

16 There were windows that narrowed inward through the walls along both sides of the passageway and along the guardroom walls. The windows were also in the exit and in the entrance halls. The pillars were decorated with palm tree decorations.

17 And so we passed through the passageway to the court inside. A stone pavement ran around the

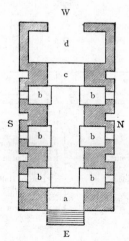

EAST OUTER PASSAGEWAY

inside of the walls, and thirty rooms were built against the walls, opening onto this pavement.

18   This was called "the lower pavement." It extended out from the walls into the court the same distance as the passageway did.

19   Then he measured across to the wall on the other side of this court (which was called "the outer court" of the Temple)³ and found that the distance was 175 feet.

20   As I followed, he left the eastern passageway and went over to the passage through the northern wall and measured it.

21   Here too there were three guardrooms on each side; and all the measurements were the same as for the east passageway—87½ feet long and 43¾ feet from side to side across the top of the guardrooms.

22   There were windows, an entry hall and the palm tree decorations just the same as on the east side. And there were seven steps leading up to the doorway to the entry hall inside.

23   Here at the north entry, just as at the east, if one walked through the passageway into the court, and straight across it, he came to an inner wall and a passageway through it to an inner court. The distance between the two passageways was 175 feet.

24   Then he took me around to the south gate and measured the various sections of its passageway and found they were just the same as in the others.

25   It had windows along the walls as the others

---

³Implied.

did, and an entry hall. And like the others, it was 87½ feet long and 43¾ feet wide.

26 It too had a stairway of seven steps leading up to it, and there were palm tree decorations along the walls.

27 And here again, if one walked through the passageway into the court and straight across it, he came to the inner wall and a passageway through it to the inner court. And the distance between the passageways was 175 feet.

28 Then he took me over to the inner wall and its south passageway. He measured this passageway and found that it had the same measurements as the passageways of the outer wall.[4]

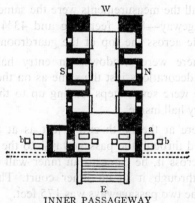

INNER PASSAGEWAY

29, 30 Its guardrooms, pillars and entrance and exit hall were identical to all the others; and so were the

---

[4]Some manuscripts add: "And the arches around it were 37½ feet by 8¾ feet broad."
[5]Verse 30, omitted in the Septuagint and several other of the ancient manuscripts, reads, "There were vestibules round about, and they were 37½ feet long and 8¾ feet broad."

windows along its walls and entry. And, like the others, it was 87½ feet long by 43¾ feet wide.

31 The only difference was that it had eight steps leading up to it instead of seven. It had palm tree decorations on the pillars, just as the others.

32 Then he took me along the court to the eastern entrance of the inner wall, and measured it. It too had the same measurements as the others.

33 Its guardrooms, pillars and entrance hall were the same size as those of the other passageways, and there were windows along the walls and in the entry hall; and it was 87½ feet long by 43¾ feet wide.

34 Its entry hall faced the outer court and there were palm tree decorations on its columns, but there were eight steps instead of seven going up to the entrance.

35 Then he took me around to the north gate of the inner wall, and the measurements there were just like the others:

36 The guardrooms, pillars and entry hall of this passageway were the same as the others, with a length of 87½ feet and a width of 43¾ feet.

37 Its entry hall faced towards the outer court, and it had palm tree decorations on the walls of each side of the passageway, and there were eight steps leading up to the entrance.

38 But a door led from its entry hall into a side room where the flesh of the sacrifices was washed before being taken to the altar;

39 On each side of the entry hall of the passageway

there were two tables where the animals for sacrifice were slaughtered for the burnt offerings, sin offerings and guilt offerings to be presented in the Temple.

40 Outside the entry hall, on each side of the stairs going up to the north entrance, there were two more tables.

41 So, in all, there were eight tables, four inside and four outside, where the sacrifices were cut up and prepared.

42 There were also four stone tables where the butchering knives and other implements were laid. These tables were about 2⅝ feet square and 1¾ feet high.

43 There were hooks, three or four inches long, fastened along the walls of the entry hall; and on the tables the flesh of the offering was to be laid.

44 In the inner court, there were two one-room buildings, one beside the northern entrance, facing south, and one beside the southern entrance, facing north.

45 And he said to me: "The building beside the inner northern gate is for the priests who supervise the maintenance.

46 The building beside the inner southern entrance is for the priests in charge of the altar—the descendants of Zadok—for they alone of all the Levites may come near to the Lord to minister to Him."

47 Then he measured the inner court (in front of the Temple)[7] and found it to be 175 feet square, and

_____
[7]Implied.

there was an altar in the court, standing in front of the Temple.

48, 49 Then he brought me to the entrance hall of the Temple. Ten steps led up to it from the inner court. Its walls extended up on either side to form two pillars, each of them 8¾ feet thick. The entrance was 24½ feet wide with 5¼ foot walls. Thus the entry hall was 35 feet wide and 19¼ feet long.


# CHAPTER 41


A fterwards he brought me into the nave, the large main room of the Temple, and measured the pillars that formed its doorway. They were 10½ feet square.

2 The entrance hall was 17½ feet wide and 8¾ feet deep. The nave itself was 70 feet long by 35 feet.

3 Then he went into the inner room at the end of the nave and measured the columns at the entrance and found them to be 3½ feet thick; its doorway was 10½ feet wide, with a hallway 12¼ feet deep behind it.

4 The inner room was 35 feet square. "This," he told me, "is the Most Holy Place."

5 Then he measured the wall of the Temple and found that it was 10½ feet thick, with a row of rooms along the outside, each room was seven feet wide.

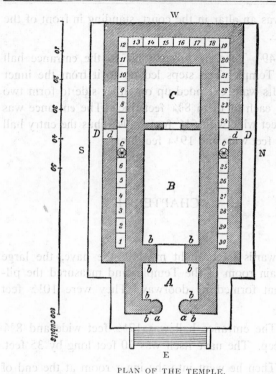

PLAN OF THE TEMPLE.

6 These rooms were in three tiers, one above the other, with 30 rooms in each tier. The whole structure was supported by girders and not attached to the Temple wall for support.

7 Each tier was wider than the one below it, corresponding to the narrowing of the Temple wall as it rose higher. A stairway at the side of the Temple led up from floor to floor.

8 I noticed that the Temple was built on a terrace and that the bottom row of rooms extended out 10½ feet onto the terrace.

9 The outer wall of these rooms was 8¾ feet thick, leaving a free space of 8¾ feet out to the edge of the terrace, the same on both sides.

10 Thirty-five feet away from the terrace, on both sides of the Temple, was another row of rooms down in the inner court.

11 Two doors opened from the tiers of rooms to the terrace yard, which was 8¾ feet wide; one door faced north and the other south.

12 A large building stood on the west, facing the Temple yard, measuring 122½ feet wide by 157½ feet long. Its walls were 8¾ feet thick.

13 Then he measured the Temple and its immediately surrounding yards. The area was 175 feet square.

14 The inner court at the east of the Temple was also 175 feet wide,

15, 16 And so was the building west of the Temple, including its two walls. The nave of the Temple and the Holy of Holies and the entry hall were paneled, and all three had recessed windows. The inner walls of the Temple were paneled with wood above and below the windows.

17, 18 The space above the door leading into the Holy of Holies was also paneled. The walls were decorated with carvings of cherubim, each with two faces, and of palm trees alternating with the cherubim.

19, 20 One face—that of a man—looked toward the palm tree on one side, and the other face—that of a young lion—looked toward the palm tree on the other side. And so it was, all around the inner wall of the Temple.

21 There were square doorposts at the doors of the nave, and in front of the Holy of Holies was what appeared to be an altar, but it was made of wood.

22 This altar was 3½ feet square, and 5¼ feet high; its corners, base and sides were all of wood. "This," he told me, "is the Table of the Lord."[8]

23 Both the nave and the Holy of Holies had double doors,

24 Each with two swinging sections.

25 The doors leading into the nave were decorated with cherubim and palm trees, just as on the walls. And there was a wooden canopy over the entry hall.

26 There were recessed windows and carved palm trees on both sides of the entry hall, the hallways beside the Temple, and on the canopy over the entrance.

## CHAPTER 42

Then he led me out of the Temple, back into the inner court to the rooms north of the Temple yard, and to another building.

2 This group of structures was 175 feet long by 87½ feet wide.

---

[8]Literally, "the table which is before the Lord."

3   The rows of rooms behind this building were the inner wall of the court. The rooms were in three tiers, overlooking the outer court on one side, and having a 35-foot strip of inner court on the other.

4   A 17½-foot walk ran between the building and the tiers of rooms, extending the entire length; with the doors of the building facing north.

5   The upper two tiers of rooms were not as wide as the lower one, because the upper tiers had wider walkways beside them.

6   And since the building was not built with girders as those in the outer court were, the upper stories were set back from the ground floor.

7, 8   The north tiers, next to the outer court, were 87½ feet long—only half as long as the inner wing that faced the Temple court, which was 175 feet long. But a wall extended from the end of the shorter wing, parallel to the longer wing.

9   And there was an entrance from the outer court to these rooms from the east. On the opposite side of the Temple a similar building composed of two units of tiers was on the south side of the inner court, between the Temple and the outer court, arranged the same as the other.

11   There was a walk between the two wings of the building, the same as in the other building across the court—the same length and width and the same exits and doors—they were identical units.

12   And there was a door from the outer court[9] at the east.

---

[9]Implied.

13 Then he told me: "These north and south tiers of rooms facing the Temple yard are holy; there the priests who offer up the sacrifices to the Lord shall eat of the most holy offerings and store them—the cereal offerings, sin offerings, and guilt offerings, for these rooms are holy.

14 When the priests leave the Holy Place—the nave of the Temple—they must change their clothes before going out to the outer court. The special robes in which they have been ministering must first be removed, for these robes are holy. They must put on other clothes before entering the parts of the building open to the public."

15 When he had finished making these measurements, he led me out through the east passageway to measure the entire Temple area.

16-20 He found that it was in the form of a square, 875 feet long on each side, with a wall all around it to separate the restricted area from the public places.[1]

## CHAPTER 43

Afterwards he brought me out again to the passageway through the outer wall leading to the east.

2 And suddenly the glory of the God of Israel appeared from the east. The sound of His coming was like the roar of rushing waters and the whole landscape lighted up with His glory.

---

[1]Literally, "between the holy and the common."

3   It was just as I had seen it in the other visions, first by the Chebar Canal, and then later at Jerusalem[2] when He came to destroy the city. And I fell down before Him with my face in the dust.

4   And the glory of the Lord came into the Temple through the eastern passageway.

5   Then the Spirit took me up and brought me into the inner court; and the glory of the Lord filled the Temple.

6   And I heard the Lord speaking to me from within the Temple (the man who had been measuring was still standing beside me).

7   And the Lord said to me: "Son of dust, this is the place of My throne, and My footstool, where I shall remain, living among the people of Israel forever. They and their kings will not defile My holy Name any longer through the adulterous worship of other gods or by worshiping the totem poles erected by their kings.

8   They built their idol temples beside Mine, with only a wall between, and worshiped their idols. Because they sullied My holy Name by such wickedness, I consumed them in My anger.

9   Now let them put away their idols and the totem poles[3] erected by their kings, and I will live among them forever.

10   Son of dust, describe the Temple I have shown you to the people of Israel. Tell them its appearance and its plan so they will be ashamed of all their sins.

11   And if they are truly ashamed of what they

---

[2]Implied.
[3]Literally, "stellae."

have done, then explain to them the details of its construction—its doors and entrances—and everything about it. Write out all the directions and the rules for them to keep.

12   And this is the basic law of the Temple: *Holiness!* The entire top of the hill where the Temple is built is *holy.* Yes, this is the primary law concerning it.

13   And these are the measurements of the altar: The base is 21 inches high, with a nine-inch rim around its edge, and it extends 21 inches beyond the altar on all sides.

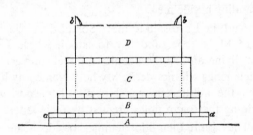

ALTAR OF BURNT-OFFERING.

14   The first stage of the altar is a stone platform 3½ feet high. This platform is 21 inches narrower than the base block on all sides. Rising from this is a narrower platform, 21 inches narrower on all sides, and seven feet high.

15   From it a still narrower platform rises seven feet, and this is the top of the altar, with four horns projecting 21 inches up from the corners.

16   This top platform of the altar is 21 feet square.

17   The platform beneath it is 24½ feet square with a 10½-inch curb around the edges. The entire platform extends out from the top 21 inches on all sides. On the east side are steps to climb the altar.

18   And He said to me: Son of dust, the Lord God says: These are the measurements of the altar to be made in the future, when it is erected for the burning of offerings and the sprinkling of blood upon it.

19   At that time the Zadok family of the Levite tribe, who are my ministers, are to be given a bullock for a sin offering.

20   You shall take some of its blood and smear it on the four horns of the altar and on the four corners of the top platform and in the curb around it. This will cleanse and make atonement for the altar.

21   Then take the bullock for the sin offering and burn it at the appointed place outside the Temple area.

22   The second day, sacrifice a young male goat without any defects—without sickness, deformities, cuts or scars—for a sin offering. Thus the altar shall be cleansed, as it was by the bullock.

23   When you have finished this cleansing ceremony, offer another perfect bullock and a perfect ram from the flock.

24   Present them before the Lord, and the priests shall sprinkle salt upon them as a burnt offering.

25   Every day for seven days a male goat, a bullock and a ram from the flock shall be sacrificed as a sin offering. None are to have any defects or unhealthiness of any kind.

26   Do this each day for seven days to cleanse and make atonement for the altar, thus consecrating it.

27   On the eighth day, and on each day afterwards, the priests will sacrifice on the altar the burnt offerings and thank offerings of the people, and I will accept you, says the Lord God."

## CHAPTER 44

Then the Lord brought me back to the outer wall's eastern passageway, but it was closed.

2   And He said to me: "This gate shall remain closed; it shall never be opened. No man shall pass through it; for the Lord, the God of Israel, entered here and so it shall remain shut.

3   Only the prince—because He is the prince—may sit inside the passageway to feast there before the Lord. But he shall go and come only through the entry hall of the passage."

4   Then he brought me through the north passageway to the front of the Temple. I looked and saw that the glory of the Lord filled the Temple of the Lord, and I fell to the ground with my face in the dust.

5   And the Lord said to me: "Son of dust, notice carefully; use your eyes and ears. Listen to all I tell you about the laws and rules of the Temple of the Lord. Note carefully who may be admitted to the Temple, and who is to be excluded from it.

6   And say to these rebels, the people of Israel: The Lord God says: O Israel, you have sinned greatly,

7   By letting the uncircumcised—they who have no heart for God—when you offer Me My food, the fat and the blood. Thus you have broken My covenant in addition to all your other sins.

8   You have not kept the laws I gave you concerning these holy affairs, for you have hired foreigners to take charge of My sanctuary.

9   The Lord God says: No foreigner of all the many among you shall enter My sanctuary if he has not been circumcised and does not love the Lord.

10   And the men of the tribe of Levi who abandoned Me when Israel strayed away from God to idols must be punished for their unfaithfulness.

11   They may be Temple guards and gatemen; they may slay the animals brought for burnt offerings and be present to help the people.

12   But because they encouraged the people to worship other gods, causing Israel to fall into deep sin, I have raised My hand and taken oath, says the Lord God, that they must be punished.

13   They shall not come near Me to minister as priests; they may not touch any of My holy things, for they must bear their shame for all the sins they have committed.

14   They are the Temple caretakers, to do maintenance work and to assist the people in a general way.

15   However, the sons of Zadok, of the tribe of Levi, they continued as My priests in the Temple when Israel

abandoned Me for idols. These men shall be My ministers; they shall stand before Me to offer the fat and blood of the sacrifices, says the Lord God.

16    They shall enter My sanctuary and come to My Table to minister to Me; they shall fulfill My requirements.

17    They must wear only linen clothing when they enter the passageway to the inner court, for they must wear no wool while on duty in the inner court or in the Temple.

18    They must wear linen turbans and linen trousers; they must not wear anything that would cause them to perspire.

19    When they return to the outer court, they must take off the clothes they wear while ministering to Me, leaving them in the sacred chambers, and put on other clothes lest they consecrate the people by touching them with this clothing.

20    They must not let their hair grow too long, nor shave it off. Regular, moderate haircuts are all they are allowed.

21    No priest may drink wine before coming to the inner court.

22    He may marry only a Jewish maiden, or the widow of a priest; he may not marry a divorced woman.

23    He shall teach My people the difference between what is holy and what is secular, what is right and what is wrong.[5]

---

[5]Literally, "between what is ritually clean and ritually unclean."

24   They will serve as judges to resolve any disagreements among My people. Their decisions must be based upon My laws. And the priests themselves shall obey My rules and regulations at all the sacred festivals, and they shall see to it that the Sabbath is kept a sacred day.

25   A priest must not defile himself by being in the presence of a dead person, unless it is his father, mother, child, brother or unmarried sister. In such cases it is all right.

26   But afterwards he must wait seven days before he is cleansed and able to perform his Temple duties again.

27   The first day he returns to work and enters the inner court and the sanctuary, he must offer a sin offering for himself, the Lord God says.

28   As to property, they shall not own any, for I am their heritage! That is enough![6]

29   Their food shall be the gifts and sacrifices brought to the Temple by the people—the cereal offerings, the sin offerings and the guilt offerings. Whatever anyone gives to the Lord shall be the priests'.

30   The first of the first-ripe fruits and all the gifts for the Lord shall go to the priests. The first samples of each harvest of grain shall be donated to the priests too, so that the Lord will bless your homes.

31   Priests may never eat meat from any bird or animal that dies a natural death or that dies after being attacked by other animals.

----

[6]Implied.

## CHAPTER 45

When you divide the land among the tribes of Israel, you shall first give a section of it to the Lord as His holy portion. This piece shall be 8⅓ miles long and 6⅔ miles wide. It shall all be holy ground.

2 A section of this land, 875 feet square, shall be designated for the Temple. An additional 87½-foot strip all around is to be left empty.

3 The Temple shall be built within the area which is 8⅓ miles long and 3⅓ miles wide.

4 All this section shall be holy land; it will be used by the priests, who minister in the sanctuary, for their homes and for My Temple.

5 The strip next to it, 8⅓ miles long and 3⅓ miles wide, shall be the residence area for the Levites who work at the Temple.

6 Adjacent to the holy lands will be a section 8⅓ miles by 1⅔ miles for a city open to everyone in Israel.

7 Two special sections of land shall be set apart for the prince—one on each side of the holy lands and city; it is contiguous with them in length, and its eastern and western boundaries are the same as those of the tribal sections. (See map.)

8 This shall be his allotment. My princes shall no longer oppress and rob My people, but shall assign all the remainder of the land to the people, giving a portion to each tribe.

9 For the Lord God says to the rulers: Quit robbing and cheating My people out of their land, and expelling them from their homes. Always be fair and honest.

10 You must use honest scales, honest bushels, honest gallons.

11 A homer[7] shall be your standard unit of measurement, for both liquid and dry measure. Smaller units shall be the ephah (one-tenth of a homer) for dry measure, and the bath (one-tenth of a homer) for liquid.

12 The unit of weight shall be the silver shekel (about half an ounce); it must always be exchanged for 20 gerahs, no less; five shekels shall be valued at five shekels, no less; and ten shekels at ten shekels! Fifty shekels shall always equal one maneh.

13 This is the tax you must give to the prince: a bushel of wheat or barley for every 60 you reap;

14 And one per cent of your olive oil;

15 From each 200 sheep in all your flocks in Israel, give him one sheep. These are the meal offerings, burnt offerings and thank offerings to make atonement for those who bring them, says the Lord God.

16 All the people of Israel shall bring their offerings to the prince.

17 The prince shall be required to furnish the people with sacrifices for public worship—sin offerings, burnt offerings, meal offerings, drink offerings and thank offerings—to make reconciliation for the people

---

[7] The homer was about 220 litres, or 6½ bushels.

of Israel. This shall be done at the time of the religious feasts, the new moon ceremonies, the sabbaths and all other similar occasions.

18    The Lord God says: On each New Year's Day* sacrifice a young bull with no blemishes, to purify the Temple.

19    The priest shall take some of the blood of this sin offering and put it on the door posts of the Temple and upon the four corners of the base of the altar and upon the walls at the entry of the inner court.

20    Do this also on the seventh day of that month for anyone who has sinned through error or ignorance; and so the Temple will be cleansed.

21    On the fourteenth day of the same month, you shall celebrate the Passover. It will be a seven-day feast. Only bread without yeast shall be eaten during those days.

22    On the day of Passover the prince shall provide a young bull for a sin offering for himself and all the people of Israel.

23    On each of the seven days of the feast he shall prepare a burnt offering to the Lord. This daily offering will consist of seven young bulls and seven rams without blemish. A young goat will also be given each day for a sin offering.

24    And the prince shall provide 14 bushels of grain for the meal offering—one bushel for each bullock and ram; and 21 gallons of olive oil—1½ gallons to go with each bushel.

25    Early in October, during each of the seven days

---

*April was the first month of the Hebrew year.

of the annual feast, he shall provide these same sacrifices for the sin offering, burnt offering, meal offering and oil offering.

## CHAPTER 46

The Lord God says, the inner wall's eastern entrance shall be closed during the six work days but open on the Sabbath and on the days of the new moon celebrations.

2   The prince shall enter the outside entry hall of the passageway and proceed to the inner wall at the other end while the priest offers his burnt offering and peace offering. He shall worship inside the passageway and then return back to the entrance, which shall not be closed until evening.

3   The people shall worship the Lord in front of this passageway on the Sabbaths and on the days of the new moon celebrations.

4   The burnt offering which the prince sacrifices to the Lord on the Sabbath days shall be six lambs and a ram, all unblemished.

5   He shall present a meal offering of one bushel of flour to go with the ram, and whatever amount he is willing for, to go with each lamb. And he shall bring 1½ gallons of olive oil for each bushel of flour.

6   At the new moon celebration, he shall bring one young bull, in perfect condition; six lambs and one ram, all without any blemish.

7 With the young bull, he must bring a bushel[8] of flour for a meal offering. With the ram, he is to bring one bushel[8] of flour. With the lamb, he is to bring whatever he is willing[9] to give. With each bushel he is to bring 1½ gallons of olive oil.

8 The prince shall go in at the entry hall of the passageway and out the same way;

9 But when the people come in through the north passageway to sacrifice during the religious feasts, they must go out through the south passageway. Those coming in from the south must go out by the north. They must never go out the same way they come in, but must always use the opposite passageway.

10 The prince shall enter and leave with the common people on these occasions.

11 To summarize: At the special feasts and sacred festivals the meal offering shall be one bushel with the young bull; one bushel with the ram; as much as the prince is willing to give with each lamb; and 1½ gallons of oil with each bushel.

12 Whenever the prince offers an extra burnt offering or peace offering to be sacrificed to the Lord, the inner eastern gate shall be opened up for him to enter and he shall offer his sacrifices just as on the Sabbaths. Then he shall turn around and go out, and the passage shall be shut behind him.

13 Each morning a yearling lamb must be sacrificed as a burnt offering to the Lord.

---

[8]Literally, one ephah.
[9]Literally, "his hand shall attain unto."

14, 15   And there must be a meal offering each morning—⅙ bushel of flour with half a gallon of oil with which to mix it. This is a permanent ordinance—the lamb, the grain offering and the olive oil shall be provided every morning for the daily sacrifice.

16   The Lord God says: If the prince gives a gift of land to one of his sons, it will belong to him forever.

17   But if he gives a gift of land to one of his servants, the servant may keep it only until the Year of Release (every 7th year) when he is set free; then the land returns to the prince. Only gifts to his sons are permanent.

18   And the prince may never take anyone's property by force. If he gives property to his sons, it must be from his own land, for I don't want My people losing their property and having to move away."

19, 20   After that, using the door through the wall at the side of the main passageway, he led me through the entrance to the block of sacred chambers that faced north. There, at the extreme west end of these rooms, I saw a place where, my guide told me, the priests boil the meat of the trespass offering and sin offering and bake the flour of the flour offerings into bread. They do it here to avoid the necessity of carrying the sacrifices through the outer court, in case they sanctify the people.

21, 22   Then he brought me out to the outer court again and led me to each of the four corners of the court. I saw that in each corner there was a room 70 feet long by 52½ feet wide, enclosed by walls.

23 Around the inside of these walls there ran a line of brick boiling vats, with ovens underneath.

24 He said these rooms were where the Temple assistants—the Levites—boil the sacrifices the people offer.

## CHAPTER 47

Then he brought me back to the door of the Temple. I saw a stream flowing eastward from beneath the Temple and passing to the right of the altar, that is, on its south side.

2 Then he brought me outside the wall through the north passageway[2] and around to the eastern entrance, where I saw the stream flowing along on the south side (of the eastern passageway).[3]

3 Measuring as he went, he took me 1,500 feet east along the stream and told me to go across. At that point the water was up to my ankles.

4 He measured off another 1,500 feet and told me to cross again. This time the water was up to my knees.

5 Fifteen hundred feet after that it was up to my waist. Another 1,500 feet and it had become a river so deep I wouldn't be able to get across unless I were to swim. It was too deep to cross on foot.

6 He told me to keep in mind what I had seen, then led me back along the bank.

---

[2]The eastern passageway was closed.
[3]Implied.

7  And now, to my surprise,[3] many trees were growing on both sides of the river!

8  He told me: This river flows east through the desert and the Jordan Valley to the Dead Sea, where it will heal the salty waters and make them fresh and pure.

9  Everything touching the water of this river shall live. Fish will abound in the Dead Sea, for its waters will be healed. Wherever this water flows, everything will live.

10  Fishermen will stand along the shores of the Dead Sea, fishing all the way from Engedi to Eneglaim. The shores will be filled with nets drying in the sun. Fish of every kind will fill the Dead Sea just as they do the Mediterranean!

11  But the marshes and swamps will not be healed; they will still be salty.

12  All kinds of fruit trees will grow along the river banks. The leaves will never turn brown and fall, and there will always be fruit. There will be a new crop every month—without fail! For they are watered by the river flowing from the Temple. The fruit will be for food and the leaves for medicine.

\*     \*     \*     \*     \*

13  The Lord God says: Here are the instructions for dividing the land to the twelve tribes of Israel: The tribe of Joseph (Ephraim and Manesseh)[4] shall be given two sections.

---

[3]Implied.
[4]Implied.

14 Otherwise, each tribe will have an equal share. I promised with hand raised in oath of truth to give the land to your fathers, and you shall inherit it now.

15 The northern boundary will run from the Mediterranean toward Hethlon, then on through Labweh[5] to Zedad;

16 Then to Berothah and Sibraim, which are on the border between Damascus and Hamath, and finally to Hazar-hatticon, on the border of Hauran.

17 So the northern border will be from the Mediterranean to Hazar-enon, on the border with Hamath to the north and Damascus to the south.

18 The eastern border will run south from Hazar-enon to Mount Hauran, where it will bend westward to the Jordan at the southern tip of the Sea of Galilee, and down along the Jordan River separating Israel from Gilead, past the Dead Sea to Tamar.

19 The southern border will go west from Tamar to the springs at Meribath-Kadesh and then follow the course of the Brook of Egypt (Wadi el-Arish) to the Mediterranean.

20 On the west side, the Mediterranean itself will be your boundary, from the southern boundary to the point where the northern boundary begins.

21 Divide the land within these boundaries among the tribes of Israel.

22 Distribute the land as an inheritance for yourselves and for the foreigners who live among you with their families. All children born in the land—whether

---

[5]The present village on this site is so named. It was originally called Lebo-Hamath.

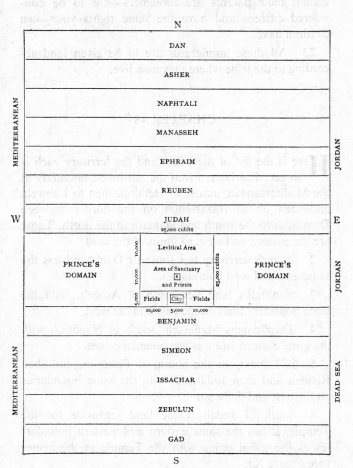

ALLOTMENT OF THE LAND

or not their parents are foreigners—are to be considered citizens and have the same rights your own children have.

23    All these immigrants are to be given land according to the tribe where they now live.

## CHAPTER 48

Here is the list of the tribes and the territory each is to get: For Dan: From the northwest boundary at the Mediterranean, across to Hethlon, then to Labweh, and then on to Hazar-enon on the border between Damascus to the south and Hamath to the north. Those are the eastern and western limits of the land.

2    Asher's territory lies south of Dan's and has the same east and west boundaries.

3    Naphtali's land lies south of Asher's, with the same boundary lines on the east and the west.

4    Then comes Manasseh, south of Naphtali, with the same eastern and western boundary lines.

5, 6, 7    Next, to the south, is Ephraim, and then Reuben and then Judah, all with the same boundaries on the east and the west.

8    South of Judah is the land set aside for the Temple. It has the same eastern and western boundaries as the tribal units, with the Temple in the center (see Figure X).

9    This Temple area will be 8⅓ miles long and 6⅔ miles wide.

10   A strip of land measuring 8⅓ miles long by 3⅓ miles wide, north to south, surrounds the Temple.

11   It is for the priests, that is, the sons of Zadok who obeyed Me and didn't go into sin when the people of Israel and the rest of their tribe of Levi did.

12   It is their special portion when the land is distributed, the most sacred land of all. Next to it lies the area where the other Levites will live.

13   It will be of the same size and shape as the first. Together they measure 8⅓ miles by 6⅔ miles.

14   None of this special land shall ever be sold or traded or used by others, for it belongs to the Lord; it is holy.

15   The strip of land 8⅓ miles long by 1⅔ miles wide, south of the Temple section, is for public use—homes, pasture and parks, with a city in the center.

16   The city itself is to be 1½ miles square.

17   Open land for pastures shall surround the city for approximately* a tenth of a mile.

18   Outside the city, stretching east and west for three miles alongside the holy grounds, is garden area belonging to the city, for public use.

19   It is open to anyone working in the city, no matter where he comes from in Israel.

20   The entire area—including sacred lands and city lands—is 8⅓ miles square.

21, 22   The land on both sides of this area, extending clear out to the eastern and western boundaries of Israel, shall belong to the prince. This land, lying

*Literally, "437½ feet" in every direction.

between the sections alloted to Judah and Benjamin, is 8⅓ miles square on each side of the sacred and city lands.

23    The sections given to the remaining tribes are as follows:

Benjamin's section extends across the entire country of Israel, from its eastern border clear across to the western border.

24    South of Benjamin's area lies that of Simeon, also extending out to these same eastern and western borders.

25    Next is Issachar, with the same boundaries.

26    Then comes Zebulun, also extending all the way across.

27, 28    Then Gad, with the same borders on east and west, while its south border runs from Tamar to the Spring at Meribath-Kadesh, and then follows the Brook of Egypt (Wadi el-Arish) to the Mediterranean.

29    These are the allotments to be made to each tribe, says the Lord God.

30, 31    Each city gate will be named in honor of one of the tribes of Israel. On the north side, with its 1½ mile wall, there will be three gates, one named for Reuben, one for Judah and one for Levi.

32    On the east side, with its 1½ mile wall, the gates will be named for Joseph, Benjamin and Dan.

33    The south wall, also the same length, will have the gates of Simeon, Issachar and Zebulun;

34    On the 1½ miles of the west side, they will be named for Gad, Asher and Naphtali.

35   The entire circumference of the city is 6 miles. And the name of the city will be "The City of God."[6]

---

[6]Literally, "Jehovah-Shammah," "The Lord is there."

*Notes*

*Notes*

*Notes*

*Notes*

*Notes*

*Notes*

*Notes*

*Notes*

# Notes